FUTURE POLICING

Future Policing examines how technologies such as facial recognition, quantum computing, virtual reality, data integration, artificial intelligence, robot cops, electrocardiograms, predictive policing, and investigative genetic genealogy are transforming the practice and governance of contemporary law enforcement.

Bringing together interdisciplinary scholars from eight countries, this 20-chapter volume offers empirically grounded analyses of how technologies are adopted, implemented, regulated, and experienced in practice. Chapters synthesize research evidence, operational experience, and theoretical debate to evaluate claims of efficiency, objectivity, and innovation, while identifying the social, legal, and ethical consequences that accompany digital transformation. At a critical moment when police agencies are investing heavily in technological solutions while navigating a fast-moving landscape of evolving tools, claims, and expectations, this volume provides a much-needed evidence base for understanding what these systems change in practice and what outcomes they realistically produce. And by bringing sustained critical investigation and scrutiny to rapidly institutionalizing tools, the collection establishes a foundation for the next generation of policing scholarship.

Rigorous and accessible, *Future Policing* provides students, researchers, practitioners, and policymakers, among others, with the insight required to critically assess technological change and understand how innovation is reshaping what policing is, how it is done, and whom it serves.

Laura Huey is a Professor of Sociology at Western University, Editor of *Police Practice & Research*, Editor of *Evidence Base*, alumnus of the College of New Scholars, Artists and Scientists of the Royal Society of Canada (RSC), and a member of the Canadian Council of Academies' expert panels on Cybercrime and Policing. Her current research focuses on public order policing, critical incident response, police downloading, policing and mental health, and missing persons.

Lorna Ferguson is an Assistant Professor of Criminology and Criminal Justice at the University of Regina, the Founder of the Missing Persons Research Hub, and the Senior Managing Editor for *Evidence Base*. Dr. Ferguson's specialization is police responses to missing persons. Her broader research program extends to related areas of policing, including incident command, evidence-based policing, technology and innovation, police data and intelligence, cybercrime, responses involving persons with mental illness, and police reform.

Ian T. Adams is an Associate Professor of Criminology and Criminal Justice at the University of South Carolina, where he is a 2025 McCausland Faculty Fellow in recognition of excellence in research and teaching. He has been involved in law enforcement and policing for over 20 years as an officer, a labour executive, and a scholar. Dr. Adams' research addresses practical police concerns, focusing on technology, policy, and behaviour. He is a leading academic voice in the ongoing development of evidence-based practices in policing.

Routledge Series on Practical and Evidence-Based Policing

Books in the *Routledge Series on Practical and Evidence-Based Policing* disseminate knowledge and provide practical tools for law enforcement leaders and personnel to protect and serve the public and reduce crime. With an aim to bridge the "translation gap" between frontline policing and academic research, books in this series apply sound scientific methods as well as practical experience to make everyday police work safer and smarter. These books are an invaluable resource for police practitioners, academic researchers, public policymakers, and students in law enforcement and criminology programs to guide best practices in all aspects of policing.

Reframing Police Education and Freedom in America
Martin Alan Greenberg and Beth Allen Easterling

Gold Medal Policing
Operational Readiness and Performance Excellence, Second Edition
Judy M. McDonald

Understanding Police Operational Performance
James E. McCabe, Paul E. O'Connell, Demosthenes Long, and Carol Rasor-Cordero

Cutting Crime Using the Rule of the Few
Shannon Linning, Daniel W. Gerard, and John E. Eck

Future Policing
Technology and Transformation
Laura Huey, Lorna Ferguson, and Ian T. Adams

FUTURE POLICING

Technology and Transformation

Edited by Laura Huey, Lorna Ferguson, and Ian T. Adams

Routledge
Taylor & Francis Group
NEW YORK AND LONDON

Designed cover image: Getty Images

First published 2027
by Routledge
605 Third Avenue, New York, NY 10158

and by Routledge
4 Park Square, Milton Park, Abingdon, Oxon, OX14 4RN

Routledge is an imprint of the Taylor & Francis Group, an informa business

Library of Congress Cataloging-in-Publication Data
Names: Huey, Laura editor | Ferguson, Lorna (Criminologist) editor | Adams, Ian T. editor
Title: Future policing : technology and transformation / edited by Laura Huey, Lorna Ferguson, and Ian T. Adams.
Description: Abingdon, Oxon ; New York, NY : Routledge, 2027. | Series: Routledge series on practical and evidence-based policing | Includes bibliographical references and index. |
Identifiers: LCCN 2026020105 (print) | LCCN 2026020106 (ebook) | ISBN 9781041137498 hardback | ISBN 9781041137481 paperback | ISBN 9781003671312 ebook
Subjects: LCSH: Police--Technological innovations | Law enforcement--Technological innovations
Classification: LCC HV7921 .F889 2027 (print) | LCC HV7921 (ebook)
LC record available at https://lccn.loc.gov/2026020105
LC ebook record available at https://lccn.loc.gov/2026020106

ISBN: 978-1-041-13749-8 (hbk)
ISBN: 978-1-041-13748-1 (pbk)
ISBN: 978-1-003-67131-2 (ebk)

DOI: 10.4324/9781003671312

Typeset in Times New Roman
by KnowledgeWorks Global Ltd.

CONTENTS

CONTRIBUTORS

Ian T. Adams is an Associate Professor of Criminology and Criminal Justice at the University of South Carolina, where he is a 2025 McCausland Faculty Fellow in recognition of excellence in research and teaching. He has been involved in law enforcement and policing for over 20 years as an officer, a labour executive, and a scholar. Dr. Adams' research addresses practical police concerns, focusing on technology, policy, and behaviour. He is a leading academic voice in the ongoing development of evidence-based practices in policing.

Abdulwahab Alasfour is an Assistant Professor in Electrical Engineering at Kuwait University. His research interests include biomedical signal processing, focusing on neural and cardiac signal analysis. He is a board member of the Sabah Al-Ahmad Center for Giftedness and Creativity and an Associate Editor for *Signal, Image, and Video Processing*.

Nasser AlSabah is a doctoral candidate at John Jay College and a police practitioner with 10+ years of experience in Kuwait's National Police Force. Nasser's research focuses on police performance and culture, and criminal justice in the Middle East. He has published in prominent journals, including *Police Quarterly and Policing: An International Journal.*

Michael Arntfield is a Professor of Forensic Literature and Criminology at Western University and a Fulbright scholar who has served as a visiting Professor or Chair at international universities. He is a former police detective and homicide scholar and has produced and appeared as an expert in 20+ television documentaries.

Kaan Boke, PhD, is an AI & Machine Learning Engineer and independent researcher based in Finland, whose work bridges applied AI, evaluation, and public policy implementation. His research spans AI in policing, use-of-force investigations, police reform, and violent extremism, employing advanced quantitative methods to translate empirical findings into actionable policy guidance. https://orcid.org/0000-0002-3042-9436

Mehzeb Chowdhury is an Assistant Professor of Policing at Northumbria University. An innovator in AI, VR, AR, and pioneering forensic technologies, he developed, among others, the MABMAT crime scene rover. His research explores the intersection of science, technology, justice, and emergent cyber futures. https://orcid.org/0000-0001-8989-9355

Jordan I. Cline is an MA student in Criminology at the University of Nebraska Omaha. After getting his BS in Criminal Justice at Wichita State University, he moved to Omaha to study policing and procedural justice in the Violence Intervention and Policing Research (VIPR) Lab. https://orcid.org/0009-0005-7267-5554

Aidan K. Comeau is a doctoral candidate in the School of Kinesiology at the University of British Columbia. He has been a long-term research assistant within the Aging and Innovation Research Program and is recognized as highly qualified personnel within the AGE-WELL Network of Centres of Excellence.

Antonio Miguel Cruz is an Associate Professor, Department of Occupational Therapy, University of Alberta, and Adjunct Professor in the School of Public Health Sciences, University of Waterloo. He leads the PEAR Lab, focusing on how digital health interventions and health data can enhance the health and well-being of older adults. https://orcid.org/0000-0003-1618-8733

Christine Daum is a Research Assistant Professor in the School of Public Health Sciences at the University of Waterloo and holds an adjunct appointment in the Faculty of Rehabilitation Medicine at the University of Alberta. Her research utilizes qualitative and community-based methodologies, focusing on older adults and their care partners. https://orcid.org/0000-0001-5555-3698

Naomi Davis-Crane is a Senior Lecturer in Policing Studies at Liverpool John Moores University with a background in counter terrorism intelligence analysis, border security, major crime investigation, and prisons intelligence. Her research interests include organizational behaviour, leadership and culture in law enforcement, including their implications for strategic and tactical decision making. https://orcid.org/0009-0009-0956-7269

Simon Davis-Crane is a member of the UK Civil Service specializing in the development of cyber security policy for a large Government department. A skilled cyber practitioner, with a background in police information technology, Simon blends knowledge of cyber best practice with understanding of the realities of law enforcement. https://orcid.org/0009-0000-5825-3068

Eric Dlugolenski is an Assistant Professor of Criminology and Criminal Justice at Central Connecticut State University and a former police sergeant. He is an applied policing researcher, a Policing Fellow with the National Policing Institute, and a Law Enforcement Advancing Data and Science (LEADS) alumnus focused on police practice, policy, and emergent technologies. https://orcid.org/0000-0002-4621-7526

Alexis R. Fabila is a PhD student in Criminology and Criminal Justice at the University of South Carolina. Her research examines police and government organizations, discretion, victimization, and the governance of emerging technologies in criminal justice institutions.

Lorna Ferguson is an Assistant Professor of Criminology and Criminal Justice at the University of Regina and is the Founder of the Missing Persons Research Hub. Lorna has a broad interest in policing research and the development of evidence-based approaches to policing and crime prevention, including issues related to search and rescue, incident command, technologies, crime concentration, cybercrime, and individuals with mental illness. Her specialization is police responses to missing person cases. https://orcid.org/0000-0002-4077-9501

Meaghan Furlano is a PhD student in the Department of Sociology at the University of Western Ontario. She is a feminist Sociologist who uses qualitative methods to examine gender inequality, (anti)feminisms, digital femininities, and women's role in mainstreaming far-right and reactionary politics. Her work has been published in *Media, Culture & Society*, *European Journal of Cultural Studies*, and *Culture, Health & Sexuality*.

Ahmet Guler, PhD, is an Associate Teaching Professor in the Department of Sociology and Criminology at the Pennsylvania State University, University Park. His research examines criminal justice policy, policing, terrorism, criminal justice reform, information technology in criminal justice, and transnational crime. https://orcid.org/0000-0002-2739-7824

Cassidy B. Haigh is an Assistant Professor of Criminal Justice and Human Security at the University of Bridgeport. Her research and teaching interests include eyewitness identification, wrongful conviction, and criminal justice policy. https://orcid.org/0000-0001-7363-2189

Cole Heffren is a Police Sergeant and member of the Peel Regional Police. He is also currently a PhD student in the Department of Sociology at the University of Western Ontario. His research interests include the development and implementation of evidence-based strategies, such as place-based programs, incident command, leadership, and emerging technologies, as well as their intersection with police crime prevention initiatives.

Marius Hoggenmueller is a Lecturer in Interaction Design in the School of Architecture, Design and Planning at the University of Sydney. His research interests include the design of interactive urban technologies such as service robots and autonomous vehicles. His research has been published at key human-computer interaction (HCI) venues, including ACM CHI Conference on Human Factors in Computing Systems (CHI), ACM Designing Interactive Systems Conference (DIS), and ACM/IEEE International Conference on Human-Robot Interaction. https://orcid.org/0000-0002-8893-5729

Laura Huey is a Professor of Sociology at the University of Western Ontario and the Editor in Chief of two international journals: *Police Practice & Research* and *Evidence Base*. She is an alumnus of the College of New Scholars, Artists and Academics of the Royal Society of Canada, and sat on the RSC Covid Taskforce as the Chair of its working group on mental health and policing. She also founded the Canadian Society of Evidence Based Policing and was a member of the Board of SERENE-RISC (a NCE-funded cybercrime research consortium), a Senior Research Fellow at the US National Police Foundation, and a Senior Researcher and University Representative for the Canadian Network for Research on Terrorism, Security and Society. She has also been a member of the Canadian Council of Academies' Expert Panels on the Future of Canadian Policing and Cybercrime, respectively, and has sat on numerous boards and working groups related to community safety.

Anmol Jassal is an undergraduate student pursuing a BSc in Health Studies at the University of Waterloo. Anmol's work focuses on understanding the lived experiences of persons living with dementia, their care partners, and service providers, and how these experiences can help estimate and manage the risk of missing incidents.

Natasha N. Johnson is an Assistant Professor in the Department of Research, Counseling, and Curriculum in the College of Education and Human Development at Augusta University. https://orcid.org/0000-0001-8145-2153

Thaddeus L. Johnson is a senior fellow for the Council on Criminal Justice and Assistant Professor of Criminal Justice and Criminology at Georgia State University. https://orcid.org/0000-0002-2908-7897

Ardavan M. Khoshnood, MD, PhD, is an Associate Professor of Emergency Medicine and researcher at the Centre for Intelligence Studies at Lund University. He holds academic degrees in Criminology, Political Science, Police Work, and Intelligence Analysis. He has published extensively in the fields of intelligence and counterintelligence. https://orcid.org/0000-0002-3142-4119

Lisanne Kleygrewe, PhD, is a Senior Specialist in Modelling and Simulation at the Royal Netherlands Army Simulation Centre. Her research interests focus on human performance, training, and education, and the use of immersive and simulation-based technologies to support decision-making, learning, and operational readiness in military and police. https://orcid.org/0000-0001-9685-4198

Sedat Kula, PhD, is a senior researcher at the Global Centers for Security Studies. His research specializes in police management and behaviour, criminal justice policy, terrorism, and fear of crime. https://orcid.org/0000-0002-2488-423X

Jennifer Lavoie, PhD, is an Associate Professor in the departments of Psychology and Criminology at Wilfrid Laurier University and leads the Mental Health and Crisis Response (MHCR) program, a required de-escalation training program for police officers in Ontario, Canada. She conducts research centered on the nexus between policing and mental health crisis, primarily focusing on the design of police scenario-based training. https://orcid.org/0000-0002-0101-0732

Kai Lin is a Senior Lecturer in the Faculty of Design and Society at the University of Technology Sydney in Sydney, Australia. His research interests include the etiology of interpersonal violence, international and comparative criminology, policing, and cybercrime. His publications have appeared in journals such as the *Journal of Criminal Justice*, *Policing & Society*, *Asian Journal of Criminology*, *Journal of Criminology*, *Crime & Delinquency*, *Criminology & Criminal Justice*, *Police Practice & Research*, *Policing: An International Journal*, and *Policing: A Journal of Policy and Practice*. https://orcid.org/0000-0003-3966-0009

Lili Liu is Dean (Faculty of Health), and Professor (School of Public Health Sciences), University of Waterloo. Liu's research focuses on evaluation of innovations to support aging in place of choice, including communities. Liu leads Aging and Innovation Research Program and leads AGE-WELL's Autonomy and Independence Challenge Area. https://orcid.org/0000-0001-7082-4898

Maria Lungu is a legal scholar and public administration researcher with the Digital Technology for Democracy Lab at the University of Virginia. Her work examines the intersection of law, public administration, and artificial intelligence

(AI), with a focus on the use of AI in policing and the courts. Her research addresses how these systems shape decision-making, efficiency, and justice in administrative governance. https://orcid.org/0000-0003-0331-8658

Aili Malm is a Professor and Director of the School of Criminology, Criminal Justice and Emergency Management at California State University, Long Beach. Her research centers on the assessment and evaluation of policing strategies and intelligence. https://orcid.org/0000-0001-6059-0258

Kyle McLean is an Associate Professor in the Department of Sociology, Anthropology, and Criminal Justice at Clemson University. Dr. McLean works with law enforcement officers across the country to assess and recommend evidence-based practices for police departments.

John E. Muñoz, PhD, is an Assistant Professor of User Experience Design at Wilfrid Laurier University and director of the BioAdaptive Interface Lab. His research focuses on physiological computing, virtual reality, and adaptive biofeedback systems for training, rehabilitation, and mental health, with ongoing collaborations with police services and clinical partners. https://orcid.org/0000-0002-6161-9443

Nahanni Pollard, PhD, is the national Director of Public Safety at Deloitte Canada with over 20 years of experience advising police agencies on operational and organizational strategy and operations. Her work centers on implementing large-scale transformation within the public safety sector and applying evidence-based approaches to system excellence. She has taught policing at the post-secondary level for over 15 years and has published in the areas of policing, crime analysis, and public safety, including the textbook *Canadian Policing* (Oxford University Press). The views expressed in this work are those of the author alone.

Alan T. Pope, PhD, is a human factors scientist and former NASA Langley researcher whose work focuses on physiological computing, neuroergonomics, and adaptive automation. He is widely known for foundational contributions to biocybernetic adaptation, and the use of psychophysiological measures to support human performance in high-demand operational and training environments. https://orcid.org/0009-0002-4436-7341

Daniel J. Robinson is a Professor and Associate Dean in the Faculty of Information and Media Studies at Western University. He is the author of *Cigarette Nation: Business, Health, and Canadian Smokers, 1930–1975*, (McGill-Queen's University Press). His recent research examines the role of genealogy in society and culture.

Fraser Sampson LL.B.(Hons)., LL.M., MBA., PhD., Solicitor. Professor of Governance and National Security at the Centre for Excellence in Terrorism, Resilience, Intelligence & Organised Crime Research (CENTRIC), Sheffield Hallam University. He was the UK's first joint Biometrics and Surveillance Camera Commissioner, and is a strategic advisor to the Centre for Emerging Technology and Security (CETaS) at the Alan Turing Institute and a columnist for Biometric Update.

Ivan Y. Sun is a Professor in the Department of Sociology and Criminal Justice at the University of Delaware. His research interests include police attitudes and behaviour, public opinion on legal authorities, and crime and justice in Asian societies. His recent publications on policing have appeared in *Human Behavior and Law*, *Crime and Delinquency*, *Criminal Justice and Behavior*, *Journal of Interpersonal Violence*, *Police Quarterly*, and *Terrorism and Political Violence*. https://orcid.org/0000-0002-5679-196X

Wei Wang is a doctoral student in the Department of Sociology and Criminal Justice at the University of Delaware. Her research interests include health, psychology, and criminology. Her recent publications have appeared in *Psychology in School*, *International Journal of Environmental Research and Public Health*, and *Asian Journal of Criminology*. https://orcid.org/0000-0003-4467-902X

Seth Watts, PhD, is an Assistant Professor at Texas State University in the School of Criminal Justice and Criminology. He studies policing, technological innovation, and public health. https://orcid.org/0000-0002-5108-9055

Michael D. White, PhD, is a Professor in the School of Criminology and Criminal Justice at Arizona State University and is Associate Director of ASU's Center for Violence Prevention and Community Safety. Dr. White's primary research interests involve the police, including use of force, technology, and innovation. https://orcid.org/0000-0002-6151-6399

Lisa Whittingham, PhD, is an Assistant Professor in the Department of Applied Disability Studies at Brock University and a lead of the Mental Health Crisis Response (MHCR) program. Her research interests center around disability, the law, and crisis responses, as well as understanding the construction of disability and embodied experiences in police professionals and other first responders.

Qiuming Zhang is a PhD student in the School of Architecture Design and Planning at the University of Sydney. Her research interests include human-robot interaction (HRI), community engagement, community safety perception, and the integration of robotics in smart cities. Her recent studies have been accepted at Human-Computer Interaction (HCI) conferences, including the Australian Conference on Human-Computer Interaction (OzCHI) and ACM CHI Conference on Human Factors in Computing Systems (CHI). https://orcid.org/0009-0005-2502-3369

You Zhou is a Lecturer in the School of Law and Justice at the University of Newcastle in Australia. His research interests include cybercrime, future crimes, youth violence, criminological theories, and mixed methods. His recent studies have been published in cross-disciplinary journals including *Computers in Human Behavior*, *Law, Innovation and Technology*, *Crime & Delinquency*, *Behavioral Sciences & the Law*, and *Asian Journal of Criminology*. https://orcid.org/0000-0002-9255-5403

1

THE FUTURE IS NOW

An Introduction

Laura Huey, Lorna Ferguson, and Ian T. Adams

In 2013, the Government of Canada commissioned the Canadian Council of Academies (CCA) to convene an expert panel to draft a comprehensive statement on the 'future of policing'. One of us, with a direct view of the activities involved, likened the exercise to watching bureaucrats trying to herd cats while demanding the cats guess the number of angels dancing on the head of a hypothetical pin. The subsequent report, as is often the case with work commissioned by governments, fell somewhat short of its intended mark and was not known to be widely consulted by policymakers or police leaders. One of the reasons for this failure is undoubtedly that the panel, composed mainly of older academics and senior police leaders, was not particularly tech-savvy. Thus, references to new and emergent technology are scant throughout the document, couched in generic language, most frequently found in relation to cybercrime or in arguments for increased IT skills among police personnel (CCA, 2014). Written seven years after the launch of the Apple iPhone, the report urged police to adopt smartphones and laptops as tools for freeing up policing resources. Thus, one of the most significant revolutions in human history – the fourth industrial revolution (information technology) – was largely relegated to mentions of cybercrime, smartphones, and record management systems. Writing in 2026, at a time of ChatGPT, Meta glasses, facial recognition software, and Bitcoin, among other technologies increasingly populating our contemporary and future landscapes, such an oversight seems nothing less than mind-boggling.

Of course, it is always easy with the benefit of hindsight to identify failures in prophecy. Predicting the future *is* something of a tricky business. That said, this book takes up this challenge, exploring the present and future of public policing as this institution is shaped by new and emergent technologies. Drawing on the

DOI: 10.4324/9781003671312-1

scholarship of a cadre of international researchers, we present a collection of reports of cutting-edge research on technological innovations that could or will change the future of law enforcement for better or for worse.

Some of the technologies discussed in the chapters to follow include those that were known and/or in operation in 2014 when one of us was sitting through interminable meetings on the 'future of policing'. These include concepts such as 'cyberspace' and 'robots', as well as 'body-worn video', which was first piloted in the US in 2012. Indeed, much of the software discussed in this book is driven by artificial intelligence (AI), a research field established in academia in the 1950s. Automated facial recognition, today powered by AI, was pioneered in the 1960s. While it is the case that in 2014 AI was not at everyone's fingertips, thanks to Steve Jobs and the other gurus of mobile technology, some of the technologies discussed here *were* commercially available for policing and other uses in 2014, although they had yet to be perfected. Certainly, any qualitative researcher in 2014 would love to have had access to reasonably accurate 'voice to text' software. Today, voice to text translation has been greatly improved, and is now considered a standard feature of police body-worn camera systems. These innovations were knowable in 2014, just as the development of new technologies today can give us some insights into a possible future some ten years from now, if we have imagination.

The authors in this collection have imagination. Their work represents the cutting edge of thinking and research into the still nascent field where technology intersects with criminal justice. Drawing on empirical observations, they paint for us a policing future that is variously intriguing, concerning, hopeful, and troubling. Their work raises fundamental questions about such things as the nature of 'work', who 'owns' or can use your likeness from captured public images, and whether technology can improve or exacerbate racial equity issues in the criminal justice space, among others.

Several of the chapters highlight what can only be considered desirable benefits of the new technologies. For example, a chapter (5) by **Cruz, Daum, Comeau, Jassal, and Liu** examines the possibilities offered by improved data integration in cases involving individuals living with dementia. Increased data and data-sharing, they argue, can be used in ways to enhance the safety of this vulnerable population. Investigative genetic genealogy offers families and other loved ones the hope of resolving cases that have long gone cold, as **Arntfield and Robinson** discuss in their chapter (19) on this latest use for forensic DNA.

New technologies also offer the potential of significant improvements, such as greater efficiencies in public policing. **AlSabah and Alasfour** in Chapter 9 document how physiological instruments, such as the electrocardiogram, and AI-assisted assessments, can enhance officer readiness, training effectiveness, and stress mitigation. In an analysis of AI for more mundane tasks, **Fabila, Adams, and McLean** (Chapter 18) argue that while AI is unlikely to revolutionize policing, it appears poised to "reshape documentation practices, supervisory review, and feedback structures" – no small feat for anyone familiar with police paperwork. AI can also help improve officer performance and oversight through tools that analyze officers' behaviour during rare or unique citizen encounters, as **Watts, White, and Malm** point out in Chapter 14. De-escalation and use of force are also central concerns of 'The Heart of the Matter' by **Muñoz, Lavoie, Kleygrewe, Whittingham, and Pope** (Chapter 15). Reporting the results of four experimental studies, these authors examine the various training and other benefits that come from the pairing of virtual reality systems with bio-tracking. That said, as **Guler, Boke, and Kula** make explicit in Chapter 4, and as several contributors reiterate throughout this volume, the expansion of AI in policing requires more than technological enthusiasm, including robust, evidence-based policy frameworks grounded in empirical research and attentive to governance, accountability, and public trust.

Not all of the chapters in this collection are laudatory of the new technologies. Several authors present work here that should rightly spark concerns among readers. These include **Huey, Ferguson, Heffren, and Furlano**'s exploratory study of the state of police readiness to address the misuse of AI by terrorists and other malicious actors (Chapter 7). In Chapter 10, **Cline** examines the moral, ethical, and metaphysical dilemmas posed by predictive policing systems premised on the possibility of near-perfect forecasting. **Haigh and Dlugolenski** (Chapter 11) relay several potential harms associated with AI assistance in suspect identification, including accuracy, weaponization, and concerns about authority and power. Chapter 8 by **Davis-Crane and Davis-Crane** highlights ongoing warnings about weaknesses in security architecture that pose significant threats to cyberspace. Another chapter (12) by **Huey, Heffren, and Ferguson** raises critical questions about the rise of misinformation in the cybersphere and its potential misuse by political actors to damage police and other democratic institutions. **Khoshnood**'s chapter (13) looks at a different type of threat: the ways in which corrupt police 'insiders' can manipulate both technological and human vulnerabilities – from leaking data to compromising police operations. Khoshnood concludes that the best defense against such threats will lie with human and not technology-focused solutions.

A third cluster of chapters focuses our attention on both the benefits and drawbacks of new technologies. One of the first of its kind to explore the employment of police robots, **Lin, Zhou, Zhang, Hoggenmueller, Wang, and Sun**'s paper (Chapter 3) surveys Chinese police officers' attitudes towards their AI-powered counterparts, finding mixed attitudes to their usefulness. In another groundbreaking paper, **Johnson and Johnson** (Chapter 20) examine the crime deterrent and other effects of facial recognition technology, including answering timely questions as to whether this technology contributes to gaps in arrest disparities between Black and White citizens. In 'About Face' (Chapter 16),

Sampson similarly explores facial biometrics, but his work raises a different set of important questions, including whether they will become completely unnecessary in a world in which everyone carries surveillant power. **Pollard**'s piece (Chapter 2) on AI integration in policing focuses on, like the chapter by Fabila and colleagues (18), the role technology can play in improving operational efficiencies in law enforcement. She, too, recognizes that efficiency is important, but argues that this need must be balanced by equal concern for civil liberties and justice and equity concerns. Looking at the current and future use of quantum systems in law enforcement (Chapter 6), **Chowdhury** similarly sees both potential improvements in policing and what he takes to be serious moral and technical issues, including privacy violations, potential abuses, and systemic biases. Turning to predictive policing, **Lungu** (Chapter 17) emphasizes the necessity of sustained collaboration and meaningful community input in the design and deployment of predictive models, arguing that digital tools must be developed and implemented in ways that align law enforcement practices with the public interest rather than undermine it.

This collection appears at an uneasy time. We are in the early Spring of an innovation cycle following the 'AI winter' of the 1990s, which itself followed the first wave of AI promise beginning in the 1950s (Haigh, 2025). What's old is new again. Hundreds of vendors are selling unproven promises to thousands of agencies with billions in public funding at stake. Agentic software is gaining momentum, with the potential to shift routine decision work towards systems that act autonomously, learn from feedback, and scale quickly across organizations. That trajectory matters for policing, but it is not confined to policing. It reaches any public or private domain where work depends on information processing, prediction, writing, triage, and code. At the same time, quantum computing sits near the edge of commercial plausibility after decades of alternating hype and dread. Nearly every week brings a new promise of transformation alongside a warning of collapse. Those paired narratives are not noise. They reflect a genuine feature of technological change: the same tools that can expand capacity and reduce certain harms can also widen discretion, deepen opacity, and redistribute power in ways that are hard to reverse.

With history as a guide, most specific predictions in this volume will land somewhere between partly right and plainly wrong (Nilsson, 2009). That is not a defect. It is the cost of thinking ahead in a domain where adoption depends on budgets, procurement rules, vendor ecosystems, labour agreements, courts, and politics, not just technical feasibility. Policing rarely changes simply because a technology exists. It changes when technologies align with organizational incentives and when legal and administrative constraints either permit or compel new practices. The future tends to arrive unevenly: fast in some places and functions, slow in others, with unintended consequences concentrated where oversight is weakest.

Being wrong is the wage of being early, but early work still has value when it forces clearer questions. Some contributors here may prove more prophetic than they intend, if only because they specify the trade-offs precisely enough to be tested as adoption unfolds. The chapters that follow move beyond gadgets to the institutional choices that will determine whether new capacities improve documentation, supervision, and accountability; strengthen responses to urgent vulnerabilities (as in search and rescue or missing persons); or expand surveillance, entrench bias through poorly governed data systems, and outsource judgement to tools that are difficult to interrogate. Readers should treat the claims in this book as hypotheses about mechanisms: what new technologies make easier, what they fail to deliver, what they make tempting, and what they make harder to see. Readers have the opportunity, and the responsibility, to bring principled scrutiny to those trade-offs: to ask what problems are being solved, for whom, with what evidence, and under what constraints. The only inevitability is that policing will change. The open question is whether that change will be governed deliberately or absorbed by default.

AI Usage Acknowledgment

The editors and authors acknowledge the use of ChatGPT (GPT-4, OpenAI) during the preparation of Chapter 13 of this manuscript. The tool was used to support language refinement, structural suggestions, editing, and synthesis of author-provided content, with the aim of enhancing clarity, coherence, and readability. It was not used to generate original research ideas or theoretical frameworks. All outputs were critically reviewed, edited, and verified by the chapter author, who takes full responsibility for the final content. This use complies with the Taylor & Francis policy on the responsible use of generative AI in scholarly publishing: https://taylorandfrancis.com/our-policies/ai-policy/.

References

Canadian Council of Academies. (2014). *Policing Canada in the 21st century: new policing for new challenges*. Council of Canadian Academies.

Haigh, T. (2025). Artificial intelligence then and now. *Communications of the ACM*, *68*(2). https://doi.org/10.1145/3708554

Nilsson, N. J. (2009). *The quest for artificial intelligence*. Cambridge University Press. https://doi.org/10.1017/CBO9780511819346

2

THE ALGORITHMIC BEAT

Navigating the Double-Edged Sword of AI in Modern Policing

Nahanni Pollard

Introduction

The integration of artificial intelligence (AI) into policing represents a pivotal, and perilous, moment in the history of law enforcement. AI tools ranging from predictive policing algorithms and facial recognition systems to generative report-writing software promise to make policing more efficient, objective, and data-driven. Yet this very promise conceals a fundamental contradiction, one that this chapter terms the paradox of precision: the simultaneous capacity of AI to enhance public safety through data-driven efficiency while systematically threatening police legitimacy through algorithmic bias, opacity, and new forms of unaccountable power.

This paradox is not merely a technical problem to be engineered away. It is a governance challenge rooted in the social history of policing itself. AI systems do not operate in a vacuum; they inherit and amplify the values, priorities, and inequities (Lum & Isaac, 2016; Richardson et al., 2019) embedded in the data on which they are trained. When that data reflects decades of racially disparate enforcement, when the systems that generate outputs are owned by private corporations shielded by trade ownership, and when the humans who act on algorithmic recommendations are subject to well-documented cognitive biases, the promise of objective precision dissolves into a more complex and troubling reality (Barocas & Selbst, 2016; Harcourt, 2007; O'Neil, 2016).

In light of these challenges, the path forward involves not only technological advancements but also community engagement and legislative reform. Proposed changes, such as the establishment of comprehensive regulations governing AI use in policing, are gaining traction at both the state and local levels, reflecting a

DOI: 10.4324/9781003671312-2

broader recognition of the necessity of oversight in automated decision-making processes (National Academies of Sciences, Engineering, and Medicine, 2017). Additionally, fostering public trust through transparency and accountability measures will be crucial as law enforcement agencies navigate the ethical complexities of AI deployment (Whittaker et al., 2018).

Ultimately, the future of policing with AI integration hinges on law enforcement's ability to strike a balance between operational efficiency and the protection of civil liberties. As the dialogue surrounding AI technologies evolves, a collaborative approach involving community stakeholders and advocacy groups will be essential to ensure that innovations in policing are implemented in ways that promote justice and equity for all (National Academies of Sciences, Engineering, and Medicine, 2017; Whittaker et al., 2018).

This chapter does not attempt a comprehensive survey of all AI technologies used in policing. That broader mapping and evaluative work is already being undertaken, often with greater technical and jurisdictional breadth, by scholars and policy institutions examining the full range of police AI applications, their empirical performance, and emerging governance responses (see most recently Perrin et al., 2026). Building on this growing body of work, the aim here is more selective and analytic: to use representative, high-impact examples to identify the deeper governance dynamics that recur across otherwise distinct technologies.

This chapter advances a specific analytical argument: the adoption of AI in policing generates three mutually reinforcing core tensions that cannot be resolved by technological improvement alone but must be actively managed through deliberate governance. These tensions are the conflict between *Efficiency* and *Equity*, the struggle between *Transparency* and *Security*, and the dilemma of *Accountability* versus *Automation*. Understanding how these tensions interact and compound one another is essential for any police leader, policymaker, or scholar seeking to navigate the algorithmic future responsibly.

The chapter proceeds in four parts. The first part traces the historical and conceptual trajectory that brought policing to this technological moment, establishing the intellectual context for the paradox of precision. The second part provides a functional typology of the AI tools now deployed across the law enforcement process, from crime prediction to post-incident investigation. The third part, the analytical core of the chapter, examines each of the three core tensions in depth, drawing on recent empirical research to illustrate how each manifests in practice and why each resists easy resolution. The fourth part proposes a governance framework organized around the HALT principles (Human-in-the-Loop, Auditable, Lawful, and Trainable) as a practical foundation for responsible AI adoption. The chapter concludes by arguing that technology alone cannot resolve the paradox of precision; only a renewed commitment to the foundational values of democratic policing can.

From Intuition to Inference: The Making of the Algorithmic Beat

To understand why AI creates such profound challenges for policing, one must first understand the century-long trajectory that prepared the ground for it. Modern policing has always been an information enterprise, but the nature and scale of that information have been transformed repeatedly by technology.

For much of the early twentieth century, the police officer's primary information system was their own embodied knowledge. The beat officer knew a neighbourhood's rhythms, its residents, and its tensions (Kelling & Moore, 1988). The advent of the automobile and two-way radio fundamentally disrupted this model. By untethering officers from geographic beats and routing them through a central dispatch, the so-called dial-a-cop model shifted the primary driver of police activity from proactive community knowledge to reactive management of incidents recorded in a call log (Sparrow, 2014). The focus moved from knowing a community to processing its emergencies.

The next major shift arrived with CompStat in the 1990s. Not an AI system, it was nonetheless the philosophical forerunner of today's algorithmic tools. By harnessing crime statistics with geographic information systems (GIS), CompStat empowered commanders to identify crime hotspots and deploy resources with unprecedented speed (Bratton & Knobler, 1998). Its core logic, that policing could be managed and improved through data, institutionalized a culture of quantitative accountability. Yet CompStat also revealed the perils of data-driven management: intense pressure to demonstrate crime reductions, incentivized aggressive enforcement tactics, and, critics argued, outright data manipulation (Eterno & Silverman, 2012). The organizational appetite for data it created, along with the governance problems it produced, are the direct antecedents of the AI dilemmas that law enforcement faces today.

These shifts were further reinforced by the rise of Evidence-Based Policing (EBP), which advocated that law enforcement practices be guided by rigorous scientific evidence of what works (Sherman, 2013). EBP cemented the idea that the craft of policing could and should be transformed into a science, a project that AI now pursues with far greater computational power than any of its predecessors.

AI represents the latest and most powerful iteration of this decades-long transformation, introducing what this chapter calls the Algorithmic Beat. This is not simply a new technology added to an existing system; it represents a qualitatively new mode of police decision-making, one that reshapes administrative discretion and professional judgment in ways that earlier technological changes did not (Brayne, 2021; Meijer & Wessels, 2019). The critical leap is the transition from descriptive and diagnostic analytics, concerned with what happened and why, to predictive and prescriptive analytics: what will likely happen next, and what should be done about it (Hardyns & Rummens, 2019; Lee et al., 2024). On the Algorithmic Beat, computational inference shapes police work before a crime occurs through hotspot prediction, during a critical incident through real-time facial recognition, and after the fact through AI-assisted forensic analysis. The officer's intuition has been translated into an algorithm, and in that translation, much is at risk. Scholars of public administration have argued that algorithmic systems in high-stakes domains are simultaneously eroding the two foundations on which institutional legitimacy rests: professional expertise and public accountability (Busuioc, 2020; Grimmelikhuijsen et al., 2022). It is precisely these foundations – transparency, equity, and accountability – that democratic policing requires.

The AI Arsenal: A Functional Typology

The landscape of policing AI is not monolithic. It is a diverse ecosystem of tools intervening at different stages of the law enforcement process. This section categorizes these technologies by function, before, during, and after a crime, to clarify both their capabilities and the specific governance challenges each raises.

Predictive and Proactive AI (Before the Act)

The most prominent and controversial category of policing AI aims to forecast and prevent crime before it occurs. Place-based forecasting, commonly known as predictive policing, uses historical crime data to calculate where and when future crimes are most likely to occur. Drawing on criminological principles such as near-repeat theory, which posits that the risk of a similar crime in the vicinity is elevated for a short period following an initial offence (Townsley et al., 2003), these algorithms generate daily forecasts displayed as high-risk geographic areas or hotspots that patrol officers are directed to target (Mohler et al., 2015). The underlying logic represents a deliberate shift from descriptive and reactive analysis toward pre-emptive forecasting: rather than explaining past crime, these systems prescribe future enforcement actions (Hardyns & Rummens, 2019). Modern systems are increasingly sophisticated, integrating live Internet of Things (IoT) data and grounding predictions in established criminological theory. The Guardians of Tomorrow framework, for example, transforms environmental factors into predictive features based on Situational Crime Prevention theory, modelling crime across dimensions of criminal effort, risk, reward, and opportunity (Sun et al., 2025).

The evidence base for these systems is promising in narrow conditions but considerably more limited than their widespread adoption suggests. A systematic review of hundreds of predictive policing studies found that only a handful provided strong real-world evidence of effectiveness, with those showing localized reductions in property crime but no consistent effect on violent crime, and none examining ethical concerns, including algorithmic bias or over-policing (Meijer & Wessels, 2019). Ethnographic research conducted inside a police department found that big data adoption does not replace prior police practices so much as it amplifies them, quantifying risk assessments that officers previously made by discretion and dramatically lowering the threshold for inclusion in law enforcement databases to encompass individuals with no direct police contact (Brayne, 2017; 2021). The result is a system that simultaneously promises greater precision and widens the net of algorithmic suspicion.

A more contentious application involves person-based forecasting: assessing the predicted risk level of specific individuals. Law enforcement agencies have developed strategic subject lists using algorithms that weigh risk factors such as arrest history, known associations, and history of victimization (Saunders et al., 2016). The most analytically sophisticated of these tools draws on network science research, specifically the social contagion model of gun violence developed by Green et al. (2017), which demonstrated that an individual's position within co-offending networks is a significant predictor of future gunshot victimization. Chicago's Strategic Subject List (SSL) incorporated this logic, using co-arrest data to map social ties and assign risk scores based on network proximity to violence.

The stated goal of these programs is proactive intervention rather than arrest, but the practice raises profound ethical, legal, and empirical concerns. Direct empirical analysis of the SSL found that its algorithmically derived risk scores predict the race and ethnicity of the arrested person even after controlling for local spatial conditions, including poverty and racial composition – evidence that the system encodes racial bias despite its claims to scientific objectivity (DaViera et al., 2024). Legal scholars have documented the constitutional dimensions of this problem: because person-based tools substitute statistical probability for the individualized suspicion required under jurisprudence rules, they risk eroding the presumption of innocence and generating a self-fulfilling prophecy in which the identification of an individual as high-risk changes how police interact with them, thereby increasing their actual exposure to the criminal justice system independent of their behaviour (Slobogin, 2025; National Academies of Sciences, Engineering, and Medicine, 2024).

Perceptive and Responsive AI (During the Act)

The second category augments law enforcement's situational awareness during real-time events. Automated sensing tools, including acoustic gunshot detection systems, Automated License Plate Readers (ALPRs), and real-time facial recognition, process data at speeds and scales impossible for human officers, and agencies have invested substantially in these capabilities in response to genuine operational needs. Their performance claims are, however, unevenly supported by evidence. A 2025 systematic review and meta-analysis found no significant relationship between gunshot detection deployment and crime reduction across evaluations (Huff et al., 2026), and a 2024 New York City government audit found that 80–92% of alerts resulted in no confirmed shooting (Office of the NYC Comptroller, 2024). ALPRs offer more established investigative utility, but their rapid expansion has outpaced regulatory frameworks, with data retention periods varying from weeks to years across states and no federal standard in place (Berris et al., 2025).

Real-time facial recognition is the most powerful and contested of these tools, with documented utility in identifying suspects and locating missing persons alongside serious and empirically established risks. Benchmark testing has found error rates approaching 35% for darker-skinned women versus below 1% for lighter-skinned men (Buolamwini & Gebru, 2018), and National Institute of Standards and Technology benchmarking shows performance degradation on low-quality probe images, and civil society commenters argue these failure modes have significant implications for due process and accountability (Grother & Ngan, 2014; Electronic Privacy Information Center, 2024). These limitations have contributed to documented wrongful arrests, reflecting both algorithmic bias and procedural failures in how officers act on algorithmic outputs (American Civil Liberties Union, 2024; Sanford, 2024). Several departments have responded by requiring corroborating evidence before acting on a match, pointing toward governance solutions rather than wholesale rejection of the technology.

Real-Time Crime Centers (RTCCs) have emerged as the organizational response to data overload: centralized hubs fusing live 911 data, officer GPS, ALPR feeds, gunshot detections, video streams, and criminal records onto a single operational display. Early empirical evidence is cautiously positive, with quasi-experimental research finding improved case clearance rates (Arrietti, 2024; Guerette et al., 2025). Adoption has nonetheless consistently outpaced evaluation, and the absence of federal standards governing data retention and access leaves the long-term civil liberties implications of this centralized infrastructure without clear institutional answers.

Investigative and Analytical AI (After the Act)

Post-incident investigative AI has substantially transformed detective work. Retrospective facial recognition involves taking a still image of an unknown suspect and comparing it against large databases, including driver's licence photos and, controversially, images scraped from social media, to generate investigative leads from evidence that would previously have been unidentifiable (Garvie & Wessler, 2016). AI also accelerates DNA analysis, helping forensic scientists disentangle complex mixtures with greater speed and accuracy (Phan et al., 2021). These biometric tools are supplemented by automated fingerprint recognition, multi-biometric fusion systems, and AI-driven tools for generating facial composites.

Digital forensics represents another rapidly expanding frontier. Natural Language Processing (NLP) algorithms can scan thousands of emails, text messages, and documents to identify keywords, named entities, themes, and sentiment, flagging relevant evidence for human review; working systems have been validated on real-world communications corpora covering fraud, organized crime, and cyber-offences (Damevski et al., 2023; Adkins et al., 2024; Sun et al., 2021). Large-scale social network analysis platforms extend this further, mapping the structure of criminal enterprises from call records, financial transactions, and social media connections to identify hierarchies, brokers, and communication patterns obscured by sheer data volume (Sparrow, 1991). Simulation studies on real criminal networks have found that targeting actors ranked by betweenness centrality, their role as structural brokers between disconnected subgroups, is the most consistently effective disruption strategy (Ficara et al., 2020). These tools nonetheless carry significant methodological limits: criminal network data derived from arrest records and intercepted communications is structurally incomplete and shaped by investigative priorities rather than network reality, and research shows that missing data can render centrality-based targeting strategies ineffective, while criminal organizations tend to reorganize and adapt in response to disruption (Bright et al., 2021). What unites these tools is the ambition to find the signal in the noise, transforming investigative work from a slow, human-paced process into rapid, algorithmic triage, though the reliability of that triage depends directly on the quality and completeness of the underlying data.

Administrative AI (Operational Support)

A growing category of policing AI targets not crime-fighting but operational efficiency. For example, Generative AI (GenAI) tools are using Large Language Models (LLMs) to synthesize body-worn camera footage and officer notes into initial drafts of police reports in real time (Brems, 2025). These tools are touted as being capable of reducing report-writing time, which can account for a substantial proportion of an officer's shift, by half or more, with some departments reporting time savings above that (Adams et al., 2024).

Independent research has complicated these claims considerably. A preregistered randomized controlled trial involving 85 officers and 755 reports found that AI assistance did not significantly reduce the time required to complete reports, and a follow-up difference-in-differences analysis across thousands of reports over a full year confirmed the null finding (Adams et al., 2024). At the same time, follow-on survey evidence suggests a perception-performance gap: officers and supervisors reported generally favourable views of AI-assisted report writing, including perceived time savings among a substantial subset of treated officers, despite the objective time-use findings (Boehme et al., 2025). This divergence between perceived and actual efficiency is itself analytically significant, as it reflects the automation bias discussed herein, wherein officers defer to and trust AI-assisted processes even when objective evidence does not warrant that confidence.

The Crucible of Implementation: Three Core Tensions

The AI arsenal described earlier offers law enforcement a suite of powerful capabilities. Its deployment, however, forces a confrontation with deep-seated ethical, legal, and social challenges. It is in the crucible of implementation, where the idealized precision of the algorithm meets the complex and contested reality of the street, that the paradox of precision becomes manifest.

This section analyzes the three core tensions that this confrontation generates. These are not discrete technical problems amenable to engineering solutions; they are enduring governance dilemmas that interact with and amplify one another. How police agencies, courts, and communities navigate them will determine whether AI becomes a tool for enhanced public safety or a catalyst for diminished public trust. These tensions are further intensified by an evolving external threat environment: the same AI capabilities being adopted by law enforcement are being weaponized by malicious actors, creating a new class of AI-enabled crime, including deepfakes, learning-based cyberattacks, and automated fraud, that is scalable, disruptive, and difficult to counter (Caldwell et al., 2020). The urgency to deploy AI thus itself becomes a pressure that can undermine careful governance.

Efficiency versus Equity: The Bias in the Machine

The primary justification for investing in police AI is the promise of efficiency: allocating patrol officers to precisely the locations they are most needed, identifying investigative leads in minutes from large volumes of data, and focusing crime prevention on the highest-risk individuals. This logic of optimization, however, runs directly into the historical and social complexities of policing, creating a tension in which the drive for efficiency can systematically undermine the pursuit of equity.

The foundational problem lies in the data on which AI systems are built. Police data is not a neutral, objective record of societal crime; it is a record of police priorities and enforcement actions (Harcourt, 2007). An algorithm trained on this data will inevitably learn historical patterns, producing a dangerous algorithmic feedback loop (Lum & Isaac, 2016; Richardson et al., 2019). A systematic review of algorithmic fairness research in predictive policing finds that police actions are a major contributor to model discrimination, and that meaningful fairness interventions remain challenging and incomplete across protected attributes (Almasoud & Idowu, 2025).

The mechanics of this feedback loop are well documented and have been formally modelled. Ensign et al. (2018) developed a mathematical model that proves why the loop occurs: a system trained on discovered crime data (arrests generated by officer presence) will reliably converge on sending officers back to the same neighbourhoods regardless of the true underlying crime rate, and the severity of the divergence is quantitatively linked to the initial disparity in enforcement across areas. The result, empirically demonstrated through simulation police data, is that the system directs policing overwhelmingly toward low-income minority communities, even when independent survey data shows drug use is distributed relatively evenly across the population (Lum & Isaac, 2016). Attempts to break the loop by replacing arrest data with victim crime reports have not resolved the problem: Akpinar et al. (2021) showed that victim reporting rates are themselves racially and spatially unequal, producing comparable disparities through a different route. The result is a self-reinforcing dynamic in which algorithm and police operations validate each other, making the over-policing of a community appear to be an objective, data-driven necessity when it is, in fact, a mathematical amplification of prior injustice (Brantingham, 2018).

This feedback loop is exacerbated by cognitive mechanisms at the street level. Dittmann et al. (2025) describe a cycle of bias in AI-assisted police work in which biased information from AI tools can shape officers' initial impressions under time pressure, increasing reliance on cognitive shortcuts. Officers may then interact with members of the public in ways that reflect those biased impressions, potentially escalating encounters through self-reinforcing expectations. Finally, incident reports can reflect confirmation bias – becoming sparse, vague, or selectively detailed – and these reports can then help reproduce the same patterns in downstream records and decision processes. In this account, bias is not a flaw in the algorithm alone; it is a property of the broader sociotechnical system, including the human decision-makers embedded within it.

Even when developers consciously exclude protected variables such as race from a model, systems can engage in proxy discrimination. Variables such as postal code, income level, or consumer behaviour, which may be strongly correlated with race in some areas, can allow algorithms to produce racially disparate outcomes without ever using race as an input (Barocas & Selbst, 2016). The absence of explicit race data in an algorithm's features, therefore, provides no assurance of equitable outcomes.

The equity challenge extends beyond predictive policing to the real-time deployment of AI in sensitive situations. Research on public acceptance of AI-powered CCTV for suicide prevention found broad acceptance in principle, but qualitative data revealed deep concerns about racial bias in both the AI analysis itself and the police response it triggers (Hardy et al., 2024). Participants from non-White backgrounds specifically highlighted how intersecting identities, including race, gender, and Indigenous status, could expose them to compounded discrimination when AI systems miscategorize their behaviour. Several respondents argued that systems designed to protect public safety would be more effective if medical professionals, rather than police, were alerted, noting that calling police in response to a person in crisis can place that person at greater risk (Hardy et al., 2024). This critique is analytically significant because it extends the bias argument beyond the passive perpetuation of historical data to the active misinterpretation of human distress by automated systems, where the speed of an automated alert can produce a highly inequitable and potentially lethal response.

The bias risk extends even to administrative AI. Generative AI systems used to draft police reports are trained on massive datasets that reflect societal biases and stereotypes. The Fair and Just Prosecution (2025) policy brief warns that AI-generated reports present serious threats to accuracy and due process, documenting cases in which AI hallucinated information, including naming officers who were not present and misattributing actions to individuals. If the official account of a police encounter is partly authored by a system that can generate factually incorrect content, the implications for judicial outcomes are profound.

Researchers have also begun to propose AI-driven solutions to human bias at the point of enforcement. Noriega (2020) argues that deploying AI as an interviewer in police interrogations could create a more neutral environment designed to mitigate racial and gender disparities in false confession statistics. The core premise is that a machine, if properly designed and maintained, can provide more consistent information gathering than a human interrogator whose confirmation bias is demonstrably influential. While theoretically compelling, this proposal itself illustrates the paradox of precision: the solution to human bias is an algorithm, which introduces its own opacity and accountability challenges, the very problems examined in the sections that follow.

Across all of these applications, the evidence suggests that the efficiency gains promised by AI risk being purchased at the cost of equity, and that the communities least able to absorb that cost are consistently those asked to bear it. A 2025 empirical study using structural equation modelling found that public perceptions of procedural justice, specifically whether AI policing tools are seen as neutral, voice-giving, and trustworthy, fully mediate the relationship between AI knowledge and public support for these technologies (Guler et al., 2025). In other words, efficiency gains that are not accompanied by demonstrable fairness will erode the public legitimacy on which policing ultimately depends.

Transparency versus Security: The Black Box Dilemma

For police to be considered legitimate in a democratic society, their actions must be transparent and understandable to the public they serve. Procedural justice theory holds that authority is perceived as legitimate when it is exercised fairly, consistently, and with explanation (Tyler, 2006). The increasing reliance on AI introduces a powerful counter-current of opacity. This is commonly referred to as the black box problem, and it operates at three distinct and compounding layers.

The first layer is technical opacity. Many powerful AI models, particularly those using deep learning or neural networks, are inherently inscrutable. Unlike rule-based programs, these models learn by identifying patterns across millions of data points, creating a complex web of weighted variables that cannot be easily translated into human-readable logic. A system may assign a high-risk score to a neighbourhood or an individual, but it may be technically impossible even for the system's designers to articulate the precise combination of factors that led to that conclusion (Burrell, 2016). The system produces outputs; the reasoning behind those outputs remains opaque. For certain classes of deep learning models, this inscrutability is an inherent feature of how they work rather than a temporary limitation to be overcome.

The second layer is commercial opacity. The vast majority of AI tools used by law enforcement are developed by private corporations that treat their source code, training data, and algorithmic logic as proprietary trade secrets. When a police department procures such a system, it typically does so without gaining full access to its internal mechanics. When pressed by courts or community oversight boards to explain potentially biased outcomes, police agencies can only deflect, stating that the information is proprietary. This creates a severe accountability gap in which the public interest in understanding how consequential decisions are made is subordinated to the vendor's commercial interest in protecting competitive advantage (Whittaker et al., 2018; Grimm et al., 2021). The design of some AI report-writing tools illustrates this with particular clarity. Investigations into commercially deployed systems have found that AI-generated drafts may be permanently deleted once a report is exported, making it architecturally impossible to audit the AI's contribution to the final document (Guariglia, 2025). Ferguson (2025) identifies this as a foundational legal challenge, arguing that LLM-assisted police reports risk infecting the criminal justice system's foundational documents with unverifiable AI-generated content. California and Utah have responded with state legislation: California's SB 524 requires departments to retain the first AI-generated draft for judicial and defence review and prohibits vendors from selling data provided by police to the AI, while Utah's SB 180 mandates a disclaimer when reports contain AI-generated content and requires officer certification of accuracy (Ferguson, 2025).

The third layer is institutional opacity. Police and intelligence agencies traditionally argue that full transparency about their methods would compromise public safety: if the precise weightings of a predictive policing algorithm were made public, sophisticated offenders could exploit that knowledge. Similarly, revealing the capabilities and vulnerabilities of facial recognition tools could allow adversaries to develop countermeasures. This concern has genuine merit and is amplified by the contemporary threat environment. When AI is leveraged by criminal organizations to create learning-based cyberattacks, or when adversarial states use AI-generated disinformation to undermine democratic institutions (Caldwell et al., 2020; Mohammad et al., 2025), the argument for maintaining operational secrecy becomes more acute. However, institutional opacity is also routinely invoked as a blanket justification to resist legitimate public inquiry into the fairness and efficacy of AI systems (Ferguson, 2017). The result is a governance vacuum in which the public, courts, and oversight bodies cannot assess whether the tools being used in their name are working as claimed.

The demand for Explainable AI (XAI) represents the most promising technical response to these challenges. XAI encompasses methods and frameworks designed to make algorithmic outputs understandable to human users and auditors, prioritizing interpretable models over opaque ones for sensitive public-sector tasks (Goncalves et al., 2022; Hoffman et al., 2018). Research on contestable AI for criminal intelligence analysis argues that systems used in investigations must be designed so that human investigators can understand and challenge the system's reasoning, reframing explainability not merely as a technical aspiration but as a democratic requirement (Maoro & Geierhos, 2025). However, XAI cannot resolve the commercial and institutional dimensions of opacity; those require legal and regulatory intervention.

The most significant regulatory development in this space is the *European Union AI Act*, which became fully operational in February 2025. The Act classifies real-time remote biometric identification by police as permissible only under strict conditions, including a mandatory fundamental rights impact assessment, and prohibits AI systems that assess the risk of an individual committing a criminal offence based solely on profiling (European Parliament & Council of the European Union, 2024). Practical guidance developed under the Act for European law enforcement agencies explicitly distinguishes between institutional accountability, borne by the law enforcement agency, and personal responsibility, borne by the individual officer, providing a regulatory framework for addressing the diffusion of responsibility that AI introduces (CYCLOPES Project, 2025). In the United Kingdom, a government consultation launched in December 2025 acknowledged that the Metropolitan Police made 962 arrests using live facial recognition in a single year while also acknowledging legitimate public concerns about proportionality and biometric data governance (United Kingdom Home Office, 2025). In the United States, 15 states had enacted some form of facial recognition legislation by early 2025, with several prohibiting arrest warrant applications based solely on facial recognition results, a direct legislative response to documented wrongful arrests (Garvie & Wessler, 2016; National Conference of State Legislatures, 2026).

The consequences of multi-layered opacity are profound for due process. When police justify patrol decisions by citing algorithmic outputs without being able to explain the reasoning behind them, it frustrates any attempt at genuine accountability. More critically, it poses a direct challenge to fundamental legal principles governing disclosure of evidence. Courts are increasingly confronting the question of whether prosecutors must disclose information about an AI system's error rates, potential biases, and underlying methodology when that system was used to identify a suspect (Ferguson, 2017; Grimm et al., 2021). Without such transparency, defendants are left to challenge an accuser whose reasoning they cannot access or scrutinize, a situation that strains the most basic requirements of a fair trial.

Accountability versus Automation: The Ghost in the Machine

The entire structure of modern police accountability, from civilian oversight and internal affairs to judicial review, is built on the premise of human agency. It assumes that officers exercise discretion, that supervisors make strategic decisions, and that these humans can be held responsible for the outcomes of their choices. The integration of AI fundamentally disrupts this model by inserting a non-human actor into the chain of command, creating what scholars of automated systems have termed a "moral crumple zone": a structural dynamic in which the nearest human operator absorbs moral and legal responsibility for outcomes they did not fully control, while the technological system itself is insulated from blame (Elish, 2019). When an AI-guided action leads to a harmful outcome, the question of who is responsible has no clear answer, and empirical research suggests that citizens are themselves less likely to demand accountability from public institutions when harms are algorithmic rather than human in origin, compounding rather than correcting the governance gap (Grimmelikhuijsen et al., 2025).

This challenge is rooted in the well-documented psychological phenomenon of automation bias: the human tendency to over-rely on and uncritically accept suggestions from automated systems, even in the face of contradictory evidence (Parasuraman & Manzey, 2010). An officer may treat an individual with greater suspicion if a real-time risk assessment has flagged them as high-risk. An analyst may confirm a facial recognition match with less scrutiny if the system reports a high confidence score, affording the machine's output an authority that a tip from a human informant would not receive. The machine's output is perceived as objective and authoritative, subtly shifting the locus of decision-making from the officer to the system.

This shift carries significant implications for legal accountability. When an adverse outcome follows an officer's action on a high-risk algorithmic alert, responsibility is diffused among the human officer, the procuring agency, and the private company that built the tool, and is, in practice, held by none of them with adequate clarity. The officer argues they were following the data; the department argues the vendor's system was at fault; the vendor argues their system produced only a probability score, not an instruction to act.

The accountability problem is vividly illustrated in the context of AI-enabled crisis intervention. Australian police officers discussing the deployment of AI for real-time suicide detection expressed concern not primarily about ethics but about their own liability when the system fails. Officers asked explicitly whether a failure to act on an AI alert could be used against them in a subsequent review (Hardy et al., 2024). This anxiety reflects a precise accountability trap: the AI's promise of objective accuracy creates an expectation of omniscience, and when the system generates a false negative or misclassifies a situation, blame shifts to the human officer. The ghost in the machine becomes a tool for shifting institutional responsibility rather than bearing it.

A growing body of research suggests, however, that AI can also be deployed to resolve accountability failures by providing objective oversight of police conduct, reversing the usual direction of algorithmic surveillance. Arnav and Ensari (2024) used computer vision algorithms applied to publicly available traffic cameras to automatically detect and report illegal parking violations, then tracked the NYPD's resolution of those complaints in real time. Their findings empirically documented a widespread failure of accountability: of complaints closed by officers, 52.2% were resolved while the vehicle was still illegally parked, and complaint resolutions were frequently submitted within five minutes, suggesting officers were closing cases without on-site verification. The system provided a quantitative, verifiable record of discrepancies between official resolution descriptions and actual on-the-ground conditions, creating an irrefutable basis for accountability that self-reporting could never provide.

A simulation study on AI and police workforce automation adds a further dimension to these concerns, finding that large numbers of police employees face full or partial automation risk, with civilian back-office roles most affected while frontline policing is more likely to be augmented than fully replaced (Halford, 2026). As more elements of the policing process are delegated to automated systems, the accountability gap at each delegation point widens. Designing AI specifically to audit human police conduct, rather than only to direct it, represents a design choice that police agencies and policymakers could make deliberately. Agencies that deploy AI to surveil communities without simultaneously deploying mechanisms for algorithmic oversight of their own operations are making a choice about who bears the burden of the technology's risks.

Governing the Algorithmic Beat: A Framework for Responsible Innovation

The challenges of bias, opacity, and diffused accountability are not inevitable outcomes of technological progress; they are failures of governance. Confronting the paradox of precision requires a deliberate, multi-faceted strategy that treats the adoption of AI as a profound policy decision rather than a routine technical procurement. This section proposes a governance framework organized around the HALT mnemonic (Human-in-the-Loop, Auditable, Lawful, and Trainable) as a practical foundation for responsible AI adoption in policing. While elements of this framework echo established principles in responsible AI and police governance, particularly human oversight, auditability, and legality (see INTERPOL & UNICRI, 2020; Organisation for Economic Co-operation and Development, 2019; National Institute of Standards and Technology, 2023), the HALT framework advances a more compact and operational synthesis tailored specifically to the institutional realities of policing. Its contribution lies not in introducing new ethical concepts, but in integrating them into a governance test that is actionable, cumulative, and resistant to purely technical fixes. This framework is broadly consistent with the Police AI Covenant recently published by the UK National Police Chiefs' Council, which similarly grounds responsible AI deployment in principles of lawfulness, transparency, explainability, accountability, and evidence-led practice (National Police Chiefs' Council, 2023).

The HALT Principle

Human-in-the-Loop (H). The most critical governance backstop is ensuring that AI serves as a decision-support tool rather than the decision-maker itself. The ultimate moral and legal authority for any police action must rest with a human being. Policy should mandate that no person be stopped, searched, or arrested based solely on the output of an algorithmic system. AI-generated leads should be treated as any other investigative tip, requiring independent, human-led corroboration before action is taken (INTERPOL & UNICRI, 2020). Beyond policy mandate, the human-in-the-loop principle requires a recalibration of officer mindset. Training and interface design should position AI as a limited collaborator rather than an authoritative decision-maker, actively encouraging officers to maintain professional skepticism toward algorithmic outputs (Hoffman et al., 2018). Halford's (2025) Transformer Led Policing (TLP) model, which structures AI integration around a three-tier framework of Devise, Discuss, and Deploy, offers a practical institutional template for embedding this principle into operational practice. The TLP model explicitly incorporates procedural fairness and legitimacy considerations at each stage, demonstrating that human oversight and operational efficiency are complementary rather than competing goals.

Auditable (A). Vendor contracts that forbid independent auditing are inherently problematic to the premise of auditability. Before and during deployment, all AI systems should be subjected to regular audits by independent third parties that test not only for accuracy and effectiveness but explicitly for discriminatory impact against protected groups using the agency's own local data. Summary results of these audits should be made public, balanced against legitimate operational security needs (Whittaker et al., 2018). The concept of auditability should also extend to human officers. As demonstrated by Arnav and Ensari (2024), technological tools can objectively verify whether officers' reported actions align with real-world outcomes.

Lawful (L). Legal compliance must be a proactive rather than reactive consideration. Prior to procurement, every AI tool should undergo a thorough legal and ethical review assessing its potential impact on constitutional and statutory rights, including privacy, due process, and equal protection. In the Canadian context, this assessment should explicitly engage rights guaranteed under the Canadian Charter of Rights and Freedoms (Ferguson, 2017; Scassa, 2023; Veale & Binns, 2017). Jurisdictions should mandate the creation of an Algorithmic Impact Assessment (AIA) before any new AI system is acquired: a public document outlining the technology's purpose, data sources, potential negative impacts on privacy and equity, and specific mitigation steps (Reisman et al., 2018). The EU AI Act's mandatory fundamental rights impact assessment for high-risk policing applications provides a legislative model for this requirement (European Parliament & Council of the European Union, 2024).

Trainable (T). Training for AI systems cannot be limited to technical proficiency. Officers and analysts must be comprehensively educated on the tool's limitations: the specific data it was built on, its known error rates, its statistical margins of error, and its potential for bias. Training curricula must address the psychology of automation bias, teaching officers to treat algorithmic recommendations with the same professional skepticism they would apply to any other form of evidence (Parasuraman & Manzey, 2010). The goal is not technical competence alone but a professional culture of informed and critical AI use.

Public Legitimacy Through Engagement

Internal governance alone is insufficient. Because police AI directly impacts public life and liberty, its legitimacy can only be secured through genuine public engagement. Research consistently shows that perceptions of procedural justice, specifically whether communities view AI policing tools as neutral, voice-giving, and trustworthy, are the primary determinants of public support for these technologies (Guler et al., 2025). Policies governing AI and surveillance technologies should therefore be developed in active consultation with community oversight boards and civil liberties organizations (National Academies of Sciences, Engineering, and Medicine, 2017).

The Algorithmic Impact Assessment process should be treated not as a regulatory hurdle but as an opportunity to co-design the technological future of policing with the communities it serves. This imperative is especially acute given the disparate impacts documented previously. Communities that have historically borne the greatest burden of aggressive policing face the greatest risk of harm from biased algorithms and the least access to redress when that harm occurs. Meaningful engagement requires not only that police agencies publish information about the AI systems they use but that they create genuine mechanisms for community input before, during, and after deployment.

Conclusion: Technology as a Societal Choice

This chapter has argued that the integration of AI into policing is best understood not as a technological upgrade but as a set of governance dilemmas organized around three core tensions: Efficiency versus Equity, Transparency versus Security, and Accountability versus Automation. These tensions are not discrete problems; they interact and compound one another in ways that make each more difficult to manage in isolation. Opacity makes bias harder to detect. Diffused accountability makes bias harder to redress. The urgency of countering AI-enabled crime creates pressure to deploy AI quickly, undermining the deliberative governance that equitable implementation requires. Understanding this interdependence is essential to navigating the algorithmic future responsibly.

The paradox of precision is ultimately a paradox of data. AI systems do not generate objective knowledge; they generate inferences from historical records. When those records encode decades of racially disparate enforcement, when the systems that generate outputs are shielded from scrutiny by commercial secrecy, and when the humans who act on algorithmic recommendations are subject to cognitive biases that automation amplifies rather than corrects, the pursuit of precision risks becoming a mechanism for reproducing injustice at scale and speed.

The HALT framework and the principles of public engagement outlined earlier do not resolve these tensions; no governance framework can eliminate them. What good governance can do is render them manageable, ensuring that the burden of the technology's risks is not borne disproportionately by those who already bear the greatest burden of aggressive policing, that commercial secrecy does not become a permanent barrier to democratic accountability, and that the diffusion of responsibility created by automation does not become a permanent shield against institutional responsibility.

The legislative and policy responses emerging in 2025, from the EU AI Act's mandatory rights assessments to California and Utah's AI report-writing disclosure requirements and the UK's consultation on facial recognition governance, suggest that the regulatory environment is beginning to catch up with the pace of technological deployment. These developments are encouraging, but legislation alone is insufficient. The deeper challenge is cultural: building police organizations in which human judgment, professional ethics, and community accountability are understood as the irreplaceable foundations on which any technological tool must rest.

AI offers no simple solutions for the complex challenges of modern policing. It is not a technological silver bullet but a societal choice. The same capabilities that promise to predict the next crime can systematically target communities based on the last century's injustices. The same systems that offer new forms of police oversight can, if ungoverned, become new instruments of unaccountable power. Navigating this future successfully will require more than better code or faster processors. It will require a renewed and unwavering commitment to the foundational principles of democratic policing, ensuring that the human values of justice, fairness, and legitimacy always guide the algorithmic beat.

References

Adams, I., Barter, M., McLean, K., Boehme, H., & Geary, I., Jr. (2024). *No man's hand: Artificial intelligence does not improve police report writing speed*. CrimRxiv. https://doi.org/10.21428/cb6ab371.4a6d42e9

Adkins, J., Al Bataineh, A., & Khalaf, M. (2024). Identifying persons of interest in digital forensics using NLP-based AI. *Future Internet*, *16*(11), Article 426. https://doi.org/10.3390/fi16110426

Akpinar, N.-J., De-Arteaga, M., & Chouldechova, A. (2021). The effect of differential victim crime reporting on predictive policing systems. In *Proceedings of the 2021 ACM Conference on Fairness, Accountability, and Transparency (FAccT '21)* (pp. 838–849). Association for Computing Machinery. https://doi.org/10.1145/3442188.3445877

Almasoud, A. S., & Idowu, J. A. (2025). Algorithmic fairness in predictive policing. *AI and Ethics*, *5*, 2323–2337. https://doi.org/10.1007/s43681-024-00541-3

American Civil Liberties Union. (2024). *Wrongful arrests from facial recognition technology: Documented cases*. ACLU.

Arnav, B., & Ensari, E. (2024). *Automated illegal parking monitor for 311 based on publicly available data*. New York University. https://ultraviolet.library.nyu.edu/records/1vs56-e3h85

Arrietti, R. (2024). Do real-time crime centers improve case clearance? An examination of Chicago's strategic decision support centers. *Journal of Criminal Justice*, *90*. https://www.ojp.gov/ncjrs/virtual-library/abstracts/do-real-time-crime-centers-improve-case-clearance-examination

Barocas, S., & Selbst, A. D. (2016). Big data's disparate impact. *California Law Review*, *104*(3), 671–732.

Berris, P. G., Finklea, K., & Sidhu, D. S. (2025, July 21). *Automated license plate readers: Background and legal issues* (IF13068). Congressional Research Service. https://www.congress.gov/crs-product/IF13068

Boehme, H., Adams, I., Barter, M., Geary, I., Jr., & McLean, K. (2025). Writing at the speed of hype: Officers' post-experimental perceptions of AI report writing. *Journal of Experimental Criminology*, 1–13. https://doi.org/10.1007/s11292-025-09679-4

Brantingham, P. J. (2018). The logic of data bias and its impact on place-based predictive policing. *Ohio State Journal of Criminal Law*, *15*(2), 473–486.

Bratton, W., & Knobler, P. (1998). *Turnaround: How America's top cop reversed the crime epidemic*. Random House.

Brayne, S. (2017). Big data surveillance: The case of policing. *American Sociological Review*, *82*(5), 977–1008. https://doi.org/10.1177/0003122417725865

Brayne, S. (2021). *Predict and surveil: Data, discretion, and the future of policing*. Oxford University Press.

Brems, R. (2025). Transforming police reporting with generative AI: Insights from the Oklahoma City Police Department. *The Police Journal: Theory, Practice and Principles*, *99*(1), 86–102.

Bright, D., Koskinen, J., & Malm, A. (2021). Using social network analysis to study crime: Navigating the challenges of criminal justice records. *Social Networks*, *66*, 50–64. https://doi.org/10.1016/j.socnet.2021.01.006

Buolamwini, J., & Gebru, T. (2018). Gender shades: Intersectional accuracy disparities in commercial gender classification. *Proceedings of Machine Learning Research*, *81*, 77–91.

Burrell, J. (2016). How the machine "thinks": Understanding opacity in machine learning algorithms. *Big Data & Society*, *3*(1), 1–12. https://doi.org/10.1177/2053951715622512

Busuioc, M. (2020). Accountable artificial intelligence: Holding algorithms to account. *Public Administration Review*, *81*, e13293. https://doi.org/10.1111/puar.13293

Caldwell, M., Andrews, J. T. A., Tanay, T., & Griffin, L. D. (2020). AI-enabled future crime. *Crime Science*, *9*(1), Article 14. https://doi.org/10.1186/s40163-020-00123-8

CYCLOPES Project. (2025). *Deploying AI in law enforcement: Practical guidelines for European agencies*. European Union Horizon 2020 Programme. https://www.cyclopes-project.eu

Damevski, K., Ahmed, I., Imran, M. M., & Ali, H. (2023). *Natural language processing for digital forensics* [Conference presentation]. Digital Forensics Research Workshop (DFRWS). https://dfrws.org/presentation/natural-language-processing-for-digital-forensics/

DaViera, A. L., Uriostegui, M., Gottlieb, A., & Onyeka, O. C. (2024). Risk, race, and predictive policing: A critical race theory analysis of the Strategic Subject List. *American Journal of Community Psychology*, *73*(1–2), 91–103. https://doi.org/10.1002/ajcp.12671

Dittmann, A. G., Dobson, K. S. H., & Schweitzer, S. (2025). How behavioural science interventions can disrupt the cycle of bias in AI-assisted police work. *Behavioural Science & Policy*, *10*(2), 8–15. https://doi.org/10.1177/23794607241300788

Elish, M. C. (2019). Moral crumple zones: Cautionary tales in human-robot interaction. *Engaging Science, Technology, and Society*, *5*, 40–60. https://doi.org/10.17351/ests2019.260

Ensign, D., Friedler, S. A., Neville, S., Scheidegger, C., & Venkatasubramanian, S. (2018). Runaway feedback loops in predictive policing. *Proceedings of Machine Learning Research*, *81*, 160–171. http://proceedings.mlr.press/v81/ensign18a.html

Eterno, J. A., & Silverman, E. B. (2012). *The crime numbers game: Management by manipulation*. CRC Press.

European Parliament & Council of the European Union. (2024). *Regulation (EU) 2024/1689 of the European Parliament and of the Council of 13 June 2024 laying down harmonized rules on artificial intelligence (Artificial Intelligence Act)*. EUR-Lex. https://eur-lex.europa.eu/eli/reg/2024/1689/oj/eng

Electronic Privacy Information Center. (2024). *Comments of EPIC to the U.S. Commission on Civil Rights on facial recognition technology*. https://epic.org/documents/comments-of-epic-to-u-s-commission-on-civil-rights-on-facial-recognition-technology/

Fair and Just Prosecution. (2025, June 24). *AI-generated police reports: High-tech, low accuracy, big risks*. https://fairandjustprosecution.org/press-releases/new-fjp-issue-brief-warns-of-risks-with-ai-generated-police-reports/

Ferguson, A. G. (2017). *The rise of big data policing: Surveillance, race, and the future of law enforcement*. NYU Press.

Ferguson, A. G. (2025). Generative suspicion and the risks of AI-assisted police reports. *Northwestern University Law Review*, *120*(2). https://scholarlycommons.law.northwestern.edu/nulr/vol120/iss2/9

Ficara, A., Fiumara, G., Liotta, A., & De Meo, P. (2020). Disrupting resilient criminal networks through data analysis: The case of Sicilian Mafia. *PLoS ONE*, *15*(8), e0236476. https://doi.org/10.1371/journal.pone.0236476

Garvie, C., & Wessler, N. F. (2016). *Facial recognition and the Fourth Amendment*. American Civil Liberties Union.
Goncalves, J., Vitorino, J., & Maia, E. (2022). Explainable artificial intelligence for law enforcement: A systematic review. *IEEE Access*, *10*, 110516–110535.
Green, B., Horel, T., & Papachristos, A. V. (2017). Modeling contagion through social networks to explain and predict gunshot violence in Chicago, 2006 to 2014. *JAMA Internal Medicine*, *177*(3), 326–333. https://doi.org/10.1001/jamainternmed.2016.8245
Grimm, P. W., Grossman, M. R., & Cormack, G. V. (2021). Artificial intelligence as evidence. *Northwestern Journal of Technology and Intellectual Property*, *19*(1), 9–75. https://scholarlycommons.law.northwestern.edu/njtip/vol19/iss1/2/
Grimmelikhuijsen, S., Meijer, A., & Brandsma, G. J. (2022). Algorithmic transparency and accountability in public administration. *Public Administration Review*, *82*(4), 791–802.
Grimmelikhuijsen, S., Peeters, R., & Faber, L. (2025). Algorithmic discrimination in public service provision: Understanding citizens' attribution of responsibility for human versus algorithmic discriminatory outcomes. *Journal of Public Administration Research and Theory*, *35*(4), 469–487.
Grother, P., & Ngan, M. (2014). *Performance of face identification algorithms* (NIST Interagency Report 8009). National Institute of Standards and Technology. https://nvlpubs.nist.gov/nistpubs/ir/2014/NIST.IR.8009.pdf
Guariglia, M. (2025, December 23). *AI police reports: Year in review*. Electronic Frontier Foundation. https://www.eff.org/deeplinks/2025/12/ai-police-reports-year-review
Guerette, R., Przeszlowski, K., Mitchell, J., Rodriguez, J., Ramirez, J., & Gutierrez, A. (2025). An extended impact evaluation of real-time crime center (RTCC) technologies on violent crime outcomes. *Justice Evaluation Journal*, *8*, 1–17. https://doi.org/10.1080/24751979.2025.2475515
Guler, A., Kula, S., & Boke, K. (2025). Examining public support for AI in policing: The role of perceived procedural justice. *Police Practice and Research*, *26*(6), 673–695. https://doi.org/10.1080/15614263.2025.2516535
Halford, E. (2025). The Transformer led policing model: A framework for applying generative artificial intelligence in policing. *Policing: A Journal of Policy and Practice*, *19*, paaf027. https://doi.org/10.1093/police/paaf027
Halford, E. (2026). Policing in the age of artificial intelligence: A simulation study modelling workforce automation scenarios. *Police Practice and Research*, *27*(1), 164–187. https://doi.org/10.1080/15614263.2025.2577438
Harcourt, B. E. (2007). *Against prediction: Profiling, policing, and punishing in an actuarial age*. University of Chicago Press.
Hardy, R. C., Glastonbury, K., Onie, S., Josifovski, N., Theobald, A., & Larsen, M. E. (2024). Attitudes among the Australian public toward AI and CCTV in suicide prevention research: A mixed methods study. *American Psychologist*, *79*(1), 65–78. https://doi.org/10.1037/amp0001215
Hardyns, W., & Rummens, A. (2019). Predictive policing as a new tool for law enforcement? Recent developments and challenges. *European Journal on Criminal Policy and Research*, *24*(3), 201–218. https://doi.org/10.1007/s10610-017-9361-2
Hoffman, R. R., Mueller, S. T., Klein, G., & Litman, J. (2018). Metrics for explainable AI: Challenges and prospects. *arXiv*. https://arxiv.org/abs/1812.04608
Huff, J., Dunlap, B., & Pearson, R. L., Jr. (2026). Does acoustic gunshot detection technology reduce crime? A systematic review and meta-analysis. *American Journal of Criminal Justice*. https://doi.org/10.1007/s12103-025-09883-y
INTERPOL, & UNICRI. (2020). *Towards responsible AI innovation: INTERPOL's principles for the use of AI in policing*. INTERPOL.
Kelling, G. L., & Moore, M. H. (1988). *The evolving strategy of policing* (Perspectives on Policing No. 4). National Institute of Justice.

Lee, Y., Bradford, B., & Posch, K. (2024). The effectiveness of big data-driven predictive policing: Systematic review. *Justice Evaluation Journal*. https://doi.org/10.1080/24751979.2024.2371781

Lum, K., & Isaac, W. (2016). To predict and serve? *Significance*, *13*(5), 14–19. https://doi.org/10.1111/j.1740-9713.2016.00960.x

Maoro, F., & Geierhos, M. (2025). Contestable AI for criminal intelligence analysis: Improving decision-making through semantic modeling and human oversight. *Frontiers in Artificial Intelligence*, *8*, Article 1602998. https://doi.org/10.3389/frai.2025.1602998

Meijer, A., & Wessels, M. (2019). Predictive policing: Review of benefits and drawbacks. *International Journal of Public Administration*, *42*(12), 1031–1039. https://doi.org/10.1080/01900692.2019.1575664

Mohammad, A., Hoque, R., & Saleem, M. (2025). AI-generated deepfakes: The emerging cybersecurity threat and countermeasures. *ISTM Journal of Training Research and Governance*, *5*, 101–114.

Mohler, G. O., Short, M. B., Malinowski, S., Johnson, M., Tita, G. E., Bertozzi, A. L., & Brantingham, P. J. (2015). Randomized controlled field trials of predictive policing. *Journal of the American Statistical Association*, *110*(512), 1399–1411. https://doi.org/10.1080/01621459.2015.1077710

National Academies of Sciences, Engineering, and Medicine. (2017). *Proactive policing: Effects on crime and communities*. The National Academies Press. https://sites.nationalacademies.org/cs/groups/dbassesite/documents/webpage/dbasse_186649.pdf

National Academies of Sciences, Engineering, and Medicine. (2024). *Law enforcement use of predictive policing approaches: Proceedings of a workshop—in brief*. The National Academies Press. https://doi.org/10.17226/28037

National Conference of State Legislatures. (2026, March 1). *Artificial intelligence legislation database*. https://www.ncsl.org/financial-services/artificial-intelligence-legislation-database

National Institute of Standards and Technology. (2023). *AI risk management framework (AI RMF 1.0)* (NIST AI 100-1). U.S. Department of Commerce. https://www.nist.gov/itl/ai-risk-management-framework

National Police Chiefs' Council. (2023). *Covenant for using artificial intelligence (AI) in policing* (Version 1.1). https://science.police.uk/site/assets/files/4682/ai_principles_1_1_1.pdf

Noriega, M. R. (2020). The application of artificial intelligence in police interrogations: An analysis addressing the proposed effect AI has on racial and gender bias, cooperation, and false confessions. *Futures*, *117*, 102510. https://doi.org/10.1016/j.futures.2019.102510

O'Neil, C. (2016). *Weapons of math destruction: How big data increases inequality and threatens democracy*. Crown Publishers.

Office of the NYC Comptroller. (2024). *Audit report on the New York City Police Department's use of ShotSpotter gunshot detection technology*. Office of the NYC Comptroller.

Organisation for Economic Co-operation and Development. (2019). *OECD principles on artificial intelligence*. OECD Publishing. https://www.oecd.org/ai/principles/

Parasuraman, R., & Manzey, D. H. (2010). Complacency and bias in human use of automation: An attentional integration. *Human Factors*, *52*(3), 381–410. https://doi.org/10.1177/0018720810376055

Perrin, B., Liew, G., & Sweeney, I. (2026). *AI & policing: Research report on the governance and use of artificial intelligence by police in Canada*. UBC AI & Criminal Justice Initiative. https://canlii.ca/t/7nr4b

Phan, N. N., Chattopadhyay, A., Lee, T.-T., Yin, H.-I., Lu, T.-P., Lai, L.-C., Hwa, H.-L., Tsai, M.-H., & Chuang, E. Y. (2021). High-performance deep learning pipeline predicts individuals in mixtures of DNA using sequencing data. *Briefings in Bioinformatics*, *22*(6), bbab283. https://doi.org/10.1093/bib/bbab283

Reisman, D., Schultz, J., Crawford, K., & Whittaker, M. (2018). *Algorithmic impact assessments: A practical framework for public agency accountability*. AI Now Institute. https://ainowinstitute.org/aiareport2018.pdf

Richardson, R., Schultz, J. M., & Crawford, K. (2019). Dirty data, bad predictions: How civil rights violations impact police data, predictive policing systems, and justice. *New York University Law Review Online*, *94*, 192–233. https://nyulawreview.org/online-features/dirty-data-bad-predictions-how-civil-rights-violations-impact-police-data-predictive-policing-systems-and-justice/

Sanford, A. (2024, February 14). *Artificial intelligence is putting innocent people at risk of being incarcerated*. Innocence Project. https://innocenceproject.org/news/artificial-intelligence-is-putting-innocent-people-at-risk-of-being-incarcerated/

Saunders, J., Hunt, P., & Hollywood, J. S. (2016). Predictions put into practice: A quasi-experimental evaluation of Chicago's predictive policing pilot. *Journal of Experimental Criminology*, *12*(3), 347–371.

Scassa, T. (2023). Regulating AI in Canada: A critical look at the proposed Artificial Intelligence and Data Act. *Canadian Bar Review*, *101*(1), 1–48. https://cbr.cba.org/index.php/cbr/article/view/4817

Sherman, L. W. (2013). The rise of evidence-based policing: Targeting, testing, and tracking. *Crime and Justice*, *42*(1), 377–451.

Slobogin, C. (2025). *Data-driven police profiling* (SSRN Scholarly Paper No. 5220029). Social Science Research Network.

Sparrow, M. K. (1991). The application of network analysis to criminal intelligence: An assessment of the prospects. *Social Networks*, *13*(3), 251–274.

Sparrow, M. K. (2014, September). *Managing the boundary between public and private policing*. National Institute of Justice. https://nij.ojp.gov/library/publications/managing-boundary-between-public-and-private-policing

Sun, D., Zhang, X., Choo, K.-K. R., Hu, L., & Wang, F. (2021). NLP-based digital forensic investigation platform for online communications. *Computers & Security*, *104*, 102210. https://doi.org/10.1016/j.cose.2021.102210

Sun, X., Wang, Q., Qiu, L., & Xu, W. (2025). Guardians of Tomorrow: Leveraging responsible AI for early detection and response to criminal threats. *INFORMS Journal on Computing*. https://doi.org/10.1287/ijoc.2023.0488

Townsley, M., Homel, R., & Chaseling, J. (2003). Infectious burglaries: A test of the near repeat hypothesis. *British Journal of Criminology*, *43*(3), 615–633.

Tyler, T. R. (2006). *Why people obey the law*. Princeton University Press.

United Kingdom Home Office. (2025, December 4). *Consultation on a new legal framework for law enforcement use of biometrics, facial recognition and similar technologies (accessible)*. GOV.UK. https://www.gov.uk/government/consultations/legal-framework-for-using-facial-recognition-in-law-enforcement/consultation-on-a-new-legal-framework-for-law-enforcement-use-of-biometrics-facial-recognition-and-similar-technologies-accessible

Veale, M., & Binns, R. (2017). Fairer machine learning in the real world: Mitigating discrimination without collecting sensitive data. *Big Data & Society*, *4*(2), 1–17.

Whittaker, M., Crawford, K., Dobbe, R., Fried, G., Kaziunas, E., Mathur, V., Myers West, S., Richardson, R., Schultz, J., & Schwartz, O. (2018). *AI Now report 2018*. AI Now Institute. https://ainowinstitute.org/wp-content/uploads/2023/04/AI_Now_2018_Report.pdf

3

ROBOT COPS ON PATROL

Police Officers' Views of Humanoid Robots in Operational Policing

Kai Lin, You Zhou, Qiuming Zhang, Marius Hoggenmueller, Wei Wang, and Ivan Y. Sun

Introduction

With the rise of artificial intelligence (AI) in recent years, multiple countries around the world (Chia, 2021; Saseendran, 2024; Siff, 2024; Yang, 2025) have piloted the application of AI-powered robots, or "embodied AI", in operational policing, with the hope of enhancing operational efficiency (including offsetting staff shortages) as well as officer and public safety (Koper et al., 2015; Westendorf, 2022). These robots can perform tasks without much human intervention, relying on advanced software, sensors, and AI to navigate and operate in real-world environments. In China, AI-powered "police robots" have been introduced in several urban trials to perform tasks ranging from traffic enforcement and public engagement to surveillance and crime reporting (Zou, 2024). Not until very recently, however, did robots with human-like physical features (i.e., humanoid robots) appear in these trial cities (Yang, 2025). Although their current use is largely experimental, the situation is likely to change soon as the technology continues to evolve rapidly.

Globally, public discourse on the potential application of emerging AI-enhanced robotic technology in policing tends to focus on citizens' concerns and opinions, especially regarding robot safety and potential privacy invasions (Dasgupta et al., 2025). In comparison, relatively little research has examined the perspectives of frontline police officers on this issue. Considering that police officers, especially frontline officers, will be the potential partners and custodians of these humanoid machines, their views are indispensable to the ethical design and implementation of this latest technological innovation, as they did in the past with other emerging technologies (Koper et al., 2015; Lum et al., 2016).

DOI: 10.4324/9781003671312-3

Against this backdrop, the current study examines how police officers in China, a country at the forefront of AI, robotics, and their application in law enforcement, perceive the prospective integration of humanoid robots into policing operations, with a focus on comparing two different police robotic roles: service delivery versus law enforcement. This is important because introducing humanoid robots into policing carries different risks and benefits depending on their role: service delivery may improve safety, efficiency, and public trust, while law enforcement roles raise serious concerns about force, privacy, accountability, and dehumanization, yet we lack empirical evidence on how officers themselves perceive and differentially accept these applications. Drawing on a survey of 923 police officers from a mega-metropolitan area in China, this study is intended to address three research questions: (1) What are Chinese police officers' overall attitudes toward the potential application of AI-powered robots in operational policing? (2) Do officers' attitudes vary by police robot roles? (3) Do officers' digital and AI literacy, personal demographics, and professional characteristics correlate with their attitudes toward the application of police robots?

Literature Review

The Integration of AI and Robotics into Policing

Since the 2010s, police agencies globally have increasingly adopted AI to augment traditional law enforcement practices. Early applications focused on using algorithms to support behind-the-scenes operations, such as crime mapping, predictive analytics, and automated decision-support systems (Hossain et al., 2020). Empirical assessments of these systems have generally been encouraging. For example, randomized trials of ETAS (Epidemic-Type Aftershock Sequence) models in Los Angeles and Kent demonstrated substantially higher accuracy in identifying crime hotspots than human analysts, with targeted patrols in Los Angeles reducing weekly crime by 7.4% (Mohler et al., 2015). Similar benefits have been reported elsewhere, including reductions in police response times and enhanced situational awareness through real-time analytics (Westendorf, 2022).

Despite these potential gains, scholars caution that their realization depends on organizational readiness and robust ethical safeguards that protect procedural justice and public trust (Lum et al., 2017). Concerns remain regarding algorithmic bias, feedback loops, and accountability in predictive policing (Fitzpatrick et al., 2019; Shapiro, 2017). Models trained on historical crime data risk reinforcing over-policing in disadvantaged and minority communities, particularly when driven by low-level offences, and the proprietary opacity of commercial algorithms limits transparency and oversight (Fitzpatrick et al., 2019; Shapiro, 2017).

While debates about algorithmic policing persist, the rise of AI-enabled police robots marks a new and even more contentious frontier. These systems, still largely experimental, have been piloted across diverse jurisdictions with varying degrees of autonomy and public engagement. In New York City, for instance, the Knightscope K5 robot was withdrawn after a short trial due to limited utility and public concerns about surveillance and privacy (Siff, 2024). Similar initiatives in Singapore, China, and the United Arab Emirates have deployed robots for tasks ranging from issuing verbal warnings and conducting routine patrols to providing community assistance (Chen et al., 2026; Chia, 2021; Yang, 2025; Saseendran, 2024).

Although differing in design and operational scope, these robotic systems collectively reflect divergent conceptions of policing and its technological extensions. In some settings, robots emphasize surveillance and enforcement support. In contrast, in others, they serve community-oriented roles centered on communication, engagement, and service delivery. These contrasting orientations reflect the broader tension between crime-control and community-service paradigms, reviving longstanding debates about the ethical and societal implications of integrating AI into law enforcement. As Oravec (2022) argues in her analysis of "compulsory robots" in policing and security, such deployments risk extending coercive state power, raising concerns over privacy, accountability, dehumanization, and the potential for excessive force—issues that become particularly salient when distinguishing between non-coercive service roles and enforcement-oriented applications.

Police Robots and Their Roles

A substantial body of policing scholarship has long examined how officers and the public perceive the role of the police. Historically, officers have been depicted as crime fighters or guardians of public order, vested with the authority to use coercive force to maintain social control. Over time, however, this conception has expanded to encompass service-oriented and community policing functions, such as assisting citizens, building public trust, and addressing localized problems through collaborative engagement (Paoline, 2003). Within contemporary policing institutions, these dual imperatives of crime control and community service often coexist, generating both internal and operational tensions.

As AI-enabled police robots become more widely deployed, these same tensions are reemerging in technologically mediated forms (Chen et al., 2026). Like human officers, robotic systems can be designed to perform both enforcement and service-oriented tasks, such as monitoring crowds or detecting minor infractions (e.g., unauthorized vending or smoking), while also assisting with navigation or disseminating public health information (Chia, 2021). The overlap between coercive and service functions suggests that existing conceptual frameworks for understanding officers' role orientations and conflicts may also apply to robotic policing systems.

Officers' own professional orientations are likely to influence how they perceive and support different robotic roles. Despite decades of community policing reforms, many officers continue to identify more strongly with the crime-fighter role than with the service-provider role, especially in departments that emphasize measurable enforcement outcomes, proactive patrol, or zero-tolerance strategies (Fuller & Smith, 2014). Organizational factors also shape these orientations: officers in higher-level or administrative positions tend to show weaker adherence to enforcement norms, suggesting that rank is inversely related to crime-fighting attitudes (Chen, 2016; Chen et al., 2026).

Individual dispositions further reinforce these distinctions. Officers with military backgrounds or thrill-seeking tendencies are more likely to embrace the action-oriented "crime-fighter" archetype (Chen et al., 2026). Conversely, officers with community-oriented values often identify as social workers or problem-solvers, prioritizing service delivery, conflict resolution, and long-term community welfare (Sollund, 2008).

Digital and AI literacy also likely play a role in shaping officers' attitudes. According to the Technology Acceptance Model (TAM; Davis, 1989) and the Unified Theory of Acceptance and Use of Technology (UTAUT; Venkatesh et al., 2003), higher levels of digital and AI literacy tend to increase perceived ease of use and perceived usefulness of new technologies. This, in turn, promotes more positive attitudes and stronger intentions to adopt humanoid robots—especially in technically demanding enforcement roles that involve surveillance, facial recognition, and data analysis (Chen et al., 2026). At the same time, stronger literacy may help reduce anxiety, resistance, or feelings of threat among officers who lean toward traditional or community-oriented policing styles.

Robotic Policing: The Chinese Context

Robotics is a central, explicitly prioritized pillar of China's overall AI-industrial strategy, treated both as a major extension of AI technology and as a discrete industrial sector targeted for rapid upscaling and upgrading. The position of robotics is laid out in China's national AI and industrial policy stack, such as *Made in China 2025* (State Council of the People's Republic of China, 2015), the *New Generation Artificial Intelligence Development Plan* (State Council of the People's Republic of China, 2017), and the *14th Five-Year Plan for the Development of the Robotics Industry* (Ministry of Industry and Information Technology of the People's Republic of China, 2021), which integrate robotics, AI, and (smart)manufacturing to strengthen and "future-proof" China's industrial base. These industrial policies have driven rapid, large-scale growth across installations, production, market value, research and development (R&D), and patenting, turning China into the world's largest industrial-robot market with a rapidly maturing domestic supply chain and a critical hub of global robotics R&D.

With steadfast state support and an exponentially growing industry and market, comes an unmatched public enthusiasm about AI and robotics in China.

Ipsos' (2024) recent cross-national survey revealed that 80% of Chinese citizens feel "excited" about the rise of AI in society, compared to 43% in the US, most European countries, and 39% in Japan. In contrast, only 47% of the Chinese public expressed concerns about the rise of AI. It is noteworthy, however, that besides the industry's potential to generate growth and prosperity, a purely economic calculus, this high level of public optimism is also a byproduct of the state's deliberate framing of AI and robotics as markers of national pride, advancement, and strength, aligning with China's long-declared ambition to achieve "national revitalization" in the coming decades (State Council of the People's Republic of China, 2015; 2017).

In the experimentation with robotic policing specifically, 2024 and 2025 witnessed a critical shift from limited pilot initiatives to widespread implementation across multiple municipalities, indicating that robotic policing has been gradually incorporated into China's public security infrastructure (Zhang, 2024). This progression not only reflects advances in AI and robotics but also the integration of these technologies into China's centralized political structure. Robotic policing in authoritarian China serves as a tangible expression of the state's capacity to embed sophisticated surveillance and enforcement tools directly into daily urban life (Sun et al., 2022). Rather than serving as ancillary support for human officers, robotic units could function as integral elements of a vertically managed, data-driven force, predictability, order, and population control.

Methods

Research Site and Survey Instrument

A collaborative research team comprising scholars from China, the United States, and Australia initiated a study in May 2025 to examine Chinese police officers' perceptions of AI applications in policing. The team selected a large municipality in southwestern China as the study site, which provided crucial support for participant recruitment and survey distribution.

The research team developed a survey instrument to examine the role of AI in Chinese law enforcement. The survey was initially developed in English and then translated into Chinese using the back-translation method to ensure linguistic accuracy and consistency. A pilot test was conducted with a small group of Chinese police officers, resulting in minor modifications that improved the instrument's overall reliability and validity.

Data Collection and Sampling

Once finalized, the survey instrument was uploaded to Tencent Questionnaire, a widely utilized online survey platform in China. Data were collected between May and June 2025. The survey invitation, which contains a link to the online survey, was disseminated to multiple internal police WeChat groups by the researchers. WeChat is not only the largest social media and messaging app in China, but also the top workplace communications app for 90% of Chinese professionals (Jing, 2017). All group members, including both sworn officers and auxiliary officers, were invited to participate. The online survey included a cover page that explained the study's academic purpose, detailed the investigators' affiliations and contact information, emphasized the voluntary and anonymous nature of participation, and stated the strict data confidentiality. All study procedures adhered to ethical standards and received approval from the Institutional Review Board of the research team leader's institution. Informed consent was obtained electronically by having participants acknowledge that they had read the information on the cover page before they started the survey.

Participants viewed two 30-second virtual simulation videos while completing the survey. The two videos depicted hypothetical, yet realistic scenarios grounded in emerging technologies currently being developed and trialed in China. The first video depicted scenarios of a friendly-looking humanoid service robot performing tasks related to public engagement and service provision, including comforting a little girl who had lost her parents. The second video illustrated a technology-enhanced humanoid enforcement robot encountering a suspicious person in a dark alley and performing intelligence collection, facial recognition, and criminal investigation tasks. After viewing each video, participants responded to the survey questions assessing their overall attitudes toward the AI-powered robots depicted in the videos.

A total of 1,008 responses were collected from police officers in the research site. After removing 49 invalid responses (e.g., those completed under three minutes and patterned responses), the sample consisted of 959 responses. A final sample of 923 responses was used in the analysis after selecting the relevant variables, as listwise deletion was applied to missing values on any variable. As presented in Table 3.1, approximately 22% of respondents were women, 11% identified as ethnic minorities, 68% were married, and 8% reported prior military service. Over half of the participants (58%) were assigned to field stations, and 55% were based in urban districts. The median age group was 31–35 years, and the mean educational attainment was roughly equivalent to a bachelor's degree.

Measures

Dependent Variables

The three dependent variables were measured for two robot types: endorsement of capabilities, trust in robots, and willingness to adopt robots in police departments. Six dependent variables were therefore created to capture these different attitudinal dimensions across two robot types. *Endorsement of robot capabilities* and *trust in police robots* were additive scales consisting of three survey items each (1 = strongly disagree; 6 = strongly agree). *Willingness to adopt police robots* (into

TABLE 3.1 Descriptive Statistics for Variables in Regression Analysis ($N = 923$)

Variables	*M*	*SD*	*Range*	*α*
Dependent variables				
Endorse capabilities: service robot	13.92	2.79	3–18	.88
Endorse capabilities: enforcement robot	14.10	2.68	3–18	.91
Trust: service robot	12.76	2.92	3–18	.86
Trust: enforcement robot	13.10	2.88	3–18	.87
Adoption: service robot	4.47	1.12	1–6	–
Adoption: enforcement robot	4.52	1.08	1–6	–
Independent variables				
Digital and AI literacy				
Training in CS and/or IT	9.91	3.99	3–18	.93
Self-efficacy in AI knowledge	17.50	5.83	5–30	.92
Demographics				
Women	.22	.41	0–1	–
Age	3.37	1.76	1–18	–
Minority	.11	.31	0–1	–
Married	.68	.47	0–1	–
Educational attainment	4.01	.60	1–5	–
Military veteran	.08	.28	0–1	–
Professional characteristics				
Rank	2.12	.85	1–4	–
Auxiliary police	.16	.37	0–1	–
Field station	.58	.49	0–1	–
Urban assignment	.55	.50	0–1	–

Note: M = mean; SD = standard deviation; α = Cronbach's alpha.

operational policing) was measured by a single survey item (strongly disagree = 1, strongly agree = 6): "Police departments should actively promote the use of this type of police robot in policing practice." The Cronbach's alphas ranged from .88–.91, indicating excellent interitem reliability. Table 3.2 presents a complete list of the aforementioned items, which were designed by the research team and pilot-tested with a small sample prior to the implementation of the study.

Independent Variables

The independent variables fall into three domains: digital and AI literacy, personal demographics, and professional characteristics. Digital and AI literacy includes *formal training in computer science (CS) and information technology (IT)*, and *AI self-efficacy. Formal training in CS and IT* is a three-item additive scale (1 = strongly disagree, 6 = strongly agree; Cronbach's alpha = .93) measured by the following survey items: "I have received higher-education coursework in computer science, programming, or AI (e.g., university-level courses)", "I have participated in specialized training in computer science, programming,

TABLE 3.2 Dimensions of Officer Attitudes toward Service versus Enforcement Police Robots ($N = 923$)

Dimensions	*Survey items*	*Service robot*		*Enforcement robot*		
		% "agree" or "strongly agree"	*Mean*	*% "agree" or "strongly agree"*	*Mean*	*t-test*
Endorsement of robot capabilities	The police robot in the video undertakes some important policing tasks.	69.23%	4.72	70.21%	4.75	−0.74
	The police robot in the video can improve policing efficiency.	70.75%	4.77	69.23%	4.74	0.90
	The police robot in the video can effectively ensure public safety.	56.23%	4.42	63.16%	4.61	−5.74**
Trust in police robot	Police officers can trust the police robot in the video.	43.34%	4.21	53.95%	4.41	−6.75**
	The public can trust the police robot in the video.	50.05%	4.34	54.93%	4.44	−3.38**
	Using the police robot in the video will not infringe upon citizens' lawful rights and freedoms.	47.35%	4.21	49.40%	4.25	−1.16
Adoption of police robot	Police departments should actively promote the use of this type of police robot in policing practice.	55.47%	4.47	59.15%	4.52	−1.66*

Note: $^{*}p < .05$; $^{**}p < .01$

or AI (e.g., short-term coding bootcamps)", and "I have received training related to crimes involving AI". *AI self-efficacy* is a five-item additive scale (1 = strongly disagree, 6 = strongly agree; Cronbach's alpha = .92) measured by the following survey items: "I have a thorough understanding of the fundamental principles of AI technology", "I have a comprehensive understanding of how AI can be used to commit crimes", "I have a thorough understanding of the application of AI in crime prediction", "I have a thorough understanding of the use of AI in criminal investigation and case-solving", and "I have a thorough understanding of the role of AI in providing legal advisory services".

Demographic and socioeconomic characteristics included: gender (0 = male, 1 = female), marital status (0 = unmarried, 1 = married), ethnic minority status (0 = non-minority, 1 = minority), and military veteran status (0 = non-veteran, 1 = veteran). Age was measured using an eight-point ordinal scale, ranging from 1 (21–25 years) to 8 (56–60 years). Educational attainment was assessed on a six-point ordinal scale, with response options ranging from 1 (high school diploma) to 6 (graduate degree). Professional characteristics included rank (measured on a four-point ordinal scale ranging from 1 = officer/constable to 4 = senior/chief superintendent), auxiliary police status (0 = sworn police officers, 1 = auxiliary police), field station assignment (0 = non–field station, 1 = field station), and the area of station assignment (0 = prefectures or other areas outside the main urban districts, 1 = stationed in the municipality's main urban districts).

Analytic Strategy

To explore our research questions, we employed a two-step analytical approach. First, we performed a paired-samples t-test to examine differences in police officers' support between service robots and enforcement robots. Next, we estimated six regression models examining the relationships between the predictor variables and the six dependent variables. Ordinary Least Square (OLS) regression analyses were conducted on endorsement capabilities and trust in the police, whereas ordered logistic regression analyses were performed on the willingness to adopt police robots. Brant's test of parallel regression assumption indicated no violation of the proportional odds assumption of ordered logistic regression. For all regression analyses, mean and maximum Variance Inflation Factors (VIFs) were well below 5, indicating no multicollinearity issues.

Results

T-Tests Comparing Endorsement of Two Robot Types

Table 3.2 compares officers' perceptions of two simulated scenarios: one depicting a service robot and the other depicting a service robot and an enforcement robot. Overall, respondents expressed generally positive attitudes toward both types of robots. More favourable attitudes toward the enforcement robot were recorded across several dimensions. Participants perceived both robots as capable of performing important policing tasks ($t = -.74$, $p > .05$) and enhancing policing efficiency ($t = .90$, $p > .05$). A significant difference was observed in officers' perceptions of the robot's effectiveness in enhancing public safety, with respondents rating the enforcement robot significantly higher ($M = 4.61$) than the service robot ($M = 4.42$; $t = -5.74$, $p < .01$). Support for adoption of these robots in operational policing was moderately high for both conditions, though slightly greater for the enforcement robot ($M = 4.47$ vs. 4.52; $t = -1.66$, $p < .05$). Trust showed the largest divergences: officers reported significantly greater trust in the enforcement robot ($M = 4.41$) compared with the service robot ($M = 4.21$; $t = -6.75$, $p < .01$), and similarly higher perceptions that the public could trust the enforcement robot ($M = 4.44$ vs. 4.34; $t = -3.38$, $p < .01$). Perceptions regarding potential infringements on citizens' rights did not differ significantly between conditions ($t = -1.16$, $p > .05$).

Multivariate Regression Analyses

Table 3.3 summarizes the results of multivariate regression analyses across three attitudinal domains (i.e., endorsement of robot capabilities, trust in robots, and willingness to adopt robots in operational policing) and two robot types (i.e., service versus enforcement robots). Model 1 displays the estimated OLS regression coefficients of officers' endorsement of service robot capabilities. Formal training in CS or IT ($\beta = .09$, $p < .05$) and AI self-efficacy ($\beta = .17$, $p < .01$) were positively associated with perceived capabilities. Demographic and socioeconomic characteristics, as well as professional characteristics, were not significant predictors. The model was statistically significant ($F = 4.83$, $p < .01$) and explained approximately 5% of the variation in endorsement. Model 2 displays the estimated OLS regression coefficients of officers' endorsement of enforcement robot capabilities. AI self-efficacy remained a significant predictor ($\beta = .17$, $p < .01$). No background or professional characteristics were significant. The model was significant ($F = 3.98$, $p < .01$), accounting for 4% of the variance.

Model 3 displays the estimated OLS regression coefficients of officers' trust in service robots. Trust was positively associated with age ($\beta = .16$, $p < .01$), digital literacy training ($\beta = .11$, $p < .05$), and AI self-efficacy ($\beta = .12$, $p < .01$). Officers assigned to field stations also reported higher trust ($\beta = .09$, $p < .05$). Other variables were not significant. The model was significant ($F = 5.74$, $p < .01$) and explained 6% of the variance. Model 4 displays the estimated OLS regression coefficients of officers' trust in enforcement robots. Digital literacy training ($\beta = .11$, $p < .05$) and AI self-efficacy ($\beta = .13$, $p < .01$) were significant predictors. Background and professional characteristics were not significant. The model was statistically significant ($F = 4.87$, $p < .01$), with 5% of variance explained.

TABLE 3.3 Multivariate Regression Models Predicting Officer Attitudes toward Service vs. Enforcement Robots ($N = 923$)

Variables	*Model 1 Capabilities: Service Robot*		*Model 2 Capabilities: Enforcement Robot*		*Model 3 Trust: Service Robot*		*Model 4 Trust: Enforcement Robot*		*Model 5 Adoption: Service Robot*		*Model 6 Adoption: Enforcement Robot*	
	Beta	*SE*	*Beta*	*SE*	*Beta*	*SE*	*Beta*	*SE*	*OR*	*SE*	*OR*	*SE*
Digital and AI literacy												
Digital literacy training	.09*	.03	.06	0.03	.11*	.03	.11*	.03	1.04*	.02	1.04*	.02
AI self-efficacy	.17**	.02	.17**	0.02	.12**	.02	.13**	.02	1.04**	.02	1.04**	.02
Demographics												
Men	.01	.22	.01	.22	–.03	.23	–.03	.23	1.11	.16	1.04	.16
Age	.04	.08	.02	.08	.16**	.08	.08	.08	1.07	.06	1.06	.06
Minority	–.02	.31	–.02	.30	–.03	.32	–.03	.32	.91	.19	.81	.17
Married	.02	.23	.01	.22	.02	.24	.03	.24	1.16	.18	1.12	.18
Educational attainment	–.03	.17	–.04	.17	–.01	.18	–.06	.18	.94	.11	.84	.10
Military veteran	–.03	.35	–.02	.34	–.01	.36	.00	.36	.75	.18	.79	.19
Professional characteristics												
Rank	–.04	.19	–.01	.18	–.01	.20	.00	.20	1.02	.13	1.02	.13
Auxiliary police	–.04	.34	–.06	.32	–.03	.35	–.02	.35	.86	.19	.86	.20
Field station	.04	.19	.02	.18	.09**	.20	.06	.20	1.28*	.16	1.22	.16
Urban assignment	.05	.20	0.03	.19	–.06	.21	–.03	.21	1.16	.15	1.07	.14
F-test/chi-square test		4.83**		3.98**		5.74**		4.87**		44.44**		35.01**
Adjusted/pseudo R^2		.05		.04		.06		.05		.02		.01

Note: $^*p < .05$; $^{**}p < .01$

Model 5 displays the ordered logistic regression results of respondents' odds of adopting service robots. Officers with digital literacy training (OR = 1.04, $p < .05$), higher AI self-efficacy (OR = 1.04, $p < .01$), and those assigned to a field station (OR = 1.28, $p < .05$) had greater odds of adoption. Other variables were not significant. The model chi-square was significant ($\chi^2 = 44.44$, $p < .01$), with a pseudo-R^2 of .02. Model 6 displays the ordered logistic regression results, showing a pseudo-R^2 of .02. Model 6 presents the ordered logistic regression results for respondents' odds of adopting enforcement robots. Digital literacy training (OR = 1.04, $p < .05$) and AI self-efficacy (OR = 1.04, $p < .01$) increased the odds of adoption, while other variables, including field station assignment, were not significant. The model was statistically significant ($\chi^2 = 35.01$, $p < .01$), with pseudo-$R^2 = .01$.

Discussion and Conclusion

This study represents a forward-looking investigation of Chinese police officers' perceptions of the prospect of introducing two types of police robots into operational policing: service-delivery robots versus law enforcement robots. The findings revealed overall strong endorsement of both types of robots' capabilities in policing practice. In comparison, support for their adoption by the police force is weaker, trailed by perceived trust in the robots. Moreover, officers showed significantly greater endorsement of enforcement robots over service robots, especially in terms of trust. Several officer characteristics are linked to the levels of endorsement. These findings are further unpacked next.

First, Chinese officers consistently endorse the robots' capabilities to enhance policing efficiency and efficacy, with approximately seven in ten officers expressing support across both robot types. When it comes to adopting this emerging technology, which could potentially reduce workload but simultaneously result in workplace displacement of some police officers in the future, the officers' enthusiasm diminished, although a whopping 55–60% still indicated support. Such an overwhelmingly positive attitude may be attributed to the overall "pro-AI" public sentiment in Chinese society (Ipsos, 2024), rooted in the government's strategic investment in and alignment with advanced AI and robotic technologies (State Council of the People's Republic of China, 2015; 2017), including its application in public safety and security (Sun et al., 2022; Yang, 2025).

In comparison to the strong support for capability and adoption, trust in both types of robots is significantly lower, especially for service robots. This finding suggests that officers' attitudes toward robotic applications are marked by a degree of ambivalence beneath the surface of overall endorsement. While officers recognize the potential strengths and benefits of adopting these robots in police work, they may also harbour concerns about possible misuse, malfunction, or unintended consequences. For example, advanced technologies, such as electric or autonomous vehicles, have recently been involved in multiple highly publicized reports of serious accidents resulting in injuries and fatalities in China (e.g., Xue, 2025). Such incidents may reinforce skepticism toward the reliability and safety of autonomous systems more generally, including AI-powered robots. Although the simulated videos used in this study depicted futuristic humanoid robots that appear several generations beyond current technology, it remains difficult to predict their functional reliability in complex, real-world operational policing environments.

Moreover, expressing trust implies attributing trustworthiness, a human-like quality that extends beyond mechanical reliability, to these robots (Hancock et al., 2011). For officers, this anthropomorphic dimension of trust may still be hard to imagine, particularly when the robot's actions could have implications for police accountability and citizen rights. This may also explain why trust in service robots is even lower. Although the service robot was depicted as amicable and helpful, officers may perceive that its apparent friendliness masks an underlying focus on operational objectives, such as monitoring or data collection, raising concerns about covert surveillance and privacy intrusion. In contrast, the enforcement robot was depicted as more instrumental, aligning more closely with traditional policing tasks and thus eliciting higher perceived legitimacy. Notably, older officers and those stationed in local field offices expressed higher levels of trust in service police robots, in contrast to previous research on security robots, which found that age does not seem to explain similar perceptions (Ye & Robert, 2024). This pattern may reflect both greater professional experience and more frequent engagement with the public, which makes these officers more receptive to technologies that facilitate citizen interaction and service delivery. Officers at field stations may also face heavier workloads and resource constraints; for them, service robots can serve as support tools for routine administrative or community service tasks, reducing stress and workload.

Our findings also show greater willingness among officers to promote the use of enforcement robots over service robots. Officers may perceive enforcement robots, with their advanced sensory, analytical, and physical capabilities, as particularly valuable for enhancing effectiveness in intelligence gathering, offence detection, and suspect apprehension. They may also believe that robotic systems can improve officer safety by performing hazardous duties such as confronting armed suspects or handling explosive devices. Similar to trust, officers in field stations expressed relatively higher support for service robots, likely because they operate at the front lines of citizen engagement where service-oriented functions such as guiding, assisting, and de-escalating are more visible and immediately beneficial (Fuller & Smith, 2014).

Across robot types, we consistently found that police officers with greater digital literacy and self-efficacy in AI knowledge exhibited stronger endorsement, trust, and willingness to adopt police robots. This aligns with past research, which suggests that the acceptance of novel technologies is influenced by users' beliefs about their capabilities, experience, and perceived autonomy (Venkatesh & Davis, 2000). In the policing context, these dynamics are especially salient: officers' receptivity to technological innovation is significantly shaped by their attributes, such as age, education, digital literacy, and organizational role (Cochran & Worden, 2023; Koper et al., 2015). The findings from the current study could be interpreted as an extension of this literature. That said, Salehzadeh et al. (2025) found that while general self-efficacy initially predicted officers' acceptance of a teleoperated communication robot, this effect disappeared after hands-on training, suggesting that direct experience and understanding of robotic systems can supplant general confidence as the key driver of acceptance. Future research is warranted to investigate these nuances further.

Several limitations of this study should be acknowledged. First, the research relied on a convenience sample of police officers from a single mega-metropolitan area in China, limiting the generalizability of our findings. Second, although this study is exploratory and focuses primarily on digital and AI literacy, along with some basic background and organizational characteristics, the modest explanatory power (reflected in low adjusted/pseudo R^2 values) indicates that other unmeasured factors may influence officers' attitudes toward service and enforcement robots; future studies should explore these additional predictors to enhance explanatory power. Third, the use of internal police WeChat groups for survey distribution introduces potential selection bias. In China's hierarchical and centrally managed policing system, where technological modernization is a government priority, officers who engage with digital platforms and respond to AI-related surveys may constitute a self-selected group that is more technology-positive or organizationally compliant. These limitations should be considered when interpreting the study's findings.

The findings offer several practical implications for policy and implementation. First, given persistent gaps in trust, particularly toward service robots, the introduction of AI and robotic systems should be accompanied by clear ethical frameworks, transparent accountability mechanisms, and detailed operational guidelines. Second, integrating AI and digital literacy training into police education and professional development programs can enhance officers' competence and confidence in collaborating with robotic systems. Third, deployment strategies should be context-sensitive, prioritizing units such as field stations and community-policing divisions where robots can most directly alleviate workload pressures and support public engagement. Importantly, robots should be positioned as tools that augment rather than replace human judgment and effort, ensuring that decision-making authority remains firmly with human officers to preserve police legitimacy. Ultimately, successful adoption necessitates organizational readiness developed through participatory approaches that engage frontline officers in the design, testing, and evaluation of the system. Cross-sector collaboration and longitudinal monitoring are also crucial to assess the ethical, operational, and societal impacts of AI-powered robotics in policing.

References

Chen, Y., Wu, Y., Lin, K., Hoggenmueller, M., Zhang, Q., Jian, Y. S., & Sun, I. Y. (2026). Attitudes toward AI-powered robots in policing: AI literacy, organizational justice, and occupational wellbeing among Chinese police officers. *Asian Journal of Criminology*, *21*(1), 3.

Chen, Z. (2016). Measuring police role orientations in China: An exploratory study. *International Journal of Law, Crime and Justice*, *44*, 43–67. https://doi.org/10.1016/j.ijlcj.2015.05.001

Chia, O. (2021, September 5). Robots to patrol Toa Payoh for 'undesirable social behaviors' as part of trial. *Channel News Asia*. https://www.channelnewsasia.com/singapore/robots-police-patrol-smoking-toa-payoh-2157186

Cochran, H., & Worden, R. E. (2023). Police culture and officers' receptivity to body-worn cameras: A panel study. *Policing: An International Journal*, *46*(1), 24–39. https://doi.org/10.1108/pijpsm-06-2022-0076

Dasgupta, R., Mekala, S. H., Jaigirdar, F. T., Anwar, A., & Chang, L. Y.-C. (2025). Unlocking Australia's AI usage in law enforcement from human involvement perspective: A systematic literature review. *AI & Society*. https://doi.org/10.1007/s00146-025-02350-6

Davis, F. D. (1989). Perceived usefulness, perceived ease of use, and user acceptance of information technology. *MIS Quarterly*, *13*(3), 319–340. https://doi.org/10.2307/249008

Fitzpatrick, C. D., Knodler, M. A., Ryan, A., Ai, C., & Chen, D. (2019). *The application of unmanned aerial systems in surface transportation-volume II-C: Evaluation of UAS highway speed-sensing application* (No. 19-010). University of Massachusetts at Amherst. Transportation Center.

Fuller, F. & Smith, H. (2014). Police culture: Adapting to the strains of the job. *Criminal Justice Review*, *39*(4), 464–465.

Hancock, P. A., Billings, D. R., Schaefer, K. E., Chen, J. Y., de Visser, E. J., & Parasuraman, R. (2011). A meta-analysis of factors affecting trust in human-robot interaction. *Human Factors*, *53*(5), 517–527. https://doi.org/10.1177/0018720811417254

Hossain, S., Abtahee, A., Kashem, I., Hoque, M. M., & Sarker, I. H. (2020, March). Crime prediction using spatio-temporal data. In *International Conference on Computing Science, Communication and Security* (pp. 277–289). Springer Singapore.

Ipsos. (2024). The Ipsos AI monitor 2024: A 32-country Ipsos Global Advisor Survey. https://ipsos.com/sites/default/files/ct/news/documents/2024-06/Ipsos-AI-Monitor-2024-final-APAC.pdf

Jing, M. (2017, April 25). WeChat is top workplace communications app for 90 per cent of Chinese professionals. *South China Morning Post*. https://www.scmp.com/tech/apps-gaming/article/2090472/wechat-top-workplace-communications-app-90-cent-chinese

Koper, C. S., Lum, C., Willis, J. J., Woods, D. J., & Hibdon, J. (2015, December). Realizing the potential of technology in policing: A multi-site study of the social, organizational, and behavioral aspects of implementing policing technologies. In *Report to the National Institute of Justice*, US Department of Justice. Center for Evidence-Based Crime Policy, George Mason University and Police Executive Research Forum.

Lum, C., Koper, C. S., & Willis, J. J. (2016). Understanding the limits of technology's impact on police effectiveness. *Police Quarterly*, *20*(2), 135–163. https://doi.org/10.1177/1098611116667279

Ministry of Industry and Information Technology of the People's Republic of China. (2021, December 28).十四五" 机器人产业发展规划 [The 14th Five-Year Plan for the Development of the Robotics Industry]. https://www.gov.cn/zhengce/zhengceku/2021-12/28/5664988/files/7cee5d915efa463ab9e7be82228759fb.pdf

Mohler, G. O., Short, M. B., Malinowski, S., Johnson, M., Tita, G. E., Bertozzi, A. L., & Brantingham, P. J. (2015). Randomized controlled field trials of predictive policing. *Journal of the American Statistical Association*, *110*(512), 1399–1411. https://doi.org/10.1080/01621459.2015.1077710

Oravec, J. A. (2022). The long robotic arm of the law: Emerging police, military, militia, security, and other compulsory robots. In *Good Robot, Bad Robot: Dark and Creepy Sides of Robotics, Autonomous Vehicles, and AI* (pp. 125–152). Springer International Publishing.

Paoline, E. A. (2003). Taking stock: Toward a richer understanding of police culture. *Journal of Criminal Justice*, *31*(3), 199–214. https://doi.org/10.1016/S0047-2352(03)00002-3

Salehzadeh, R., Bordbar, F., Fan, X., Korivand, S., Merritt, G., Griffin, D. J., … & Jalili, N. (2025). Teleoperated communication robot: A law enforcement perspective. *ACM Transactions on Human-Robot Interaction*, *14*(2), 1–23. https://doi.org/10.1145/3697842

Saseendran, S. (2024). Dubai rolls out robot that will use facial recognition to fine e-scooter, bicycle rule violators. *Golf News*. Retrieved on June 19, 2024, from https://gulfnews.com/uae/transport/watch-dubai-rolls-out-robot-that-will-use-facial-recognition-to-fine-e-scooter-bicycle-rule-violators-1.101764432

Shapiro, A. (2017). Reform predictive policing. *Nature*, *541*(7638), 458–460. doi:https://doi.org/10.1038/541458a

Siff, A. (2024, February). NYC retires 420-pound NYPD subway surveilling robot after pilot ends. *ABC New York*. Retrieved on June 19, 2024, from https://www.nbcnewyork.com/news/local/nyc-retires-420-pound-nypd-subway-surveilling-robot-after-pilot-ends/5099973/

Sollund, R. (2008). Tough cop–soft cop? The impact of motivations and experiences on police officers' approaches to the public. *Journal of Scandinavian Studies in Criminology and Crime Prevention*, *9*(2), 119–140. https://doi.org/10.1080/14043850802475580

State Council of the People's Republic of China. (2015, May 19). *Made in China 2025*. https://www.gov.cn/zhengce/content/2015-05/19/content_9784.htm

State Council of the People's Republic of China. (2017, July 20). 新一代人工智能发展规划 [New Generation Artificial Intelligence Development Plan]. https://www.gov.cn/zhengce/content/2017-07/20/content_5211996.htm

Sun, I. Y., Wu, Y., Triplett, R., & Hu, R. (2022). Political efficacy, police legitimacy, and public support for counterterrorism measures in China. *Terrorism and Political Violence*, *34*(8), 1580–1594.

Venkatesh, V., & Davis, F. (2000). A theoretical extension of the technology acceptance model: Four longitudinal field studies. *Management Science*, *46*(2), 186–204.

Venkatesh, V., Morris, M. G., Davis, G. B., & Davis, F. D. (2003). User acceptance of information technology: Toward a unified view. *MIS Quarterly*, *27*(3), 425–478. https://doi.org/10.2307/30036540

Westendorf, T. (2022). *Artificial intelligence and policing in Australia* (Strategic Insights No. 169). Australian Strategic Policy Institute. https://www.aspi.org.au/report/ai_policing_australia

Xue, Y. (2025, April 22). China sets 'critical' rules to corral safe self-driving EVs after Xiaomi's fatal crash. *South China Morning Post*. https://www.scmp.com/business/china-evs/article/3307355/chinese-ev-makers-urged-boost-safety-self-driving-systems-after-xiaomi-crash

Yang, Y. (2025, March 4). China police robot patrols streets, capturing public attention, bringing sci-fi to life. *South China Morning Post*. https://www.scmp.com/news/people-culture/trending-china/article/3300917/china-police-robot-patrols-streets-capturing-public-attention-bringing-sci-fi-life

Ye, X., & Robert, L. P. (2024). A human–security robot interaction literature review. *ACM Transactions on Human-Robot Interaction, 14*(2), 1–36. https://doi.org/10.1145/3700888
Zhang, P. (2024, 12 December). Police in China take hi-tech rolling robot out on patrol. *South China Morning Post.* https://www.scmp.com/news/china/politics/article/3290536/officers-patrol-china-test-ball-shaped-robot-beijing-pushes-hi-tech-policing
Zou, S. (2024, 13 December). AI devices help road users obey traffic rules. *China Daily*. https://www.chinadaily.com.cn/a/202412/13/WS675b8ed4a310f1265a1d2aed.html

4

AI IN POLICING

A Systematic Review of AI Use in the US Law Enforcement

Ahmet Guler, Kaan Boke, and Sedat Kula

Introduction

Artificial intelligence (AI) is increasingly reshaping every aspect of law enforcement practices in the US AI tools such as predictive policing algorithms, facial recognition systems, and real-time surveillance are increasingly adopted to improve police operations, resource allocation, and crime prevention (Bullock, 2019; Chan, 2021). Supporters highlight their potential to enhance public safety and police efficiency (Haley & Burrell, 2025), yet critics raise concerns about algorithmic bias, lack of transparency, and erosion of civil liberties (Rowe & Muir, 2021; Joh, 2017). The US federal government has endorsed AI adoption as part of broader efforts to modernize public service delivery, but the legitimacy and effectiveness of AI in policing remain debated (Lukens, 2025; The White House, 2025).

This chapter presents a systematic review of empirical research on the effectiveness and implications of AI technologies used in US policing over the last fifteen years. The focus is on AI tools applied to crime fighting, particularly in identification and surveillance, predictive policing, and decision support, while also examining public and police perceptions of AI use in law enforcement.

Background

AI is fundamentally reshaping the way law enforcement agencies operate in the US. It is changing traditional policing models by introducing data-driven tools and analytical systems that support decision-making, enhance efficiency, and expand surveillance and investigative capacities (US Department of Justice, 2024). From predictive analytics and automated report generation to facial recognition and real-time crime mapping, AI technologies are redefining how

DOI: 10.4324/9781003671312-4

police departments allocate resources, assess risk, and engage with the public (Chan, 2021). This transformation marks a shift toward a more technologically integrated approach to public safety, one that promises greater precision (Lum et al., 2017) but also raises complex ethical, legal, and accountability challenges for modern policing (Guler et al., 2025).

AI refers to technologies that enable machines to perform tasks that typically require human intelligence, such as learning, reasoning, problem-solving, and decision-making (IBM, 2024). In both public and private sectors, AI is increasingly used to automate processes, analyze large datasets, and make complex decisions (Boke et al., 2025). The main value of AI in policing lies in its ability to organize, analyze, and interpret large amounts of data ("*big data*") to improve decision-making and public safety. Algorithms are mathematical procedures used to solve specific problems. Through their use, law enforcement agencies can detect unusual crime patterns, link suspects or incidents using shared data, and predict where crimes are likely to occur. AI and machine learning make it possible to process large volumes of police data, such as reports, social networks, and surveillance footage, in ways that were not possible before (Ferguson, 2017). These tools help police transform complex information into useful insights for crime prevention and investigation.

Within the American criminal justice system, AI applications are being deployed to support identification, surveillance, forensic analysis, predictive policing, and risk assessment (US Department of Justice, 2024). Tools such as facial recognition systems, automatic license plate readers, gunshot detection devices, video and social media analytics applications, and predictive crime mapping software are now commonly used by police departments in an effort to improve accuracy, efficiency, and public safety outcomes (Finklea, 2023).

Despite the promises and potential of AI, the use of these technologies in policing raises complex ethical, legal, and operational concerns. For example, while facial recognition systems can expedite the identification of suspects, they have also been criticized for contributing to wrongful arrests, particularly among marginalized populations, due to algorithmic bias and errors in recognition accuracy (Ray, 2020; Rowe & Muir, 2021). Predictive policing tools that rely on historical crime data may help allocate resources more efficiently, but they also risk reinforcing existing patterns of over-policing in already targeted neighbourhoods, potentially exacerbating social inequalities (Joh, 2017). Similarly, risk assessment algorithms used in pretrial decisions and sentencing have been shown to reflect racial and socioeconomic disparities embedded in their training data, leading to potential violations of due process (Simmons, 2017). These concerns emphasize the importance of careful oversight, transparency, and validation of AI systems used in law enforcement.

The US federal government has increasingly promoted the responsible adoption of AI across public services, including criminal justice. America's AI

Action Plan (The White House, 2025) outlines a strategy for accelerating the integration of AI technologies into government operations, with the goal of improving efficiency and delivering better outcomes for citizens. In line with this approach, federal agencies such as the Department of Justice are supporting AI-driven innovations that aim to enhance crime prevention and improve resource allocation. President Trump has publicly endorsed the expanded use of AI in law enforcement, particularly in relation to predictive policing and threat detection (Lukens, 2025). At the same time, the President's Task Force on 21st Century Policing (2015) emphasized that technological adoption must be guided by principles of transparency, accountability, and community engagement.

According to the National Conference of State Legislatures, law enforcement agencies use AI in three main ways (Ezeh et al., 2025, p.1): to assist humans with tasks and increase capacity, to expand human capabilities, and to replace humans entirely with fully automated processes. AI helps officers by automating routine functions, analyzing large datasets, and supporting more efficient decision-making. It also enhances human capabilities by improving surveillance, predictive policing, and pattern detection, which allows for more proactive resource allocation and investigative support. Fully autonomous systems are rare and typically operate under controlled conditions, as human oversight remains critical for ethical and effective policing.

Police departments across the US are at varying stages of AI adoption. Larger, well-funded urban departments have begun integrating AI for tasks such as predictive crime hotspot analysis, automated license plate reading, and real-time surveillance. Meanwhile, smaller departments often lack the resources or technical expertise to implement such tools, continuing to rely on more traditional methods of policing. A recent national survey (Mark43, 2025) found that 90 percent of law enforcement officials expressed support for using some form of AI technology in their operations. This level of enthusiasm suggests growing institutional interest in technological innovation. However, the actual effectiveness and societal impact of these tools remain largely untested. Many departments implement AI technologies with limited evaluation, often without the benefit of empirical evidence, demonstrating improvements in public safety or crime reduction (Boehme et al., 2025).

Despite the increasing reliance on AI technologies, there remains a lack of systematic, evidence-based evaluation of their outcomes in the policing context. Some tools, such as facial recognition and gunshot detection systems, have shown promising results in specific settings (Johnson et al., 2024), while others, including AI-assisted report writing, have not demonstrated measurable benefits in practice (Adams et al., 2024). Many AI systems remain in early stages of implementation, and their long-term effects on civil liberties, officer discretion, and community relations are still unknown. The rapid pace of technological adoption has outpaced the development of regulatory frameworks and ethical guidelines, creating a critical need for comprehensive research that can inform policy and practice.

This background emphasizes the need for an evidence-based review of AI applications in policing. It highlights the competing narratives of innovation and risk, as well as the factors that shape public and officer support for AI technologies. As the use of AI continues to expand in law enforcement, understanding its practical outcomes, ethical implications, and impact on public and officer trust becomes essential. This study addresses this need by systematically reviewing the empirical evidence on AI tools in policing, focusing particularly on the areas of AI in crime fighting, administrative decision support, and public and police attitudes toward AI use in policing.

Research Methodology

This research employs a systematic review methodology informed by *A Tailored Approach* (Cooper et al., 2024), designed to align search methods and review processes with the specific context of AI applications in US policing in the last fifteen years. The approach was iterative, reflexive, and evidence-driven, allowing the review team to adjust methods as collective understanding of the literature developed. The review focuses on empirical research examining the operational use of AI technologies in law enforcement, including patrol, investigations, surveillance, administrative decision-making, and community interaction (see also Figure 4.1).

The process began with discussion and agreement on the research question, where the team jointly explored the aims of the review and the types of information needed to address them. This stage fostered shared understanding and allowed refinement of the review scope before any formal searching began. Logic models and early discussion of key studies helped clarify the boundaries of inquiry and informed the subsequent design of the search strategy. The review team, composed of three researchers with expertise in AI and policing, brought both technical and contextual knowledge to the process. Their collaboration ensured that the research question and inclusion parameters reflected both the technological complexity of AI systems and the operational realities of policing practice. As a result, this review aimed to address the critical research question: "*How have AI technologies been utilized in American policing over the past fifteen years?*"

Following this, a scoping and immersion phase was conducted to map the landscape of existing research. The purpose of this stage was exploratory rather than exhaustive, designed to develop preliminary knowledge of the topic and refine search terminology and categorization of AI applications. The initial search on Google Scholar returned 39,100 results for "*AI in Policing*" and 46,500 results for "*AI in Law Enforcement*" in the last fifteen years. We then conducted

1. Defining the Research Question	Collaborative discussion among the team to define aims, identify information needs, and clarify the scope of AI in policing research. As a result, the main research question of this review is: *"How have AI technologies been utilized in American policing over the past fifteen years?"*
2. Scoping and Immersion in the Literature	Preliminary exploration of key databases and terminology to understand the evidence landscape and refine search terms and inclusion criteria. "AI in Policing" (39,100 results), "AI in Law Enforcement" (46,500 results) in Google Scholar.
3. Team-Based Discussion and Refinement	Review team meets to analyze scoping results, determine where evidence is concentrated, and adjust research questions or methods accordingly.
4. Testing and Selecting Search Methods	Different search strategies (e.g. database, citation check, web searches) are tested to identify which methods retrieve the most relevant studies.
5. Screening and Sampling the Evidence	Studies from scoping searches are screened collaboratively to pilot inclusion/exclusion criteria and test data extraction frameworks.
6. Running Full Searches	Prioritized search methods are applied systematically across selected databases to identify all eligible empirical studies. The first round of the final search identified 316 studies, and the second round added 132 studies, bringing the total study pool to 448.
7. Reviewing and Extracting Data	Eligible studies are analyzed and categorized by AI technology type, policing domain, and research design, ensuring transparency and accuracy.
8. Peer Review and Verification of Included Studies	All team members double-checked the included studies to confirm completeness and identify any overlooked evidence.
9. Follow-Up Searches and Refinement	Supplementary searches conducted as new insights emerge during analysis to ensure completeness and account for newly published research.
10. Synthesis and Reporting	Findings are synthesized into thematic categories (e.g., predictive analytics, surveillance, public/police attitudes) and transparently reported with full methodological documentation.

FIGURE 4.1 Steps of a Tailored Approach Systematic Literature Review

preliminary searches across multiple databases, testing keyword combinations and identifying core definitions of terms such as "predictive policing," "machine learning," and "facial recognition." Team members shared findings to develop a collective understanding of the literature's structure and to anticipate challenges, such as inconsistent terminology or overlapping study domains. The outcomes of this stage included a refined set of search terms, initial identification of relevant studies, and a clearer sense of the evidence base available.

Based on this scoping work, the team met to discuss where the most relevant evidence was likely to be found and to determine the publication types and study designs most appropriate for inclusion. This discussion stage was critical in shaping the next steps of the review, as the research question and information needs were revisited to ensure alignment with the emerging evidence landscape.

Subsequent scoping searches were then conducted using different search methods to test their capacity to identify relevant studies. The search strategy covered the period from 2010 to 2025, capturing fifteen years of technological developments and empirical research on AI applications in law enforcement. Boolean combinations of terms such as "police," "law enforcement," "artificial intelligence," "machine learning," "deep learning," "predictive policing," "facial recognition," "gunshot detection," "license plate reader," "body-worn cameras," and "drones" were employed. This stage was iterative and experimental, consistent with the principles of a Tailored Approach, which emphasizes methodological flexibility based on empirical results. Searches were performed across Criminal Justice Abstracts, PsycINFO, IEEE Xplore, Scopus, and Web of Science, with supplementary searches through Google Scholar and reference list screening. Detailed notes were maintained on all search terms used, combinations tested, and studies identified. This documentation process provided a transparent record of methodological decisions and informed later stages of fully systematic searching.

During the screening and sampling phase, the team reviewed studies identified in the scoping phase to refine inclusion and exclusion criteria. This process served to clarify the boundaries of "AI in policing" and ensure consistent interpretation of eligibility criteria. The team collectively reviewed sample studies to test the robustness of these criteria and to pilot data extraction templates. This iterative engagement helped ensure that the review would remain both rigorous and responsive to the evidence encountered.

Based on the insights gained from scoping and sampling, the team finalized the choice and order of search methods. The decision process prioritized databases and search approaches that had demonstrated effectiveness in identifying significant studies that were consistently relevant and representative of the review's aims. This staged prioritization reflects a Tailored Approach's distinction between data-producing methods, such as database searches, and data-responding methods, such as citation tracking or manual searches.

Once search methods were finalized, full searches were conducted systematically to produce a comprehensive set of studies for screening and inclusion. Inclusion criteria consisted of peer-reviewed empirical studies published in English between 2010 and 2025 examining AI applications in US law enforcement, while non-empirical works, grey literature, and studies related to judicial, correctional, or forensic contexts were excluded. Each stage of the search and selection process was documented in detail using an Excel tracking file that recorded databases searched, dates, keyword strings, inclusion decisions, and reasons for exclusion. This record-keeping provided transparency and reproducibility of the review process. The first round of the final search identified 316 studies, and the second round added 132 studies, bringing the total study pool to 448.

Screening of identified studies was then undertaken to confirm eligibility based on predefined inclusion and exclusion criteria. Peer review of the included studies list by the team was performed to verify completeness and minimize the risk of omitting relevant research. Any additional studies identified through this process were examined for inclusion and documented accordingly.

Finally, follow-up searches were conducted in parallel with data synthesis to ensure that no recent or overlooked studies were excluded. Consistent with a Tailored Approach, this final iterative step allowed the incorporation of new knowledge gained during synthesis and addressed any potential gaps identified through peer review.

Data from included studies were extracted and organized by AI technology type, research design, operational context, and key findings. Studies were categorized across core policing domains, including predictive analytics, surveillance and identification, investigative support, administrative applications, and public and police support for AI in policing. Ethical and governance issues, such as bias, transparency, privacy, and accountability, were noted where discussed.

By following the iterative, evidence-driven process outlined in a Tailored Approach, this review achieved a methodologically robust and contextually grounded synthesis of the empirical literature on AI in US law enforcement.

Results

This section presents the results of empirical studies evaluating the effectiveness, limitations, and broader implications of AI technologies in law enforcement. Drawing on empirical research in the last fifteen years, it examines five key areas: predictive policing, identification and surveillance, decision support tools, public perceptions, and police officer attitudes. The findings indicate both potential benefits and significant challenges, highlighting the importance of implementation context, transparency, and accountability in determining the outcomes of AI adoption in policing.

AI in Crime Fighting: Predictive Policing

Predictive policing relies on historical crime data to forecast potential future crimes. Predictive policing methods can be broadly classified into two main types: place-based predictions and person-based predictions. Place-based predictions focus on identifying locations and times where crimes are more likely to occur, while person-based predictions aim to identify individuals who are at risk of offending or becoming victims. Within these two overarching types, predictive methods can be divided into four specific categories (Perry et al., 2013). The first category predicts crimes by forecasting areas and times with increased risk, which is place-based. The second category predicts potential offenders, identifying individuals who may commit crimes in the future, making it person-based. The third category predicts perpetrators' identities by matching likely offenders to specific past crimes, which is also person-based. The fourth category predicts victims of crime, identifying groups or individuals at higher risk, and can involve both place-based and person-based approaches depending on the focus.

Place-based predictive policing has shown modest success when predictions are coupled with visible police presence. The Shreveport Predictive Policing Experiment (Hunt et al., 2014) found no overall statistical evidence that predictive policing districts experienced greater crime reductions than control districts, though one command that maintained higher effort initially saw a temporary 35 percent drop in property crimes. The results suggest that inconsistent implementation, reduced effort over time, and unclear intervention strategies likely limited the program's effectiveness. On the other hand, in Los Angeles and Kent (Mohler et al., 2015), predictive patrols were associated with a 7.4 percent greater reduction in crime per patrol hour compared to traditional hotspot policing. Similarly, in Philadelphia, overt police deployments in forecasted areas led to a 31 percent reduction in property crime, while covert patrols had no measurable effect (Ratcliffe et al., 2021). Harmspot policing in Indianapolis, which directed officers to areas of concentrated social harm rather than just high crime frequency, demonstrated that strategic deployment can reduce overall harm without exacerbating racial disparities (Carter et al., 2021). In Portland and Cincinnati, Lee and colleagues (2020) implemented a transparent, Excel-based algorithm using population heterogeneity and state dependence frameworks, achieving high accuracy and efficiency in forecasting crime hotspots. These studies indicate that the effectiveness of place-based predictive policing depends not only on the accuracy of the algorithm but also on how law enforcement integrates tactical deployment with the forecasts.

On the other hand, person-based predictive policing has produced more concerning outcomes. The Strategic Subjects List (SSL) in Chicago, which scored individuals considered likely to be involved in gun violence, did not reduce shootings or homicides and was associated with increased arrests (Saunders et al., 2016). Law enforcement agencies are increasingly adopting predictive policing technologies, yet many of these systems depend on data generated during times of racially biased, unfair, or otherwise problematic policing. This reliance creates the danger of "dirty data," which can reinforce existing systemic biases. A review (Richardson et al., 2019) of thirteen jurisdictions, including Chicago, New Orleans, and Maricopa County, reveals that predictive tools frequently incorporate or risk incorporating such compromised data, potentially resulting in inaccurate or discriminatory forecasts.

On the other hand, Berk and Sorenson (2020) focused on high-risk intimate partner violence offenders likely to cause injury, using police data and multiple algorithmic approaches to better identify those most likely to reoffend violently. Their findings suggest that predictive tools can help allocate prevention resources more effectively for rare violent acts, although such applications remain limited and highly context-specific.

In summary, place-based predictive policing can reduce crime under certain conditions, particularly when forecasts are combined with visible, strategic deployment and community-sensitive practices. Person-based models, however, have not reliably prevented crime and risk reinforcing inequities through increased surveillance and arrests. Machine learning techniques show promise for targeting rare, high-risk events, but careful governance, ethical oversight, and alignment with broader prevention strategies are essential to ensure these tools enhance safety without causing disproportionate harm.

AI in Crime Fighting: Identification and Surveillance

AI tools such as facial recognition, automated license plate readers (ALPRs), and acoustic gunshot detection are increasingly used to support identification efforts and enhance situational awareness in law enforcement operations. These technologies are designed to assist police in detecting criminal activity more quickly and accurately, though their effects on crime reduction and public safety vary across contexts.

Facial recognition technology has shown both potential and limitations. National analyses have produced mixed findings, with some studies linking facial recognition to higher Black arrest rates and wider racial disparities without significant reductions in overall crime (Johnson et al., 2022). However, a large-scale study later found that the adoption of facial recognition across 268 US cities was associated with a 14 percent reduction in homicides, with no increase in racial disparities or arrest rates (Johnson et al., 2024).

ALPRs have demonstrated operational advantages such as faster detection of stolen vehicles and improved situational awareness. Randomized controlled trials in Fairfax and Alexandria, however, found that ALPR patrols did not reduce auto theft or overall crime rates (Lum et al., 2011). Koper and Lum (2019) evaluated the impact of a large-scale fixed network of ALPR on police investigations in Charlotte-Mecklenburg. Findings showed some improvement in case clearances for auto theft and robbery after the ALPR network was installed, especially in areas with high ALPR concentration, but the effects were not statistically significant, indicating that further research is needed to confirm their effectiveness.

Acoustic gunshot detection systems have also shown mixed results. In Philadelphia, St. Louis, and Kansas City, these systems generated more alerts and improved evidence collection but did not lead to measurable declines in victimization or confirmed shootings (Ratcliffe et al., 2019; Mares & Blackburn,

2020; Piza et al., 2024; 2025). In Columbia, South Carolina, gunshot detection increased the number of detected shootings, firearm seizures, and faster recovery of guns in incidents without victims or property damage, while non-fatal shootings decreased and fatal shootings remained unchanged (Boehme et al., 2025). In Chicago, staggered deployment of gunshot detection improved gun recovery rates but did not reduce shootings or gun crime overall (Connealy et al., 2025). In Denver, Milwaukee, and Richmond, the technology doubled shooting alerts and increased officer workload, improving response times only in the interval between notification and officer assignment (Lawrence & Novak, 2024). Finally, a recent evaluation (Kent & Lovell, 2025) found that a gunshot detection system in Cleveland (ShotSpotter) accurately detects gunfire and enables faster police responses. However, most alerts do not lead to arrests or actionable outcomes, and the system has added strain to Cleveland's already understaffed police force while offering limited integration with other technologies. They concluded that the gunshot detection system improves situational awareness but does not directly reduce crime or significantly enhance community trust in Cleveland, Ohio.

Machine learning approaches have also been applied to crime identification and risk prediction. California uses predictive tools that analyze firearm transaction records to identify individuals at high risk for mass shootings, supporting targeted interventions alongside traditional threat assessments (Laqueur & Wintemute, 2019). Similarly, Ortiz Salazar (2024) developed a machine learning system using natural language processing to detect hate crimes in Seattle Police Department reports, which demonstrated improved identification accuracy even with imbalanced datasets.

In summary, AI tools for identification and surveillance including facial recognition, ALPR, gunshot detection, and predictive machine learning offer some operational and investigatory advantages. Facial recognition shows promise in reducing certain types of crime but carries significant risks of bias depending on oversight. ALPR and gunshot detection improve situational awareness and procedural efficiency but have not consistently demonstrated crime reduction. Machine learning applications for predictive risk assessment and crime detection can improve accuracy and support targeted interventions, although extreme events remain difficult to predict.

AI in Administrative Support

AI is increasingly being explored as a tool for improving internal police procedures, particularly in administrative and investigative functions. One major area of interest is the automation of routine tasks such as report writing. Studies by Adams et al. (2024) and Boehme et al. (2025) tested AI-assisted report writing across 755 police reports in Manchester, New Hampshire, and found no significant reduction in time spent or consistent improvements in perceived usefulness. Moreover, AI-based auditing tools have also been investigated as a method to influence officer behaviour and support accountability. Research conducted in the Aurora Police Department and the Richland County Sheriff's Department found partial evidence that AI audits could lead to changes in officer behaviour (Adams et al., 2024). However, the low explanatory power of these studies suggests that the effects were modest and inconsistent across settings.

Another emerging application of AI in administrative policing is the analysis of officer-worn body camera footage. Camp and Voigt (2024) utilized natural language processing to examine speech for politeness, emotion, and interaction quality to demonstrate how AI can transform large volumes of audio-visual data into meaningful insights. Watts et al. (2024) also studied the Truleo system, which evaluates audio for indicators of risk and professional conduct, and found that AI could support professionalism and strengthen departmental oversight, particularly given that much recorded material is rarely reviewed manually. Finally, Davies and Krame (2023) expanded this approach by combining AI with drones and other sensor technologies to enhance situational awareness and evidence collection, emphasizing the importance of ethics and privacy.

Moreover, machine learning is also being applied to predict and prevent officer misconduct. Cubitt et al. (2022) analyzed NYPD data and found that serious misconduct could be predicted with considerable accuracy for both male and female officers, though management responses often failed to prevent further incidents. Helsby et al. (2018) reported that a machine learning-based early intervention system at Charlotte-Mecklenburg improved detection accuracy, achieving 20 percent fewer false positives and 75 percent more true positives than existing systems. These applications illustrate AI's potential to support predictive oversight, informing targeted interventions, training, and policy development.

Public Support for AI in Policing

Public attitudes toward AI in policing play a key role in shaping the legitimacy and long-term success of these technologies. According to a recent survey (Pew Research Center, 2025), the majority of Americans say AI should play at least a small role in crime-related tasks, with 61 percent supporting its use to identify suspects. Previous research indicates that support for AI tools is uneven and depends heavily on the type of technology and the demographic characteristics of the population. For example, body-worn cameras and gunshot detection systems generally receive favourable views, while facial recognition and predictive policing provoke greater concern, especially regarding privacy, misuse, and potential discriminatory outcomes (Lee & Chin-Rothman, 2022). These differences suggest that public acceptance is not uniform and is closely tied to perceived risks and benefits associated with specific applications.

Trust in law enforcement emerges as a critical factor influencing public approval of AI. Individuals who report higher confidence in the police are more likely to endorse the use of AI technologies in policing (UNICRI, 2024). Cross-cultural comparisons further demonstrate variation in attitudes, with North American respondents showing more concern about AI in policing than those in Europe or Asia (Akhgar et al., 2022; Ardabili et al., 2024). Moreover, Kreps et al. (2023) identified an "AI trust paradox," in which individuals adopt AI tools despite incomplete trust. Factors driving this paradox include optimism about technological improvements, belief in efficiency gains, and concern about missing out on potential benefits, highlighting the complex psychology behind public attitudes.

Procedural justice theory provides a useful lens for understanding these dynamics, emphasizing that perceptions of fairness, neutrality, and respect in police decision-making strongly shape support for technological interventions (Guler et al., 2025). When AI is perceived as non-transparent, biased, or unaccountable, public approval declines (Crawford & Calo, 2016; Ezzeddine et al., 2023). Empirical research reinforces the importance of procedural fairness in shaping public opinion. In a recent study, Guler and colleagues (2025) found that perceptions of neutrality, public input in decision-making, and trustworthiness fully mediate the relationship between knowledge of AI and support for its use. This indicates that public approval is contingent not simply on familiarity with AI technologies but on confidence in the fairness and legitimacy of their implementation.

Studies focused on specific AI technologies show nuanced patterns of opinion. Mesch and Lam (2024) reported that public views on facial recognition technology are mixed, with people recognizing potential crime prevention benefits while expressing privacy concerns. Familiarity with technology also influences perceptions, suggesting that education and exposure can shape acceptance. Moreover, O'Shaughnessy et al. (2023) demonstrated that cultural values, including individualism, egalitarianism, risk aversion, and technoskepticism, strongly shape opinions on AI, while experts tend to hold more nuanced perspectives than the general public. Schiff et al. (2023) also found that public support is influenced more by the institutional setting than by the technology itself, with local law enforcement agencies garnering higher trust than federal law enforcement organizations.

Police Officer Support for AI in Policing

Attitudes within law enforcement agencies significantly influence the adoption and implementation of AI tools. A recent survey indicates that roughly 90 percent of officers support the use of some form of AI in their work, although support is not uniform across applications (Mark43, 2025). Officers generally favour tools that enhance operational efficiency, such as administrative automation or surveillance systems, but express more caution toward predictive analytics that could affect enforcement decisions. Concerns center on the interpretability of algorithmic recommendations and the potential impact on professional judgment and relationships with the community (Brayne & Christin, 2021; Laufs & Borrion, 2022).

Even though Adams et al. (2024) and Boehme et al. (2025) found no significant reduction in time spent or consistent improvements in perceived usefulness, 48 percent of patrol officers generally viewed AI-assisted report writing positively. However, no significant differences were observed between treatment and control groups in perceived usefulness, efficiency, or report quality. Research on body-worn camera monitoring highlights the importance of human involvement in shaping fairness perceptions. Adams (2025) examined officer views on different activation methods and review types, finding that automatic activation and AI audits were perceived as less fair, especially when combined. Officers preferred supervisor reviews and felt fairness increased when they retained control over recordings. Higher-ranking officers generally viewed policies more positively, likely reflecting their supervisory responsibilities. Similarly, White et al. (2025) examined Truleo usage in two Arizona departments and found that while officers' attitudes were largely neutral, understanding of the system improved and consistent use was observed. This suggests that maintaining human oversight and control is critical to ensuring the legitimacy and acceptance of AI monitoring tools within policing, and that such tools can be effectively integrated into routine practices when supported by adequate training and clear operational guidelines.

Discussion

This review has examined the deployment and effectiveness of AI technologies in policing over the past fifteen years, which demonstrates the multifaceted nature of the findings. While some AI tools demonstrate measurable benefits under specific conditions, others show limited impact or result in unintended consequences. Across applications, the success of AI appears highly dependent on implementation strategies, oversight, and integration with human decision-making. Place-based predictive policing illustrates this complexity. In cities such as Los Angeles and Kent, predictive patrols led to modest but meaningful reductions in crime per patrol hour compared with traditional hotspot policing (Mohler et al., 2015), and overt deployment in forecasted areas of Philadelphia resulted in significant reductions in property crime, while covert patrols had no measurable effect (Ratcliffe et al., 2021). Strategies that focus on areas of concentrated social harm, rather than solely on crime frequency, have been shown to reduce overall harm without exacerbating racial disparities (Carter et al., 2021). These findings suggest that predictive accuracy alone is insufficient and that the operational integration of forecasts with tactical deployment and community-sensitive practices is crucial.

On the other hand, person-based predictive policing, exemplified by Chicago's SSL, has consistently failed to reduce violent incidents while increasing arrests (Saunders et al., 2016), raising ethical concerns about over-policing marginalized communities. Targeted applications, such as machine learning models predicting rare but high-risk events like intimate partner violence, show potential for resource allocation but remain highly context-specific (Berk & Sorenson, 2020).

AI technologies used for identification and surveillance, including facial recognition, ALPR, and acoustic gunshot detection, offer operational benefits but inconsistent impacts on crime reduction. Facial recognition adoption across multiple US cities has been associated with reductions in homicides in some studies (Johnson et al., 2024), yet other analyses link these tools to higher arrest rates among Black populations without measurable crime reductions (Johnson et al., 2022). ALPRs improve investigative efficiency but do not consistently lower auto theft or overall crime rates (Lum et al., 2011). Gunshot detection systems enhance situational awareness and evidence collection but have not reliably reduced shootings or victimization, although they increased detection rates and improved response times in some cases (Boehme et al., 2025; Connealy et al., 2025; Kent & Lovell, 2025; Lawrence & Novak, 2024; Mares & Blackburn, 2020; Piza et al., 2024; 2025; Ratcliffe et al., 2019). Machine learning applications, such as predictive risk assessment for firearm transactions (Laqueur & Wintemute, 2019) and natural language processing for hate crime detection (Ortiz Salazar, 2024), have demonstrated improved accuracy and identification efficiency, indicating that AI can meaningfully support investigative work.

In administrative and decision-support applications, AI is being explored for report writing, auditing, and predicting officer misconduct, but efficiency gains remain modest. Studies conducted in Manchester, New Hampshire (Adams et al., 2024; Boehme et al., 2025) found that AI-assisted report writing neither reduced workload nor consistently improved perceived quality. AI auditing and misconduct prediction tools show potential to influence officer behaviour and improve oversight, although effects are highly context-dependent (Adams et al., 2024; Cubitt et al., 2022; Helsby et al., 2018). Natural language processing applied to body-worn camera footage demonstrates that AI can support supervision and situational awareness while transforming large volumes of data into actionable insights (Camp & Voigt, 2024; Davies & Krame, 2023; Watts et al., 2024). These applications suggest that AI's most promising administrative use lies in predictive, analytic, and oversight functions rather than routine task automation.

Public attitudes toward AI in policing are shaped by technology type, perceptions of procedural justice, and institutional trust. Tools perceived as enhancing transparency or safety, such as body-worn cameras and gunshot detection systems, generally receive higher support, whereas facial recognition and predictive policing prompt skepticism, particularly regarding privacy, misuse, and discriminatory outcomes (Crawford & Calo, 2016; Ezzeddine et al., 2023). Trust in law enforcement strongly mediates acceptance (UNICRI, 2024), and cross-cultural comparisons show variation in attitudes, with North Americans expressing more concern than Europeans or Asians (Akhgar et al., 2022; Ardabili et al., 2024). Procedural fairness, transparency, and accountability are central to legitimacy, and cultural values, institutional setting, and familiarity with technology further influence public opinion (Guler et al., 2025; Kreps et al., 2023; Mesch & Lam, 2024; Schiff et al., 2023; O'Shaughnessy et al., 2023).

Officer support for AI is generally high, with most endorsing some use in policing, although acceptance varies by application (Brayne & Christin, 2021; Laufs & Borrion, 2022). Officers favour tools that enhance operational efficiency but are cautious about predictive analytics that could affect discretionary decision-making. Evidence indicates that successful adoption depends on preserving procedural justice, ensuring interpretability of algorithmic outputs, and maintaining human oversight, particularly for body-worn camera monitoring and AI audits (Adams, 2025; White et al., 2025). Effective integration requires sufficient training, clear policies, and accountability structures to ensure technology enhances rather than undermines professional judgment and community trust.

In brief, AI technologies offer significant potential to improve efficiency, responsiveness, and oversight in policing, but their effects on crime reduction, fairness, and legitimacy are inconsistent and highly context-dependent. Place-based predictive policing and carefully implemented facial recognition show promise under specific conditions, while person-based predictive systems and report-writing tools have not proven effective. Transparent AI policies, public input, and evidence-based evaluation are essential to ensure that AI contributes positively to equitable and effective policing without exacerbating existing challenges in American policing.

This systematic review points to several key policy implications. First, the adoption of AI in policing should be guided by principles of transparency, accountability, and community engagement. Agencies must adopt policies requiring that algorithms are explainable, subject to external review, and regularly audited for fairness. This includes public disclosure of data sources, model logic, and evaluation metrics. Second, community engagement is essential to building public trust. Policymakers should invest in public education efforts that clarify how AI systems work, what safeguards are in place, and how individuals can voice concerns. Third, all AI tools used in policing should undergo rigorous, independent evaluation. This includes both experimental research and long-term studies that assess outcomes across diverse communities and operational contexts. Fourth, equity audits must be institutionalized to monitor for unintended consequences, especially in terms of racial or socioeconomic disparities. Policymakers should require that bias mitigation strategies be integrated into both the design and deployment phases of AI tools. Finally, police departments must provide adequate training so that officers can appropriately interpret and apply AI-generated insights. Internal accountability structures are also necessary to prevent misuse and reinforce procedural fairness.

The findings of this review highlight the necessity for future research to address existing gaps. Longitudinal studies are needed to assess the long-term impacts of AI technologies on crime, public perceptions, and institutional trust. Cross-jurisdictional comparisons can offer insights into how different governance structures and community dynamics influence outcomes. More qualitative research, including ethnographic studies, would help illuminate how AI is experienced by both police and communities, especially those historically subject to over-policing. Emerging tools such as AI-powered drones, large language models, and chatbot-based reporting systems should be evaluated with the same level of empirical rigour as more established technologies. Finally, future studies should explore how AI in policing interacts with broader social structures, including patterns of inequality and systemic bias, so that technological innovation does not inadvertently reinforce existing injustices.

In conclusion, AI technologies offer significant potential to enhance the efficiency and responsiveness of law enforcement, but their actual impact on crime reduction, fairness, and public trust remains conditional and inconsistent. The most promising tools, such as place-based predictive models and facial recognition, have shown potential under specific conditions but also carry risks that must be carefully managed. Others, particularly person-based predictive systems and acoustic gunshot detection, have produced insignificant or concerning results. Without transparent policies, evidence-based evaluation, and community accountability, AI may not only fall short of its goals but also deepen existing problems in American policing. A more cautious and evidence-based approach, grounded in principles of procedural justice and informed by interdisciplinary research, is essential for accurately assessing the effectiveness of AI tools in US policing.

Funding: This work was supported by the Penn State Criminal Justice Research Center (CJRC) through seed funding.

References

Adams, I. T., McLean, K., & Alpert, G. (2024). Improving police behaviour through artificial intelligence: Pre-registered experimental results in two large US agencies. *CrimRxiv.* https://www.crimrxiv.com/pub/q5fehcov/release/1

Adams, I. T. (2025). Automation and artificial intelligence in police body-worn cameras: Experimental evidence of impact on perceptions of fairness among officers. *Journal of Criminal Justice*, *97*, 102373.

Akhgar, B., Bayerl, P. S., Bailey, K., Dennis, R., Gibson, H., Heyes, S., Lyle, A., Raven, A., & Sampson, F. (2022). *Accountability Principles for Artificial Intelligence (AP4AI) in the internal security domain: AP4AI framework blueprint.* Europol Innovation Lab.

Ardabili, B. R., Pazho, A. D., Noghre, G. A., Katariya, V., Hull, G., Reid, S., & Tabkhi, H. (2024). Exploring public's perception of safety and video surveillance technology: A survey approach. *Technology in Society*, *78*, 102641.

Berk, R. A., & Sorenson, S. B. (2020). Algorithmic approach to forecasting rare violent events: An illustration based in intimate partner violence perpetration. *Criminology & Public Policy*, *19*(1), 213–233.

Boehme, H. M., Olson, M., Adams, I. T., & Fulmer, C. (2025). Shootings, seizures, and speed: A quasi-experimental study of gunshot detection technology in a mid-sized capital city. *Crime Science*, *14*(1), 14.

Boke, K., Guler, A., & Kula, S. (2025). AI in crime fighting: A systematic review using the framework of "what works, what doesn't, what's promising". *Police Practice and Research*, 1–17.

Brayne, S., & Christin, A. (2021). Technologies of crime prediction: The reception of algorithms in policing and criminal courts. *Social Problems*, *68*(3), 608–624.

Bullock, J. B. (2019). Artificial intelligence, discretion, and bureaucracy. *The American Review of Public Administration*, *49*(7), 751–761.

Camp, N. P., & Voigt, R. (2024). Body camera footage as data: Using natural language processing to monitor policing at scale & in depth. *Behavioral Science & Policy*, *10*(2), 16–25.

Carter, J. G., Mohler, G., Raje, R., Chowdhury, N., & Pandey, S. (2021). The Indianapolis harmspot policing experiment. *Journal of Criminal Justice*, *74*, 101814.

Chan, J. (2021). The future of AI in policing: Exploring the sociotechnical imaginaries. In *Predictive policing and artificial intelligence* (pp. 41–57). Routledge.

Connealy, N. T., Piza, E. L., Arietti, R. A., Mohler, G. O., & Carter, J. G. (2025). Staggered deployment of gunshot detection technology in Chicago, IL: A matched quasi-experiment of gun violence outcomes. *Journal of Experimental Criminology*, *21*(3), 1027–1053.

Cooper, C., Booth, A., Husk, K., Lovell, R., Frost, J., Schauberger, U., … & Garside, R. (2024). A Tailored Approach: A model for literature searching in complex systematic reviews. *Journal of Information Science*, *50*(4), 1030–1062.

Crawford, K. & Calo, R. (2016). There is a blind spot in AI research. *Nature*, *538*(7625), 311–313.

Cubitt, T. I., Gaub, J. E., & Holtfreter, K. (2022). Gender differences in serious police misconduct: A machine-learning analysis of the New York Police Department (NYPD). *Journal of Criminal Justice*, *82*, 101976.

Davies, A., & Krame, G. (2023). Integrating body-worn cameras, drones, and AI: A framework for enhancing police readiness and response. *Policing: A Journal of Policy and Practice*, *17*, paad083.

Ezeh, N., Widgery, A., & Canada, C. (2025). Artificial intelligence in law enforcement: The federal and state landscape. National Conference of State Legislatures. https://www.ncsl.org/civil-and-criminal-justice/artificial-intelligence-and-law-enforcement-the-federal-and-state-landscape

Ezzeddine, Y., Bayerl, P. S., & Gibson, H. (2023). Safety, privacy, or both: Evaluating citizens' perspectives around artificial intelligence use by police forces. *Policing and Society*, *33*(7), 861–876.

Ferguson, A. G. (2017). *The rise of big data policing: Surveillance, race, and the future of law enforcement*. New York University Press.

Finklea, K. (2023, December 15). *Law enforcement use of artificial intelligence and directives in the 2023 Executive Order* (CRS Insight No. IN12289). Congressional Research Service.

Guler, A., Kula, S., & Boke, K. (2025). Examining public support for AI in policing: The role of perceived procedural justice. *Police Practice and Research*, 1–23.

Haley, P., & Burrell, D. N. (2025). Using artificial intelligence in law enforcement and policing to improve public health and safety. *Law, Economics and Society*, *1*(1), 46.

Helsby, J., Carton, S., Joseph, K., Mahmud, A., Park, Y., Navarrete, A., … & Ghani, R. (2018). Early intervention systems: Predicting adverse interactions between police and the public. *Criminal Justice Policy Review*, *29*(2), 190–209.

Hunt, P., Saunders, J., & Hollywood, J. S. (2014). *Evaluation of the Shreveport predictive policing experiment*. Rand Corporation.

IBM. (2024). What is AI? https://www.ibm.com/think/topics/artificial-intelligence

Joh, E. E. (2017). Artificial intelligence and policing: First questions. *Seattle UL Rev.*, *41*, 1139.

Johnson, T. L., Johnson, N. N., McCurdy, D., & Olajide, M. S. (2022). Facial recognition systems in policing and racial disparities in arrests. *Government Information Quarterly*, *39*, 101753.

Johnson, T. L., Johnson, N. N., Topalli, V., McCurdy, D., & Wallace, A. (2024). Police facial recognition applications and violent crime control in U.S. cities. *Cities*, *155*, 105472.

Kent, S. K., & Lovell, R. E. (2025, August). *Evaluation of the Cleveland Division of Police's implementation of ShotSpotter*. Criminology Research Center, Levin College of Public Affairs and Education, Cleveland State University.

Koper, C. S., & Lum, C. (2019). The impacts of large-scale license plate reader deployment on criminal investigations. *Police Quarterly*, *22*(3), 305–329.

Kreps, S., George, J., Lushenko, P., & Rao, A. (2023). Exploring the artificial intelligence "Trust paradox": Evidence from a survey experiment in the United States. *Plos one*, *18*(7), e0288109.

Laqueur, H. S., & Wintemute, G. J. (2019). Identifying high-risk firearm owners to prevent mass violence. *Criminology & Public Policy*, *19*(1), 109–127.

Lawrence, D. S., & Novak, K. J. (2024). Firearm shootings and the police response: Examining the impact of gunshot detection technology. *Police Practice and Research*, 1–20.

Laufs, J., & Borrion, H. (2022). Technological innovation in policing and crime prevention: Practitioner perspectives from London. *International Journal of Police Science & Management*, *24*(2), 190–209.

Lee, N. T., & Chin-Rothmann, C. (2022). *Police surveillance and facial recognition: Why data privacy is imperative for communities of color*. The Brookings Institution. Erişim adresi: https://www.brookings.edu/research/police-surveillance-and-facial-recognition-why-data-privacy-is-an-imperative-for-communities-of-color.

Lee, Y. J., SooHyun, O., & Eck, J. E. (2020). A theory-driven algorithm for real-time crime hot spot forecasting. *Police Quarterly*, *23*(2), 174–201.

Lukens, P. (2025). *How President Trump's recent actions could impact law enforcement: From reversing police reform orders to promoting AI and expanding police resources*, here's what has unfolded since January 20. Police1. https://www.police1.com/chiefs-sheriffs/how-president-trumps-recent-actions-could-impact-law-enforcement

Lum, C., Hibdon, J., Cave, B., Koper, C. S., & Merola, L. (2011). License plate reader (LPR) police patrols in crime hot spots: An experimental evaluation in two adjacent jurisdictions. *Journal of Experimental Criminology*, *7*(4), 321–345.

Lum, C., Koper, C. S., & Willis, J. (2017). Understanding the limits of technology's impact on police effectiveness. *Police Quarterly*, *20*(2), 135–163.

Mares, D., & Blackburn, E. (2020). Acoustic gunshot detection systems: A quasi-experimental evaluation in St. Louis, MO. *Journal of Experimental Criminology*, *17*(2), 193–215.

Mark43. (2025). *The 2025 U.S. Public Safety Trends Report*. https://mark43.com/2025-public-safety-trends-report/

Mesch, G., & Lam, I. (2024). Public perceptions about the police's use of facial recognition technologies. *AI & SOCIETY, 40*(5), 3869–3879.

Mohler, G. O., Short, M. B., Malinowski, S., Johnson, M., Tita, G., Bertozzi, A. L., & Brantingham, P. J. (2015). Randomized controlled field trials of predictive policing. *Journal of the American Statistical Association, 110*(512), 1399–1411.

Ortiz Salazar, A. (2024). Detecting hate crimes through machine learning and natural language processing. *Police Practice and Research, 26*(6), 746–768.

O'Shaughnessy, M. R., Schiff, D. S., Varshney, L. R., Rozell, C. J., & Davenport, M. A. (2023). What governs attitudes toward artificial intelligence adoption and governance?. *Science and Public Policy, 50*(2), 161–176.

Perry, W. L., McInnis, B., Price, C. C., Smith, S. C., & Hollywood, J. S. (2013). *Predictive policing: The role of crime forecasting in law enforcement operations*. RAND Corporation.

Pew Research Center. (2025, September 17). *How Americans view AI and its impact on people and society*. Pew Research Center. https://www.pewresearch.org/wp-content/uploads/sites/20/2025/09/PS_2025.9.15_AI-and-its-impact_report.pdf

Piza, E. L., Hatten, D. N., Mohler, G. O., Carter, J. G., & Cho, J. (2024). Gunshot detection technology's effect on gun violence in Kansas City, Missouri: A microsynthetic control evaluation. *Criminology & Public Policy, 23*(4), 863–892.

Piza, E. L., Arietti, R. A., Carter, J. G., & Mohler, G. O. (2025). The effect of gunshot detection technology on evidence collection and case clearance in Kansas City, Missouri. *Journal of Experimental Criminology, 21*(1), 127–152.

Ratcliffe, J. H., Lattanzio, M., Kikuchi, G., & Thomas, K. (2019). A partially randomized field experiment on the effect of an acoustic gunshot detection system on police incident reports. *Journal of Experimental Criminology, 15*(1), 67–76.

Ratcliffe, J. H., Taylor, R. B., Askey, A. P. et al. (2021). The Philadelphia predictive policing experiment. *Journal of Experimental Criminology*, 17, 15–41.

Ray, R. (2020, February 20). *5 questions policymakers should ask about facial recognition, law enforcement, and algorithmic bias*. The Brookings Institution. https://www.brookings.edu/research/5-questions-policymakers-should-ask-about-facial-recognition-law-enforcement-and-algorithmic-bias/

Richardson, R., Schultz, J. M., & Crawford, K. (2019). Dirty data, bad predictions: How civil rights violations impact police data, predictive policing systems, and justice. *NYUL Rev. Online, 94*, 15.

Rowe, M. & Muir, R. (2021). Big data policing: Governing the machines? In *Predictive policing and artificial intelligence. Routledge Frontiers of Criminal Justice* (pp. 254–268). Taylor & Francis.

Saunders, J., Hunt, P., & Hollywood, J. S. (2016). Predictions put into practice: a quasi-experimental evaluation of Chicago's predictive policing pilot. *Journal of Experimental Criminology, 12*(3), 347–371.

Schiff, K. J., Schiff, D. S., Adams, I. T., McCrain, J., & Mourtgos, S. M. (2023). Institutional factors driving citizen perceptions of AI in government: Evidence from a survey experiment on policing. *Public Administration Review.* doi:10.21428/cb6ab371.ad39582c

Simmons, R. (2017). Big data and procedural justice: Legitimizing algorithms in the criminal justice system. *Ohio St. J. Crim. L., 15*, 573.

The President's Task Force on 21st Century Policing. (2015). *Final report of the president's task force on 21st century policing*. U.S. Department of Justice, Office of Community Oriented Policing Services. https://cops.usdoj.gov/pdf/taskforce/taskforce_finalreport.pdf

The White House. (2025, July 23). *Winning the race: America's AI Action Plan. U.S. Executive Office of the President*. https://www.whitehouse.gov/wp-content/uploads/2025/07/Americas-AI-Action-Plan.pdf

UNICRI. (2024). *Not Just Another Tool: Public perceptions on the police use of artificial intelligence*. United Nations Interregional Crime and Justice Research Institute. https://unicri.org/sites/default/files/2024-11/Public-Perceptions-Police-Use-Artificial-Intelligence.pdf

US Department of Justice. (2024). *Artificial intelligence and criminal justice*. https://www.justice.gov/olp/media/1381796/dl

Watts, S., White, M. D., & Malm, A. (2024). Automating body-worn camera footage review through AI: Baseline attitudes from a multisite randomized control trial. *Policing: A Journal of Policy and Practice*, *18*, paae107.

White, M. D., Watts, S., Malm, A., & Navarrete, G. B. (2025). Officer acceptance and use of AI-driven body-worn camera footage review. *American Journal of Criminal Justice*, 1–22.

5

DATA INTEGRATION ACROSS AGENCIES TO ENHANCE THE SAFETY OF PERSONS LIVING WITH DEMENTIA

Antonio Miguel Cruz, Christine Daum, Aidan K. Comeau, Anmol Jassal, and Lili Liu

Introduction

Dementia is an escalating public health challenge. Globally, it is estimated that more than 150 million people will be affected by this condition by 2050 (Nichols et al., 2022). In Canada, approximately 700,000 individuals are currently living with dementia, and this number is projected to double by 2050 as the population ages (Alzheimer Society of Canada, n.d.). This anticipated growth presents a challenge to health systems and highlights a societal imperative to safeguard the quality of life of those affected.

Canada's national dementia strategy reflects this priority by emphasizing three key objectives: *preventing dementia*, *advancing therapies*, and *enhancing the quality of life* for people living with dementia and their caregivers (Public Health Agency of Canada, 2024). Quality of life in this context encompasses more than clinical outcomes; it includes the ability of a person living with dementia to participate in meaningful activities, maintain social connections, and engage with their community (Craig et al., 2024). However, as dementia progresses, cognitive changes such as memory loss, disorientation, and impaired judgment can elevate the risks associated with daily activities (Kumar et al., 2024). One of the most concerning risks associated with dementia is becoming lost and going missing. While the majority of reported cases fortunately result in safe recovery, the potential consequences can be severe, ranging from emotional distress for the person and care partners to injury or death in time-sensitive situations (Kikuchi et al., 2019). Even when resolved safely, these incidents require rapid mobilization and coordination, placing significant operational demands on police and search and rescue organizations due to the resource-intensive and specialized nature of search efforts (Ferguson & Huey, 2023a).

DOI: 10.4324/9781003671312-5

Police play a critical role in locating missing individuals, but may overlook the complex *demographic*, *psychopathological*, and *environmental factors* that contribute to missing incidents involving persons living with dementia (Gambier-Ross et al., 2023). A public health approach reframes missing incidents as events that first responders react to, to events that can be prevented through shared responsibility and collaboration among community and social care agencies, to support those at risk of getting lost. At its core, the public health approach emphasizes prevention strategies, moving beyond reactive search efforts to proactive interventions. This includes primary prevention to stop missing incidents from occurring, secondary prevention through early intervention to prevent re-occurrence (e.g., tailored therapies or counselling), and tertiary prevention to manage ongoing cases through collaborative care (e.g., return to home interview (Pona et al., 2019)). This conceptual shift recognizes police as vital "*public health interventionists*" in social issues, even though this role is largely untested in the context of missing persons (Gambier-Ross et al., 2023), including in dementia-related missing incidents.

Prevention, early detection, and rapid resolution of missing incidents require access to accurate, timely, and relevant data (Ferguson & Huey, 2023a). However, the data needed to anticipate or respond effectively to missing incidents is often fragmented across multiple sectors (Miguel Cruz et al., 2022). Healthcare providers hold medical information and information about a person's behaviour and function. Additionally, police and other first responders (ambulance, fire, search and rescue), search and rescue teams, and not-for-profit organizations (e.g., MedicAlert® (MedicAlert Foundation Canada, n.d.)) maintain records of past incidents and search patterns. Yet among agencies that collect data on medical and demographic information, some is poorly reported (e.g., gender, ethnicity) (Ferguson, 2022). Data from police services are unstructured, siloed, and not standardized (Ferguson & Huey, 2023a). This is compounded when several levels of police (e.g., municipal, provincial, national) are involved. Without integration, each agency must operate with an incomplete picture, limiting the capacity for coordinated and proactive interventions.

Emerging privacy-preserving technologies offer a transformative opportunity to integrate data and modernize responses to missing persons cases. Fully homomorphic encryption enables analysis of encrypted data across healthcare, police, volunteer search and rescue, and community systems without exposing personal information. Rather than forcing agencies to relinquish control of sensitive records, fully homomorphic encryption supports secure, cross-sector risk modelling and decision-support while maintaining confidentiality. Its adoption signals a shift toward future policing-data-driven, anticipatory, and prevention-focused, where police are equipped not only to respond to crises but to identify and mitigate risk before harm occurs. When embedded within robust governance and community oversight, such innovation can strengthen public trust and align safety with rights protection. In this model, policing evolves from reactive incident management to a collaborative, evidence-informed public health partner (Future of Police Institute, n.d.).

This chapter examines the potential of cross-agency data integration. It explores the nature of missing incidents in dementia, outlines the current landscape of data sources relating to these incidents, and discusses how linking these sources can enhance prevention, search efficiency, and reduce negative outcomes. Particular attention is given to privacy-preserving technological solutions, including fully homomorphic encryption. By demonstrating how fully homomorphic encryption can support encrypted analytics, cross-agency risk modelling, and interoperable data systems, the chapter situates this technological innovation within broader ethical, legal, and operational considerations. Technical and ethical dimensions are reviewed alongside practical implementation strategies, with a view to informing policy and practice.

A central contribution of this chapter is its proposal to integrate fully homomorphic encryption into cross-agency missing-person data infrastructures. While prior discussions of data integration in policing and public health have emphasized governance and interoperability (Jones et al., 2024; van Dijk et al., 2019), to the best of our knowledge, research on how advanced cryptographic methods can operationalize such collaboration and data integration is lacking. By advancing a privacy-by-design framework grounded in fully homomorphic encryption, this chapter contributes to emerging models of future policing that are anticipatory, data-informed, and rights-respecting, demonstrating how innovation can simultaneously enhance public safety and strengthen public trust.

Understanding Lost and Missing Concepts in Dementia

Not all missing people are lost. A missing person is broadly defined as anyone whose whereabouts are unknown after being reported to the police, regardless of the circumstances of the person's disappearance (Royal Canadian Mounted Police, 2021). In contrast, a lost person is an individual who is temporarily disoriented and wishes to be found. In other words, a lost person is characterized by an inability to identify or orient oneself to known locations or to use effective reorientation methods, often leading to specific behaviour, known as *lost person behaviour* (Koester, 2008).

Lost person behaviour refers to the "*predictable patterns*" of movement, decision-making, and location choices exhibited by individuals after they become disoriented (Koester, 2008). In search and rescue contexts, it describes how different categories of people, such as children, hikers, or persons living with dementia, tend to act once they become lost. These patterns are based on empirical data from past incidents and are influenced by factors such as *demographic*, *psychopathological*, and *environmental factors* (Cruz et al., 2024; Miguel-Cruz et al., 2024).

Persons living with dementia face increased risks of becoming lost and going missing (Kikuchi et al., 2019). Neurocognitive deficits that accompany the progression of dementia significantly predispose individuals to an inability to safely navigate their environment and find their way. These include *memory loss* (remembering facts and events, and short-term memory for recent events and contexts), *anosognosia* (a lack of awareness or insight into one's cognitive deficits and functional impairments), *executive function impairments*, and *changes to visuospatial and visuoperceptual processing*, all of which can manifest as difficulty with navigation, especially in unfamiliar and familiar locations (Rowe et al., 2015).

Prevalence and Characteristics of Persons Living with Dementia Who Go Missing: Insights from Multi-Database Police Data in the Canadian Context

Estimation of the prevalence of missing incidents among persons living with dementia has been difficult to make due to methodological and data limitations. Studies differ in how they define and measure missing incidents, with estimates in prevalence ranging from 11% to 60% depending on definitions, datasets, time frames, and populations studied (Cruz et al., 2024; Perez et al., 2024). Prior attempts to characterize missing incidents have been constrained by small sample sizes, inconsistent data quality, and limited retention of police or registry records (Cruz et al., 2024). Furthermore, reliance on subscription databases (e.g., MedicAlert®) or selective samples can result in underrepresentation of certain groups, raising concerns about generalizability. Our recent multi-database study, which included analyses of four police organizations, albeit with limitations, aimed to close this gap by providing more accurate prevalence estimates in addition to characterizing demographic, psychopathological, and environmental factors associated with dementia-related missing incidents.

Dataset

The dataset included Edmonton Police Service (2015–2021), Service de police de la Ville de Montréal (2019–2021), Waterloo Regional Police Service (2010–2023), and Regina Police Service (2010–2021). A total of 7,333 police cases were screened for inclusion, with 1,674 (22.8%). These 1,674 incidents were included in subsequent analyses.

Population

The sample was comprised primarily of older adults, with 84.5% over the age of 65 (mean 76.3, SD 10.6). Slightly more than half were female (54.2%), and the majority were Caucasian (81.7%). In 79.2% of cases, individuals spoke at least one of Canada's official languages (English or French). Most participants

(98.1%) resided in urban areas, reflecting the predominance of cases drawn from municipal police services. Most reported living with a family member (64.1%). A diagnosis of dementia, including Alzheimer's disease or other dementias, was present in 90.0% of the sample. For clarity, Alzheimer's disease is the most common subtype of dementia; dementia is an umbrella term describing a syndrome of cognitive decline caused by various underlying conditions, of which Alzheimer's disease is one. Most individuals were reported to be living with mild dementia (40.6%).

Locations

Locations were analyzed in terms of point last seen or where the person was located. They were located mostly in outdoor public spaces (60.8%) and private homes in the community (15.3%), the vast majority in urban areas (97.7%).

Mode of Mobility

While missing, the most common way of travelling was on foot (79.6%). The second most common mode of mobility was driving (12.9%). In terms of intended destination, people got lost when they intended to go to a private residence in the community – Home (house, condo, apartment) of a family member, friend, acquaintance (37.8%) – and outdoor public space – non-specific (e.g., going for a walk) (24.0%).

Temporality (Time and Seasonality)

In general, missing incidents occurred mostly in the evening (39.1%) and the morning (36.9%), while the most common seasons for these incidents were summer, followed by spring (32.1% and 25.5%, respectively). In other words, missing incidents occurred primarily during the warmest months of the year, comprising 57.6% of cases.

Outcomes of the Missing Incidents

In 100% of cases, the persons involved in missing incidents were found. In terms of survivability, only 0.2% of cases reported that the missing person was deceased, and 5.7% of cases the missing persons were found with an injury.

Subject Profile

Table 5.1 shows statistics for the lost subject profile. The analysis shows clear patterns in how long individuals are missing and how far they tend to travel.

Lost Time (Reported Missing to Found)

Most individuals were located quickly. Half were found within 1.3 hours of being reported, and three-quarters within 3.25 hours. However, a small number of cases extended much longer, with 5% lasting more than 16 hours. This means police search and rescue teams can expect most cases to be resolved within the first few hours, but remain prepared for extended search operations.

Search Duration (Search Started to Found)

Searches typically took about 1 hour to conclude, with 75% finishing within 2.7 hours. A small subset requires much longer, stretching beyond 14 hours. For planning, teams should allocate enough resources for rapid resolution but also ensure capacity for sustained searches when necessary.

Distance from Home

Most individuals were found close to home. The median distance is under 1.8 km, and 75% were located within 6 km. However, a few cases extended much farther, pushing the average up to over 29 km. Search efforts should prioritize the immediate area around the home, but remain ready to expand outward significantly if the subject is not located early.

Distance from Last Seen Location (IPP)

Similarly, most subjects are found within 5 km of where they were last seen, with a median distance of 1.7 km. Only a small fraction was found much farther away (17.4 km), but these cases could require a broad search radius.

TABLE 5.1 Characteristics of Missing Incidents (Subject Profile) (n = 1,674)

Characteristics	*Valid Cases*	*Percentiles*			
	Mean (SD)	*25*	*50 (Median)*	*75*	*95*
Lost time, in Hours (Time between Reported & Found (Hours) **[valid cases, n = 1,353]**)	4.47 (16.20)	0.48	1.34	3.25	16.07
Search hours, in Hours (Time between Search Started & Found) **[valid cases, n = 850]**	3.37 (13.53)	0.39	1.05	2.73	14.06
Distance Between Home and Found (in km) **[valid cases, n = 1372]**	14.41 (141.42)	0.50	1.84	6.00	29.70
Distance From IPP (Distance Between Last Seen and Found (in km) **[valid cases, n = 1,267]**)	8.91 (107.49)	0.48	1.66	4.96	17.36

TABLE 5.2 Dementia Versus No Dementia: Characteristics of Missing Incidents (Subject Profile) (n = 1,674)

Characteristics	*Dementia*				*No Dementia*			
	Percentiles				*Percentiles*			
	25	*50*	*75*	*95*	*25*	*50*	*75*	*95*
Lost time, in Hours (Time between Reported & Found (Hours) **[valid cases, n = 1256]**)	0.45	1.25	2.94	13.39	1.15	3.00	7.58	34.37
Search hours, in Hours (Time between Search Started & Found) **[valid cases, n = 792]**	0.38	0.99	2.45	10.76	0.73	2.19	5.34	32.00
Distance Between Home and Found (in km) **[valid cases, n = 1263]**	0.49	1.66	5.42	20.91	0.78	3.02	9.25	26.16
Distance From IPP (Distance Between Last Seen and Found (in km) **[valid cases, n = 1178]**)	0.46	1.52	4.21	15.61	0.69	2.52	6.90	18.16

TABLE 5.3 Younger Versus Older than 65 Years Old: Characteristics of Missing Incidents (Subject Profile) (n = 1,674)

Characteristics	*Younger than 65*				*65+*			
	Percentiles				*Percentiles*			
	25	*50*	*75*	*95*	*25*	*50*	*75*	*95*
Lost time, in Hours (Time between Reported & Found (Hours) **[valid cases, n = 1340]**)	0.74	2.06	5.58	32.27	0.46	1.29	2.99	14.07
Search hours, in *Hours* (Time between Search Started & Found) **[valid cases, n = 838]**	0.51	1.99	5.33	21.65	0.38	0.98	2.47	13.07
Distance Between Home and Found (in km) **[valid cases, n = 1368]**	0.84	0.84	0.84	0.84	0.45	0.45	0.45	0.45
Distance From IPP (Distance Between Last Seen and Found (in km) **[valid cases, n = 1262]**)	0.72	3.33	7.08	20.84	0.43	1.50	4.22	16.47

Challenges of Leveraging Missing Incident Data for Public Health Purposes

Effective prevention and response to missing incidents in dementia depends on timely access to relevant data. However, the data necessary to understand risk, guide search strategies, and evaluate outcomes is dispersed across multiple agencies and systems. Each agency collects information for its own operational purposes, often in isolation from others, creating silos that limit the potential for coordinated action (Miguel Cruz et al., 2022). Mapping this current landscape is a crucial first step in recognizing both the opportunities and the challenges of cross-agency integration.

Healthcare Data

Healthcare providers document the clinical and functional risk factors associated with missing incidents. Medical records may contain useful pieces of data such as *diagnoses of dementia*, *cognitive assessments*, *comorbidities* (such as visual impairment or reduced mobility), and information about *behavioural symptoms* like restlessness or exit-seeking. Occupational and physical therapy data from interventions may also provide insights into an individual's *mobility capacity*, *daily routines*, and *environmental adaptations* at home (Orellano et al., 2012). These details could be invaluable in anticipating risk or guiding search efforts.

Despite its immense value in the context of missing incidents, healthcare data is typically stored within electronic medical record systems that are designed primarily for clinical care, not inter-agency communication (Vos et al., 2020). Privacy regulations restrict access, and systems are rarely interoperable across regions or institutions. As a result, police or the community of first responders often lack access to clinical insights that might refine their understanding of the person's vulnerabilities or likely behaviours during a dementia-related missing incident.

Police Data

Police services maintain detailed records on missing persons, including incident reports, demographic information, circumstances of the missing incidents, and outcomes of search and rescue operations. In cases involving a person living with dementia, such reports may reveal patterns, such as the times of day when individuals are most likely to go missing or the types of environments where they are eventually found.

However, these records are not typically used for systematic analysis or prevention planning (Ferguson & Huey, 2023a). Data quality can also vary considerably. Some demographic fields and clinical information in the psycho-pathological domain may be inconsistently completed. In our experience, after extracting data from police reports regarding dementia-related missing incidents, key variables were inconsistently reported or frequently missing, undermining the potential for robust data analysis. For example, gender identity was absent in 99.1% of police records, while within the psychopathological domain, the *level of dementia* was missing in 56.9% of cases and *medication use* in nearly 80%. Situational details such as the *probable cause of the missing incident* were missing in 63% of cases, and weather-related variables in over 90%. These gaps highlight the urgent need for standardized reporting and investment in infrastructure if police data are to meaningfully inform public health approaches to the safety of persons living with dementia. Importantly, they also demonstrate why cross-agency data integration is not only valuable but essential, as pooling diverse datasets can help overcome individual reporting limitations and create a more complete picture of an individual's risk.

The process of extracting meaningful information from police reports is inherently slow and resource-intensive, limiting the timely use of this critical data. For example, over a three-year period, our team manually screened 9,882 police reports across six agencies, ultimately extracting 1,734 relevant cases. This painstaking effort, far exceeding the routine capacity of police organizations, underscores the resource-intensive nature of transforming raw police records into usable data. Fully leveraging police information requires substantial time and expertise to clean, manage, and analyze, which poses major challenges for agencies already operating under stretched resources (Law Enforcement Forecasting Group, 2012).

Volunteer Search and Rescue Data

While the police service of jurisdiction retains primary responsibility for missing persons investigations, volunteer search and rescue organizations play an indispensable supporting role (Ferguson et al., 2021). When mobilized under police authority, these volunteer teams bring trained personnel who expand search capacity, particularly in complex or high-risk cases.

A key contribution of volunteer search and rescue organizations lies in the collection and recording of field data during active searches. Volunteers are trained to conduct systematic grid searches, document search coverage, and log environmental conditions and sightings. Using mapping technologies, they generate real-time data that helps police incident commanders assess search effectiveness, identify coverage gaps, and direct subsequent deployments.

Beyond live operations, volunteer search and rescue groups also contribute to after-action reporting and case databases. Their reports often capture details about search environments, distances travelled by missing persons, and behavioural patterns observed in the field. In some regions, these data are shared with larger repositories, such as the *International Search and Rescue Incident Database*

(ISRID) (International Search & Rescue Incident Database (ISRID), n.d.), which is used globally to refine *lost person behaviour* profiles (Koester, 2008).

Integration of volunteer search and rescue data with *healthcare* and *law enforcement* records remains limited. Developing mechanisms to incorporate these datasets into broader cross-agency frameworks would strengthen both immediate response capacity and long-term prevention strategies.

Community Organizations and Services Data

Community organizations, including Alzheimer societies and registries, collect valuable information about persons living with dementia and their caregivers. For example, MedicAlert® datasets include *demographic*, *psychopathological*, and *environmental factors* from the subscriber and missing incidents data from summary notes made by hotline call operators. Both datasets are linked through a unique Medic-Alert® subscriber identification number. Despite their potential value, these datasets are rarely integrated with other agencies and access may be limited to voluntary disclosure by families or caregivers, and data sharing with police or healthcare providers often depends on ad hoc communication rather than formalized protocols.

Cross-Agency Data Integration: From Silos to Systems

The fragmentation of healthcare, police, volunteer search and rescue, and community organization data creates significant barriers to protecting persons living with dementia who are at risk of going missing. While each agency captures valuable information, the absence of mechanisms for integration means that no single agency has a complete picture of an individual's risk profile or the best strategies for intervention. Cross-agency data integration could offer a powerful way to bridge these silos, enabling more coordinated *prevention*, *faster responses*, and ultimately *better outcomes* for people with dementia and their families.

Enhancing Prevention and Early Intervention

One of the most compelling reasons to integrate data is the potential to shift from reactive to proactive management of missing incidents. Healthcare providers routinely assess and document cognitive function, behavioural symptoms, and mobility, all of which can be associated with missing risk. If these risk factors could be shared, in a privacy-compliant manner, with community organizations and police registries, proactive safety planning could be possible. For example, a person identified as showing frequent exit-seeking behaviour in a clinical setting could be automatically flagged for inclusion in a vulnerable persons registry, or caregivers could be connected with geofencing technologies (e.g., GPS (Liu et al., 2017, 2018)) before an incident occurs.

Integration also supports the development of data-driven models. By combining clinical variables (e.g., dementia severity, comorbidities) with historical police data on missing incidents and volunteer search and rescue records on lost person behaviour, it becomes possible to identify high-risk individuals or environments. These insights can inform caregiver education, targeted interventions, and resource allocation at the community level.

Improving Emergency Response and Search Efficiency

When a missing incident occurs, time is critical. Case-series evidence shows that the risk of serious harm (including death) rises markedly when a person living with dementia is not located within the first 24 hours (McShane et al., 1998; Rowe et al., 2011). Our research shows that after seven hours of being lost, the likelihood of harm increases 2.8 times. The effectiveness of a search, therefore, depends on the amount and quality of information available to responders. Integrated data systems would provide police and volunteer search and rescue teams with richer information at the outset: clinical details that may influence mobility, community knowledge of frequently visited locations, and information from previous missing incidents' last known positions.

Such integration allows responders to establish high-probability search areas more quickly and to tailor the tactics of their response to the individual who is missing. For example, if data reveals that the person has impaired mobility and a history of hiding in small, enclosed spaces, searchers can prioritize nearby sheds, bushes, or garages. If geofencing alerts indicate direction of travel, resources can be deployed more strategically.

Facilitating Coordination Across Agencies

Cross-agency integration is not solely about data; it also fosters collaboration. Shared systems encourage agencies to work from the same information set, reducing duplication of effort and miscommunication. For instance, police and healthcare providers often rely on families providing information during an incident. While the families and loved ones are critical partners, the stress of a missing episode may compromise their ability to recall accurate details (Ferguson & Huey, 2023b). Integrated systems would relieve some of this burden by ensuring that essential information is already available to all responders.

Moreover, volunteer search and rescue organizations often document extensive operational data during searches; however, this information may not be shared with healthcare providers or community services after an incident has occurred. Integrated data frameworks and formal data sharing agreements would create feedback loops, allowing lessons learned from one incident to inform prevention and care planning for the future.

Strengthening Resource Allocation and Policy Planning

At a broader level, integrated data supports system-wide planning and resource allocation. Policymakers and senior leaders require accurate, comprehensive data to understand the scale of the issue, identify geographic hotspots, and justify investment in prevention programs or technological supports. Currently, the absence of integrated data obscures the true prevalence of missing incidents in dementia and limits the ability to calculate associated social and monetary costs.

By consolidating healthcare, police, search and rescue, and community data, a clearer picture emerges, one that can inform funding decisions, policy frameworks, and public awareness campaigns. For example, if integrated data show that missing incidents cluster around certain residential care facilities or during specific times of day, targeted training and prevention initiatives can be implemented. Prevention initiatives can include, for example, examining case records and operational data to uncover recurring patterns that can guide prevention initiatives for populations or regions at elevated risk. Such analyses can also support the creation of data-informed risk assessment tools and the application of geographic profiling techniques to detect spatial trends, thereby identifying hotspots where targeted community engagement may be most effective (Ferguson & Huey, 2023a).

Bridging Data Silos to Prevent Missing Incidents in Dementia: A Privacy-Preserving Approach Using Fully Homomorphic Encryption

While the benefits of integrating data across healthcare, law enforcement, volunteer search and rescue, and community are clear, the question remains: *how can this integration be achieved in practice?*

Technologically, it can be achieved through *fully homomorphic encryption.* It is a form of encryption that allows data to remain encrypted throughout its entire lifecycle, including during processing and analysis (Gentry, 2009). Similarly, *Private Set Intersection* enables matching of records (e.g., identifying if a healthcare patient also appears in a police vulnerable persons registry) without revealing non-matching information (De Cristofaro & Tsudik, 2010). Unlike traditional encryption, where data must be decrypted before use, fully homomorphic encryption enables mathematical operations (such as addition, multiplication, and even full machine learning models) to be performed directly on encrypted data. This means that different agencies can each encrypt their datasets, send them to a secure computing environment, and perform joint analysis without ever exposing the underlying data. Only the final results (for example, a risk score or predictive model) are decrypted and shared.

Machine learning models and data analytics with fully homomorphic encryption capabilities can be conducted over two types of technical models of integration, namely, *centralized* or *federated* data systems (Kurniawan & Mambo, 2022). In a centralized model, data from multiple agencies is collected and stored in a single repository. This creates a unified source of data that can be accessed by authorized users across sectors. Centralized systems can simplify analysis, enable real-time dashboards, and support predictive modelling by pooling diverse datasets in one place. For example, a centralized registry could combine healthcare records, police missing persons reports, and community service information to generate comprehensive risk profiles. Federated approaches offer an alternative by allowing agencies to retain control over multiple agencies' data while enabling queries across systems. In this model, data remains with the originating agency, but standardized protocols allow authorized users to access relevant information when needed (Li et al., 2020). For example, a federated query could pull key variables from police and healthcare databases to generate a risk assessment without physically moving data from its original source.

BOX 5.1 CASE SCENARIO. WHAT IF WE COULD HAVE SEEN IT COMING?

A Privacy-Preserving Look at How Fully Homomorphic Encryption **Could Help Prevent Future Missing Incidents**

On an unseasonably warm day in December 2021, Mary (pseudonym), a 79-year-old woman living with dementia went missing in rural Nova Scotia, dressed in lightweight clothing, while on a walk with her new dog. In the weeks leading up to this occurrence, a rapid succession of events, all recognized in retrospect as risk factors (the death of her long-time dog followed by a difficult adjustment to a new one, flood damage that forced her to change her walking route, etc.), contributed to this tragic event. Mary's husband and police searched for a week, but their efforts were hindered by severe weather conditions. Mary was never found.

Now imagine a future where **privacy-preserving technologies** allow for earlier intervention **without ever compromising Mary's privacy and autonomy.**

In that future:

- Mary's healthcare provider has encrypted notes indicating recent signs of disorientation and emotional distress following the death of her pet and changes to her routine.

- Police systems hold encrypted reports showing her prior missing incidents and their outcomes, including patterns of location, weather conditions, and timing.
- Both datasets are **never shared in plain form**, but instead processed using **Fully Homomorphic Encryption.**
- In a secure computing environment, a predictive model trained on similar cases detects a **rising risk score** for Mary based on the combination of recent health notes and past incident patterns.
- The output (also encrypted) is flagged and decrypted **only by authorized professionals**, such as a dementia care coordinator or local community support team.
- Mary and her husband receive a **gentle wellness check** or an outreach call (e.g., perhaps offering respite services, routine support, or just a check-in walk along her altered path).

Nothing personal was ever exposed. Yet **everything important was seen in time**.

Fully homomorphic encryption represents a paradigm shift in how we think about data collaboration. By enabling computation on encrypted data, it allows us to harness the full potential of cross-sector datasets. For missing incidents in dementia, this opens the door to a future where risk can be predicted before harm occurs, where interventions are proactive rather than reactive, and where privacy is not an obstacle but an integral part of the solution. When properly governed and thoughtfully implemented, fully homomorphic encryption offers a privacy-preserving foundation for building a safer environment for people living with dementia at risk of getting lost and going missing.

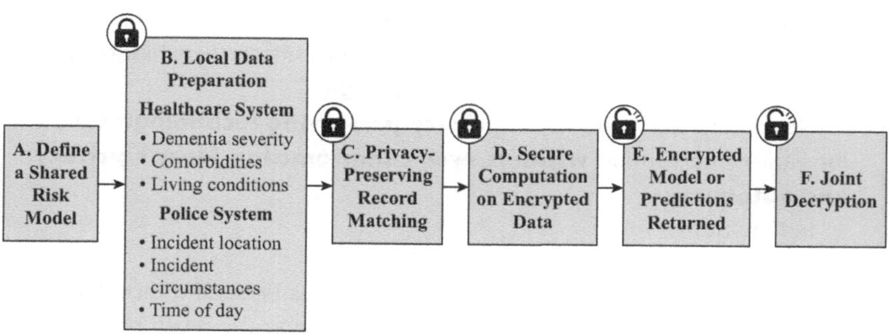

FIGURE 5.1 Privacy-Preserving Pipeline Using Fully Homomorphic Encryption

Technical Challenges and Limitations of Fully Homomorphic Encryption

Despite its promise, fully homomorphic encryption is not without limitations. Its biggest hurdle remains *computational performance* (Gong et al., 2024). Running even simple operations on encrypted data is still significantly slower than performing them on plaintext, although this gap is gradually shrinking with recent advances in hardware (e.g., *Field-Programmable Gate Array*) (Yang et al., 2022) and software (e.g., algorithm optimization) (Gupta et al., 2024).

Additionally, fully homomorphic encryption is not trivial to implement. It requires specialized *cryptographic knowledge* and often demands infrastructure that can handle intensive mathematical operations. Most open-source libraries for fully homomorphic encryption, such as *Concrete-ML* (Python library developed by Zama), *TenSEAL* (Python software around Microsoft SEAL), and *PySEA* (a community-maintained Python software for Microsoft SEAL), are still evolving and require careful parameter tuning to balance security, accuracy, and performance (Gong et al., 2024).

Beyond technical complexity, fully homomorphic encryption does not automatically solve data integration problems. If datasets need to be matched at the individual level, tools like *Private Set Intersection* (a cryptographic protocol that allows two parties to determine which items they have in common without revealing any other information about the rest of their data (Morales et al., 2023)) must be layered in, adding further architectural complexity. Governance also remains a challenge: managing shared encryption keys, defining who can decrypt results, and ensuring transparency in usage are all essential for responsible deployment.

Finally, while fully homomorphic encryption supports privacy by design, legal, and regulatory frameworks, such as the Personal Information *Protection and Electronic Documents Act (Canada)* (PIPEDA) (Office of the Privacy Commissioner of Canada, 2024) or *General Data Protection Regulation (European Union)* (GDPR) (Wolford, n.d.) may still lack explicit guidance. This means organizations must proactively engage legal, ethics, and data protection teams when deploying fully homomorphic encryption-based systems in topics such as *vulnerabilities to key-recovery attacks* (Chaturvedi et al., 2022), *tradeoff between verifiable computing and server function confidentiality* (Viand et al., 2023), *circular security of evaluation keys* (Gentry, 2010), and the issues that input data cannot be *audited for quality control or traceability purposes* (Weinkauf, 2023).

At the same time, dementia-related missing incidents raise a deeper ethical question: when time-sensitive information sharing may directly influence survival, how should organizations balance the protection of personal data with the duty to protect life? Privacy legislation is intended to safeguard individuals from misuse of their information, yet rigid or overly cautious interpretations may inadvertently delay access to data critical for search and rescue operations. Most data protection frameworks contain provisions permitting disclosure where there is imminent risk of serious harm (e.g., Canada's PIPEDA (Minister of Justice, 2000)); however, uncertainty around interpretation can generate institutional hesitation. In this context, fully homomorphic encryption and related privacy-preserving technologies should not be viewed as mechanisms that privilege data protection over safety, but rather as tools that enable proportionate data sharing, allowing essential information to inform urgent response while minimizing unnecessary exposure. Properly governed, such systems can align the protection of the person with the protection of their data, reframing what might appear as competing priorities into mutually reinforcing objectives.

Harmonization and Data Framework

Building systems that enable healthcare, police, ambulance and fire volunteer search and rescue, and community agencies to share information is not only a technical challenge but also a conceptual one. Different sectors collect data for their own purposes, often using their own definitions and formats. The result is a patchwork of information that cannot easily be compared or combined. To move beyond fragmented datasets, there is a need for a *foundational data framework* that harmonizes the way dementia-related missing incidents are recorded across agencies. Such a data framework must capture the multiple, intersecting factors that shape risk, response, and outcomes, while remaining feasible for organizations with limited resources.

At its core, a harmonized data framework should begin with *demographic* and *socioeconomic* data. Basic details such as age, sex, gender, and cultural background are essential for understanding levels and types of risk and for identifying inequities in both prevention and response. Yet, in practice, these fields are often incomplete or inconsistently entered in police records (Ferguson, 2022). By adopting common standards for demographic data, agencies could create a clearer picture of vulnerable groups and tailor interventions more effectively.

Equally important are the clinical and *psychopathological dimensions* (Ferguson, 2022). Healthcare providers document diagnoses, dementia subtypes, comorbidities, and behavioural symptoms, but this information rarely reaches police during an incident. Without a standardized mechanism for sharing key clinical factors, such as the stage of cognitive decline, history of restlessness, or use of medications that influence alertness, responders are left with only a partial understanding of the person they are searching for. Linking these clinical insights with operational records could transform search strategies, making them more targeted and efficient.

Patterns of behaviour and daily routines form another critical domain. Families and caregivers often know the routes a person likes to walk, the landmarks they are drawn to, or the times of day when they are most restless. These details, however, are not systematically recorded in either health or police systems. When they are collected consistently, behavioural patterns can be integrated into geographic profiling models, helping responders predict where a missing person is most likely to be found (i.e., lost person behaviour (Koester, 2008)).

The *environment* itself also shapes the dynamics of a missing incident. Whether the individual lives in an urban neighbourhood, a suburban setting, or a remote rural area can influence both the likelihood of becoming lost and the challenges of conducting a search. Contextual features such as nearby waterways, forests, or highways create specific hazards, while weather and seasonal conditions can alter survival or harm outcomes (Larsson et al., 2025). Capturing environmental context as part of a harmonized framework, a researcher ensures that data are not stripped of these extrinsic factors that shape risk and response. *Social support* context must be recognized as part of the environment. The presence of a reliable caregiver, the degree of caregiver stress, and participation in programs all influence the risk of a missing incident and the likelihood of a safe recovery. However, even with reliable care partners and substantial support in place, individuals may still go missing. These dimensions are often invisible in police datasets. For example, in our own experience, data such as consent to disclose missing incident on media, recommendation to other organization (after conclusion of search), or consent to refer to outside organization (e.g., warm handover) were poorly reported. Including caregiver and support information within a unified framework would highlight the role of social determinants and open new avenues for prevention through caregiver support.

Every missing incident generates *operational information*, yet this data is typically siloed within police case files or search and rescue after-action reports. Time of disappearance, circumstances of the event, elapsed time until reporting, search methods deployed, condition upon recovery, and outcomes are rarely pooled across jurisdictions. Without harmonization, we cannot assess response effectiveness or learn systematically from past cases. A common framework would allow operational data to be standardized and compared, enabling continuous improvement.

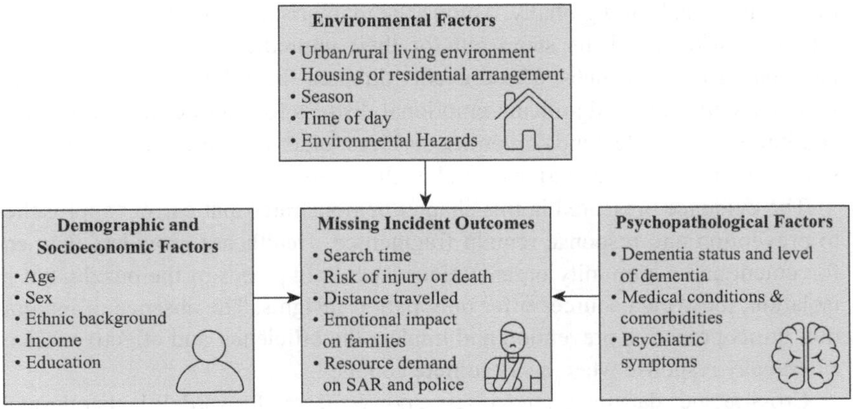

FIGURE 5.2 Determinants Influencing Outcomes of Dementia-Related Missing Incidents

Linking Data Domains to Determinants of Health

Conceptualization of these domains through the lens of the determinants of health would allow integration of diverse sources of information. Determinants of health are the broad conditions (i.e., individual behaviours, demographic, psychopathological, and environmental factors) that influence health risks and outcomes across populations (Masters et al., 2017; National Academies of Sciences et al., 2021). Missing incidents in dementia are not simply a consequence of cognitive decline; they arise from the intersection of clinical vulnerability with social factors, caregiving supports, environmental hazards, and community resources. For example, demographic and socioeconomic variables align with the social determinants of health, highlighting how income, education, and cultural context shape both risk exposure and access to protective supports such as GPS-enabled technologies or caregiver respite. Clinical and behavioural domains reflect biomedical determinants, linking neuropathology with observable behaviours that increase vulnerability. Environmental data connect directly to the physical determinants of health, showing how neighbourhood design, rurality, or climate conditions amplify risk. Finally, caregiver context exemplifies the importance of social and relational determinants, underscoring how stress, social support, and service access influence both prevention and response.

Framing a harmonized data system around determinants of health can ensure that the analysis of missing incidents is not reduced to isolated clinical events but understood as complex, multifactorial phenomena. This perspective also strengthens the link between public health and policing, making clear that preventing harm requires attention not only to immediate operational response but also to antecedent factors that shape vulnerability over time.

Conclusion and Recommendations

Dementia presents a pressing public health challenge, with prevalence rising rapidly in Canada and globally. Among the many risks associated with the condition, missing incidents stand out for their unpredictability and potentially devastating consequences. These events threaten the safety of persons living with dementia, cause significant emotional distress for families and caregivers, and impose heavy demands on police services, other first responders, volunteer search and rescue organizations, and health systems.

The evidence presented in this chapter demonstrates that current approaches to prevention and response remain fragmented. Healthcare providers, law enforcement and community organizations each hold pieces of the puzzle, but in isolation, these data sources offer only partial insights. The absence of integration limits proactive prevention and hinders the efficiency and effectiveness of emergency response when every minute counts.

Cross-agency data integration offers a powerful way forward. Whether through centralized repositories, federated systems, or privacy-preserving technologies, integration enables a shift from reactive to proactive strategies. It allows responders to act more quickly, policymakers to allocate resources more effectively, and communities to learn from each incident, thereby improving future safety. Importantly, integration need not come at the expense of privacy. With thoughtful governance, ethical safeguards, and transparent communication, it is possible to protect both safety and dignity.

Contemporary discussions of "future policing" increasingly call for models that are intelligence-led, collaborative, technologically sophisticated, and grounded in public legitimacy. Dementia-related missing incidents illuminate how these aspirations can be operationalized in practice. By leveraging privacy-preserving innovations such as fully homomorphic encryption, policing can move beyond reactive response toward anticipatory, data-informed prevention without compromising civil liberties. Bridging data silos through secure, encrypted collaboration (e.g., law enforcement and public health) demonstrates that modernization need not erode privacy. Instead, it offers a pathway toward a form of policing that is predictive yet principled, efficient yet ethical, and that defines the evolving landscape of future public safety.

In conclusion, data integration across agencies is a public health necessity. By breaking down silos and creating coordinated, ethical, and secure systems, Canada has the opportunity to set a global example of how to safeguard vulnerable populations while respecting their autonomy. The task ahead is challenging, but the potential gains, in lives saved, families supported, and communities strengthened, make it an urgent and worthy priority.

Conflicts of interest: We have no conflicts of interest to declare.

Funding: This work was supported by the Search and Rescue New Initiative Fund (SAR NIF) program, Public Safety Canada [grant number 22005].

References

Alzheimer Society of Canada. (n.d.). *Dementia numbers in Canada*. Alzheimer Society. Retrieved August 14, 2025, from https://alzheimer.ca/en/about-dementia/what-dementia/dementia-numbers-canada

Chaturvedi, B., Chakraborty, A., Chatterjee, A., & Mukhopadhyay, D. (2022). *A practical full key recovery attack on TFHE and FHEW by inducing decryption errors* (No. 2022/1563). Cryptology ePrint Archive. https://eprint.iacr.org/2022/1563

Craig, S., Halloran, P. O., Mitchell, G., Stark, P., & Wilson, C. B. (2024). Dementia friendly communities (DFCs) to improve quality of life for people with dementia: A realist review. *BMC Geriatrics*, *24*(1), 776. https://doi.org/10.1186/s12877-024-05343-0

Cruz, A. M., Perez, H., Rutledge, E., Daum, C., & Liu, L. (2024). Factors associated with a history of critical wandering among Medic-Alert subscribers. *BMC Geriatrics*, *24*(1), 564. https://doi.org/10.1186/s12877-024-05162-3

De Cristofaro, E., & Tsudik, G. (2010). Practical private set intersection protocols with linear complexity. In R. Sion (Ed.), *Financial cryptography and data security* (pp. 143–159). Springer Berlin Heidelberg.

Ferguson, L. (2022). Risk factors and missing persons: Advancing an understanding of "risk." *Humanities and Social Sciences Communications*, *9*(1), 101. https://doi.org/10.1057/s41599-022-01113-8

Ferguson, L., Gaub, J. E., & Huey, L. (2021). *Exploring the roles and function of police search and rescue (SAR) teams in Canadian agencies*. https://doi.org/10.21428/cb6ab371.33399969

Ferguson, L., & Huey, L. (2023a). Outroduction to police search and rescue. In L. Ferguson & Huey, L. (2023) (Eds.), *Police search and rescue response to lost and missing persons* (pp. 93–103). Springer International Publishing. https://doi.org/10.1007/978-3-031-44077-9_7

Ferguson, L., & Huey, L. (2023b). The organization of police search and rescue. In L. Ferguson & L. Huey (Eds.), *Police search and rescue response to lost and missing persons* (pp. 13–22). Springer International Publishing. https://doi.org/10.1007/978-3-031-44077-9_2

Future of Police Institute. (n.d.). Retrieved Febraury 20, 2026, from https://www.futurepolicing.org/

Gambier-Ross, K., Apps, J., & Wayland, S. (2023). Shared responsibility: Conceptualising how a public health approach may enhance police response to missing persons. *International Journal of Missing Persons*, *1*(1), 26. https://doi.org/10.55917/2769-7045.1001

Gentry, C. (2009). Fully homomorphic encryption using ideal lattices. *Proceedings of the Forty-First Annual ACM Symposium on Theory of Computing*, 169–178. https://doi.org/10.1145/1536414.1536440

Gentry, C. (2010). Computing arbitrary functions of encrypted data. *Commun. ACM*, *53*(3), 97–105. https://doi.org/10.1145/1666420.1666444

Gong, Y., Chang, X., Mišić, J., Mišić, V. B., Wang, J., & Zhu, H. (2024). Practical solutions in fully homomorphic encryption: A survey analyzing existing acceleration methods. *Cybersecurity*, *7*(1), 5. https://doi.org/10.1186/s42400-023-00187-4

Gupta, S., Cammarota, R., & Šimunić, T. (2024). MemFHE: End-to-end computing with fully homomorphic encryption in memory. *ACM Trans. Embed. Comput. Syst.*, *23*(2), 28:1–28:23. https://doi.org/10.1145/3569955

International Search & Rescue Incident Database (ISRID). (n.d.). *International Search & Rescue Incident Database (ISRID)*. dbS Productions. Retrieved July 31, 2025, from https://www.dbs-sar.com/SAR_Research/ISRID.htm

Jones, H., Bandyopadhyay, A., Kennedy, N., Brophy, S., Evans, J., Bellis, M., Rowe, B., McNerney, C., & Moore, S. (2024). Investigating methods of sharing data between police, health, education, and social services: Semi-structured interviews with police service areas in Wales. *The Police Journal: Theory, Practice and Principles*, 97(4), 731–741. https://doi.org/10.1177/0032258X231220864

Kikuchi, K., Ijuin, M., Awata, S., & Suzuki, T. (2019). Exploratory research on outcomes for individuals missing through dementia wandering in Japan. *Geriatrics & Gerontology International*, *19*(9), 902–906. https://doi.org/10.1111/ggi.13738

Koester, R. J. (2008). *Lost person behavior: A search and rescue guide on where to look for land, air, and water*. dbS Productions.

Kumar, A., Sidhu, J., Lui, F., & Tsao, J. W. (2024). Alzheimer disease. In *StatPearls [Internet]*. StatPearls Publishing. https://www.ncbi.nlm.nih.gov/books/NBK499922/

Kurniawan, H., & Mambo, M. (2022). Homomorphic encryption-based federated privacy preservation for deep active learning. *Entropy*, *24*(11), 1545. https://doi.org/10.3390/e24111545

Larsson, M., Årestedt, K., Svensson, A., Andersson, H., & Wolmesjö, M. (2025). Missing incidents and the risk of harm in persons living with dementia reported to the Swedish police – A nationwide retrospective registry study. *BMC Geriatrics*, *25*(1), 153. https://doi.org/10.1186/s12877-025-05809-9

Law Enforcement Forecasting Group. (2012). *Increasing analytic capacity of state and local law enforcement agencies: Moving beyond data analysis to create a vision for change*. U.S. Department of Justice. https://bja.ojp.gov/sites/g/files/xyckuh186/files/Publications/LEFGIncreasingAnalyticCapacity.pdf

Li, T., Sahu, A. K., Talwalkar, A., & Smith, V. (2020). Federated learning: Challenges, methods, and future directions. *IEEE Signal Processing Magazine*, *37*(3), 50–60. https://doi.org/10.1109/MSP.2020.2975749

Liu, L., Miguel Cruz, A., & Juzwishin, D. (2018). Caregivers as a proxy for responses of dementia clients in a GPS technology acceptance study. *Behaviour & Information Technology*, *37*(6), 634–645. https://doi.org/10.1080/0144929X.2018.1470672

Liu, L., Miguel Cruz, A., Ruptash, T., Barnard, S., & Juzwishin, D. (2017). Acceptance of Global Positioning System (GPS) technology among dementia clients and family caregivers. *Journal of Technology in Human Services*, *35*(2), 99–119. https://doi.org/10.1080/15228835.2016.1266724

Masters, R., Anwar, E., Collins, B., Cookson, R., & Capewell, S. (2017). Return on investment of public health interventions: A systematic review. *Journal of Epidemiology and Community Health*, *71*(8), 827–834. https://doi.org/10.1136/jech-2016-208141

McShane, R., Gedling, K., Keene, J., Jacoby, R., Hope, T., & Fairburn, C. (1998). Getting lost in dementia: A longitudinal study of a behavioral symptom. *International Psychogeriatrics*, *10*(3), 253–260. https://doi.org/10.1017/S1041610298005365

MedicAlert Foundation Canada. (n.d.). *MedicAlert® Connect Protect Program®*. MedicAlert Foundation Canada. Retrieved July 31, 2025, from https://www.medicalert.ca/safe-and-found

Miguel Cruz, A., Marshall, S., Daum, C., Perez, H., Hirdes, J., & Liu, L. (2022). Data silos undermine efforts to characterize, predict, and mitigate dementia-related missing person incidents. *Healthcare Management Forum*, *35*(6), 333–338. https://doi.org/10.1177/08404704221106156

Miguel-Cruz, A., Perez, H., Choi, Y., Rutledge, E., Daum, C., & Liu, L. (2024). The prevalence of missing incidents and their antecedents among older adult MedicAlert subscribers: Retrospective descriptive study. *JMIR Aging*, *7*, e58205. https://doi.org/10.2196/58205

Minister of Justice. (2000). Personal Information Protection and Electronic Documents Act (S.C. 2000, c.5). 2000. Accessed February 3, 2026. http://laws-lois.justice.gc.ca.

Morales, D., Agudo, I., & Lopez, J. (2023). Private set intersection: A systematic literature review. *Computer Science Review*, *49*, 100567. https://doi.org/10.1016/j.cosrev.2023.100567

National Academies of Sciences, E., Medicine, N. A. of, Nursing 2020–2030, C. on the F. of, Flaubert, J. L., Menestrel, S. L., Williams, D. R., & Wakefield, M. K. (2021). Social determinants of health and health equity. In *The future of nursing 2020–2030: Charting a path to achieve health equity*. National Academies Press (US). https://www.ncbi.nlm.nih.gov/books/NBK573923/

Nichols, E., Steinmetz, J. D., Vollset, S. E., Fukutaki, K., Chalek, J., Abd-Allah, F., Abdoli, A., Abualhasan, A., Abu-Gharbieh, E., Akram, T. T., Al Hamad, H., Alahdab, F., Alanezi, F. M., Alipour, V., Almustanyir, S., Amu, H., Ansari, I., Arabloo, J., Ashraf, T., … Vos, T. (2022). Estimation of the global prevalence of dementia in 2019 and forecasted prevalence in 2050: An analysis for the Global Burden of Disease Study 2019. *The Lancet Public Health*, *7*(2), e105–e125. https://doi.org/10.1016/S2468-2667(21)00249-8

Office of the Privacy Commissioner of Canada. (2024, May 1). *PIPEDA requirements in brief*. https://www.priv.gc.ca/en/privacy-topics/privacy-laws-in-canada/the-personal-information-protection-and-electronic-documents-act-pipeda/pipeda_brief

Orellano, E., Colón, W. I., & Arbesman, M. (2012). Effect of occupation- and activity-based interventions on instrumental activities of daily living performance among community-dwelling older adults: A systematic review. *The American Journal of*

Occupational Therapy: Official Publication of the American Occupational Therapy Association, *66*(3), 292–300. https://doi.org/10.5014/ajot.2012.003053

Perez, H., Miguel Cruz, A., Neubauer, N., Daum, C., Comeau, A. K., Marshall, S. D., Letts, E., & Liu, L. (2024). Risk factors associated with missing incidents among persons living with dementia: A scoping review. *Canadian Journal on Aging/La Revue Canadienne Du Vieillissement*, *43*(3), 370–384. https://doi.org/10.1017/S0714980823000776

Pona, I., Raws, P., & Chetwynd, H. (2019). *The first step: How return home interviews can improve support and safeguarding for missing young people*. The Children's Society. https://www.childrenssociety.org.uk/sites/default/files/2020-10/the-first-step.pdf

Public Health Agency of Canada. (2024, November). *A dementia strategy for Canada: Together we achieve* [Education and awareness]. Goverment of Canada. https://www.canada.ca/en/public-health/services/publications/diseases-conditions/dementia-strategy-annual-report-parliament-2024.html

Rowe, M. A., Vandeveer, S. S., Greenblum, C. A., List, C. N., Fernandez, R. M., Mixson, N. E., & Ahn, H. C. (2011). Persons with dementia missing in the community: Is it wandering or something unique? *BMC Geriatrics*, *11*(1), 28. https://doi.org/10.1186/1471-2318-11-28

Rowe, M., Houston, A., Molinari, V., Bulat, T., Bowen, M. E., Spring, H., Mutolo, S., & McKenzie, B. (2015). The concept of missing incidents in persons with dementia. *Healthcare*, *3*(4), 1121–1132. https://doi.org/10.3390/healthcare3041121

Royal Canadian Mounted Police. (2021, December 31). *Missing persons unit*. Royal Canadian Mounted Police. https://www.rcmp-grc.gc.ca/ab/scb-sdcg/mpu-geppd-eng.htm

van Dijk, A. J., Herrington, V., Crofts, N., Breunig, R., Burris, S., Sullivan, H., Middleton, J., Sherman, S., & Thomson, N. (2019). Law enforcement and public health: Recognition and enhancement of joined-up solutions. *Lancet* (London, England), *393*(10168), 287–294. https://doi.org/10.1016/S0140-6736(18)32839-3

Viand, A., Knabenhans, C., & Hithnawi, A. (2023). *Verifiable fully homomorphic encryption* (No. arXiv:2301.07041). arXiv. https://doi.org/10.48550/arXiv.2301.07041

Vos, J. F. J., Boonstra, A., Kooistra, A., Seelen, M., & van Offenbeek, M. (2020). The influence of electronic health record use on collaboration among medical specialties. *BMC Health Services Research*, *20*(1), 676. https://doi.org/10.1186/s12913-020-05542-6

Weinkauf, D. (2023, October 24). *Privacy tech-know blog: Computing while blindfolded – Lifting the veil on homomorphic encryption*. Office of the Privacy Commissioner of Canada. https://www.priv.gc.ca/en/blog/20231024

Wolford, B. (n.d.). *A guide to GDPR data privacy requirements*. GDPR.EU. Retrieved September 4, 2025, from https://gdpr.eu/data-privacy/

Yang, Y., Kuppannagari, S. R., Kannan, R., & Prasanna, V. K. (2022). FPGA accelerator for homomorphic encrypted sparse convolutional neural network inference. *2022 IEEE 30th Annual International Symposium on Field-Programmable Custom Computing Machines (FCCM)*, 1–9. https://doi.org/10.1109/FCCM53951.2022.9786115

6

QUANTUM LEAP

Strategic and Ethical Dimensions of Next Generation Technologies in Law Enforcement

Mehzeb Chowdhury

Introduction

In recent times, quantum computing has been posited to be a disruptive force across industries, particularly in defence and intelligence (How & Cheah, 2023). Specifically, within the realms of policing, the potential of quantum computing has received limited attention, with the focus predominantly on cryptography and encryption systems (Ajala et al., 2024). There have been concerns about the use of quantum methodologies to make contemporary encryption standards obsolete (Ganesh et al., 2025). These concerns have garnered conversations in technology circles but only represent a limited use case landscape for quantum computing, which has the potential to impact everything from the way police organizations run and govern themselves and to investigative practices (Inglesant et al., 2016). There are also implications for the use, or misuse, of this new technical frontier in the government sphere and what it means for the legitimacy of state power (Rose & Miller, 2017). This chapter examines these aspects and argues that quantum computing's ultimate potential lies in its ability to open new horizons for law enforcement organizations across cryptography, communications, sensing, analytics, and decision-making in their macro and micro tasks.

Quantum computing, operating on well-established physics principles such as superposition, entanglement, and probabilistic measurement, can perform a class of computation that differs markedly from traditional systems (Horowitz & Grumbling, 2019). While many have suggested that this makes the former universally superior, almost guaranteeing deterministic outcomes (even though quantum systems are inherently probabilistic), the reality is that speed, optimization, and signal detection that quantum computing offers can be advantageous

DOI: 10.4324/9781003671312-6

in marked circumstances where uncertainty is prevalent (Yazdi, 2024). If considering the use case for policing, the correlation becomes clear. A significant part of law enforcement activities involves incomplete information, probabilistic inferences, and time-critical decision-making (Phillips & Burrell, 2009). Uncertainty has been a matter of contention for state mechanisms of control since the inception of the organized police force, and in recent years, the forensic science community has had to contend with it (Williams, 2012). These issues are augmented by challenges surrounding explainability, evidential reliability, and governance that might need to be updated in the face of shifts in conventional algorithmic systems (De Bruijn et al., 2022).

This chapter explores quantum technologies within the wider policing landscape, examining the potential implementation trajectory of these tools. The transition period between inception and adoption is likely not to arrive as a singular threshold moment but be part of a prolonged period of asymmetry in which existing technologies co-exist with quantum tools and experimental deployment paves the way for a more quantum future (Somani et al., 2023). The transition period is likely to highlight capability gaps, where pressures to adopt the latest gear (backed by either political or public pressure) can create evidential, ethical, and legal implications (Burton et al., 2020).

Therefore, treating this impending quantum future as an abstract risk, the approach should be to adopt a pragmatic orientation, where policymakers and stakeholders determine where quantum technologies and policing practice plausibly intersect (Ten Holter, 2023). This chapter, therefore, argues that before deployment can be conceived, current scientific evidence and its claims would be required to not only be fulfilled, but exceeded, and governance frameworks would be put into place. This would ensure readiness, and with risk and responsibility assessments flanking the approach, quantum computing could only then be a viable and beneficial tool for policing (Johnson, 2019).

Cryptography and Encryption Systems in the Age of Quantum Computing

In modern times, policing has relied increasingly on cryptographic systems where secure communications, digital evidence storage, systems of authentication, and intelligence databases form inter-agency data-sharing arrangements, and data transfers are built around classical computation encryption schemes (Griffiths, 2022). One such is public-key encryption infrastructures, where secure exchanges over open networks provide assurances of integrity and confidentiality (Schmeh, 2006). Its reliance and wide-scale adoption have been documented, and so too has a challenge to its mathematical assumptions by emerging quantum computing systems (Mellese et al., 2026). The supposition is that quantum computing holds the advantage in both processing and robustness, capable of dethroning traditional encryption mechanisms, thereby exposing long-term security risks around sensitive policing data (Zornetta, 2024).

Shor's algorithm indicates that with an adequately powerful quantum computer, it could be possible, at least in principle, to efficiently factor large integers and solve discrete logarithm problems, undermining public-key systems such as the widely popular Rivest-Shamir-Adleman (RSA) and elliptical curve cryptographies, which currently protects everything from police radio backhaul networks, to digital evidence vaults (Shor, 1999). The threat extends to potential data breaches, information interceptions, and decryption of previously encrypted data sets, as users could use quantum machines to do what is known as 'harvest now, decrypt later', and unlock operational, legal, and personal sensitive data, held long-term by the police, causing a particular form of temporal asymmetry that would affect both isolated and networked law enforcement systems (Olutimehin et al., 2025).

Quantum search algorithms hold the potential to reduce effective security margins by exposing shorter encryption keys and requiring increasingly longer ones to maintain equivalent resistance to attack (Fathalla & Azab, 2024). While it does not indicate the immediate obsolescence of symmetric encryption, it exposes a potential future risk and need for continuous vigilance with regard to existing systems (Manpearl, 2017). The challenge centres around conceptualizing and operationalizing quantum-resistant algorithms in a climate where police are often the last to adopt the latest and greatest in terms of technologies, often using legacy software, engulfed in long procurement cycles, and being constrained by ever-shrinking budgets, all of which would complicate and constrict progress in an approaching age of cryptographic change (Willis et al., 2020).

There also exists what is known as a capability gap between the high-budget, well-resourced metropolitan forces or federal/national agencies, and the smaller, rural local forces (Mendel et al., 2017). Due to the emerging nature of quantum computer systems, the expertise in the area remains scarce, with the hardware itself expensive and difficult to adopt (De Leon et al., 2021). The likelihood is that, at least in the short term, only the elite units in organizations would prospectively be able to utilize the technology, creating a form of quantum divide, where quality of digital data security and investigative capability would be geographically determined (Gercek & Seskir, 2025). This could create particular vulnerability within underfunded jurisdictions where more sophisticated cyber threats run a particular risk of breach, and advanced analytical tools are only available to their larger counterparts on whom they succumb to reliance (George et al., 2024).

Encryption choices are often also not a matter of technical considerations (Distler et al., 2020). The reality is that they shape investigatory access, cross-border cooperation schemes, and evidential disclosure obligations, which tie in directly with public trust (Abraha, 2021). Matters with regard to quantum systems therefore have far-reaching consequences in both computational hardware and software landscapes, but also in how governance infrastructures are built around these to ensure security, legality, and institutional legitimacy (Perrier, 2022).

Quantum Computer and the Future Communication Landscape

Quantum technologies also carry challenges for law enforcement through advancements in communications (Minbaleev et al., 2024). For example, quantum key distribution (QKD), often referred to as a fundamentally secure method of exchanging cryptographic keys, is based on physical principles as opposed to computational hardness (Broadbent & Schaffner, 2016). The idea is that in controlled conditions, any attempt to intercept or observe quantum states will create detectable disturbances, thus alerting communicating parties that there has been an attempt to eavesdrop (Fuchs & Fuchs, 1998). In the case of police and law enforcement, as well as intelligence agencies, these advances in quantum computing could reinforce long-held concerns about the robustness and reliability of current cryptographic communication systems (Ren et al., 2025). It could also, on the other hand, inspire worry in stakeholder circles that using quantum mechanisms, law enforcement, or state bodies could intercept and access private information otherwise thought to be secure among private parties (Lodge, 2010).

QKD offers strong protection for key exchange, but it is important to understand that some of these guarantees run the risk of being theoretical (Bozzio et al., 2025). The operational reality is that in the quantum age, no communication system can be dependably classed as invulnerable (Shahanas & Thampi, 2025). The practicality of any deployment and its eventual reliability would be dictated by hardware choices, secure endpoints, and implementation practices that are well-crafted and suitable for the needs of the organization (Brotherston et al., 2024). Often, compromises at the device level, coupled with poor key management and shoddy integration with legacy networks, are the principal culprits in breaches of security (Shastry & Mohan, 2024). With the maturing of these technologies, though, interception of encrypted traffic would invariably be more difficult, especially without direct access to endpoints or cooperation with service providers (de Carné de Carnavalet & van Oorschot, 2023).

In policing, this matter risks amplification because criminal networks and other hostile actors have a history of exploiting encrypted communication platforms, either to gather information on investigations or to obscure surveillance attempts (Landau, 2011). In a quantum future, secure channels using the technology, combined with tailored and decentralized infrastructures, could prevent lawful surveillance attempts from law enforcement and affect the feasibility of passive communication interception (Parlov et al., 2021). The state itself could adopt quantum mechanisms of communication where sensitive data is transmitted and held without the risk of immediate breach (Harmon, 2022). Its vast ability to also intercept traditionally encrypted, but now less-secured, data using the latest quantum systems could raise questions around surveillance, security, and their overlap with civil liberties (Wimmer & Moraes, 2022).

While police organizations would benefit from the increased robustness in security and data integrity, they could face similar resistance from others who may adopt comparable measures (Lavorgna, 2015). It could also reduce openness from these organizations, as well as other state actors who could keep potentially damaging political information from stakeholders, thus preventing, particularly, media organizations or civil society from uncovering their nefarious activities (Bakir, 2018). Managing such tensions will involve clear articulation of proportionality, oversight, and lawful access frameworks, as well as a means of accessing data through freedom of information mechanisms (Birkinshaw, 2006).

QML: Beyond Machine Learning

Machine learning has a long history of use within policing contexts, particularly for crime pattern analysis, facial recognition, risk assessment, and resource allocation (Berk et al., 2019). Quantum Machine Learning (QML) could lead to a further acceleration of these capabilities, with faster optimization, improved handling of high-dimensional data, and innovative approaches to discern patterns (Khurana et al., 2024). The data environments being as vast for policing, the heterogeneous and noisy nature of the data itself would be well-suited to quantum machines (Sanders and Sheptycki, 2017). However, most contemporary QML is a combination of classical and quantum computers, with the latter itself having limited current capabilities (Markoska & Markoski, 2025).

The hybrid nature of these infrastructures lends credence to concerns that housing these often-unstable quantum hardware(s) within police data centres could be impractical and cost-ineffective (Fedorov, 2023). The more likely deployment strategy would be accessing quantum processing units (QPUs) through dedicated and secure cloud interfaces to accelerate specific and fit-for-purpose computational tasks (Minarini, 2025). This approach has been successful for traditional computing, especially in the realm of graphics processing units (GPUs), which, at the time of writing, have been useful for deep learning and artificial intelligence (AI) tasks, as well as for virtualization, gaming, and image/video processing (Madiajagan & Raj, 2019). What would prevent headway in this path would be, along with the prohibitive cost of expensive hardware, the unavailability of secure and high-bandwidth offering providers, and the lack of specialized, trained talent required to translate policing problems into quantum-ready algorithms capable of solving them (Atmakuri, 2025; Lin, 2025).

There is limited empirical evidence that QML consistently outperforms classical machines, even the state-of-the-art ones; there are only theoretical models that suggest real-world optimization and sampling (Ficara et al., 2022; Khan & Robles-Kelly, 2020), which could be advantageous to police datasets (Cavadas et al., 2015).

Then there is the matter of data encoding costs, potentially high error rates, and the difficulty of benchmarking quantum systems, meaning their performance gains would face measurement difficulties, and any advantages would be task-specific and incremental (at least in the short run) rather than transformative (Resch & Karpuzcu, 2021). It is therefore premature to classify QML as a direct replacement for classical analytics, and care should be taken to make any such classifications without measuring and quantifying utility (Machireddy, 2023).

However, it has to be said that even incremental performance improvements in predictive and prioritization systems would carry significant implications for policing, especially in decisions about patrol deployment, suspect prioritization, and investigative focus (Camacho-Collados & Liberatore, 2015). These would have a direct effect on who is observed, questioned, taken into custody, and what is prioritized during active investigations (Sachoulidou, 2023). The potential of QML to provide faster and more granular analysis, therefore, carries wide-ranging potential, despite long-held concerns about potential bias, feedback loops, and the automation and quelling of discretion (Van Der Haegen, 2023). The need for accuracy, though great, could be outstripped by the want for contestable, explainable, and proportionate results that fit within the legal and ethical frameworks of the jurisdiction where the technology is adopted (Luís-Ferreira & Loureiro-Rodrigues, 2025; Ali, 2020).

This caution also needs to extend to claims that quantum systems would decisively resolve current incapabilities regarding deepfake and AI detection, as well as behaviour prediction (Barczak, 2023). History has consistently demonstrated a continuing tug-of-war between technology improvement and potential detection and countermeasure (Ekblom, 2013), meaning any developments brought forward by quantum machines could well be countered by innovations on the other side (Weinberg & Faccia, 2024). Police forces and other law enforcement organizations could therefore be tempted to adopt the latest and greatest technology just to keep up with bad actors (Manning, 2001; Wall, 1998), leaving a governance gap, where experimental, partially understood systems are integrated without the requisite audit and validation (Joh, 2025; Lum et al., 2017). Therefore, robust oversight, transparency, and accountability frameworks must be in place before quantum-enhanced analytics and its algorithmic outputs are allowed to guide operational decisions or, more importantly, be used as evidence in court (Kolapo & Oyewole, forthcoming).

Forensic Science in the Era of Quantum Systems

Technological innovation has been the driving force of forensic science and its applicability and utility in criminal justice (Kloosterman et al., 2015). This can be attributed to advances in measurement, sensitivity, and signal interpretation, which have drastically reduced sample analysis and detection rates (Nickell & Fischer, 2014). Quantum processing can radically improve sample matching times from DNA and fingerprint comparison to facial recognition (Salari et al., 2023). Quantum technologies have long been touted as the next phase in unprecedented sensitivity and detection of physical traces, creating tangible opportunities for evidential enhancement, particularly in technically complex cases (Krelina, 2021). For instance, quantum sensors could exploit quantum states to measure physical properties of magnetism, gravity, and even time with extreme precision, which can be used to improve detection of trace evidence, understand evidence degradation from even most subtle environmental disturbances, or to locate otherwise undetectable artefacts (Bass & Doser, 2024; Stray et al., 2022). However, something to remember is that increased sensitivity would not automatically translate to improved certainty, as longstanding issues around evidence transfer, persistence, and context-specific interpretation would still remain (Reed et al. 2018; Wells, 2025). It could even cause ambiguity and concern from detecting irrelevant signals or patterns (Murphy, 2007; Biedermann & Vuille, 2016).

There is consensus that evidence must not only be reliable for admission but must also be capable of being understood (Saks & Faigman, 2008). Scientific validity should be communicable, and as such, quantum-enhanced methods would also need to be transparent in addition to establishing reliability (Zednik & Boelsen, 2022). In its early deployment stages, quantum-enhanced evidence could face a form of adversarial scrutiny, derailing cases, and causing unintended extra-legal consequences (Chintalapati et al., 2025). Based on recent memory, expert testimony would likely become even more dependent on specialized technical knowledge, and the gap between scientific capability and legal comprehension could widen significantly (Imwinkelried, 1988; Jasanoff,1997; Mnookin, 2008).

In law enforcement contexts, restraint would be in the best interests of stakeholders, at least until the technology is more mainstream and public comprehension is at a level where both judges and jurors have at least an awareness of the nature of the systems at play (Adam, 2016). The legal aspects here, beyond the knowledge gap, relate to a need for robust validation studies, long-term error rate detection, and a methodology that is transparent and challengeable from both sides inside the courtroom (Córcoles et al., 2019). The risk lies in early adoption with the misconception that quantum technologies are the magic bullet to resolving forensic uncertainty (Nguyen & Costa, 2022). The recommended path forward is therefore to view it more as an extension of current evidential practices and operationalizing it in a limited capacity within the existing legal framework with a view to future amendment of the law (Murphy, 2013).

Beyond the Eye: Hidden Detection Through Quantum Sensing

There are further applications for the technology in advancing everything from magnetometers to gravimeters and related measurement devices (Veryaskin, 2021). In defence and even law enforcement contexts, the utility of such advances is great, particularly in relation to detecting concealed objects, mapping underground structures, and identifying anomalies that evade traditional detection methods. Quantum magnetometers could, in principle, enable passive detection of concealed weapons without the need for active scanning or physical checkpoints (Coy, 2025). These are, however, only laboratory tested, and translating these to crowded public spaces where substantial environmental noise is accompanied by real-world uncertainty around magnetic signatures could lead to a plethora of false positives.

Beyond weapons detection, improvements in quantum sensing could lead to a wider scope in locating hidden spaces, monitoring structural integrity, and enhancing situational awareness in complex and unknown environments where more detailed information could lead to better safety and save lives (Czipott & Iwanowski, 1997). It could allow law enforcement to have a considerably wider reach into domains where they have historically had limited access for observation (Schultz, 2007).

The risks and implications of these systems are, however, consequential, due to the potentially invasive nature of the technology. It could mean a future where regulation of public spaces is intensified with widespread surveillance and an imbalance between prevention and intrusion (Chowdhury, 2022). Passive screening can blur the line between observation and search, especially when deployed covertly and at scale (Wang et al., 2019). Questions of consent, proportionality, and utility are directly tied with state authorities systematically scanning bodies and/or belongings, even when no images or personal identifiers are collected (Mironenko, 2011). Considered calibration along with systems capable of deciphering contextual cues would also be needed to avoid often innocuous objects from being flagged, or worse, particular population groups being targeted due to historic prejudices or systemic biases (Nazer et al., 2023).

Operational Deployment and the Advantages of Quantum Optimization

Law enforcement has long struggled with logistical challenges, particularly in patrol routing, custody transport, shift allocation, response coordination, and prioritization of resources under time pressure (Samanta et al., 2022). Quantum and quantum-enhanced optimization techniques have marked potential to bring incremental improvements in these realms, with the risks being comparatively low (El Gaily & Imre, 2021). They can address combinatorial difficulties that often become intractable at scale for traditional computing systems, tangibly speeding up these tasks due to the ability to handle multiple problems and combinations of problems at the same time through the utilization of quantum states (Abbas et al., 2024). It could translate into more efficient deployment of officers, reduced response times, and improved coordination across jurisdictional lines (Chase et al., 2017). Optimization, therefore, represents a practical and pragmatic entry into quantum technologies for otherwise traditional organizations like law enforcement, where cautious experimentation could lead to tangible gains (Acín et al., 2018).

Still, there needs to be awareness that even seemingly neutral optimization could lead to material distributive effects (Schleich et al., 2016). Decisions on resource allocation could affect visibility, support, and enforcement of particular communities, especially if historical patterns and institutional priorities are not revised with critical scrutiny (Min, 2023). Current AI technologies have already shown the dangers of algorithmic biases, and this should be a cautionary tale for police bodies who must remain vigilant about potentially improved logistics obscuring transparency, oversight, and the values embedded in organizational functions (Jackson, 2021).

Regulation and Regulatory Frameworks

It is thus, given the risks, hazards, and dangers associated with the technology, a necessity, rather than a preference, that policies that facilitate experimental adoption be shifted towards a more principled regulatory framework. The disruptive nature of quantum computing, in particular, its ability to render modern encryption standards almost obsolete, presents risks to institutional legitimacy and civil liberties. Therefore, without clear and robust ethical guardrails, the inherent technical opacity and probabilistic nature of such systems could lead to unchecked institutional power, the erosion of already dwindling public trust, and the lack of accountability and challenge in the justice system. The looming threat of harvest now, decrypt later attacks creates a temporal asymmetry that requires immediate and mandatory standards for cryptographic resilience. This should not be a mere technical necessity, but an essential requirement to ensure that quantum tools are used proportionately, transparently, and within existing legal frameworks.

The path towards regulation is however a complex one, given the global regulatory landscape that has traditionally struggled to translate over abstract principles into binding rules. At the international level, the G7 Hiroshima AI Process (2023) and the NATO Quantum Technologies Roadmap (2023) established high-level political and military commitments to address cryptographic threats and shared security standards. Their operationalization through technical benchmarks, most notably the NIST Post-Quantum Cryptography Standards (FIPS 203, 204, 205), was finalized in August 2024 (National Institute of Standards and Technology, 2024). In the meantime, the International Telecommunication Union (n.d.) developed standards for quantum key distribution (QKD) to govern future communications infrastructure. These are in addition to the Wassenaar Arrangement (1996), which historically coordinated export controls for dual-use technologies. However, geopolitical shifts fractured this consensus, leading many states to pursue independent national controls to protect their domestic quantum interests.

The National Quantum Initiative Act (NQI Act) in the United States (US) became the foundational statute in 2018, with reauthorization to extend through 2034 and significant funding increases for research and coordination. It has been supported by the CHIPS and Science Act (2022), which identified quantum as a critical technology for national security and created a direct talent pipeline from academia to the federal workforce. The National Security Memorandum 10 (NSM-10; White House, 2022) and the Quantum Computing Cybersecurity Preparedness Act (2022) also mandated that federal agencies audit their systems and transition to quantum-resistant algorithms by 2035. Other developments, such as the BIS Interim Final Rule (September 2024), imposed stringent export controls on quantum hardware and software, while the Quantum Encryption Readiness and Resilience Act (2025) sought to benchmark the readiness of both the public and private sectors against international competitors.

Elsewhere, the United Kingdom (UK) and European Union (EU) adopted similarly structured approaches that emphasized economic strategy and security-driven oversight. The UK National Quantum Strategy (Department for Science, Innovation and Technology, 2023) contains a ten-year roadmap for a quantum-enabled economy, working in tandem with the National Security and Investment Act 2021 to block hostile foreign acquisitions of sensitive quantum intellectual property. In a similar vein, the EU Dual-Use Regulation (updated in September 2025; European Commission, 2025a) formally adopted quantum computers in export control lists, harmonizing previously fragmented national approaches. The EU Quantum Strategy (European Commission, 2025b) and the proposed EU Quantum Act (European Commission, forthcoming) aimed to establish a sovereign European ecosystem with binding regulations on supply chain security and market access. Such efforts have been bolstered by the NIS2 Directive (European Union, 2022) and the Cyber Resilience Act (European Union, 2024), which required critical infrastructure operators and product manufacturers to adopt state-of-the-art cryptographic security to withstand emerging quantum threats.

The Way Forward

The collective function of these is to ensure that the transition to a quantum-enabled future remains principled and that organizations implement a strategy of intentioned decision-making. Agencies should therefore prioritize cryptographic audits to address vulnerabilities within sensitive databases and digital evidence vaults. These would, however, need to be adopted for law enforcement use; require the establishment of rigorous forensic validation standards so that evidence remains scientifically reliable, transparent, and communicable for judicial scrutiny; and avoid the misconception that these technologies are a magic bullet for forensic uncertainty. Institutions should also leverage national talent pipelines to bridge the widening gap between scientific capability and legal comprehension. Integration of advanced analytics must be accompanied by ethical regulations to prevent feedback loops and the automation of discretion, so that civil liberties are protected, and institutional legitimacy remains intact. A pragmatic transition should favour incremental optimization in low-risk operational areas, such as logistics and patrol routing, while maintaining cautious evaluation for more invasive technologies. Within the confines of existing and upcoming regulatory frameworks, law enforcement can, and should, ensure that advancements serve as instruments for justice rather than a catalyst for the erosion of public trust. In the current state, the regulations and regulatory frameworks stem from a place of national anxiety about cryptographic breaches and quantum technology hijack (Liman & Weber, 2023). Once national and international borders are secured in these regards, internal frameworks could be developed in a more structured and introspective manner.

Conclusion

Quantum technologies hold great potential in the state securitization apparatus. There is a way to go, especially with the development of computational, communicative, and sensing capabilities of these technologies, with the principal challenge being how their results are going to be interpreted, governed, and integrated into existing frameworks and operational practices. This chapter has argued that quantum computing, post-quantum cryptography, quantum communication, quantum-assisted optimization, and quantum sensing are each promising near-future tools that can transform policing, but also carry varying levels of risk. While some demand immediate preparatory action, others warrant cautious experimentation, all underpinned by a need for evidential reliability, governance implications, and potential societal impact.

The recurring theme in existing works and in the current trajectory of quantum systems is legitimacy, where visibility of reasoning, the ability to challenge decisions, and the proportional exercise of power all rely heavily on allowing police authority to remain lawful. Lack of technical opacity and overreliance on probabilistic processes could undermine this authority, and so, considered design and oversight are needed; the absence of which could lead to an amplification of already lopsided institutional power, and the erosion of public trust and legal accountability. Comprehensive regulatory frameworks are, therefore, an essential response to this undesired potential of unchecked technological power. Mandates act as necessary guardrails that ensure the exercise of state power remains proportional and institutional legitimacy is derived from clear legal and ethical standards. The transition from reactive adoption to a governed, intentional strategy can assist states to secure a future where quantum advancements fundamentally serve the interests of justice and the protection of civil liberties.

Encouraging evidence exists that a quantum future, though not inevitable, could be on the horizon for law enforcement. The real challenge for adopting organizations is not acquiring the machines or training staff, but implementing meaningful mechanisms of evaluation and self-reflection, sometimes even refusing technological interventions, should the risks outweigh the benefits. There are futures of great hope tied in with dark dystopias, and what will separate the two and prevent one from the other would depend on power and utility, balanced with risk and accountability.

References

Abbas, A., Ambainis, A., Augustino, B., Bärtschi, A., Buhrman, H., Coffrin, C., ... & Zoufal, C. (2024). Challenges and opportunities in quantum optimization. *Nature Reviews Physics*, 1–18.

Abraha, H. H. (2021). Law enforcement access to electronic evidence across borders: mapping policy approaches and emerging reform initiatives. *International Journal of Law and Information Technology*, *29*(2), 118–153.

Acín, A., Bloch, I., Buhrman, H., Calarco, T., Eichler, C., Eisert, J., ... & Wilhelm, F. K. (2018). The quantum technologies roadmap: A European community view. *New Journal of Physics*, *20*(8), 080201.

Adam, C. (2016). *Forensic evidence in court: Evaluation and scientific opinion*. John Wiley & Sons.

Ajala, O. A., Arinze, C. A., Ofodile, O. C., Okoye, C. C., & Daraojimba, A. I. (2024). Exploring and reviewing the potential of quantum computing in enhancing cybersecurity encryption methods. *Magna Scientia Advanced Research and Reviews*, *10*(1), 321–329.

Ali, S. (2020). Coming to a battlefield near you: Quantum computing, artificial intelligence, & machine learning's impact on proportionality. *Santa Clara J. Int'l L.*, *18*, 1.

Atmakuri, N. B. (2025). Democratizing advanced technology: How edge AI in embedded systems transforms everyday life. *Journal of Multidisciplinary*, *5*(8), 253–263.

Bakir, V. (2018). *Intelligence elites and public accountability: Relationships of influence with civil society*. Routledge.

Barczak, A. (2023). Artificial intelligence: Challenges and threats. *Studia Informatica: Systems and Information Technology*, *2*.

Bass, S. D., & Doser, M. (2024). Quantum sensing for particle physics. *Nature Reviews Physics*, *6*(5), 329–339.

Berk, R., Berk, D., & Drougas, D. (2019). *Machine learning risk assessments in criminal justice settings* (pp. 1–178). Springer.

Biedermann, A., & Vuille, J. (2016). Digital evidence, 'Absence' of data and ambiguous patterns of reasoning. *Digital Investigation*, *16*, S86–S95.

Birkinshaw, P. (2006). Freedom of information and openness: Fundamental human rights. *Admin. L. Rev.*, *58*, 177.

Bozzio, M., Crépeau, C., Wallden, P., & Walther, P. (2025). Quantum cryptography beyond key distribution: Theory and experiment. *Reviews of Modern Physics*, *97*(4), 045006.

Broadbent, A., & Schaffner, C. (2016). Quantum cryptography beyond quantum key distribution. *Designs, Codes and Cryptography*, *78*(1), 351–382.

Brotherston, L., Berlin, A., & Reyor III, W. F. (2024). *Defensive security handbook*. O'Reilly Media, Inc.

Burton, S., Habli, I., Lawton, T., McDermid, J., Morgan, P., & Porter, Z. (2020). Mind the gaps: Assuring the safety of autonomous systems from an engineering, ethical, and legal perspective. *Artificial Intelligence*, *279*, 103201.

Camacho-Collados, M., & Liberatore, F. (2015). A decision support system for predictive police patrolling. *Decision Support Systems*, *75*, 25–37.

Cavadas, B., Branco, P., & Pereira, S. (2015). Crime prediction using regression and resources optimization. In *Portuguese Conference on Artificial Intelligence* (pp. 513–524). Springer International Publishing.

Chase, J., Du, J., Fu, N., Le, T. V., & Lau, H. C. (2017, November). Law enforcement resource optimization with response time guarantees. In *2017 IEEE Symposium Series on Computational Intelligence (SSCI)* (pp. 1–7). IEEE.

Chintalapati, A., Enkhbat, K., Annamalai, R., Amali, G. B., Ozaydin, F., & Noel, M. M. (2025). Quantum-enhanced algorithmic fairness and the advancement of AI integrity and responsibility. *Quantum Reports*, *7*(3), 36.

CHIPS and Science Act of 2022, Pub. L. No. 117-167, 136 Stat. 1366 (2022).

Chowdhury, M. (2022). Trajectories of automation in policing. *Contemporary Issues in Global Criminal Justice*, *87*.

Córcoles, A. D., Kandala, A., Javadi-Abhari, A., McClure, D. T., Cross, A. W., Temme, K., … & Gambetta, J. M. (2019). Challenges and opportunities of near-term quantum computing systems. *Proceedings of the IEEE*, *108*(8), 1338–1352.

Coy, L. J. (2025). *Assessing quantum magnetometry as an emerging detection modality for strategic anti-submarine warfare* [Doctoral dissertation, Massachusetts Institute of Technology].

Czipott, P. V., & Iwanowski, M. D. (1997). Magnetic sensor technology for detecting mines, UXO, and other concealed security threats. In *Terrorism and counter-terrorism methods and technologies* (Vol. 2933, pp. 67–76). SPIE.

De Bruijn, H., Warnier, M., & Janssen, M. (2022). The perils and pitfalls of explainable AI: Strategies for explaining algorithmic decision-making. *Government Information Quarterly*, *39*(2), 101666.

De Carné de Carnavalet, X., & van Oorschot, P. C. (2023). A survey and analysis of TLS interception mechanisms and motivations: Exploring how end-to-end TLS is made "end-to-me" for web traffic. *ACM Computing Surveys*, *55*(13s), 1–40.

De Leon, N. P., Itoh, K. M., Kim, D., Mehta, K. K., Northup, T. E., Paik, H., … & Steuerman, D. W. (2021). Materials challenges and opportunities for quantum computing hardware. *Science*, *372*(6539).

Department for Science, Innovation and Technology. (2023). *UK national quantum strategy*. HM Government.

Distler, V., Lallemand, C., & Koenig, V. (2020, September). Making encryption feel secure: Investigating how descriptions of encryption impact perceived security. In *2020, IEEE European Symposium on Security and Privacy Workshops (EuroS&PW)* (pp. 220–229). IEEE.

Ekblom, P. (2013). How to police the future: Scanning for scientific and technological innovations which generate potential threats and opportunities in crime, policing and crime reduction. In *Crime Science* (pp. 27–55). Willan.

El Gaily, S., & Imre, S. (2021). Constrained quantum optimization for resource distribution management. *International Journal of Advanced Computer Science and Applications*, *12*(8).

European Commission. (2025a). *Commission delegated regulation amending Regulation (EU) 2021/821 as regards the list of dual-use items*. Official Journal of the European Union.

European Commission. (2025b, July). *Quantum Europe Strategy: Quantum Europe in a changing world*. Quantum Flagship. https://qt.eu/media/pdf/Quantum_Europe_Strategy_July_2025.pdf

European Commission. (Forthcoming). *The EU quantum act.*

European Union (2022) *Directive (EU) 2022/2555 of the European Parliament and of the Council of 14 December 2022 on measures for a high common level of cybersecurity across the Union (NIS2 Directive). Official Journal of the European Union.* https://eur-lex.europa.eu/eli/dir/2022/2555/oj/eng

European Union (2024) *Regulation (EU) 2024/2847 of the European Parliament and of the Council of 10 October 2024 on horizontal cybersecurity requirements for products with digital elements (Cyber Resilience Act). Official Journal of the European Union.* https://eur-lex.europa.eu/eli/reg/2024/2847/oj/eng

Fathalla, E., & Azab, M. (2024). Beyond classical cryptography: A systematic review of post-quantum hash-based signature schemes, security, and optimizations. *IEEE Access.*

Fedorov, A. K. (2023). Deploying hybrid quantum-secured infrastructure for applications: When quantum and post-quantum can work together. *Frontiers in Quantum Science and Technology, 2*, 1164428.

Ficara, A., Fiumara, G., De Meo, P., & Catanese, S. (2022, November). Classical and quantum random walks to identify leaders in criminal networks. *In International Conference on Complex Networks and Their Applications* (pp. 190–201). Springer International Publishing.

Fuchs, C. A., & Fuchs, C. A. (1998). Information gain vs. state disturbance in quantum theory. *Fortschritte der Physik: Progress of Physics, 46*(4–5), 535–565.

G7. (2023). *G7 Hiroshima AI process: G7 leaders' statement and Hiroshima process international guiding principles for organizations developing advanced AI systems.* https://digital-strategy.ec.europa.eu/en/library/g7-leaders-statement-hiroshima-ai-process

Ganesh, R., Khan, B. U. I., Khan, A. R., & Kamsin, A. B. (2025). A panoramic survey of the advanced encryption standard: From architecture to security analysis, key management, real-world applications, and post-quantum challenges. *International Journal of Information Security, 24*(5), 216.

George, A. S., Baskar, T., & Srikaanth, P. B. (2024). Cyber threats to critical infrastructure: Assessing vulnerabilities across key sectors. *Partners Universal International Innovation Journal, 2*(1), 51–75.

Gercek, A. A., & Seskir, Z. C. (2025). *Navigating the quantum divide(s)*. IEEE Engineering Management Review.

Griffiths, C. T. (2022). *Interagency communication, collaboration, and interoperability within police services and between police services and other emergency services.* School of Criminology, Simon Fraser University.

Harmon, P. (2022). Data breach notification laws and the quantum decryption problem. *Wash. & Lee L. Rev., 79*, 475.

Horowitz, M., & Grumbling, E. (Eds.). (2019). *Quantum computing: progress and prospects.* https://www.nationalacademies.org/projects/DEPS-AFSB-16-01/publication/25196

How, M. L., & Cheah, S. M. (2023). Business renaissance: Opportunities and challenges at the dawn of the Quantum Computing Era. *Businesses, 3*(4), 585–605.

Imwinkelried, E. J. (1988). The bases of expert testimony: The syllogistic structure of scientific testimony. *NCL Rev., 67*, 1.

Inglesant, P., Hartswood, M., & Jirotka, M. (2016). *Thinking ahead to a world with quantum computers: The landscape of responsible research and innovation in quantum computing*. University of Oxford.

International Telecommunication Union. (n.d.). *Focus group on quantum information technology for networks (FG-QIT4N) technical reports.* https://www.itu.int/en/ITU-T/focusgroups/qit4n/Pages/default.aspx

Jackson, M. C. (2021). Artificial intelligence & algorithmic bias: The issues with technology reflecting history & humans. *J. Bus. & Tech. l., 16*, 299.

Jasanoff, S. (1997). *Science at the bar: Law, science, and technology in America* (Vol. 9). Harvard University Press.
Joh, E. E. (2025). Police technology experiments. *Columbia Law Review, 125*(1), 1–28.
Johnson, W. G. (2019). Governance tools for the second quantum revolution. *Jurimetrics, 59*(4), 487–522.
Khan, T. M., & Robles-Kelly, A. (2020). Machine learning: Quantum vs classical. *IEEE Access, 8*, 219275–219294.
Khurana, S., Nene, M., & Nene, M. J. (2024). Quantum machine learning: Unraveling a new paradigm in computational intelligence. *Quantum, 74*(1).
Kloosterman, A., Mapes, A., Geradts, Z., van Eijk, E., Koper, C., van den Berg, J., … & van Asten, A. (2015). The interface between forensic science and technology: How technology could cause a paradigm shift in the role of forensic institutes in the criminal justice system. *Philosophical Transactions of the Royal Society B: Biological Sciences, 370*(1674), 20140264.
Kolapo, A. A., & Oyewole, B. (Forthcoming). *The roadmap to quantum-enhanced financial forensics: Opportunities and challenges*.
Krelina, M. (2021). Quantum technology for military applications. *EPJ Quantum Technology, 8*(1), 24.
Landau, S. (2011). *Surveillance or security? The risks posed by new wiretapping technologies*. MIT Press.
Lavorgna, A. (2015). Organised crime goes online: Realities and challenges. *Journal of Money Laundering Control, 18*(2), 153–168.
Liman, A., & Weber, K. (2023). Quantum computing: Bridging the national security–digital sovereignty divide. *European Journal of Risk Regulation, 14*(3), 476–483.
Lin, L. S. (2025). Integrating artificial intelligence in police education: An analysis of the top-down approach at Taiwan's Central Police University. In *Transforming vocational education and training using AI* (pp. 131–164). IGI Global Scientific Publishing.
Lodge, J. (2010). *Quantum surveillance and 'shared secrets'. A biometric step too far?* CEPS Centre for European Policy Studies.
Luís-Ferreira, F., & Loureiro-Rodrigues, C. (2025). *Ethical challenges in the current digital landscape: AI, robotics and quantum computing*. https://www.preprints.org/manuscript/202505.0507
Lum, C., Koper, C. S., & Willis, J. (2017). Understanding the limits of technology's impact on police effectiveness. *Police Quarterly, 20*(2), 135–163.
Machireddy, J. R. (2023). Data quality management and performance optimization for enterprise-scale ETL pipelines in modern analytical ecosystems. *Journal of Data Science, Predictive Analytics, and Big Data Applications, 8*(7), 1–26.
Madiajagan, M., & Raj, S. S. (2019). Parallel computing, graphics processing unit (GPU) and new hardware for deep learning in computational intelligence research. In *Deep learning and parallel computing environment for bioengineering systems* (pp. 1–15). Academic Press.
Manning, P. K. (2001). Technology's ways: Information technology, crime analysis and the rationalizing of policing. *Criminal Justice, 1*(1), 83–103.
Manpearl, E. (2017). Preventing going dark: A sober analysis and reasonable solution to preserve security in the encryption debate. *U. Fla. JL & Pub. Pol'y, 28*, 65.
Markoska, R., & Markoski, A. (2025). Quantum vs classical computing: Technologies in tandem. *International Journal of Recent Research in Mathematics, Computer Science, and Information Technology, 11*(2).
Mellese, D. W., Tefera, Z. G., Belay, M. B., Seffa, G. H., Negewo, A. G., Acham, Z. G., … & Adamu, D. M. (2026). A systematic literature review of lattice-based key encapsulation mechanisms and digital signatures: Current status, research gaps, and future directions. *IEEE Access, 14*, 9624–9643.

Mendel, J., Fyfe, N. R., & den Heyer, G. (2017). Does police size matter? A review of the evidence regarding restructuring police organisations. *Police Practice and Research, 18*(1), 3–14.

Min, A. (2023). Artificial intelligence and bias: Challenges, implications, and remedies. *Journal of Social Research, 2*(11).

Minarini, F. (2025). *Green computing for particle physics*. [Doctoral thesis. University of Bologna.]

Minbaleev, A., Zenin, S., & Evsikov, K. (2024). Prospects for legal regulation of quantum communication. *BRICS Law Journal, 11*(2), 11–54.

Mironenko, O. (2011). Body scanners versus privacy and data protection. *Computer Law & Security Review, 27*(3), 232–244.

Mnookin, J. (2008). Expert evidence, partisanship and epistemic competence. *Brooklyn Law Review, 73*(587), 8–12.

Murphy, E. (2007). The new forensics: Criminal justice, false certainty, and the second generation of scientific evidence. *Calif. L. Rev., 95*, 721.

Murphy, E. (2013). The mismatch between twenty-first-century forensic evidence and our antiquated criminal justice system. *S. Cal. L. Rev., 87*, 633.

NATO. (2023). *NATO quantum technologies roadmap*. Science and Technology Organization. North Atlantic Treaty Organization.

National Institute of Standards and Technology. (2024). *Statutory post-quantum cryptography standards (FIPS 203, 204, 205)*. U.S. Department of Commerce.

National Quantum Initiative Act of 2018, Pub. L. No. 115-368, 132 Stat. 5092 (2018, as amended).

National Security and Investment Act 2021, c. 25 (UK).

Nazer, L. H., Zatarah, R., Waldrip, S., Ke, J. X. C., Moukheiber, M., Khanna, A. K., … & Mathur, P. (2023). Bias in artificial intelligence algorithms and recommendations for mitigation. *PLOS Digital Health, 2*(6), e0000278.

Nguyen, C., & Costa, A. (2022). Digital forensics challenges in quantum computing era. *ITSI Transactions on Electrical and Electronics Engineering, 11*(1), 1–7.

Nickell, J., & Fischer, J. F. (2014). *Crime science: Methods of forensic detection*. University Press of Kentucky.

Olutimehin, A. T., Joseph, S., Ajayi, A. J., Metibemu, O. C., Balogun, A. Y., & Olaniyi, O. O. (2025, February 17). Future-proofing data: Assessing the feasibility of post-quantum cryptographic algorithms to mitigate 'harvest now, decrypt later' attacks. *Decrypt Later' Attacks*.

Parlov, N., Sičaja, Ž., Katulić, T., & Luša, R. (2021). Information security and the lawful interception of communications through telecom service providers infrastructure: advanced model system architecture. *Policija i sigurnost, 30*(1/2021), 112–130.

Perrier, E. (2022). The quantum governance stack: Models of governance for quantum information technologies. *Digital Society, 1*(3), 22.

Phillips Jr, W. E., & Burrell, D. N. (2009). Decision-making skills that encompass a critical thinking orientation for law enforcement professionals. *International Journal of Police Science & Management, 11*(2), 141–149.

Quantum Computing Cybersecurity Preparedness Act 2022, Pub. L. No. 117-260, 136 Stat. 2351 (2022).

Quantum Encryption Readiness and Resilience Act of 2025, H.R. [Introduced 2025].

Reed, J. E., Howe, C., Doyle, C., & Bell, D. (2018). Simple rules for evidence translation in complex systems: A qualitative study. *BMC Medicine, 16*(1), 92.

Ren, S. Z., Wahab, N. H. B. A., Quan, B. L. Y., Fadila, J. N., Razali, N. F., & Wong, K. Y. (2025, May). Resilience of smart contracts towards quantum computing: Threats, solutions, and research directions. In *2025 2nd International Conference on Smart City and Information System (ICSCIS)* (pp. 97–101). IEEE.

Resch, S., & Karpuzcu, U. R. (2021). Benchmarking quantum computers and the impact of quantum noise. *ACM Computing Surveys (CSUR)*, *54*(7), 1–35.
Rose, N., & Miller, P. (2017). Political power beyond the state: Problematics of government. In *Foucault and law* (pp. 191–224). Routledge.
Sachoulidou, A. (2023). Going beyond the "common suspects": To be presumed innocent in the era of algorithms, big data and artificial intelligence. *Artificial Intelligence and Law*, 1–54.
Saks, M. J., & Faigman, D. L. (2008). Failed forensics: How forensic science lost its way and how it might yet find it. *Annual Review of Law and Social Science*, *4*(1), 149–171.
Salari, V., Paneru, D., Saglamyurek, E., Ghadimi, M., Abdar, M., Rezaee, M., … & Karimi, E. (2023). Quantum face recognition protocol with ghost imaging. *Scientific Reports*, *13*(1), 2401.
Samanta, S., Sen, G., & Ghosh, S. K. (2022). A literature review on police patrolling problems. *Annals of Operations Research*, *316*(2), 1063–1106.
Sanders, C. B., & Sheptycki, J. (2017). Policing, crime and 'big data'; Towards a critique of the moral economy of stochastic governance. *Crime, Law and Social Change*, *68*(1), 1–15.
Schleich, W. P., Ranade, K. S., Anton, C., Arndt, M., Aspelmeyer, M., Bayer, M., … & Zoller, P. (2016). Quantum technology: From research to application. *Applied Physics B*, *122*(5), 130.
Schmeh, K. (2006). *Cryptography and public key infrastructure on the Internet*. John Wiley & Sons.
Schultz, J. J. (2007). Using ground-penetrating radar to locate clandestine graves of homicide victims: Forming forensic archaeology partnerships with law enforcement. *Homicide Studies*, *11*(1), 15–29.
Shahanas, I. N., & Thampi, S. M. (2025). Secure communication protocols: Safeguarding information in the digital age. In *Securing the connected world: Exploring emerging threats and innovative solutions* (pp. 157–221). Springer Nature Switzerland.
Shastry, K. A., & Mohan, S. G. (2024). Internet of things security: Techniques and challenges. In *Blockchain for IoT Systems* (pp. 39–62). Chapman and Hall/CRC.
Shor, P. W. (1999). Polynomial-time algorithms for prime factorization and discrete logarithms on a quantum computer. *SIAM Review*, *41*(2), 303–332.
Somani, A., Horsch, A., & Prasad, D. K. (2023). *Interpretability in deep learning* (Vol. 2). Springer.
Stray, B., Lamb, A., Kaushik, A., Vovrosh, J., Rodgers, A., Winch, J., … & Holynski, M. (2022). Quantum sensing for gravity cartography. *Nature*, *602*(7898), 590–594.
Ten Holter, C. (2023). *Towards a methodology for prospective governance in quantum computing technologies* [Doctoral dissertation, University of Oxford].
Van Der Haegen, M. (2023). Quantitative legal prediction as a dispute resolution mechanism. *European Review of Private Law*, *31*(2/3).
Veryaskin, A. V. (2021). *Gravity, magnetic and electromagnetic gradiometry: Strategic technologies in the 21st century*. IOP Publishing.
Wall, D. S. (1998). Catching cybercriminals: Policing the internet. *International Review of Law, Computers & Technology*, *12*(2), 201–218.
Wang, Z., Chang, T., & Cui, H. L. (2019). Review of active millimeter wave imaging techniques for personnel security screening. *IEEE Access*, *7*, 148336–148350.
Wassenaar (1996). Arrangement on Export Controls for Conventional Arms and Dual-Use Goods and Technologies. Multilateral Export Control Regimes.
Wells, W. (2025). Battlefield evidence in the age of artificial intelligence-enabled warfare. *Chi. J. Int'l L.*, *26*, 217.
White House, The. (2022). National security memorandum on promoting United States leadership in quantum computing while mitigating risks to vulnerable cryptographic systems (NSM-10).

Williams, R. (2012). Policing and forensic science. In *Handbook of policing* (pp. 788–821). Willan.

Willis, J. J., Koper, C. S., & Lum, C. (2020). Technology use and constituting structures: Accounting for the consequences of information technology on police organisational change. *Policing and Society*, *30*(5), 483–501. https://doi.org/10.1080/10439463.2018.1557660

Wimmer, M., & Moraes, T. G. (2022). Quantum computing, digital constitutionalism, and the right to encryption: Perspectives from Brazil. *Digital Society*, *1*(2), 12.

Weinberg, A. I., & Faccia, A. (2024). Quantum algorithms: A new frontier in financial crime prevention. arXiv preprint arXiv:2403.18322.

Yazdi, M. (2024). Application of quantum computing in reliability analysis. In *Advances in computational mathematics for industrial system reliability and maintainability* (pp. 139–154). Springer Nature Switzerland.

Zednik, C., & Boelsen, H. (2022). Scientific exploration and explainable artificial intelligence. *Minds and Machines*, *32*(1), 219–239.

Zornetta, A. (2024). Quantum-safe global encryption policy. *International Journal of Law and Information Technology*, *32*.

7

"WE ARE NOT READY FOR THAT"

Police Views on the Use of Generative AI to Create Public Security Threats

Laura Huey, Lorna Ferguson, Cole Heffren, and Meaghan Furlano

Introduction

Thousands of protestors, many with families in tow, have arrived from across the country to raise public awareness for their cause. Police have gathered intelligence to suggest that most will leave after a day or two. However, intelligence estimates also suggest that a few hundred will remain, occupying a prominent section of the nation's capital, disrupting traffic, local businesses, and government affairs until their demands are met. There is no intelligence to suggest they pose a significant security threat, and police liaison teams are actively working to build rapport in the hopes of convincing the protestors to leave or relocate. As the protest drags on, pressure to have the protest area shut down increases, with some vocal media and political critics raising concerns about the presence of children in the protest camp. While some protestors are nervous about the possibility of being forcibly moved or having their access to essential goods cut off by a police cordon around the site, the majority are committed to remaining and are hopeful for a peaceful solution. Protestor spirits are buoyed by the fact that their efforts are receiving international media coverage, generating waves of funding and other support from across the country and globe.

Something then happens to change the tenor of the protest completely: a two-minute video titled "HELP US!! They're taking our kids" is released on X (formerly Twitter), Facebook, and other social media platforms. The video, which purports to have been uploaded by one of the protestors, appears to show police officers dragging screaming children away from their parents, bundling them into unmarked vans. Parents who try to resist are depicted as being beaten by police wielding batons. The video goes viral almost immediately, inflaming millions of

DOI: 10.4324/9781003671312-7

viewers, who, a growing number of cause supporters have urged to take some form of direct action against what they see as a brutal example of state oppression. In security parlance, the video has created a "flashpoint" – that is, a moment in time at which significant levels of violence and disorder become very real threats. Only in the hours after the video has already been consumed by millions of viewers, some of whom may have chosen to act in response to their outrage, do government officials scramble to announce the video was a "deepfake," a wholly created product of artificial intelligence (AI). This protest scenario is hypothetical and entirely fictitious, but it nevertheless demonstrates the chaos and public security threat that AI can pose for civil society. Policing, as a civil force responsible for the prevention and detection of unlawful activity, thus has a key role to play in responding to AI-related crimes and public security threats. But do police officials see these threats? And if they do, how equipped do they feel to deal with them?

In this exploratory study, we raise the spectre of the potential misuse of AI with interviewees as a means of examining the extent to which Canadian police are prepared for this potential security threat. In-depth qualitative interviews were conducted with twenty-two (n = 22) municipal, regional, provincial, and national police leaders from across Canada. In these interviews, we asked police officials for their views on 1) whether public police see the malicious use of generative AI as a legitimate public safety concern; and 2) the extent to which Canadian policing is equipped to respond to the use of deepfakes as a public security threat. Analysis of the interview data collected reveals that, while there have been some, at best, preliminary discussions at provincial and federal levels among police and policy leaders, Canadian policing remains inadequately prepared for this threat. To help contextualize both the threat and the resulting national security gap Canadians face, this study is informed by Cronin's (2022) work on the adoption of open technological innovations by terrorist groups, as well as other recent papers on innovation by individuals and groups posing security threats (Logan et al., 2019; Lubrano, 2023; Chávez & Swed, 2024). In the pages that follow, we draw upon this work to present our findings in greater detail, as well as consider what potential steps can be taken to ameliorate this gap and related gaps in national security.

Context and Theory

Lethal Empowerment Theory

In a recent analysis of how political actors can exploit the benefits of open technological innovation to engage in armed conflict, Audrey Kurth Cronin (2022) presents a theory that neatly explains the potential diffusion and use of AI by terrorists and other proponents of political violence. Cronin's work, we note, draws heavily on a landmark paper by Christensen and Bower (1996; see also Christensen, 1997), in which the authors set out to explain the failure of larger, successful companies to adapt to changes in the marketplace. To do so, Christensen and Bower (1996) differentiate between "sustaining" and "disruptive" innovations. Sustaining innovations are those technologies that allow individuals and/or organizations to better meet identified needs through improvements or enhancements to existing processes. The use of QR codes to create contactless ordering from digital restaurant menus is just one such example. Disruptive innovations shake up the existing marketplace by creating new consumers, introducing radically new technologies, or offering services. An example of the latter is the introduction of digital streaming services, which completely reinvented how people consume music, television, and movies. While most consumers might agree that digital streaming has been a net benefit, other disruptive technologies, in the hands of malicious actors, have the potential to pose serious threats to public safety (Cronin, 2020, 2021). Cronin thus argues that one way open technology can disrupt the marketplace is by creating new consumers, individuals, and groups who might otherwise have lacked access to deadly technologies. Whereas in previous generations deadly technology – that is, technology with the capability of inflicting mass casualties – was developed mainly for military purposes and held under strict state control, the rapid pace of open technologies means that today, "disruptive technologies often democratize access to lethal capabilities, shifting unprecedented power into the hands of civilians" (Cronin, 2022, p. 7).

Cronin's "lethal empowerment theory" states that disruptive technologies may be vulnerable to misuse by bad actors when they meet several key criteria. The twelve criteria she lists are:

1. Accessibility
2. Affordability
3. Ease of use
4. Transportable
5. Concealability
6. Effectiveness
7. Open to multiple uses
8. Easily purchased
9. Not a brand new (and thus largely unknown) technology
10. Able to be converted into unexpected uses
11. Part of a cluster of other new technologies
12. Symbolically resonant

Suppose we return to the example of the New Orleans New Year's Day terrorist attack. In that case, we can see how this event illustrates how important issues such as concealability and accessibility can be to potential terrorists and others bent on imperilling public safety. The use of a vehicle as a weapon in that attack meets almost every single one of the criteria enumerated previously. When the vehicle as a weapon is combined with the use of improvised explosive devices

(IEDs)[1] and META smart glasses for pre-scoping potential targets (Madani, 2025); arguably, the attack meets each of Cronin's criteria.

AI as a Potentially Deadly Technology

Nowadays, it is nearly impossible to navigate online spaces without encountering the influence of AI. Whether submitting a query on Google or scrolling through one's social media feed, our experiences are shaped by AI systems (Gillespie, 2014; Mendes & Furlano, 2026; Noble, 2018; Sumpter, 2018). Algorithms, the basic building blocks of AI, are "a sequence of instructions or commands that a computer can work through to solve a task" (Vallejos et al., 2021, p. 2). Algorithms are inherently social products (Tacheva, 2022), shaped by the ideologies, biases, and political intentions of their designers and users (Bennett & Livingston, 2020; Linvill & Warren, 2020; Noble, 2018; Safieddine, 2020), which ultimately have offline implications. For one, AI tools contribute to a broader ecosystem of "information pollution," which is an umbrella term encompassing various forms of problematic information, including misinformation and disinformation (Cotter et al., 2022). Misinformation refers to the unintentional spread of false information, whereas disinformation occurs when false information is intentionally disseminated to deceive (Tsfati et al., 2020). Both have negative implications for public safety and democratic discourse, but disinformation, due to its intentional nature and deployment to serve malicious agendas, presents the most serious threat. While humans are the primary architects of disinformation, AI tools are increasingly being used to produce and disseminate it (Bontridder & Poullet, 2021; Shin et al., 2024). Scholars observe that the production and diffusion of disinformation have become colossal in scale, such that we are living in an age of disinformation (Grohmann & Ong, 2024; Carmi et al., 2020), or what the World Health Organization (2020) refers to as an "infodemic".

AI plays a central role in exacerbating information pollution and the "infodemic". First, AI tools can generate plausible but inaccurate information and visuals, thereby undermining scientific integrity and public understanding (De Angelis et al., 2023; van Dis et al., 2023). Next, algorithmic sorting fragments users into discrete epistemic communities, which may share little in common in terms of content or perspective (Stewart et al., 2022). This phenomenon intensifies echo chambers and polarizes public discourse, sometimes to the detriment of public health and safety. For instance, individuals may be algorithmically exposed to dangerous misinformation, such as false claims that chlorine dioxide can prevent or cure COVID-19 (Chejfec-Ciociano et al., 2022). Compounding these issues is that most users cannot reliably distinguish between content generated by AI and content produced by humans. To demonstrate, Kreps et al. (2022) find that AI-generated text is frequently mistaken for human-authored material, while Momeni (2024) notes that people also struggle to identify deepfake videos as inauthentic.

Deepfakes are highly realistic AI-generated media designed to misrepresent people or events and are particularly concerning due to their potential to manipulate public opinion and erode trust in media (Momeni, 2024). Although Vaccari and Chadwick (2020) suggest that people are often more uncertain than outright misled by deepfakes, visual content is nevertheless particularly effective in spreading disinformation – and the technologies creating this content are becoming more sophisticated by the day. Research suggests that images are more persuasive than text, and that people exhibit lower cognitive resistance, or "mental immunity," to visual misinformation (Norman, 2021; Newman et al., 2015). Weikmann and Lecheler (2023) argue that visual disinformation differs from textual forms in its production, processing, and impact, as it is often deliberately designed to deceive. In response, governments worldwide have begun to consider legal and regulatory interventions, such as the criminalization of deepfake production and the establishment of specialized task forces (Radu, 2020). However, many of these efforts remain nascent and uneven. At present, platform companies often place the burden of verification on users rather than addressing the structural conditions that enable the spread of false information (Cotter et al., 2022).

The failure of platform governance mechanisms is especially alarming given AI's capacity to scale existing crimes and facilitate new digital transgressions (Hayward & Maas, 2021). Scholars have linked AI to a wide range of criminal activities, including fraud, forgery, and identity theft (King et al., 2019). Hayward and Maas (2021) categorize the criminal use of AI into three main types: 1) AI used to commit crimes; 2) crimes committed against AI, such as tampering with systems for malicious purposes; and 3) crimes committed by AI itself, particularly following manipulation or "injection" by bad actors. One example of the latter involves social bots, AI programs designed to mimic human behaviour in online interactions. These bots have been shown to amplify disinformation, manipulate public discourse, and incite emotional responses on social media platforms (Bradshaw & Howard, 2019; Lamo & Calo, 2018; Daume et al., 2023).

Building on these wide-ranging societal implications, an underexplored area of concern surrounds the weaponization of AI in ways that go beyond disinformation and into the realm of deliberate, high-impact manipulation. In particular, the use of generative AI technologies, such as deepfakes, to create persuasive, emotionally charged, and potentially destabilizing content is becoming an urgent area for scholarly and policy investigation. These applications raise critical public safety issues that intersect with national security, radicalization, and extremism, and pose serious challenges for law enforcement and intelligence communities. Despite these risks, the academic literature has only begun to grapple with the role of generative AI in shaping and amplifying extremist narratives, especially in ways that may spark real-world consequences.

To situate this concern within the broader scholarship, it is important to recognize that much of the existing literature on malicious uses of AI has centred on areas such as powered autonomous terrestrial and aerial vehicles (Cronin, 2022), AI-enabled radicalization and recruitment (Esmailzadeh & Motaghi, 2024), and AI-driven cyberattacks (Iturbe et al., 2024). These remain critical domains of inquiry. However, our focus here shifts to a comparatively overlooked threat: the use of AI-generated technology to create impactful propaganda that could spark public order flashpoints. To date, few scholars have explored this possible use in any depth, and when they do, it is often mentioned only in passing as a hypothetical scenario[2]. One exception is a recent report by Copeland (2024), which specifically examines the question of whether AI tools are currently capable of creating realistic images, videos, and text for terrorist propaganda. Copeland concludes, and we agree, that AI generators are not, at present, capable of creating the type of realistic output likely to provoke large-scale public outrage without some form of human input in the image creation process. That said, given the significant funding being poured into the development of enhanced AI by Google, Meta, Amazon, and other major companies (Cronin, 2020), it is likely that quality issues will be resolved in subsequent program iterations. Thus, without access limits in place, we can expect AI to not only allow violent extremists to produce and disseminate significant volumes of realistic content but also to be used to identify and "hypertarget" population segments that may be more vulnerable to specific messaging (Copeland, 2024). Another exception can be found in a recent report by Nelu (2024), who argues that not only are violent extremist groups aware of the potential uses of generative AI for creating propaganda, but that some groups – notably the Islamic State – have begun publishing guidelines for leveraging this tool and others have been doctoring images and video using AI to create "fake news" (see also Soufan Center, 2024).

Method of Inquiry

This study examines the readiness of Canadian policing to respond to significant public safety threats involving the use of AI by malicious actors, ranging from inciting terrorism to disseminating misinformation aimed at undermining public order. To do so, this chapter draws on an analysis of data from in-depth qualitative interviews to answer two research questions:

Q1: Do respondents see the malicious use of generative AI as a credible public safety threat?

Q2: Is Canadian policing currently equipped to respond to scenarios involving the misuse of AI (deepfakes) in a public order/public security context?

Data

Our data derive from in-depth, qualitative interviews conducted with twenty-two (n = 22) sworn and civilian police leaders from across Canada. These interviews are part of a larger research project examining ongoing security threats and other issues related to public order and safety. As police will be among the first responders tasked with responding to such incidents, as well as being involved in identifying and countering generative AI propaganda aimed at undermining public safety, we decided to focus our efforts by exploring police perspectives on this topic.

To identify prospective research participants, we employed a two-pronged approach. First, we approached individuals within our research networks who fit one of four criteria: police leaders (from both Chiefs and rank and file associations), police executive members (Chiefs and Deputy Chiefs), public order and/or critical incident commanders (Inspectors and Superintendents), and/or Directors of Information Technology at police organizations (civilians). Second, we advertised the study and its aims on our professional X (formerly Twitter) and LinkedIn and invited individuals to contact us for more information.

The interviews were semi-structured and employed a mix of closed and open-ended questions. Interviewers used an informal interview guide, comprised of questions related to the following topics: 1) information regarding a participant's role and police experience; 2) individuals' thoughts, beliefs, and knowledge of recent major public protests (such as the 2022 Freedom Convoy 'Ottawa Occupation'); 3) respondents' views on other potential threats to public order and/or public security; 4) the role of new forms of technology in generating misinformation online and the ability of police and governments to combat fabricated, inaccurate, and/or dangerously misleading information that might threaten public order; 5) potential solutions to the misuse of technology by bad actors. Interviews were conducted by phone and typically lasted between 30 and 60 minutes. Each participant provided their consent and was audio-recorded. All interviews were then transcribed verbatim. To increase data reliability, transcripts were sent to the interviewees for comment and/or correction. To further ensure the reliability of this work, we also sent copies of this and other project papers to interviewees for verification.

All research for this study was conducted with the approval of a university Research Ethics Board and in compliance with Tri-Council guidelines on the ethical treatment of research participants. To ensure the anonymity of participants, all identifying information was removed from any quotations, and participants are generally identified only by their rank or role. In a handful of cases, where identifying a participant's descriptive details (e.g., gender) might increase the risk of exposing their identity, we have changed such information.

Sample

Our final sample consisted of twenty-two (n = 22) police personnel from eleven police services across Canada. Three (n = 3) representatives were from a national police organization, and the remaining nineteen (n = 19) were from municipal or regional agencies from one of three provinces (British Columbia, Alberta, Ontario).

All participants in this study hold a leadership role within policing, whether as a civilian Director of an agency, a representative of a police association, a public order or critical incident commander, or a police executive. Nineteen (n = 19) interviewees were sworn officers; three (n = 3) were civilian members. The ranks held by the former include Constable, Sergeant, Staff Sergeant, Inspector, Superintendent, Chief Superintendent, Deputy Chief, and Chief of Police. Years of service ranged from nine to thirty-five years. Despite multiple attempts to diversify the sample, the majority were white and male. Only one participant was female.

Analysis

For this study, data were analyzed using Braun and Clarke's (2006) six-step approach to thematic analysis. The steps involved require researchers to become familiar with the data, generate a set of initial codes, search for themes and sub-themes, review the themes, define and name them, and then present and discuss the results (Braun & Clarke, 2006). Our process thus began with the first author conducting an initial inductive, exploratory manual review of the interview data, searching for and noting any initial codes, an approach known as open-focused coding. Then, the first author moved to focused coding to further develop, refine, and compare the initial codes. This led to the sorting and grouping of these themes into overarching themes or major themes and sub-themes (Braun & Clarke, 2006), which were then named and defined. Independent of the first author, the fourth author also participated in coding a subset of ten interviews, and the results were compared. Any discrepancies were resolved through consensus discussions. To increase reliability, after the first author finalized and completed the coding, the second author reviewed the work and independently verified the coding.

Results

In this section, we present an analysis of the interviewee responses concerning the two research questions that guided this study. To reiterate, we asked whether Canadian police consider the malicious use of generative AI to be a legitimate public safety concern and the extent to which they feel equipped to respond to the use of deepfakes as a public security threat.

Do Respondents See the Malicious Use of Generative AI as a Credible Public Safety Threat?

Each of the twenty-two participants stated they saw AI as a tool that malicious actors could use to generate public safety threats. As one national police leader stated, "The evolution of AI, and especially this deepfake technology, is a credible threat." Some interviewees felt the potential threat was already present. To illustrate this point, one police leader cited the ability of anyone with basic computer literacy skills to access the internet and generate misinformation. "I see it in my social media feeds … I've seen the same motivational speech apparently in a video delivered by Morgan Freeman, Keanu Reeves, Scarlett Johansson. All of them are doing the same, word for word, and it's all fake." This officer worried that, because "technology is so good now," AI could be used as a tool to "inflame or create just crazy things." This point was shared by a police leader at another agency. Speaking of the history of many large-scale public protests, he observed, "sadly, in many cases, they are also infiltrated or perhaps influenced by a smaller group of folks with nefarious intent or perhaps even criminal intent." With malevolent actors becoming increasingly engaged in the "tactical use of social media, technology to try to influence a point," he worried "there's a greater risk" of individuals and groups using AI content to create public order flashpoints.

As one of the central concerns animating this study was the malevolent use of AI to spark major public order crises, we made a specific point to interview public order commanders to learn their thoughts. While none of those interviewed could cite a direct experience, each felt that it was a matter of time before AI would be used to generate misinformation that could inflame a public order situation. "I haven't seen artificial intelligence [used]," a commander in Ontario stated, "but it's coming". A public order commander at another agency raised another related issue: the use of AI to seed the internet with false information intended to mislead police intelligence efforts. As he explained:

> As AI advances, is there a chance that there are groups out there that could try to source multiple AI fictitious reports or suggestions that, to the average analyst and the average police service, would come across as corroborated intelligence? And then what is the response to that? And if that then is deemed to be—let's say, we do show up at something, or we do act on something that then is later deemed to be—was inaccurate the entire time, what is our investigative ability to ultimately determine who is responsible for that?

In discussing AI as a tool that can pose threats to public safety, several interviewees naturally raised dimensions of AI that relate to five key elements of lethal empowerment theory: accessibility, affordability, ease of use, effectiveness, and concealability. Of these, the most frequently cited (n = 7) was effectiveness. In the discussion, interviewees saw effectiveness in two interrelated ways. First, it can deceive targeted audiences into believing what they are seeing or hearing is genuine, and second, it motivates social media users to reshare and thus spread misinformation. Concerning the former, a police leader observed, "When people see pictures, or, God forbid, video or something, they think it's true." This is not the case with just deepfakes, he noted, but also "cheap fakes" – that is, images or videos that have been edited or posted out of context. When it comes to the ability of misinformation to go viral, officers were keenly aware of the problems they faced in combating AI-generated content. "You lose the initiative very quickly," one executive said, "when it's been out there for five minutes, the compounding interest on that is incredible. And our ability to reel that back even 24 hours later is difficult."

Accessibility, and relatedly, ease of use, are also concerns (n = 2). "Someone like me," a public order commander noted, "can program something without ever taking a programming course by using AI." "I've used it myself," another commander said, "'Create a police on a horse, doing this, this,' and it creates a police officer … and this is free, so I'm not paying for it." Recognizing the benefits of this technology, which he described as "having the smartest person next to you anytime you have a question," an interviewee also acknowledged "it's also like having the biggest and baddest criminal next to you and teaching you how to crack codes and how to rip people off and how to hurt people and how to build bombs." To his mind, AI has already "democratized criminality." What this officer and others were referring to is not just the current crop of free online tools available, which most agree is not, yet, sufficiently sophisticated for creating highly realistic content, but the "technology that was once held in very close circles by governments and large tech companies." A representative from a major police association advised, "you can now actually go online and pay somebody to get the app or get access to the app to do all this stuff."

Issues with concealability were also raised, with two participants (n = 2) expressing concern about the ability of malevolent actors to create sufficiently realistic images, audio, and video that would make it difficult for both police and targeted audiences to authenticate the content. Aside from concerns over the growth of AI tools that can escape current detection software, respondents cited the anonymity of the internet and the lack of robust authentication of digital users on social media platforms. As one police IT Director stated, "I think there's a fundamental problem where there's no attribution or authentication of user accounts. I could create 20 Facebook accounts with 20 different email addresses." A national police leader shared the same concern. Without a regulatory framework that supports authentic digital IDs, he noted, "it's so hard to find someone who posts something … and how do you go about chasing them down?" He then observed, "The capacity to be able to investigate promptly to stop something from growing and becoming viral is challenging."

Is Canadian Policing Currently Equipped to Respond to Scenarios Involving the Misuse of AI in a Public Security Context?

When asked whether Canadian law enforcement was presently equipped to respond to AI-related security threats, twenty-one (n = 21) of the twenty-two respondents agreed with the sentiments expressed by one police leader, who opined, "We are not ready for that." An association leader at another organization stated, "I don't think really we've even touched upon … what the ramifications are," before adding, "other than the academics, nobody in our business has really thought about it." The only exception to this general trend was a national police leader who felt his organization was "on the curve" in terms of beginning to think through the ramifications of malevolent AI use. However, he also stated he "wouldn't say we're ahead of the curve, that's for sure."

To further unpack the issue of police preparedness for AI-generated security threats, we asked respondents to what extent, if at all, their police services had begun to consider the issue. Four respondents (n = 4) from three organizations reported that their agencies had established AI committees, while others were in the early stages of developing committees or workplace policies. However, when pressed as to whether these committees were exploring possible security threats resulting from misuse by bad actors, none were aware of such discussions. Instead, the focus of AI committee work was essentially "on how AI impacts the day-to-day operations," as an association leader observed. Those day-to-day operations included issues such as using AI to generate reports and deploying "AI tools to help us catch bad guys." As a police IT expert explained, "AI is on our radar more from a usability perspective." For the police personnel interviewed for this study, AI is so "new … fresh" that law enforcement was simply more focused on "using it for good" rather than on how potential bad actors could subvert it. Perhaps not surprisingly, then, none of the police commanders interviewed for this project were members of an AI committee.

On a more reassuring note, a handful of interviewees stated that they had participated in and/or were aware of discussions on malevolent AI among police leaders and policymakers at both provincial and federal levels. For instance, a police leader advised, "I can say that there are those discussions happening at a provincial level, at a national level, international level about how AI is going to impact public safety and policing." However, as both this respondent and others observed, governments and law enforcement struggle to keep pace with the rate of technological change. "It's evolving at such an exponential rate," he said, "it's challenging to keep up with what's potentially out there and try to stay on top of the criminals or any individual that would want to utilize it for nefarious purposes." Another senior officer agreed, "AI moves at this speed [moves hands far apart] and government and committees move at this [moves hands much closer] … Yeah, it's too slow."

Discussion

Given the limited scholarly attention to the malicious use of technologies such as AI for the creation and dissemination of propaganda, and its implications for policing, this exploratory study sought to elicit insights from senior Canadian police leaders. As these leaders are responsible for guiding the strategic direction of their organizations in both the present and foreseeable future, their perspectives provide a critical foundation for future empirical inquiry. Theoretically, this study contributes to the growing body of research on AI by engaging with Cronin's (2022) *Lethal Empowerment Theory*, which identifies accessibility, affordability, ease of use, effectiveness, and concealability as key factors driving the democratization of technology. These dimensions, according to participating police leaders, can enable bad actors to engage in harmful behaviour that was previously beyond reach. On a practical level, the study highlights the current state of police leaders' awareness regarding the malicious use of technology, as well as the fragility of their organizations' preparedness to address these emerging threats. Many participants expressed concern that bad actors are already exploiting these tools for nefarious purposes. One particularly alarming scenario raised was the release of an AI-generated deepfake or "cheap fake" video during a high-tension public protest, which could incite violence between police and the public, an event for which current organizational responses are inadequate. The results of this study are timely for several reasons.

First, with the expansion of AI into near-universal use cases, conversations around identifying future threats, anticipating potential responses, and codifying procedures and investigative techniques will be paramount for Canadian police organizations to respond effectively to the novel crimes that will emerge. Indeed, deepfake technology has reached a sophistication level that has already had real-world consequences such as an attempted coup of the president of Gabon in 2019 (Langa, 2021; Momeni, 2024), Pizzagate – where a US citizen stormed a pizza shop believing the online claims that Hillary Clinton was sexually exploiting children there (Fisher et al., 2016; Chesney & Citron, 2019), and a UK company that lost $243,000 to an AI-synthesized voice (Farid, 2022). Although senior police leaders indicated that there are ongoing discussions about the use of malevolent AI, many also acknowledged that public safety institutions are unable to keep pace with the near-exponential increase in technology. As a greater number of these examples occur, the police will need to explicate procedures to investigate incidents locally as well as organize national and international processes to assist with the borderless nature of online criminal activity.

Second, bad actors have human nature and psychology on their side. Humans rely inordinately on the use of heuristics or shortcuts when processing information and making decisions (Tversky & Kahneman, 1974). These heuristics require lower cognitive loads (Shin et al., 2024), generally made without systematic analysis. In a tense protest environment, such as the one depicted in the introduction of this chapter, the release of a deepfake video on social media makes the public more likely to believe it for several reasons. Research demonstrates that misleading visuals are more likely to elicit false perceptions based on the realism heuristic, because they appear real and believable (Fallis, 2020; Frenda et al., 2013; Sundar et al., 2021; Vaccari & Chadwick, 2020). Furthermore, if the material in the video aligns with the protesters' pre-existing beliefs, it can reinforce and further entrench their worldview, prompting them to take action (Lewandowsky et al., 2012; Paul & Matthews, 2016; Momeni, 2024; Vaccari & Chadwick, 2020). Relatedly, first impressions are remarkably resilient, and people generally favour the initial information received over any subsequent corrections (e.g., the deepfake video over potential police attempts to dispute it; Lewandowsky et al., 2012; Jerit & Zhao, 2020). Collectively, these factors contribute to the creation of potential flashpoints and underscore their importance as considerations for countering AI-generated propaganda, which police organizations should include in any future discussions. Public Order Commanders should also prepare contingency plans for responding appropriately to incidents as described.

Finally, interviewees highlighted the importance of identifying bad actors, determining culpability for novel offences committed by AI, and creating and/or strengthening national and international extradition practices as future discussion points for policing. For example, utilizing AI as an intermediary to criminal offences (i.e., programming an AI bot to seek out and purchase drugs or other illicit items on the dark web) poses serious questions for determining both the *actus reus* (voluntariness) and the *mens reus* (criminal intent) of the offence (Hayward & Maas, 2021; King et al., 2019). If police are unable to track, arrest, and prosecute potential offenders, they risk losing public confidence as an institution and further eroding democratic principles.

Limitations and Future Research

We should note that, as was employed in this study, non-probability sampling can introduce bias to the study. For example, self-selection bias can be introduced if those who feel sufficiently motivated by the study topic are more likely to participate. Therefore, the sample may be represented by individuals with strong opinions, and it may not accurately reflect the views of police officers. Given the exploratory nature of this work, there is no intention to generalize beyond the current study. Instead, the findings from this study provide initial signposts for future research directions in this area, utilizing a variety of different methodologies. One area that could benefit from further empirical research is the exploration of how disinformation (and indirectly, misinformation) has impacted police operations both nationally and internationally. This study highlighted the stark reality that police organizations in Canada do not yet have a successful means of countering any disinformation propagated through social media. With the rich body of evidence of mis- and disinformation literature from the fields of political and media sciences (Benzie & Montasari, 2022; Bontridder & Poullet, 2021; Cotter et al., 2022; De Angelis et al., 2023; Jerit & Zhao, 2020; Lewandowsky et al., 2012; Linvill & Warren, 2020; Paul & Matthews, 2016; Radu, 2020; Shin et al., 2024), there is a lacuna on how disinformation can and will affect police organizations' credibility or ability to operate when a deepfake video calls their "observed" behaviour into question. Therefore, we hope to see more research conducted in this area so that the police (and other professions and political figures) can quickly identify false narratives and respond with factual reports prior to a flashpoint incident.

Second, this study has only scratched the surface of the ways AI can be utilized for malicious purposes. Further research is needed to examine each of these crimes (deepfakes, jailbreaking of Large Language Models, spear phishing, and others), both independently and in combination, so that police organizations can develop a firm understanding of the threats they face in the coming months and years. By developing an overview of the potential crimes, police can then determine the appropriate threat level and allocate resources to support the investigation of these crimes. These same leaders can then also arm themselves with the current knowledge to lobby legislators to codify these new offences into law as they arise. Indeed, it is only through collaborative effort that public safety organizations will be prepared to respond to the growing threats posed by the malicious use of AI.

Policy Recommendations

At the time of writing this chapter, Canadian news outlets are reporting on the use of ChatGPT for discussing violent ideas by the individual responsible for a school shooting in the small community of Tumbler Ridge. This case represents a terrible example of the unintended consequences of commercial technologies and why it is critical for regulators, police, and tech companies to put serious and sustained effort into working out how best to respond to threats posed by malevolent actors newly empowered or aided by access to technologies that can be used for lethal ends. To date, the ramifications of these new forms of lethal empowerment have attracted far too little attention from public policymakers, police, and others.

To begin countering the threats discussed earlier, police leaders should consider allocating resources to developing policies and procedures that address the investigative steps necessary to combat these novel crimes effectively. Given the almost endemic nature of limited resources in most police services, this requirement will necessitate a balanced approach between staffing current operations and preparing for the future. Additionally, taking the lead on creating a community of practice that brings together relevant industry partners, including members of the prosecution, governmental agencies with legislative authority, academics, and technical experts capable of providing knowledge and guidance on applicable solutions, should also be a focus.

Practically, police services should begin to explore training for their investigators on the threats described earlier. Typically, specialty units within medium to large-sized organizations investigate technological crimes; however, generalist investigators may not currently possess the requisite knowledge, skills, or abilities to conduct successful prosecutable investigations. As these novel crimes become more commonplace with increased usage, more trained officers will be required. Proactively providing this training can help keep pace with technological advancements.

Police services and associations also need to consider the increasingly critical role of communications in the modern era and how quickly false stories can go viral across multiple platforms, reaching millions of people before the truth is revealed. Police services need to improve training and policy for guiding communications staff and police leaders in how best to effectively and efficiently respond to misinformation. In our other work on critical incident and public order response, we found that communications staff are often not part of the incident team, found in the command room or even adequately briefed until much later during an event. Rethinking incident command and the role of communications is a necessary step in addressing AI-generated potential flashpoints and other public safety threats.

Commercial tech companies such as Microsoft, Google, or Facebook need to be reminded of the long history of how paradigm-shifting, brilliant innovations are often misused, regardless of the inventors' intent. In July 2019, Microsoft invested $1 billion in OpenAI, which aims to create artificial general intelligence that rivals the human brain. Amazon and Google are also avidly competing in this area: AI is integral to Amazon's e-commerce, and Google owns the AI company DeepMind. As these companies compete to advance their platform capabilities, they bear some social responsibility for protecting their consumers and the public, whether through altruistic motives or legislative decree (Mendes & Furlano, 2026). Some of the potential solutions discussed by scholars for use by these tech companies include tagging/removing/de-prioritizing deepfakes or disinformation on social media platforms (Bontridder & Poullet, 2021; Cotter et al., 2022; Momeni, 2024; Westerlund, 2019), or mandating that deepfake applications embed digital watermarking, hashing, or utilize blockchain technology (De Angelis et al., 2023; Jones, 2023; Momeni, 2024; Westerlund, 2019). Another solution is the use of community notes, as found on X, which allows credible members of a social media platform to post warning messages about the reliability of content found on a site.

Notes

1 Interestingly, news reports suggest the IEDs located were made with a "very rare explosive compound" not typically seen in terrorist attacks (Lowrey, 2025).
2 See, for example, Sim et al. (2024).

References

Bennett, W. L., & Livingston, S. (Eds.). (2020). *The disinformation age*. Cambridge University Press.

Benzie, A., & Montasari, R. (2022). Artificial intelligence and the spread of mis- and disinformation. In *Artificial intelligence and national security* (pp. 1–18). Springer International Publishing. https://doi.org/10.1007/978-3-031-06709-9_1

Bontridder, N., & Poullet, Y. (2021). The role of artificial intelligence in disinformation. *Data & Policy*, *3*, 1–21.

Bradshaw, S., & Howard, P. N. (2019). Social media and democracy in crisis. In M. Graham & W. H. Dutton (Eds.), *Society and the internet: How networks of information and communication are changing our lives* (pp. 212–227). Oxford University Press.

Braun, V., & Clarke, V. (2006). Using thematic analysis in psychology. *Qualitative Research in Psychology*, *3*(2), 77–101.

Carmi, E., Yates, S. J., Lockley, E., & Pawluczuk, A. (2020). Data citizenship: Rethinking data literacy in the age of disinformation, misinformation, and malinformation. *Internet Policy Review*, *9*(2), 1–22.

Chávez, K., & Swed, O. (2024). The empirical determinants of violent nonstate actor drone adoption. *Armed Forces and Society*, *50*(4), 883–912. https://doi.org/10.1177/0095327X231164570

Chejfec-Ciociano, J. M., Martínez-Herrera, J. P., Parra-Guerra, A. D., Chejfec, R., Barbosa-Camacho, F. J., Ibarrola-Peña, J. C., & González-Ojeda, A. (2022). Misinformation about and interest in chlorine dioxide during the COVID-19 pandemic in Mexico identified using Google Trends data: Infodemiology study. *JMIR Infodemiology*, *2*(1), 1–11.

Chesney, B., & Citron, D. (2019). Deep fakes: A looming challenge for privacy, democracy, and national security. *California Law Review*, *107*(6), 1753–1820. https://doi.org/10.15779/Z38RV0D15J

Christensen, C. (1997). *The innovator's dilemma*. Harvard Business Review Press.

Christensen, C. M., & Bower, J. L. (1996). Customer power, strategic investment, and the failure of leading firms. *Strategic Management Journal*, *17*(3), 197–218.

Copeland, S. (2024). *Terrorist exploitation of artificial intelligence: Current risks and future applications*. https://www.poolre.co.uk/terrorism-threat-publications/report-terrorist-exploitation-of-artificial-intelligence-current-risks-and-future-applications/

Cotter, K., DeCook, J. R., & Kanthawala, S. (2022). Fact-checking the crisis: COVID-19, infodemics, and the platformization of truth. *Social Media + Society*, *8*(1), 1–13.

Cronin, A. (2020). Technology and strategic surprise: Adapting to an era of open innovation. *Parameters*, *50*(3), 71–84.

Cronin, A. (2021). US Counter-terrorism: Moving beyond global counter-insurgency to strongpoint defence. *Survival*, *63*(5), 97–120.

Cronin, A. (2022). *Power to the people: How open technological innovation is arming tomorrow's terrorists*. Oxford University Press.

Daume, S., Galaz, V., & Bjersér, P. (2023). Automated framing of climate change? The role of social bots in the Twitter climate change discourse during the 2019/2020 Australia bushfires. *Social Media + Society*, 1–16.
De Angelis, L., Baglivo, F., Arzilli, G., Privitera, G. P., Ferragina, P., & Rizzo, C. (2023). ChatGPT and the rise of large language models: The new AI-driven infodemic in public health. *Frontiers in Public Health, 11*, 1–8.
Esmailzadeh, Y., & Motaghi, E. (2024). *International terrorism and social threats of artificial intelligence*. https://ssrn.com/abstract=4893952
Fallis, D. (2020). The epistemic threat of deepfakes. *Philosophy & Technology, 34*(4), 623–643. https://doi.org/10.1007/s13347-020-00419-2
Farid, H. (2022). Creating, using, misusing, and detecting deep fakes. *Journal of Online Trust & Safety, 1*(4). https://doi.org/10.54501/jots.v1i4.56
Fisher, M., Cox, J. W., & Hermann, P. (2016, December 6). Pizzagate: From rumor, to hashtag, to gunfire in D.C. *The Washington Post*. https://www.washingtonpost.com/local/pizzagate-from-rumor-to-hashtag-to-gunfire-in-dc/2016/12/06/4c7def50-bbd4-11e6-94ac-3d324840106c_story.html
Frenda, S. J., Knowles, E. D., Saletan, W., & Loftus, E. F. (2013). False memories of fabricated political events. *Journal of Experimental Social Psychology, 49*(2), 280–286. https://doi.org/10.1016/j.jesp.2012.10.013
Gillespie, T. (2014). The relevance of algorithms. In T. Gillespie, P. J. Boczkowski, & K. A. Foot (Eds.), *Media technologies: Essays on communication, materiality, and society* (pp. 167–194). MIT Press.
Grohmann, R., & Ong, J. C. (2024). Disinformation-for-hire as everyday digital labor: Introduction to the special edition. *Social Media + Society, 10*(1), 1–9.
Hayward, K. J., & Maas, M. M. (2021). Artificial intelligence and crime: A primer for Criminologists. *Crime, Media, Culture, 17*(2), 209–233.
Iturbe, E., Llorente-Vazquez, O., Rego, A., Rios, E., & Toledo, N. (2024). Unleashing offensive artificial intelligence: Automated attack technique code generation. *Computers & Security, 147*, Article 104077. https://doi.org/10.1016/j.cose.2024.104077
Jerit, J., & Zhao, Y. (2020). Political misinformation. *Annual Review of Political Science, 23*(1), 77–94. https://doi.org/10.1146/annurev-polisci-050718-032814
Jones, N. (2023). How to stop AI deepfakes from sinking society — and science. *Nature (London), 621*(7980), 676–679. https://doi.org/10.1038/d41586-023-02990-y
King, T. C., Aggarwal, N., Taddeo, M., & Floridi, L. (2019). Artificial intelligence crime: An interdisciplinary analysis of foreseeable threats and solutions. *Science and Engineering Ethics, 26*, 89–120.
Kreps, S., McCain, R. M., & Brundage, M. (2022). All the news that's fit to fabricate: AI-generated text as a tool of media disinformation. *Journal of Experimental Political Science, 9*(1), 104–117.
Lamo, M., & Calo, R. (2018). Regulating bot speech. *UCLA Law Review*, 1–37.
Langa, J. (2021). Deepfakes, real consequences: Crafting legislation to combat threats posed by deepfakes. *Boston University Law Review, 101*(2), 761–801.
Lewandowsky, S., Ecker, U. K. H., Seifert, C. M., Schwarz, N., & Cook, J. (2012). Misinformation and its correction: Continued influence and successful debiasing. *Psychological Science in the Public Interest, 13*(3), 106–131. https://doi.org/10.1177/1529100612451018
Linvill, D. L., & Warren, P. L. (2020). Troll factories: Manufacturing specialized disinformation on Twitter. *Political Communication, 37*(4), 447–467.
Logan, M., Ligon, G., & Derrick, D. (2019). Measuring tactical innovation in terrorist attacks. *Journal of Creative Behavior, 54*(4), 926–939.
Lowrey, E. (2025). *New Orleans terror attack suspect used 'explosive compound' never used in US, Europe attacks before, NBC reports*. https://www.wdsu.com/article/new-orleans-terror-attack-new-explosive-compound/63333833.

Lubrano, M. (2023). Navigating terrorist innovation: A proposal for a conceptual framework on how terrorists innovate. *Terrorism and Political Violence*, *35*(2), 248–263.

Madani, D. (2025). New Orleans attacker filmed visits to city weeks earlier, wore Meta smart glasses during attack. *NBC News*. https://www.nbcnews.com/news/us-news/new-orleans-attacker-meta-glasses-prior-visits-rcna186293

Mendes, K., & Furlano, M. (2026). Digital spaces, algorithms of oppression, and the path forward. In V. M. Esses, J. F. Dovidio, J. Jetten, D. Sekaquaptewa, & K. West (Eds.), *The Sage handbook of psychological perspectives on diversity, equity, and inclusion* (pp. 531–547). Sage.

Momeni, M. (2024). Artificial intelligence and political deepfakes: Shaping citizen perceptions through misinformation. *Journal of Creative Communications*, 1–16.

Nelu, C. (2024). *Exploitation of generative AI by terrorist groups*. https://icct.nl/publication/exploitation-generative-ai-terrorist-groups

Newman, E. J., Garry, M., Unkelbach, C., Bernstein, D. M., Lindsay, D., & Nash, R. A. (2015). Truthiness and falsiness of trivia claims depend on judgmental contexts. *Journal of Experimental Psychology*, *41*(5), 1337–1348.

Noble, S. U. (2018). *Algorithms of oppression: How search engines reinforce racism*. New York University Press.

Norman, A. (2021). *Mental immunity: Infectious ideas, mind-parasites, and the search for a better way to think*. Harper Wave.

Paul, C., & Matthews, M. (2016). The Russian "Firehose of Falsehood" propaganda model: Why it might work and options to counter it. In *Policy File*. RAND Corporation.

Radu, R. (2020). Fighting the 'infodemic': Legal responses to COVID-19 disinformation. *Social Media + Society*, 1–4.

Safieddine, F. (2020). History of fake news. In Y. Ibrahim & F. Safieddine (Eds.), *Fake news in an era of social media: Tracking viral contagion* (pp. 1–27). Rowman & Littlefield.

Shin, D., Koerber, A., & Lim, J. S. (2024). Impact of misinformation from generative AI on user information processing: How people understand misinformation from generative AI. *New Media + Society*, 1–31.

Sim, S., Hartunian, E., & Milas, P. (Eds.). (2024). *Emerging technologies and terrorism: An American perspective*. US Army War College Press. https://press.armywarcollege.edu/monographs/967

Soufan Center. (2024). *Terrorist groups looking to AI to enhance propaganda and recruitment efforts*. https://thesoufancenter.org/intelbrief-2024-october-3/

Stewart, H., Cichocki, E., & McLeod, C. (2022). A perfect storm for epistemic injustice: Algorithmic targeting and sorting on social media. *Feminist Philosophy Quarterly*, *8*(3/4), 1–28.

Sumpter, D. (2018). *Outnumbered: From Facebook and Google to fake news and filter-bubbles—the algorithms that control our lives*. Bloomsbury Sigma.

Sundar, S. S., Molina, M. D., & Cho, E. (2021). Seeing is believing: Is video modality more powerful in spreading fake news via online messaging apps? *Journal of Computer-Mediated Communication*, *26*(6), 301–319. https://doi.org/10.1093/jcmc/zmab010

Tacheva, Z. (2022). Taking a critical look at the critical turn in data science: From "data feminism" to transnational feminist data science. *Big Data & Society*, *9*(2), 1–5.

Tsfati, Y., Boomgaarden, H. G., Strömbäck, J., Vliegenthart, R., Damstra, A., & Lindgren, E. (2020). Causes and consequences of mainstream media dissemination of fake news: Literature review and synthesis. *Annals of the International Communication Association*, *44*(2), 157–173.

Tversky, A., & Kahneman, D. (1974). Judgment under uncertainty. *Science*, 185(4157), 1124–1131.
Vaccari, C., & Chadwick, A. (2020). Deepfakes and disinformation: Exploring the impact of synthetic political video on deception, uncertainty, and trust in news. *Social Media & Society*, *6*(1), 1–13.
Vallejos, E. P., Dowthwaite, L., Creswich, H., Portillo, V., Koene, A., Jirotka, M., & McAuley, D. (2021). The impact of algorithmic decision-making processes on young people's well-being. *Health Informatics Journal*, *27*(1), 1–21.
van Dis, E. A. M., Bollen, J., Zuidema, W., van Rooij, R., & Bockting, C. L. (2023) ChatGPT: Five priorities for research. *Nature*, *614*(7947), 224–226.
Weikmann, T., & Lecheler, S. (2023). Visual disinformation in a digital age: A literature synthesis and research agenda. *New Media & Society*, *25*(12), 3696–3713.
Westerlund, M. (2019). The emergence of deepfake technology: A review. *Technology Innovation Management Review*, *9*(11), 39–52. https://doi.org/10.22215/timreview/1282
World Health Organization. (2020). *Munich security conference*. https://www.who.int/director-general/speeches/detail/munich-security-conference

8

CYBERCRIME AND CYBERSECURITY

Naomi Davis-Crane and Simon Davis-Crane

Introduction

Digital technology shapes the lives of a significant portion of the world's population. As technology advances, this effect will expand in tandem, resulting in gargantuan quantities of data being continually produced and yielding detailed insight into patterns of living on multiple levels. Insights which may be exploited for criminal gain. Therefore, as digital capability and capacity grow, so too do the range and complexity of potential cybercrime offences.

Cybercrime constitutes the deliberate use of digital technology to trespass upon, obtain, manipulate or sabotage information held within computing systems. Incorporating the commission of offences through digital means and attacks on information technology capabilities. Cybercrime presents a significant threat to states and their institutions (Baranovska et al., 2024), including law enforcement. This chapter explores a range of threats posed by cybercrime, including key investigative considerations and analysis of the ways in which law enforcement may increase cyber resilience when facing capable, motivated digital threat actors.

The Threat and Risk of Cybercrime

Global e-retail sales reached USD $4.4 trillion in 2023 (Forrester, 2024), whilst approximately 68% of the global population used the internet in 2024 (International Telecommunications Union, 2025). Cybercrime criminality is increasingly being provided as a service by experts in cybercriminal operations, including provision of ransomware, phishing and systems exploitation via a business model founded upon prospering online markets in which cybercriminals openly trade data, malware and services (Canadian Centre for Cybersecurity, 2025).

DOI: 10.4324/9781003671312-8

Various factors enable cybercrime as a service to thrive. For example, global interconnectivity allows perpetrators to be located remotely from a victim and their whereabouts masked by virtual private networking, lowering the perceived risk to the offender. Likewise, the online world offers significant opportunities for anonymity, including the use of deep fake technology and artificial intelligence (AI) in establishing alias identities. Whilst also offering offenders opportunities to access a significantly wider pool of potential victims with lower barriers to entry than in the physical world, where effort and expense would be incurred in travelling to engage with a prospective victim. Cybercrime is therefore arguably more efficient than real-world offending, particularly where automation is deployed to enable continuous acquisition of funds at scale with limited requirement for action by the offender beyond the initial setup. Finally, cybercrime as a service thrives due to the limited impact of disruption activity. Though site takedowns may briefly interrupt operations, capabilities are frequently quickly resumed under new identifiers and in alternative locations, placing an emphasis therefore on the real-world detection and prosecution of offenders.

Cybercrime as a service takes many forms, including a range of different forms of cyberattack, of which ransomware is particularly prevalent.

Cyberattacks

Ransomware may enter a victim's systems by multiple routes and cause different forms of disruption, but it is uniquely characterized by a demand for payment in return for a cessation of the assault. Small and medium-sized organizations are increasingly targeted for ransomware attacks due to the perceived likelihood of their having less capable cyber defences (Awan & Alam, 2025). Victim selection is further influenced by the capability of the initial access broker (IAB), a specialist in network penetration who provides a point of entry for exploitation to other cyber criminals. Alongside a cost-benefit analysis of the effort necessary to access the victim's systems versus the likelihood and size of any payout, with limited security, they are therefore particularly attractive (Europol, 2024).

Ransomware as a service describes a business model in which ransomware developers write software which is then sold to perpetrators, thereby eliminating the requirement for the latter to gain the necessary developer skills (Alwashali et al., 2021). Historically, ransomware operators extorted ransom payments from organizations through the use of encryption to deny their access to the resources necessary to run their business. However, as organizations increasingly back up their data and refuse to accede to demands, ransomware groups have shifted to threatening to publish the victim organization's data, which has the potential to inflict substantial reputational damage upon the business. In turn, perpetrators resort to publicly denouncing targeted organizations, post countdowns as to the time of data release and engage with clients of the targeted company whose data is at risk of publication (Pearson, 2024).

Law enforcement impact is mediated by the dissolution and regeneration of ransomware groups, increasing the challenges of disruption. Meanwhile, source code leaks have likely contributed to the development of new variants by providing threat actors with the knowledge to develop their own malware, particularly due to their concurrence with the significant expansion in the use of AI for code writing (Europol, 2024). Consequently, ransomware as a service is likely to remain a profitable business model into the 2030s.

Attack types similar to ransomware include phishing, by which perpetrators use social engineering to lead victims into providing sufficient sensitive information to enable exploitation, or to enable the installation of malware into a system (Zieni et al., 2023). Phishing remains a common attack method in the perpetration of online fraud (Europol, 2024), and when provided as a service, enables organized crime groups to conduct significant fraud with limited technical expertise, thereby presenting a potentially consistent and resilient funding stream.

Alternatively, advanced persistent threat (APT) attacks target specific entities with a view to obtaining non-public information. APT attacks are by the covert infiltration and exploitation of a system, and the exfiltration of its contents, whilst the system owner remains unaware, often until a threat to release the information online and an associated ransom is received (Sharma et al., 2023). Finally, distributed denial of service attacks involves the targeting of one or more services within the victim's network in order to disrupt normal operations, often accompanied by data exfiltration and a ransom demand (Bergamini de Neira et al., 2023).

Cybercrime as a service thus encompasses a breadth of offending models with the common qualities of data compromise and financial extortion, as enabled by a range of human and systems factors.

Cybercrime Enablers

Cybercriminals use multiple tactics and tools to access and exploit victims' systems, trade data and services, and acquire knowledge and connections to further their criminal enterprise. For example, cybercriminals often use segmentation of the process to facilitate anonymity and reduce the detection risk (Sarkar & Shukla, 2023). Further, open-source information is commonly used in preparing cyberattacks, including in identifying the prospective victim and strategy development (Zhang et al., 2022). The victim's data may be acquired through their unwitting engagement with the attacker, through the latter's digital surveillance, or both. This culminates in the criminal having sufficient information to develop a strategy targeted at vulnerabilities in the victim's defences and enabling the insertion of malware via these routes with the objective of either covertly exfiltrating information and/or instigating a denial of service (Hutchins et al., 2010).

In line with routine activity theory (RAT), inadequate defences enable cybercriminality, including insufficient digital protection and potential victim laxity in protecting their personal data. When coupled with the wide availability of suitable targets and motivated offenders, the other dimensions of RAT, the rationale for complexity, impact and prevalence of cybercrime, become apparent. Albeit at deeper levels of analysis, there are challenges with applying RAT to cyber-criminality (Leukfeldt & Yar, 2016).

Cryptocurrencies are commonly used in cybercrime networks, and most frequently appear in investment fraud investigations. Their use is driven by the increased value of specific cryptocurrencies and media attention as to the potential dividends associated with crypto investment. Money laundering via cryptocurrency is enabled through networks operating on end-to-end encrypted messaging services (Europol, 2024) and the absence of many of the protective controls designed to prevent money laundering, which exist within mainstream financial services (Dote-Pardo & Espinosa-Jaramillo, 2025). This absence of protective control additionally demonstrates the potential application of RAT to a cybercrime context.

The Dark Web similarly features regularly in cybercrime cases with forums used to promote illicit markets, share modus operandi and advertise services including malevolent large language models with capabilities such as the generation of phishing emails. These forums are often of limited lifespan to evade law enforcement agency attention. Individual behaviour in such forums has been interpreted via Matza's (1990) drift theory, highlighting the ease with which individuals may drift between criminal and non-criminal activities in a liminal context where adherence to legal expectations is diaphanous (Goldsmith & Brewer, 2015). However, more generally, identifying risk factors for individual engagement in cybercrime is problematic.

Cybercrime Offenders

Establishing cyber offender typologies is challenged by the typically anonymous nature of the crime and low detection rates (Curtis & Oxburgh, 2022). The cyber offender community comprises networks and lone actors spanning a broad range of capabilities, and continues to grow due to the increased opportunity and accessibility of cybercriminal knowledge, though wider societal influences also play a role. For example, Dearden et al. (2021) identify greater propensity toward cyber-offending amongst those most and least influenced by institutional anomie, incorporating material success associated with an achievement focus, individualism, universalism and the prioritization of monetary gain. This involves a focus on financial accumulation being demonstrated in the degree to which individuals with specialist skills in network penetration and software development are a key asset to organized crime groups conducting cyber operations (Europol, 2024). Moreover, the anonymity afforded by online crime may reduce behavioural inhibitions to re-offending by enabling the offender to separate their criminal identity from themselves (Slonje & Smith, 2008), further lowering the barrier to engagement in cyber offending.

Victims

From a victim perspective, human users are typically the most vulnerable element within a digital system and, therefore, are frequently targeted as an entry point by cyber-attackers via deception, manipulation of decisions or exploitation of behaviours, such as reusing passwords. The consequences for a victim may be considerable, including financial losses and emotional strain. However, as with offenders, challenges exist in defining typologies for victims of cybercrime, with extant research indicating that whilst younger adults are at a greater risk of cybercrime, those aged over 75 years are at a higher risk of repeat victimization and experience greater financial losses. Further, men are more likely to be victimized, potentially due to a greater propensity for engagement in risky activities (Havers et al., 2024). However, other work conflicts with respect to the age ranges of the most common victim groups, but overall demonstrates a similar bias toward older persons, potentially attributable to lower levels of awareness and familiarity with virtual environments.

Cybervictimization may be exacerbated by the online disinhibition effect, whereby individuals disclose greater levels of personal information in virtual settings compared to real-world engagement (Suler, 2004), enhancing the risk of exploitation (Nurse, 2019). Other risk factors include low self-esteem (Mobin et al., 2017), low emotional regulation (Hemphill & Heerde, 2014) and high submissiveness (Alseadoon et al., 2012). The extent of these influences will be contingent upon the nature of the cyber-criminality and subject to change as the cybercrime landscape evolves.

Looking Forward

The cyber threat landscape is growing in size and complexity, including the continued expansion of the threat actor community, which is in turn continually developing novel attack methods, collaborating and sharing insights (Canadian Centre for Cybersecurity, 2025). The criminal market for cybercrime services remains buoyant (Europol, 2024) and resilient to law enforcement disruption, at least in part due to its global distribution, whilst the lucrative returns catalyze its continued development and expansion (Canadian Centre for Cybersecurity, 2025).

Looking to the future, cyber threat actors will attempt to further increase productivity using AI to enhance the efficiency of the attack process. Generative AI presents opportunities for the development of increasingly sophisticated social engineering operations, in addition to enhancing the quality of phishing communications and removing previously telltale indications commonly relied upon as warning signs (Canadian Centre for Cybersecurity, 2025). Elsewhere, unethical large language models have been developed, and AI is already being used to generate more effective malware, including by organized crime groups, to reduce their reliance on technical experts. AI thereby lowers the entry barrier to cyber-criminality (Europol, 2024). Consequently, the challenge of detecting and disrupting cybercrime continues to grow, both in terms of size and complexity.

The Challenge of Policing Cybercrime

Law enforcement is increasingly establishing specialist cybercrime units in recognition of the associated complexities. Yet successful cybercrime prosecutions are minuscule compared to the volume of reported offences, which itself only represents a limited proportion of the actual offences committed, demonstrating the unique challenges cybercrime presents for law enforcement spanning technological, knowledge and cultural domains, to which this chapter will now turn.

For example, officers may perceive cybercrime as distinct compared to traditional criminality, which limits their perceived ability to translate existing investigative skills to a cybercrime context (Burruss et al., 2019). Alternatively there may be cases of cultural rejection of cybercrime investigation as 'real' police work (Holt et al., 2015, 2019) or limited awareness of cybercrime as a serious dimension of criminality (De Paoli et al., 2021), alongside underreporting (Button & Cross, 2017) and jurisdictional complexity (Boes & Leukfeldt, 2016) all acting to impede the effectiveness of police cybercrime investigation.

To take a specific example, at the outset, the investigation of cybercrime typically requires recognition by a victim who reports the offence to law enforcement, presenting a twofold challenge as a victim may not be aware that an offence has taken place due to the covert nature of some forms of cyber-criminality. Further, the victim must have sufficient confidence in law enforcement to respond to the crime such that it outweighs any reservations about reporting, particularly where the victimization may be associated with shame or embarrassment, such as in cases of sextortion (Ray & Henry, 2024). Yet even once an offence has been reported, other major challenges in investigating cybercrime are those of volume versus resources, establishing jurisdiction, and maintaining legislative adequacy.

Volume and Resourcing

Cybercrime presents investigators with multiple issues of volume. Firstly, potentially automated offending across a global network may result in a large number of offences for investigation (Yar & Steinmetz, 2019), whilst the associated volume of data to be reviewed and analyzed within a single case may be overwhelming (Dodge et al., 2019), further slowing the investigation (albeit AI offers significant potential in this field; Balusamy et al., 2025). The expansion of cloud computing has further added complexity, simultaneously providing users with greater storage, data sharing and processing capabilities which may be used to facilitate criminality, in addition to increasing vulnerabilities by expanding the number of devices which may be affected in an attack (Wall, 2017).

From an organizational perspective, financial constraints and performance cultures threaten cybercrime investigations, which may be complex, resource-intensive and lengthy, creating a risk of investigators prioritizing less complex cases. Moreover, the wide range of data service providers potentially implicated in a cybercrime investigation adds further complexity via the need to gain evidence from multiple sources, likely requiring multiple different requests and resulting in the receipt of a range of different data formats to be synthesized and analyzed, making the establishment of a clear picture of the offence particularly challenging. Consequently, the volume and resource complexities associated with cybercrime investigation necessitate multi-agency collaboration, including partnerships with the private sector, academia and security services to enable the cross-proliferation of knowledge and skills, whilst simultaneously establishing an environment in which to cultivate innovation in cybercrime investigation.

Jurisdiction

Cybercrime's global footprint creates challenges for territorial police forces operating within national criminal legal frameworks (Steinmetz et al., 2023). Consequently, states have sought to extend their criminal jurisdictions to encompass cyber-criminality committed abroad, where there is connectivity of varying degrees to the prosecuting state. For example, Section 4 of the UK Computer Misuse Act 1990 provides that liability for the requisite offences requires proof of a significant link to England or Wales, which may include the presence of the offender, victim or a server associated with the offence in either nation. Similar jurisdictional provisions are contained within the Council of Europe Convention on Cybercrime (the Budapest Convention) and the United Nations Convention Against Cybercrime, and are arguably necessary given the supranational nature of cybercrime, allowing for the flexibility to prosecute offenders irrespective of the perpetrator's location. However, arguments against expansive jurisdictional frameworks include their incompatibility with principles of justice and state sovereignty, potentially extensive resource requirements and the challenges of achieving justice in such cases (Arnell & Faturoti, 2022).

Consequently, international consistency and collaboration in combating cybercrime are key to long-term impact, yet legal frameworks relating to cybercrime vary substantially between jurisdictions (Wicki-Birchler, 2020). Some jurisdictions have established specific cybercrime offences, contrasting with others preferring to apply existing law to the novel circumstances of digital criminality, to limited effect. Thus, cybercrime is at least in part enabled by the existence of lacunae in national and international law, though efforts at harmonization continue.

The Budapest Convention is an international concord to address the challenges posed by digital offending via a cooperative and consistent approach, including in offence definitions, procedures, pathways for international collaboration and capability building initiatives. Originally a Council of Europe initiative, the Convention was opened to ratification by European Union and non-member states. However, even wider engagement and collaboration will be required to fully address the challenge of cybercrime (Buçaj & Idrizaj, 2024), as recognized by the UN in the adoption of the Convention Against Cybercrime by the General Assembly in December 2024.

The Convention opened for signature in October 2025, aiming to unify signatory states in tackling cybercrime via enhanced international cooperation, capability building and technical support. The Convention obliges states to claim jurisdiction for crimes committed within their territories, but enables them to also do so where offences committed from overseas have an impact on their nationals, target the State itself or are committed by their own citizens. Whilst the effectiveness of the Convention remains to be seen, concerns exist as to the broad scope of some of its powers (Bartoli, 2025). Further, the Budapest Convention has been criticized for falling behind technological change and inconsistent implementation by signatory states, creating further legal voids which may be exploited by cyber criminals (Buçaj & Idrizaj, 2024). The absence of enforcement provisions in the UN Convention may render this new treaty vulnerable to the same fate (Hoffman et al., 2022).

Legislation

The rapid evolution of technology and consequential new cyber threats creates particular challenges for legislators, given the frequently protracted processes of establishing and updating criminal frameworks. Further, technological innovation also yields new forms of data which may be used in prosecution or defence cases, thereby necessitating parallel regular updates and amendments to codes of practice relating to trial and evidence procedures. In short, cybercrime has the potential to place additional strain upon an already stretched criminal justice system.

Soft law presents opportunities for addressing international cybercrime via guidelines, codes of conduct and voluntary standards as a more responsive and flexible tool than formal legal provisions, which typically require extensive negotiation and ratification (Buçaj & Idrizaj, 2024). However, soft law inherently lacks deterrent impact and therefore may not be as effective as criminalization in preventing offences. Yet the prevalence of cybercrime versus detection rates in nations with robust criminal frameworks may suggest that 'hard law' has limited deterrent impact. Consequently, soft law may be more effective in establishing principles and standards for business and industry in respect of cybersecurity measures. Further, responsibility for cybercrime prevention is arguably more oriented toward the private sector than the state when compared to real-world offending due to their respective levels of power and control. Private sector digital service companies have a substantial opportunity to address vulnerabilities across jurisdictions in ways beyond the reach of territorial policing. Arguably, it places a considerable responsibility upon them to work with law enforcement in detecting and prosecuting offenders.

Irrespective of sector responsibility, preventative strategies in cybercrime must contend with a privacy paradox (Gerber et al., 2018) – the gap between self-reported concern relating to cybercrime and the limited extent to which it manifests in preventative behaviours. It potentially arises from overconfidence in system security features (Reyns, 2015; Reyns et al., 2016), which may manifest at an individual and organizational level, requiring a considered analysis of the risks posed to an organization's digital and information assets. Law enforcement is no exception to this requirement, and the final section of this chapter will therefore explore the means by which policing may avoid falling prey to the cyber threats they seek to disrupt.

Securing Policing Against Cyberthreats

From a policing perspective, where front-line operations take priority, it is vital that organizational resilience is given the appropriate consideration to ensure continuity of service when an unplanned event occurs. Most policing organizations apply basic business continuity via backup control rooms, for example. But these alone only cater to the immediate need to communicate and operate basic digital services, such as radio links, telephone lines and core computer systems; wider services are rarely considered in the same paradigm, presenting a potentially significant vulnerability.

For example, how would a policing organization operate if its finance systems or personnel records were taken offline by a ransomware group, even for a few days, or if sensitive intelligence was leaked from its crime recording system and posted on the internet? Immediate plans may involve resorting to manual processing until services can be recovered, but these temporary fixes can only last so long, and short-term resolutions are rarely suitable in the medium to longer term. Further, even once the technological issue is addressed, the organization will inevitably need to address longer-term issues, including reputational damage, data breach investigations, loss of staff confidence and the risk of repeat victimization via an undetected system vulnerability known to the threat actor.

Whilst these primary considerations present a daunting picture for police leaders, there are mitigations for most scenarios. With the appropriate support, resourcing and commitment, organizational resilience is achievable. Whilst the technical aspects of resilience are often relatively simple to achieve, the most important element to prioritize is organizational culture, which influences cyber threat prevention and response capabilities (Sutton & Tompson, 2025). The following sections detail the key cyber vulnerabilities within policing organizations today, measures to defend against a cyber incident and strategies for managing should an event occur, all of which require a transparent and a just cyber culture.

Vulnerabilities

Key vulnerabilities affecting organizations using IT can be broken down into human, organizational and systems factors. For example, authentication attacks where threat actors attempt to impersonate legitimate organizational users are increasingly common and can be ruthlessly effective (Breda et al., 2017). The main hardware vulnerabilities to consider are related to power or data service loss, and physical building security. For example, power sources in many countries are reliable, but in times of disaster, that may not always be the case. Consequently, organizations should consider how they will operate in the scenario that grid power sources are not available for the short term. Likewise, data link loss should be prioritized appropriately. As reliance on cloud computing increases, so too does the need for fully resilient, diverse internet connections, including using different data bearers to mitigate the failure of one supplier. In respect of systems, whilst cloud computing can be seen as a resilient option to replace older IT systems, it is not infallible. Ransomware can still encrypt data stored in the cloud; users can still inadvertently share cloud-hosted data with the wrong people. Mitigations for both scenarios are therefore required.

Defence Mechanisms

Numerous defence mechanisms can help mitigate these vulnerabilities. Technical mitigations are particularly effective as they generally do not require significant user interaction, thus mitigating against human failure (Kenlie et al., 2024). Further, limiting user account access, especially administrator or privileged accounts, is vital in protecting from lateral movement attacks. Zero trust networking is of benefit here, but it must be noted that this can be expensive and difficult to implement (Adahman et al., 2022), so it is not a simple, short-term option. Limiting users' capabilities, including restricting who and what they can send email to, or what they can access online, can be implemented more easily and will improve an organization's security (National Cyber Security Centre, n.d).

Multifactor authentication (MFA) is the most useful and effective technical defence that can be implemented to prevent breaches of an organization's systems. Though there are vulnerabilities in MFA systems, these weaknesses are known and can be mitigated (Mukherjee, 2023). From a human perspective, user training is arguably one of the best defence mechanisms available today, which can mitigate many cyber vulnerabilities and does not necessarily require substantial investment or resource commitment (Trim & Upton, 2013), provided that the training offered is specific to the context and situated within a cyber secure culture.

Culture

The cyber culture of an organization encompasses the policies, processes, norms and values of the workforce in relation to digital security and serves as a prominent element of its cybersecurity armoury (Georgiadou et al., 2022). As with other elements of the organizational culture, leadership has a powerful influence upon the wider cyber culture through the decisions, actions and communications of key individuals (Aniebonam et al., 2025). If the leaders of an organization take no interest in resilience or cybersecurity, this is likely to become the tone of the wider organization.

Consequently, the following advice is presented to police leaders seeking to enhance the cybersecurity posture of their organizations for the long term:

- Promote compliance with security policy through role modelling behaviours, removal of barriers, raising awareness and transparently addressing breaches.
- Establish clear policies with simple, accessible and resource supporting infrastructure.
- Engage with subject matter experts to understand risk ahead of making decisions.
- Prioritize cyber risk at an appropriate level compared to other risks impacting upon force operations.
- Establish, communicate and rehearse plans for a range of cyber events, including total and protracted loss of all force systems.

A clear, just and active cyber-aware and cyber-secure culture will make it easier for an organization to respond to any cyber incident. Staff will know how to respond, and operational downtime can be expected to be minimized when compared to an organization that ignores its resilience and cyber risks. For policing leaders, the default approach to cybersecurity and wider organizational resilience must necessarily shift from considering the likelihood of an incident (if) to how the organization will respond to its occurrence (when). Recognizing and accepting these key points will set leaders in good stead for the future. Ensuring the resilience of an organization does not have to be difficult, nor expensive, but it must have the full support of the leadership team as key proponents of the wider cyber secure culture.

Conclusion

Cybercrime presents considerable challenges to law enforcement, spanning the need to investigate offences, protect the public and defend policing systems from capable threat actors. A ransomware attack and release of sensitive policing operational or personnel information has the potential to result in considerable real-world risk, including the potential for loss of life. Consequently, the necessity of adequate legal, procedural and digital defences in law enforcement organizations going forward cannot be understated; neither can the ability to identify and adapt quickly to new and emerging threats.

As this and other chapters in this book have shown, policing organizations require significant increases in capability to deliver policing functions for the future. The existing capability gap may increase as the pace of technological evolution outstrips the ability of policing to keep up. Whilst the employment of cybersecurity experts will help reduce this effect to some extent, the stark fact remains that a substantial proportion of attacks in organizations enter by human error at the worker level.

So, whilst the world of cybercrime is complex and complicated, there are comparatively simple steps police executives can take to mitigate risk to their own organizations. This can involve: modelling a cyber secure culture in actions, behaviours, communications and decisions; prioritizing protection of information as a key asset; and developing, rehearsing and communicating a critical incident plan predicated on the loss of all force systems. In essence, giving cyber equal prominence compared to other areas of threat and risk to force operations.

References

Adahman, Z., Malik, A. W., & Anwar, Z. (2022). An analysis of zero-trust architecture and its cost-effectiveness for organizational security, *Computers & Security*, *122*, 102911, https://doi.org/10.1016/j.cose.2022.102911.

Alseadoon, I. M., Chan, T., Foo, E., & Nieto, J. M. G. (2012). Who is more susceptible to phishing emails? A Saudi Arabian study. In *ACIS 2012: Proceedings of the 23rd Australasian conference on information systems*, (1–11).

Alwashali, A. A. M. A, Rahman, N. A. A., & Ismail, N. A (2021) Survey of ransomware as a service (RaaS) and methods to mitigate the attack. In *2021 14th International Conference on Developments in eSystems Engineering (DeSE)*, 92–96. Sharjah, United Arab Emirates. doi: 10.1109/DeSE54285.2021.9719456

Aniebonam, E. E., Chukwuba, K., Toromade, A. S., & Ekpobiet, H. (2025). Transformational leadership and cyber-security innovation: How visionary leaders drive technological progress and security. *International Journal of Multidisciplinary Research and Growth Evaluation*, *6*(1). 1729–1742. https://doi.org/10.54660/.IJMRGE.2025.6.1-1729-1742

Arnell, P., & Faturoti, B. (2022). The prosecution of cybercrime – why transnational and extraterritorial jurisdiction should be resisted. *International Review of Law, Computers and Technology*, *37*(1), 29–51. https://doi.org/10.1080/13600869.2022.2061888

Awan, M., & Alam, A. (2025). Cybersecurity threats and defensive strategies for small and medium firms: A systematic mapping study. *Administrative Sciences*, *15*(12), 481. https://doi.org/10.3390/admsci15120481

Balusamy, S., Rengasamy, R., & Aravind, J. (2025) Cybercrime investigations in the era of artificial intelligence: Automated evidence collection and analysis through the use of machine learning, *2025 Global Conference in Emerging Technology (GINOTECH)*, India, (1–6), doi: 10.1109/GINOTECH63460.2025.11076712

Baranovska, T., Savitskyi, V., Serbov, M., Stoliar, Y., & Krutik, Y. (2024). The impact of cybercrime on state and institutional security: Analysis of threats and potential protection measures. *Economic Affairs*, *69*(Special Issue), 33–42. https://doi.org/10.46852/0424-2513.1.2024.5

Bartoli, L. (2025). Cybersecurity and the fight against cybercrime: Partners or competitors? *European Journal of Risk Regulation*, *16*(2), 498–513. https://doi.org/10.1017/err.2025.31

Bergamini de Neira, A., Kantarci, B., & Nogueira, M. (2023). Distributed denial of service attack prediction: Challenges, open issues and opportunities, *Computer Networks*, 109553, https://doi.org/10.1016/j.comnet.2022.109553.

Boes, S., & Leukfeldt, E.R. (2016). Fighting cybercrime: A joint effort. In R. M. Clark & S. Hakim (Eds.), *Cyber-physical security* (pp. 185–203). Springer.

Breda, F., Barbosa, H., & Morais, T. (2017). Social engineering and cyber security. In *INTED2017 Proceedings* (4204–4211).

Buçaj, E., & Idrizaj, K. (2024). The need for cybercrime regulation on a global scale by the international law and cyber convention. *Multidisciplinary Reviews*, *8*(1), 2025024. https://doi.org/10.31893/multirev.2025024

Burruss, G., Howell, C. J., Bossler, A., & Holt, T. J. (2019). Self-perceptions of English and Welsh constables and sergeants' preparedness for online crime: A latent class analysis. *Policing: An International Journal*, *43*(1), 105–119. https://doi.org/10.1108/PIJPSM-08-2019-0142

Button, M., & Cross, C. (2017). *Cyber frauds, scams and their victims*. Routledge.

Canadian Centre for Cybersecurity. (2025). *Canadian National Cyber Threat Assessment 2025–2026*. Communications Security Establishment Canada.

Computer Misuse Act 1990 c.18. https://www.legislation.gov.uk/ukpga/1990/18/contents

Curtis, J., & Oxburgh, G. (2022). Understanding cybercrime in 'real world' policing and law enforcement. *The Police Journal*, *96*(4), 573–592. https://doi.org/10.1177/0032258X221107584

De Paoli, S., Johnstone, J., Coull, N., Ferguson, I., Sinclair, G., Tomkins, P., Brown, M., & Martin, R. (2021) A qualitative exploratory study of the knowledge, forensic, and legal challenges from the perspective of police cybercrime specialists, *Policing: A Journal of Policy and Practice*, *15*(2), 1429–1445. https://doi.org/10.1093/police/paaa027

Dearden, T. E., Parti, K., & Hawdon, J. (2021). Institutional anomie theory and cybercrime—Cybercrime and the American dream, now available online. *Journal of Contemporary Criminal Justice*, *37*(3), 311–332. https://doi.org/10.1177/10439862211001590

Dodge, A., Spencer, D., Ricciardelli, R., & Ballucci, D. (2019). "This isn't your father's police force": Digital evidence in sexual assault investigations. *Journal of Criminology*, *52*(4), 499–515. https://doi.org/10.1177/0004865819851544

Dote-Pardo, J., & Espinosa-Jaramillo, M. T. (2025). Money laundering risks of cryptocurrencies: Towards coordinated regulatory and technological strategies, *Latin American Journal of Central Banking*, 100194. https://doi.org/10.1016/j.latcb.2025.100194.

Europol. (2024). *Internet Organised Crime Assessment 2024*. Publications Office of the European Union.

Forrester. (2024). *Global online retail sales to grow 8.9% annually, reaching $6.8 trillion in 2028*. https://www.forrester.com/press-newsroom/forrester-global-online-retail-sales-to-grow-8-9-annually-reaching-6-8-trillion-in-2028

Georgiadou, A., Mouzakitis, S., Bounas, K., & Askounis, D. (2022). A cyber-security culture framework for assessing organization readiness. *Journal of Computer Information Systems*, *62*(3), 452–462. https://doi.org/10.1080/08874417.2020.1845583

Goldsmith, A., & Brewer, R. (2015). Digital drift and the criminal interaction order. *Theoretical Criminology*, *19*(1), 112–130. https://doi.org/10.1177/1362480614538645

Gerber, N., Gerber, P., & Volkamer, M. (2018). Explaining the privacy paradox: A systematic review of literature investigating privacy attitude and behavior. *Computers and Security*, *77*, 226–261. https://doi.org/10.1016/j.cose.2018.04.002

Havers, B., Tripathi, K., Burton, A., McManus, S. & Cooper, C. (2024). Cybercrime victimisation among older adults: A probability sample survey in England and Wales. *PloS one*, *19*(12), e0314380. https://doi.org/10.1371/journal.pone.0314380

Hemphill, S. A., & Heerde, J. A. (2014). Adolescent predictors of young adult cyberbullying perpetration and victimization among Australian youth. *Journal of Adolescent Health*, *55*(4), 580–587. https://doi.org/10.1016/j.jadohealth.2014.04.014

Hoffman, S. J., Baral, P., Rogers Van Katwyk, S., Sritharan, L., Hughsam, M., Randhawa, H., Lin, G., Campbell, S., Campus, B., Dantas, M., Foroughian, N., Groux, G., Gunn, E., Guyatt, G., Habibi, R., Karabit, M., Karir, A., Kruja, K., Lavis, J. N., Lee, O., Li, B., Nagi, R., Naicker, K., Røttingen, J., Sahar, N., Srivastava, A., Tejpar, A., Tran, M., Zhang, Y., Zhou, Q., & Poirier, M. J. P. (2022). International treaties have mostly failed to produce their intended effects. *Proceedings of the National Academy of Sciences of the United States of America*, *119*(32), e2122854119. https://doi.org/10.1073/pnas.2122854119

Holt, T. J., Burruss, G. W., & Bossler, A. M. (2015). *Policing cybercrime and cyberterror*. Carolina Academic Press.

Holt, T. J., Lee, J. R., Liggett, R., Holt, K. M., & Bossler, A. (2019). Examining perceptions of online harassment among constables in England and Wales. *International Journal of Cybersecurity Intelligence and Cybercrime*, *2*(1), 24–39. https://doi.org/10.52306/02010319LFQZ1592

Hutchins, E. M., Cloppert, M. J., & Amin, R. M. (2010) Intelligence-driven computer network defense informed by analysis of adversary campaigns and intrusion kill-chains. *Proceedings of the 6th International Conference on Information Warfare and Security*, Washington, DC (113–125).

International Telecommunications Union. (2025). *Statistics*. https://www.itu.int/en/ITU-D/Statistics/Pages/stat/default.aspx

Kenlie, E. A., Hendris, C. N., Nadia, N., & Adeta, F. (2024). The impact of human error in cybersecurity breaches: Understanding behavioral patterns and mitigation strategies. *2024 International Conference on Informatics, Multimedia, Cyber and Information System (ICIMCIS)* (1045–1050). https://doi.org/10.1109/ICIMCIS63449.2024.10956680

Leukfeldt, E. R., & Yar, M. (2016). Applying routine activity theory to cybercrime: A theoretical and empirical analysis. *Deviant Behavior*, *37*(3), 263–280. https://doi.org/10.1080/01639625.2015.1012409

Matza, D. (1990). *Delinquency and drift*. Routledge.

Mobin, A., Feng, C. X., & Neudorf, C. (2017). Cybervictimization among preadolescents in a community-based sample in Canada: Prevalence and predictors. *Canadian Journal Of Public Health*, *108*(5), e475–e481. https://doi.org/10.17269/CJPH.108.5878

Mukherjee, A. (2023). *Is MFA as secure as it used to be?*. Threat Intelligence. https://www.threatintelligence.com/blog/mfa

National Cyber Security Centre. (n.d.). *Identity and access management*. https://www.ncsc.gov.uk/collection/10-steps/identity-and-access-management

Nurse, J. R. (2019). Cybercrime and you: How criminals attack and the human factors that they seek to exploit. In A. Attrill-Smith, C. Fullwood, M. Keep, & D. Kuss (Eds.), *The Oxford handbook of cyberpsychology* (pp. 663–690). Oxford University Press. https://doi.org/10.1093/oxfordhb%2F9780198812746.013.35

Pearson, J. (2024). *Ransomware is more brutal than ever*. Wired. https://www.wired.com/story/state-of-ransomware-2024/

Ray, A., & Henry, N. (2024). Sextortion: A scoping review. *Trauma, Violence, & Abuse*, *26*(1), 138–155. https://doi.org/10.1177/15248380241277271

Reyns, B. W. (2015). A routine activity perspective on online victimisation: Results from the Canadian General Social Survey. *Journal of Financial Crime*, *22*(4), 396–411. DOI:10.1108/JFC-06-2014-0030

Reyns, B. W., Randa, R., & Henson, B. (2016). Preventing crime online: Identifying determinants of online preventive behaviours using structural equation modelling and canonical correlation analysis. *Crime Prevention and Community Safety*, *18*(1), 38–59. DOI:10.1057/cpcs.2015.21

Sarkar, G., & Shukla, S. K. (2023). Behavioral analysis of cybercrime: Paving the way for effective policing strategies. *Journal of Economic Criminology*, *2*, 100034. https://doi.org/10.1016/j.jeconc.2023.100034

Sharma, A., Gupta, B. B., Singh, A. K., & Saraswat, V. K. (2023). Advanced Persistent Threats (APT): Evolution, anatomy, attribution and countermeasures. *Journal of Ambient Intelligence and Humanized Computing*, *14*, 9355–9381. https://doi.org/10.1007/s12652-023-04603-y

Slonje, R., & Smith, P. K. (2008). Cyberbullying: Another main type of bullying. *Scandinavian Journal of Psychology*, *49*(2), 147–154. DOI: 10.1111/j.1467-9450.2007.00611.x

Steinmetz, K. F., Schaefer, B. P., Brewer, C. G., & Kurtz, D. L. (2023). The role of computer technologies in structuring evidence gathering in cybercrime investigations: A qualitative analysis. *Criminal Justice Review*, *50*(1), 67–84. https://doi.org/10.1177/07340168231161091

Suler, J. (2004). The online disinhibition effect. *CyberPsychology & Behavior*, *7*(3), 321–326. https://doi.org/10.1089/1094931041291295

Sutton, A., & Tompson, L. (2025). Towards a cybersecurity culture-behaviour framework: A rapid evidence review. *Computers and Security*, *148*, 104110. https://doi.org/10.1016/j.cose.2024.104110

Trim, P., & Upton, D. (2013). *Cyber security culture: Counteracting cyber threats through organizational learning and training*. Routledge. https://doi.org/10.4324/9781315575681

Wall, D. S. (2017). Towards a conceptualisation of cloud (cyber) crime. In *International Conference on Human Aspects of Information Security, Privacy, and Trust* (pp. 529–538). Springer.

Wicki-Birchler, D. (2020). The Budapest Convention and the General Data Protection Regulation: Acting in concert to curb cybercrime? *International Cybersecurity Law Review*, *1*(1–2), 63–72. https://doi.org/10.1365/s43439-020-00012-5

Yar, M., & Steinmetz, K. F. (2019). *Cybercrime and society* (3rd ed.). Sage.

Zhang, Y., Frank, R., Warkentin, N., & Zakimi, N. (2022). Accessible from the open web: a qualitative analysis of the available open-source information involving cyber security and critical infrastructure, *Journal of Cybersecurity*, *8*(1), https://doi.org/10.1093/cybsec/tyac003

Zieni, R., Massari, L., & Calzarossa, M. C. (2023). Phishing or not phishing? A survey on the detection of phishing websites, *IEEE Access*, *11*, 18499–18519. doi:10.1109/ACCESS.2023.3247135

9

THE FUTURE OF POLICE PERFORMANCE EVALUATION

Bridging Neuroscience and Policing Through EEG

Nasser AlSabah and Abdulwahab Alasfour

Introduction

Technological advancements have had a profound impact on performance across numerous fields. This is no different in policing, with recent prominent technological advancements including body-worn cameras (Lum et al., 2020), real-time crime mapping (Chainey & Ratcliffe, 2013), and statistical crime forecasting techniques (Shah et al., 2021). These innovations, and many more, have played critical roles in transforming how law enforcement agencies gather intelligence, assess threats, and establish transparency, marking a shift toward policing methods that prioritize data-driven practices. Similar advancements have been made in police training, with recent research and developments in the use of immersive virtual reality (Zechner et al., 2023) and simulators (Muñoz et al., 2020) to prepare law enforcement members for the unpredictability and dangers of their role. Supplementing these methods has been the use of psychological and physiological instruments, most commonly electrocardiogram (ECG)[1], as a means toward predicting the likelihood of success for situational performance efficacy under the influence of stress (see Andersen et al., 2024); something that has proven to be the most used physiological metric in such research (Baldwin et al., 2019; Di Nota et al., 2023). Although validated in policing studies, heart rate variability (HRV) has been shown to have limitations, particularly when compared to other more advanced methods, such as electroencephalography (EEG) (AlSabah et al., 2025, Alasfour & AlSabah, 2025).

A means through which researchers can collect and analyze the neural dynamics of individuals, EEG provides a significantly more nuanced approach toward understanding the psychophysiological underpinnings associated with

DOI: 10.4324/9781003671312-9

individuals. However, EEG, unlike ECG, is complex and costly, requiring experts skilled in both the equipment and the software needed to navigate this data-collection method. This chapter aims to highlight the current state of performance evaluation, potential of EEG as a novel tool for assessing and enhancing situational performance in law enforcement. It then details the handful of existing studies that have employed EEG methods in policing literature, providing commentary on potential directions stemming from this research. In doing so, it positions EEG not merely as a replacement for HRV, but as a potentially actionable, transformative technology capable of revealing the cognitive and affective processes that underpin officer performance under pressure. By critically engaging with current findings and technological possibilities, the chapter concludes with discussions of the future directions neurophysiological tools can take in evidence-based police training and evaluation systems, their limitations, and potential frameworks that can serve as instructional entry points to their use. However, before detailing the potential of EEG, we must first elaborate on the current state of performance evaluation and why developing EEG as a potential replacement is warranted.

The Performance Evaluation Problem in Policing

Police agencies invest heavily in training, yet a persistent gap remains between officers' performance in controlled settings and real-world situations (AlSabah & Wolff, 2025; Di Nota & Huhta, 2019). This transfer problem is most noticeable with firearms—shooting accuracy decreases significantly under stress, even among officers who pass high-level qualifications (Oudejans, 2008; Nieuwenhuys & Oudejans, 2010, 2011)—but it also impacts arrest and self-defense skills (Renden et al., 2014). These findings have led to calls for stress training and more realistic learning approaches (Kleygrewe et al., 2022; Nieuwenhuys & Oudejans, 2011), yet they also highlight a deeper measurement issue: if agencies can't assess officers' performance under stress, not just passing a qualification, then training and evaluation cannot be effectively improved.

Current approaches to measuring performance under stress each have recognized limitations. Behavioural metrics and simulation scoring capture what an officer decided, but not the processes underlying that decision—and objective shoot/no-shoot accuracy and subjective instructor-rated situational awareness follow different longitudinal trajectories, suggesting they tap different performance dimensions (Suss & Ward, 2018; Huhta et al., 2023; Saus et al., 2006; Di Nota et al., 2021). Expert ratings remain limited to externally observable behaviour (Kleygrewe et al., 2022), and self-report measures are subject to social desirability bias and cultural reluctance to acknowledge stress.

Physiological stress measures, mainly HRV, represent the most sophisticated current approach. Ambulatory monitoring has confirmed substantial cardiovascular reactivity during field encounters (Baldwin et al., 2019; Di Nota et al., 2023), and HRV-biofeedback protocols, such as the International Performance, Resilience, and Efficiency Program (iPREP), have improved use-of-force decision-making (Andersen et al., 2024). However, HRV indexes peripheral autonomic regulation, not central cognition. It is confounded by exertion, respiration, and fitness (Kim et al., 2018; Laborde et al., 2017), and cannot differentiate productive engagement from maladaptive anxiety (Quintana & Heathers, 2014). Baldwin et al. (2022) illustrate this directly: elevated heart rate predicted lethal-force errors but could not explain why some officers erred while others, at comparable arousal, did not.

These methods collectively leave a critical blind spot between stimulus and response—the attentional engagement, threat appraisal, and inhibitory control that determine decision quality in critical moments. It is this gap that EEG is possibly positioned to address.

Neurophysiological Foundations of EEG

Basic Principles of EEG

Understanding how the brain generates and regulates electrical activity is key to interpreting the mental processes that underlie police behaviour, decision-making, and performance under stress. EEG provides a direct, real-time means of observing these processes, making it an invaluable tool in modern policing research. EEG is a non-invasive method for recording electrical activity in the brain by placing electrodes across the scalp. The electrodes pick up electrical activity from millions of neurons (the basic cell unit of the brain); however, they record the aggregate activity of these neurons. Rather than recording individual voices, EEG electrodes behave like a microphone, picking up the roar of a stadium. Typically, electrodes are placed around the scalp according to a specific protocol, such as the 10–20 system.[2] The cerebral cortex, the outermost layer of the brain, is the main region where EEG electrodes record electrical activity, encompassing all higher-level functions, such as decision-making, attention, memory, thought, and language. Therefore, this modality can be particularly insightful for analyzing police personnel's thought processes across a multitude of scenarios. For example, one can determine whether there are differences in brain activity related to decision-making during a shoot or no-shoot scenario, or in memory recall during a critical incident that could be integral to determining a legal outcome.

EEG systems capture brain activity millisecond by millisecond, making it a fast enough modality to track real-time neural processes produced by police personnel, whether during training or in the field. One can think of EEG as a high-speed camera for brain activity; the more frames per second you can record, the more detail you can capture. Since EEG can capture brain activity with high fidelity, one can uncover rich detail in the signal itself. For policing purposes, these three main categories are of the most interest:

1 **Oscillatory (rhythmic) activity:** Neurons within the brain can be synchronized in their activity, producing different rhythms. Rhythmic activity can be categorized by frequency. With respect to EEG recordings, this could be summarized into four main canonical frequency bands and their associated cognitive correlates:

Band Name	*Frequency*	*Neurological Correlates*	*Possible Police Research Applications*
Delta	1–4 Hz	Deep sleep, unconscious processes.	Recovery sleep after a night shift.
Theta	5–8 Hz	Drowsiness, emotional engagement, and working memory.	Emotional engagement during intense negotiations or high-stress encounters.
Alpha	9–12 Hz	Calm focus and reduced sensory input.	Calm, focused states prior to engaging in a critical task.
Beta	13–30 Hz	Working memory and decision-making.	Decision-making during a threat encounter.

2 **Background activity:** This refers to the non-rhythmic part of the EEG signal. It can be thought of as the brain's background baseline hum, the overall level of activity that is always present even when no clear rhythms are visible. This baseline hum can inform researchers about cognitive state and neural balance.

3 **Event Related Potentials (ERPs):** ERPs are the brain's responses to specific events such as a visual cue or a decision prompt, which occur in the order of 100s of milliseconds after stimulus onset. An example of a prominent ERP is the P300 (P stands for positive, and 300 ms post-stimulus onset). The P300 could be seen in the oddball paradigm.[3]

In a potential EEG experimental paradigm, participants would be engaged with a stimulus or task (e.g. shoot/no-shoot situation), during which brain activity is recorded. Data is subsequently analyzed to extract meaningful correlations, potentially determining which type of brain activity correlates with increased likelihoods of success.

While EEG provides excellent temporal resolution and is relatively easy to deploy, it has limited ability to pinpoint the exact source of brain activity because electrical signals are blurred as they pass through the scalp and skull. Combining EEG with other measures, such as heart rate, eye-tracking, or behavioural data, can provide a more comprehensive understanding of cognitive and emotional states. Figure 9.1 illustrates the elements discussed earlier.

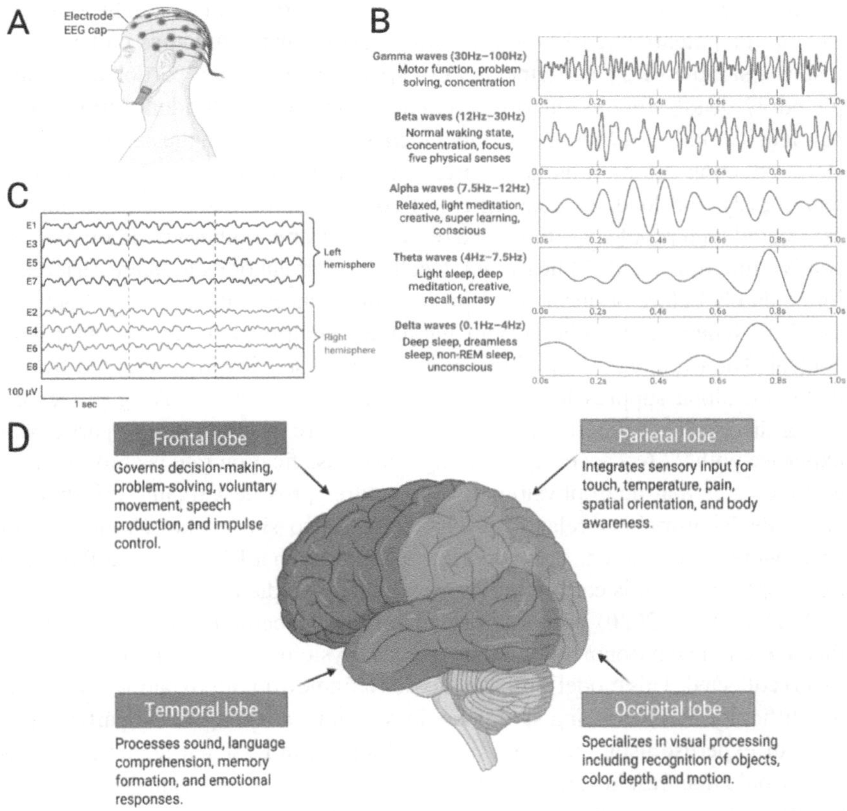

FIGURE 9.1 Overview of Electroencephalography (EEG) Brain Activity and Cortical Regions

EEG Applications in Policing Literature

As noted in this chapter's introduction, there is a significant scarcity of studies that use EEG in policing, particularly in conjunction with situational performance research.[4] As of the writing of this chapter, only five research sources investigating policing have published evidence of EEG use in situational performance under stress. Collectively, these studies represent critical advancements in merging neurophysiological monitoring with realistic policing simulations, offering novel frameworks for understanding and improving decision-making under stress. The upcoming sections will elaborate on their approaches, results, and limitations, providing insights into a potential future where this method of psychological analysis may become the standard.

The first empirical study to integrate EEG into policing research was conducted by Johnson and colleagues in 2014. Aiming to answer whether psychophysiological metrics can quantitatively distinguish expert from novice performance during situational performance simulations, they sought to elaborate on the potential of EEG in predicting performance outcomes under stress. Using a sample of 24 participants (12 experts, 12 novices), participants completed 27 deadly force scenarios (e.g. encounters with individuals armed with handguns or knives). Metrics used included: (1) engagement, the neurocognitive state reflecting information gathering, visual comprehension, and sustained attention; (2) workload, a measurement of cognitive efforts and mental demands associated with problem-solving and reasoning efforts—otherwise known as executive functions; and (3) heart rate deceleration, reductions in heart variability immediately before or during decision-making, conceptualized as psychophysiological dynamics associated with increased attentional focus and inhibitory control. Their findings showed that EEG patterns, specifically increased frontal theta and alpha suppression, distinguished expert decision-making processes. Using discriminant function analysis, the data were used to classify participant expertise with 72.6% accuracy. Although this classification rate is above chance and indicates that neurophysiological signatures provide valuable information about decision-making related to expertise, it also shows that about 25% of cases were misclassified. This serves as a reminder that EEG-based differentiation, especially at this early stage, is more indicative than conclusive.

Muñoz et al. (2020) proposed and tested a biocybernetics adaptation model that altered the environment based on psychophysiological measurements (EEG/ECG) collected. This model aimed to provide a framework for dynamically adjusting difficulty in VR training simulators in real time, adapting to the participant's level of expertise using neurophysiological and cardiovascular signals. Adaptations would manifest in various forms, including target speed, quantity, movement patterns, and others. In their efforts to provide such a model, a necessary collection and analysis were conducted as participants (n = 10) engaged in the simulation.

Their findings indicated that physiological signals effectively distinguished performance-related mental states during virtual firearms training, particularly in the frontal lobe, with both EEG and ECG reliably differentiating cognitive load and stress levels across different difficulty levels. However, it is important to recognize that these differences were correlational, derived from non-parametric group comparisons. The study did not provide classification accuracy, predictive model performance, or tests against held-out data. The biocybernetic adaptation model was presented as a theoretical framework and was not validated in a closed-loop experiment either.[5] As a result, although the findings are insightful, the operational adaptation system remains a proof of concept that needs empirical validation before any claims about its effectiveness can be made. This system offered the first promising basis for adaptive VR training tools that, if validated, could enhance learning by adjusting the level of challenge, but also illustrated how far researchers are from establishing a closed-loop system that can adjust itself to neurophysiological measures.

Alexander et al. (2024) examined oscillatory neural correlates of decision-making among experts and novices using VR—combining elements of both studies described earlier. Using a shoot/no-shoot task co-designed with firearms instructors, 27 authorized firearms officers (AFOs) and 27 age- and sex-matched novices completed virtual simulations with graded threat levels (handgun, knife, drinks can) across two phases: threat assessment/preparation (Phase 1) and shoot/no-shoot response (Phase 2). Experts responded significantly faster at both the preparation phase ($p = .023$, $d = .61$) and the shoot decision under attack ($p = .001$, $d = 1.06$). Source-localized EEG revealed that experts exhibited significantly greater frontal midline theta power in the dorsal anterior cingulate cortex (dACC) during threat assessment for both threat ($p = .006$) and no-threat ($p = .005$) conditions. However, these between-group theta differences were not significant during the shoot/no-shoot phase itself (surrender, $p = .065$; attack, $p = .126$), suggesting expertise primarily shaped preparatory assessment rather than the final action. Experts also showed significant theta differentiation between graded force levels (Taser vs. Glock, $p = .018$), a distinction absent in novices, and shorter post-response beta rebounds across multiple conditions (Phase 1 no-threat, $p = .015$; threat, $p = .006$; Phase 2 attack, $p = .003$), reflecting faster recovery and readiness for subsequent action.

AlSabah et al. (2025) examined EEG and ECG measures using video simulations at Kuwait's National Police Academy with the largest sample among EEG policing studies to date (n = 58). Cadets from three cohorts participated in a simulation featuring seven decision points, each scored during a post-simulation interview across three performance metrics: decision-making, reasoning, and memory recall. Preliminary analyses revealed significant negative correlations between frontal beta-band activation and all three metrics, indicating that higher performance was associated with lower frontal beta power, consistent with neural efficiency accounts where better performers require less cognitive load. Hierarchical linear models confirmed frontal beta as a significant predictor of decision-making ($\beta = -3.02$, $p < .01$, adj. $R^2 = .13$) and memory recall ($\beta = -8.03$, $p < .01$, adj. $R^2 = .17$), even after accounting for other brain regions and HRV. Posterior regions added no predictive value beyond what frontal electrodes captured, a finding with practical implications for deploying low-cost, frontal-only EEG systems in applied settings. ECG-based HRV demonstrated limited predictive power across all models, emphasizing EEG's advantage over standard cardiovascular measures, though incorporating HRV did strengthen the reasoning model's overall significance, suggesting it may complement rather than replace neurophysiological variables.

Building on AlSabah et al.'s (2025) experiment, Alasfour and AlSabah (2025) shifted the analysis from situational performance to perceived stress as the main outcome variable. Their analysis moved from correlational modeling to cross-validated prediction. The study showed that perceived stress can be predicted using EEG activity in police cadets during a naturalistic decision-making task. Using a nested five-fold cross-validation with ridge regression, repeated across 20 random splits, they found that a combined model, using post-stimulus delta-band EEG features and cohort membership, predicted perceived stress scores with an out-of-fold R^2 of .32. This outperformed models using only EEG features ($R^2 = .23$) or only cohort data ($R^2 = .17$). Although this combined model explains about one-third of the variance in self-reported stress, which is significant for an early ecological study, it leaves two-thirds unexplained. Furthermore, no decision threshold or classification scheme was tested, and the R^2 indicates predictive accuracy in cross-validation, not diagnostic utility at the individual level. These findings demonstrate that EEG dynamics during stressful decision-making carry information about subjective stress beyond training duration alone, laying the foundation for neurofeedback training methods to help officers manage stress responses and improve decision-making under pressure.

These five studies represent the entirety of empirical work integrating EEG into policing research—a body of literature built on approximately 119 unique participants. Despite this limited base, the studies share several commonalities. Finally, expertise—whether operationalized as years of service, training duration, or cohort membership—consistently shaped both neural patterns and performance outcomes, with better performers exhibiting more efficient cortical processing rather than greater activation. Their findings lay the groundwork for future research to refine and expand neuroadaptive systems for law enforcement training, with longer-term objectives of providing a proven framework to effectively refine officer decision-making and stress responses through more robust methods of analysis and prediction. Based on the studies mentioned earlier, an informed discussion can be held about the future of EEG use in police training, drawing on the findings and limitations outlined in the literature. However, a discussion regarding the limitations is warranted first.

Notable Limitations in EEG Literature in Policing

However, it is worth noting that these studies have also encountered notable limitations when using EEG. Some of these are unique to the methodologies used, while others apply to all (summarized in Table 9.1). Generally speaking, the sample sizes are often low, with most using bivariate pairwise comparisons to establish significant relationships between neurophysiological metrics and situational performance, rather than more robust multivariate modeling. Small samples increase the risk of overfitting, in which models focus on specific dataset details rather than general patterns. This issue is exacerbated by limited demographic and institutional diversity across studies, which often rely on single sites with predominantly male participants, thereby reducing external validity.

TABLE 9.1 Summary of Research Investigating EEG and Situational Performance in Policing

	Johnson et al. (2014)	*Muñoz et al. (2020)*	*Alexander et al. (2024)*	*AlSabah et al. (2025) and Alasfour & AlSabah (2025)*
Design Limitations	Pass/fail scoring of the shooting scenarios presented in the experiment may not capture the quality of the decision process. The officer can make the right call for the wrong reasons, and vice versa.	Exposure time for each training scenario is relatively short (three minutes for easy, medium, and hard difficulties), which limits the data's reliability. In addition, by the time the officers engage in the "hard" training scenario, they could have adapted to the training environment, which is a confound that is not fully addressed.	Officers were engaged in a shoot/no-shoot scenario while watching a highly repetitive computer-generated stimulus. This does not reflect the complexity and randomness that can occur in real-life scenarios.	Participants in the study watched a naturalistic video of stressful real-life scenarios related to police work in the field. Stress and performance metrics were obtained in a post-experiment survey. This limits the interpretability of the results since these measurements were not obtained in real time.
Measurement Limitations	An eight-channel EEG was used to record neural activity. An EEG system with low electrode count will not record brain activity from regions that could show indicators of decision-making performance.	A consumer-grade four-channel EEG was used. This limits the number of brain sites that are recorded.	No ECG activity or other physiological measures were recorded, which limited the ability to show if other physiological measures can provide information beyond the EEG.	A 32-electrode cap using dry (gel-free) sensors was used. Dry sensors are easier and faster to fit, which matters when testing 20 cadets a day, but they pick up slightly more outside interference than the wet-gel sensors, considered the research gold standard.

(*Continued*)

TABLE 9.1 (Continued)

	Johnson et al. (2014)	*Muñoz et al. (2020)*	*Alexander et al. (2024)*	*AlSabah et al. (2025) and Alasfour & AlSabah (2025)*	
Modeling Limitations	The model that was developed to distinguish between novices and experts relied on n = 12 samples per class. There is a real risk of overfitting for particular quirks for each set of individuals. In addition, the authors further segmented the data into three groups to distinguish "intermediate" expertise, thereby increasing the risk of overfitting.	The researchers proposed a system for using brain and heart data to automatically adjust training difficulty in real time. However, the results obtained in this study were never implemented in a closed-loop paradigm where there is feedback from the neurophysiological signals to the game difficulty.	Statistical analysis was focused on finding patterns in the data. However, they do not demonstrate that these patterns can be used for training or evaluation. This is usually done using cross-validation for classification or regression.	Brain activity was averaged across large regions of the scalp rather than examined electrode by electrode. This gives a broad picture but can miss finer spatial patterns. The statistical models explained only a modest share of what drives performance, suggesting many other factors are at play.	The stress-prediction model accounts for roughly one-third of what makes cadets report different stress levels—a meaningful result for an early study, but it also means two-thirds of the variation remains unexplained. The findings should be seen as a promising starting point rather than a ready-to-use assessment tool.
External Validity Limitations	The expert group included both active-duty military infantry personnel and active-duty police officers, both of whom have very different training histories. This confound can limit the impact this study has on applying the insights to active police officers. The overall sample size (n = 24) is also too low to make generalizability conclusions.	Only ten officers took part, and the group ranged from fresh academy recruits to experienced veterans. This wide range of experience, combined with the small number of participants and a single US department, means the findings are very preliminary.	Expert and novice groups were predominantly male (26 out of 27 participants in each group). This raises limitations regarding whether these findings generalize to a female cohort.	This exclusively used cadets, rather than officers. All 58 participants were male cadets at a single police academy in Kuwait. Women, serving officers, and cadets in other countries are not represented, so it is not yet known whether the same patterns would appear in more diverse groups.	

Note: Studies by Alasfour and AlSabah are from the same experiment, but different modeling and analyses were used.

It should also be noted that two studies (AlSabah et al., 2025; Alasfour & Al-Sabah, 2025) involved police cadets in training settings, while the descriptions for Johnson et al. (2014) and Muñoz et al. (2020) do not clearly state whether participants were sworn officers, cadets, or civilians. Only Alexander et al. (2024) clearly used sworn, active officers. This difference matters because cadets and sworn officers vary in selection background, exposure to real violence, organizational socialization, legal authority, and decision-making stakes—all of which can affect neurophysiological responses under stress. Findings from cadets are useful for understanding training cognition, but cannot be generalized to active-duty police without replication involving sworn officers in realistic field conditions. This is essential for the applied recommendations in this chapter, as neural signatures from academy settings may not reflect those in the more unpredictable, high-stakes environment of active duty.

Furthermore, as discussed in the introduction to this chapter, using this technology requires advanced, specialized expertise. This extends to both data collection and the analysis needed to extract the necessary information for use. Hence, using this technology with surface-level knowledge is unfeasible, whereas simpler means of physiological data collection, such as ECG measures, are not. Additionally, situational performance and officers' performance under stress depend heavily on various factors, including their physical responses to potential threats (Huhta et al., 2023). These physical aspects are challenging to work with in EEG due to its high sensitivity to movement, requiring minimal movement to collect neural data accurately—something that significantly inhibits immersion during simulations, a critical component of situational performance training (Kleygrewe et al., 2024).

Future Directions and Potential

Extensive studies discussed in this chapter have shown that the spectral, spatial, and temporal components of EEG are correlated with stress, decision-making, and performance. However, across all studies reviewed in this chapter, none have applied their results in a closed-loop real-time training or assessment paradigm. The commonality across all five sources is that frontal EEG activity is correlated with and predictive of metrics related to police performance. It is not surprising, however, that these experiments have arrived at different conclusions regarding which specific physiological metrics are most relevant, given that they differ considerably in experimental design, sample, and task demands. EEG analysis in policing is in a nascent stage, and it is therefore expected that a universal biomarker indexing officer state across contexts has not yet emerged.

There is a clear avenue to apply previous knowledge to improve both the training and evaluation of police officers. From a practical standpoint, neurofeedback systems can be developed to enhance cognitive performance and reduce stress, as previous studies have shown (Brito et al., 2022; Enriquez-Geppert et al., 2017; Hafeez et al., 2021; Trambaiolli et al., 2022; Vernon et al., 2003).[6] Just as athletes use smart watches to monitor and regulate their heart rate during exercise, police officers could potentially be trained to modulate their brain activity during stressful decision-making. However, unlike heart rate, which is a single, well-understood signal, the brain offers multiple candidate biomarkers: theta, beta, alpha oscillations, and event-related potentials, among others. The studies reviewed here each focused on different frequency bands, different brain regions, and different task formats, making it unclear which specific combination of stimulus, task, and biomarker would be most effective for training. Changing the task may change which neural signal matters most. Before any neurofeedback system can be implemented in police training, extensive testing is needed to establish that a specific pairing of task and biomarker reliably improves performance—a foundation the current literature has not yet provided. Based on these ideas, the following are actionable ideas that could enhance police readiness:

1. **Training and Simulation Enhancement:** EEG-driven VR simulations are probably the most immediate use among those discussed, building directly on proof-of-concept work by Muñoz et al. (2020). Officers could wear lightweight frontal EEG headsets during virtual reality shoot/no-shoot or crowd control exercises, receiving real-time feedback on stress indicators to adjust the difficulty level. For example, if alpha activity surpasses a certain point, the challenge could be reduced. Additional stressful scenarios, like kidnappings or hostage situations, could also be incorporated. Through repeated practice, officers might learn to control their arousal under pressure, potentially enhancing their performance in the field. However, this approach still depends on identifying the right combination of neural biomarker and stimulus that consistently correlates with training outcomes—something current research has not yet confirmed. Moreover, no study has demonstrated that adaptive EEG feedback can lead to lasting performance gains in policing, rather than just temporary neural adjustments during a single session.
2. **Personnel and Deployment Decisions:** Over the long term, portable EEG systems could inform two related personnel functions: pre-deployment readiness assessments and role assignment. For readiness, if consistent links between specific neural patterns (e.g. elevated beta activity) and impaired decision-making are established at empirically defined thresholds, this could help guide supervisory decisions about work assignments. For role placement, neural response profiles during simulated critical incidents could theoretically help identify officers best suited for high-crisis positions such as SWAT teams—particularly given that AlSabah et al. (2025) found

physiological factors to be strongly linked to performance even after controlling for training, suggesting that extended training alone does not necessarily improve handling of critical incidents. With proper validation, EEG systems integrated into helmets could also monitor cognitive overload during operations, providing real-time alerts to officers or command centers, while post-deployment review of EEG data alongside bodycam footage could examine how neural stress responses relate to decisions made in the field. However, moving from correlational findings to any of these applications requires validated neural benchmarks, known error rates, calibration across diverse populations, and governance frameworks addressing data ownership, consent, evidence admissibility, and the legal and ethical implications of using neurophysiological data in decisions affecting promotion, discipline, and career progression. Without these foundations, EEG-based personnel decisions—whether situational or structural—remain research hypotheses rather than available practical tools.

The potential applications outlined earlier, from neurofeedback-enhanced simulations to personnel and deployment decisions, share a common dependency: none can be responsibly pursued without addressing fundamental prerequisites that span technology, methodology, and institutional governance. On the technological front, EEG hardware and algorithms must improve signal quality during movement-heavy tasks, where artifacts currently compromise data reliability. Methodologically, the field needs biomarker standardization; as this chapter has shown, different studies arrive at different conclusions about which neural signals matter most, and no consensus exists on which combination of frequency band, brain region, and task paradigm best indexes officer readiness or performance. Integrating EEG with complementary measures—heart rate variability, galvanic skin response, eye tracking—may yield more robust multimodal indicators, but adds layers of analytical complexity that the current evidence base is not equipped to resolve. Most critically, any application that ties neurophysiological data to screening, assignment, or readiness assessments carries direct consequences for officers' careers, due process, and organizational liability. Clear ethical and legal frameworks must precede implementation, not follow it. This means defined data ownership, informed consent protocols, permissible uses, acceptable error thresholds, and governance structures developed collaboratively between policymakers, researchers, and the law enforcement institutions that would adopt these tools. The science reviewed in this chapter offers a genuine reason for cautious optimism—EEG can capture meaningful variation in how officers process stress and make decisions under pressure. But the distance between a significant correlation in a controlled simulation and a validated, fair, and legally defensible operational tool remains considerable. Bridging that distance is the work that lies ahead.

Notes

1 ECG is most commonly used in policing research to establish heart rate measurements during stressful encounters. Heart rate variability (HRV), derived from ECG, is used to assess autonomic nervous system balance, measuring shifts in stress, recovery, and overall physiological resilience during and after high-pressure situations.
2 The International 10–20 system is a standardized method for placing electrodes, where positions are set by measuring 10% and 20% intervals along distances between skull landmarks, ensuring consistent scalp coverage across different participants and studies.
3 In the oddball task, the brain sees one rare "different" item mixed in with many common ones. This unusual "oddball" item makes the brain react more strongly, creating the P300 response.
4 Situational performance in policing contexts refers to officers' abilities at responding to life-threatening scenarios where quick and accurate decision-making is required.
5 A "closed-loop experiment" refers to a design where real-time physiological data (like EEG) is fed back into the system to dynamically adjust the task, training environment, or intervention *as it happens*.
6 A neurofeedback system serves as a real-time training tool that monitors a person's brain activity, typically using EEG, processes the data, and provides feedback—often through visual or auditory signals—enabling individuals to learn to manage their neural patterns either consciously or unconsciously.

References

Alasfour, A., & AlSabah, N. (2025). EEG-based prediction of stress responses to naturalistic decision-making stimuli in police cadets. *Sensors*, *25*(18), 5925. https://doi.org/10.3390/s25185925

Alexander, N. A., Kelly, C. L., Wang, H., Nash, R. A., Beebe, S., Brookes, M. J., & Kessler, K. (2024). Oscillatory neural correlates of police firearms decision-making in virtual reality. *eNeuro*, *11*(7). https://doi.org/10.1523/ENEURO.0112-24.2024

AlSabah, N., AlAsfour, A., Marr, C., & Di Nota, P. M. (2025). Linking psychophysiological markers to situational performance: An EEG study of police cadets during critical incident simulations. *Applied Psychophysiology and Biofeedback*. Advance online publication. https://doi.org/10.1007/s10484-025-09736-8

AlSabah, N., & Wolff, K. T. (2025). Police academies and officer safety: Linking training structures and instruction to post-employment injury outcomes in law enforcement. *Police Quarterly*. Advance online publication. https://doi.org/10.1177/10986111251392814

Andersen, J. P., Arpaia, J., Gustafsberg, H., Poplawski, S., & Di Nota, P. M. (2024). The international performance, resilience and efficiency program protocol for the application of HRV biofeedback in applied law enforcement settings. *Applied Psychophysiology and Biofeedback*, *49*, 483–502. https://doi.org/10.1007/s10484-024-09644-3

Baldwin, S., Bennell, C., Andersen, J. P., Semple, T., & Jenkins, B. (2019). Stress-activity mapping: Physiological responses during general duty police encounters. *Frontiers in Psychology*, *10*. https://doi.org/10.3389/fpsyg.2019.02216

Baldwin, S., Bennell, C., Blaskovits, B., Brown, A., Jenkins, B., Lawrence, C., McGale, H., Semple, T., & Andersen, J. P. (2022). A reasonable officer: Examining the relationships among stress, training, and performance in a highly realistic lethal force scenario. *Frontiers in Psychology*, *12*, 759132. https://doi.org/10.3389/fpsyg.2021.759132

Brito, M. A. de, Fernandes, J. R., Esteves, N. S., Müller, V. T., Alexandria, D. B., Pérez, D. I. V., Slimani, M., Brito, C. J., Bragazzi, N. L., & Miarka, B. (2022). The effect of neurofeedback on the reaction time and cognitive performance of athletes: A systematic review and meta-analysis. *Frontiers in Human Neuroscience, 16*. https://doi.org/10.3389/fnhum.2022.868450

Chainey, S., & Ratcliffe, J. (2013). *GIS and crime mapping*. John Wiley & Sons.

Di Nota, P. M., & Huhta, J.-M. (2019). Complex motor learning and police training: Applied, cognitive, and clinical perspectives. *Frontiers in Psychology, 10*, 1797. https://doi.org/10.3389/fpsyg.2019.01797

Di Nota, P. M., Andersen, J. P., Huhta, J.-M., & Gustafsberg, H. (2021). Evidence-based instruction of police use of force: Practical methods and pedagogical principles. In E. P. Arble & B. B. Arnetz (Eds.), *Interventions, training, and technologies for improved police well-being and performance* (pp. 72–101). IGI Global. https://doi.org/10.4018/978-1-7998-6820-0.ch005

Di Nota, P. M., Huhta, J.-M., Boychuk, E. C., & Andersen, J. P. (2023). Police lethal force errors and stress physiology during video and live evaluation simulations. *Police Practice and Research*. Advance online publication. https://doi.org/10.1080/15614263.2023.2237624

Enriquez-Geppert, S., Huster, R. J., & Herrmann, C. S. (2017). EEG neurofeedback as a tool to modulate cognition and behavior: A review tutorial. *Frontiers in Human Neuroscience, 11*. https://doi.org/10.3389/fnhum.2017.00051

Hafeez, Y., Ali, S. S. A., Hasan, R. A., Adil, S. H., Moinuddin, M., Ebrahim, M., Yusoff, M. S. B., Amin, H., & Al-Saggaf, U. (2021). Development of enhanced stimulus content to improve the treatment efficacy of EEG-based frontal alpha asymmetry neurofeedback for stress mitigation. *IEEE Access, 9*, 130638–130648. https://doi.org/10.1109/ACCESS.2021.3114312

Huhta, J.-M., Di Nota, P. M., Hietanen, T., & Ropo, E. (2023). Deriving expert knowledge of situational awareness in policing: A mixed-methods study. *Journal of Police and Criminal Psychology, 38*(3), 539–554. https://doi.org/10.1007/s11896-023-09574-6

Johnson, R. R., Stone, B. T., Miranda, C. M., Vila, B., James, L., James, S. M., Rubio, R. F., & Berka, C. (2014). Identifying psychophysiological indices of expert vs. novice performance in deadly force judgment and decision making. *Frontiers in Human Neuroscience, 8*. https://doi.org/10.3389/fnhum.2014.00512

Kim, H.-G., Cheon, E.-J., Bai, D.-S., Lee, Y. H., & Koo, B.-H. (2018). Stress and heart rate variability: A meta-analysis and review of the literature. *Psychiatry Investigation, 15*(3), 235–245. https://doi.org/10.30773/pi.2017.08.17

Kleygrewe, L., Oudejans, R. R. D., Koedijk, M., & Hutter, R. I. V. (2022). Police training in practice: Organization and delivery according to European law enforcement agencies. *Frontiers in Psychology, 12*, 798067. https://doi.org/10.3389/fpsyg.2021.798067

Kleygrewe, L., Hutter, R. I. V., Koedijk, M., & Oudejans, R. R. D. (2024). Virtual reality training for police officers: A comparison of training responses in VR and real-life training. *Police Practice and Research, 25*(1), 18–37. https://doi.org/10.1080/15614263.2023.2176307

Laborde, S., Mosley, E., & Thayer, J. F. (2017). Heart rate variability and cardiac vagal tone in psychophysiological research – Recommendations for experiment planning, data analysis, and data reporting. *Frontiers in Psychology, 8*, 213. https://doi.org/10.3389/fpsyg.2017.00213

Lum, C., Koper, C. S., Wilson, D. B., Stoltz, M., Goodier, M., Eggins, E., Higginson, A., & Mazerolle, L. (2020). Body-worn cameras' effects on police officers and citizen behavior: A systematic review. *Campbell Systematic Reviews, 16*(3), e1112. https://doi.org/10.1002/cl2.1112

Muñoz, J. E., Quintero, L., Stephens, C. L., & Pope, A. T. (2020). A psychophysiological model of firearms training in police officers: A virtual reality experiment for biocybernetic adaptation. *Frontiers in Psychology, 11*. https://doi.org/10.3389/fpsyg.2020.00683

Nieuwenhuys, A., & Oudejans, R. R. D. (2010). Effects of anxiety on handgun shooting behavior of police officers: A pilot study. *Anxiety, Stress, & Coping*, *23*(2), 225–233. https://doi.org/10.1080/10615800902977494

Nieuwenhuys, A., & Oudejans, R. R. D. (2011). Training with anxiety: Short- and long-term effects on police officers' shooting behavior under pressure. *Cognitive Processing*, *12*(3), 277–288. https://doi.org/10.1007/s10339-011-0396-x

Oudejans, R. R. D. (2008). Reality-based practice under pressure improves handgun shooting performance of police officers. *Ergonomics*, *51*(3), 261–273. https://doi.org/10.1080/00140130701577435

Quintana, D. S., & Heathers, J. A. J. (2014). Considerations in the assessment of heart rate variability in biobehavioral research. *Frontiers in Psychology*, *5*, 805. https://doi.org/10.3389/fpsyg.2014.00805

Renden, P. G., Landman, A., Geusgens, A., Siu, N. K., Savelsbergh, G. J. P., & Oudejans, R. R. D. (2014). Effects of threat, trait anxiety, and state anxiety on police officers' actions during an arrest. *Legal and Criminological Psychology*, *19*(1), 44–59. https://doi.org/10.1111/j.2044-8333.2012.02063.x

Saus, E.-R., Johnsen, B. H., Eid, J., Riisem, P. K., Andersen, K., & Thayer, J. F. (2006). The effect of brief situational awareness training in a police shooting simulator: An experimental study. *Military Psychology*, *18*(Suppl.), S3–S21. https://doi.org/10.1207/s15327876mp1803s_2

Shah, N., Bhagat, N., & Shah, M. (2021). Crime forecasting: A machine learning and computer vision approach to crime prediction and prevention. *Visual Computing for Industry, Biomedicine, and Art*, *4*(1), 9. https://doi.org/10.1186/s42492-021-00075-z

Suss, J., & Ward, P. (2018). Revealing perceptual-cognitive expertise in law enforcement: An iterative approach using verbal-report, temporal-occlusion, and option-generation methods. *Cognition, Technology & Work*, *20*(4), 585–596. https://doi.org/10.1007/s10111-018-0493-z

Trambaiolli, L. R., Cassani, R., Biazoli, C. E., Cravo, A. M., Sato, J. R., & Falk, T. H. (2022). Multimodal resting-state connectivity predicts affective neurofeedback performance. *Frontiers in Human Neuroscience*, *16*. https://doi.org/10.3389/fnhum.2022.977776

Vernon, D., Egner, T., Cooper, N., Compton, T., Neilands, C., Sheri, A., & Gruzelier, J. (2003). The effect of training distinct neurofeedback protocols on aspects of cognitive performance. *International Journal of Psychophysiology*, *47*(1), 75–85. https://doi.org/10.1016/S0167-8760(02)00091-0

Zechner, O., Kleygrewe, L., Jaspaert, E., Schrom-Feiertag, H., Hutter, R. I. V., & Tscheligi, M. (2023). Enhancing operational police training in high-stress situations with virtual reality: Experiences, tools and guidelines. *Multimodal Technologies and Interaction*, *7*(2), Article 2. https://doi.org/10.3390/mti7020014

10

LAPLACE'S OFFICER

The Future of Predictive Policing

Jordan I. Cline

Introduction

Scholars and practitioners have long sought to understand the causes of crime. Since Beccaria, Lombroso, and Bentham laid the classical foundations of criminological thought, the field has grown substantially more complex (Beccaria, 1765, 2016; Garland & Sparks, 2000; Lombroso, 1876, 2006; Semple, 1993). While these texts remain foundational, the world has shifted rapidly toward technologically mediated governance (Kelly, 2016; *MIT Technology Review*, n.d.). As with policing, it is no secret that police in the 21st century are deeply reliant on technologies that have transformed how they operate: drones (Engberts & Gillissen, 2016), robots (Bendel, 2023), facial recognition (Guo & Kennedy, 2023), and some proprietary technologies like ShotSpotter (Doucette et al., 2021). The pace of change is striking: policing today looks markedly different than it did a decade ago.

Across its many institutional variations, the core mission of policing has remained constant: maintaining public order and reducing crime (Katz & Walker, 2017). Predictive policing has long attracted attention from scholars and practitioners seeking to improve police effectiveness in the field (Goldstein, 1979; Ross, 1980). Goldstein's seminal critique of "means over ends syndrome" identified a persistent tendency for tactical preoccupations to undermine the broader mission (Gaines & Cain, 1981).

The digital age has accelerated this tension considerably. Officers can now coordinate in real time, access complete criminal histories instantly, and deploy geo-coded data in ways unimaginable to earlier generations. Among the most elementary manifestations of this are CompStat and place-based policing strategies ("cops on dots"). Instantaneously now one officer can signal to their entire

DOI: 10.4324/9781003671312-10

department what is happening on their end, they can pull up an individual's entire history in a click of a button. Yet criminal enterprises have adapted in parallel, often possessing comparable technological capabilities. With this change has come the most elementary systems and methodologies for predictive policing purposes in the form of CompStat (Compare Stats) and cops on dots (Bond & Nehmens, 2015; Braga & Schnell, 2017; *Crime stats—COMPStat—NYPD*, n.d.). This dynamic of co-evolving capabilities has defined the technological arms race between police and offenders (Votey & Phillips, 1972).

Against this backdrop, advanced mathematical models now offer the prospect of genuinely proactive crime forecasting. Chief among these is the model developed by Short et al. (2008), which, along with its subsequent iterations, has meaningfully expanded the analytical possibilities for real-time policing. This development carries significant promise but also important caveats. Specifically, the model derived by Short et al. (2008) conceptualizes crime as a dynamic, spatially concentrated process shaped by offender movement, environmental attractiveness, and near-repeat victimization, thereby allowing researchers and police agencies to mathematically forecast the emergence and diffusion of crime hotspots before they fully materialize.

Three barriers impede broader uptake of this work. First, it originates in applied mathematics journals, rendering the content largely inaccessible to criminologists and practitioners. Second, the mathematical models typically cite criminological theory only superficially, lacking the contextual grounding that gives crime data meaning. Third, and most consequentially, there is no sustained synthesis between the two fields. When applied mathematicians attempt to remedy urban crime, they are working on terrain that criminologists have occupied for decades. These disciplines should not remain siloed. The present chapter attempts: (1) a dialectical synthesis and charts a path for integrating them. It also addresses the dilemmas posed by a predictive policing system capable of near-perfect prognosis. The content for academic criminologists, and especially for practitioners, is largely undigestible. There needs to be a wide-scale simplification of the research for appreciation and application to become more common. (2) The ascribed mathematical research lacks a clear criminological basis. While the studies are not entirely uninformed, there is often just a short blurb or justification as to how the research relates to criminology or criminal justice. This brings us to the final point (3) that there is a much-needed synthesis of the two fields. When applied mathematicians are aiming to remedy crime in cities, this practically calls for an upheaval by criminologists who have aimed at the same goal for years. These two fields, however, do not deserve to remain distinct in nature. This chapter shall serve as a dialectical synthesis of the two matters and set the path for approaching the subject in the future. This chapter will also address the dilemmas of a predictive policing system capable of near-perfect prognoses.

Background of Prediction

In 1814, Pierre-Simon Laplace proposed what has come to be known as his "Demon" thought experiment, in his work *A Philosophical Essay on Probabilities* (1902; 1814). The Demon posits that an omnipotent intellect, aware at any moment of the precise position and velocity of every particle in the universe, could predict all future states and recover all past ones. This thought experiment composes the material universe, that being could effectively predict the future and know the past. For if they were fully aware of the precise properties of everything within the universe, then they should know accordingly how the universe will continue to interact with itself. This principle illustrates that absolute precision in measurement is impossible, a theme that underlies many dilemmas in predictive policing.

The chapter's titular figure, "Laplace's Officer," is the criminological derivation of the Demon. The concept captures the aspirational endpoint of predictive policing: a system so informationally complete that it anticipates deviant behavior before it occurs. The sections that follow trace the recent history of predictive policing, the trajectory of its decline, and the conditions under which more capable systems might responsibly emerge. The "Laplace's Officer" is the criminological derivation of the Demon, and its connotation is as such. It stands as the proposition of the future of predictive policing; a future in which, given rapidly evolving technologies of the day, police will be able to estimate, or "predict," deviant behavior with greater accuracy. In the chapter, the recent history of predictive policing methods, the sharp decline in use, and then the expected rise in more capable systems to come will be discussed.

The UCLA Model

Minority Report, the 2002 film set in 2054, depicts a "Precrime" unit that predicts violent crime three days in advance. The film's central tension, a protagonist wrongfully accused of a future murder, illustrates with prescience the core dilemmas of any such system. Whether this is catastrophe or utopia depends entirely on the accuracy of the main character, Anderton, who is wrongfully accused of a crime that he "will" commit. Was this movie an ill manifestation of the future? Or is it a sure destiny of a peaceful society?

In 2008, applied mathematicians at UCLA published a landmark study. Short et al. (2008) put forth *A Statistical Model of Criminal Behavior*. Informed by geo-coded data from Long Beach, California, the model provides a theoretical framework for predicting where crime hotspots form. The simulation operates on a discrete lattice structure, or basically a grid. Amin (2019) provides a useful visualization of this lattice structure. Hotspot attractiveness is modeled as a function of prior victimization: each burglary incrementally increases a location's attractiveness to nearby offenders. This is designed with repeat and near-repeat victimization and broken windows theories in mind. They can generate the movement of criminals by assuming that criminals in the lattice structure will move one unit at a time, from where they were randomly generated, to a hotspot. Formulated as a "random walk," a mathematical expression whereby a variable (the criminal) will take successive steps in random directions independent of the previous step's outcome, the criminals have the chance of landing upon a hotspot depending upon how attractive it is; if it is more attractive, the criminal is drawn more toward it. This follows directly in line with that of near-repeat victimization (Chainey et al., 2018; Haberman et al., 2021; Piza & Carter, 2018; Ratcliffe & Rengert, 2008; Spaulding & Morris, 2022; Youstin et al., 2011) and broken windows theory (Gau & Pratt, 2010; Maskaly & Boggess, 2014; O'Brien et al., 2019; Pandey & Pathak, 2021) equally. These models marked a paradigm shift from induction toward deduction, reframing crime forecasting.

This work attracted rapid scholarly attention. A subsequent publication by Short et al. (2010a) refined the original framework using geo- and temporally coded data from the Long Beach Police Department. Chaturapruek et al. (2013), Jones et al. (2010), Mohler & Short (2012) and Kolokolnikov et al. (2012), among others, all quickly developed increasingly innovative models not only aimed at hotspot detection, but also modelling how burglars might flee from a crime scene (as opposed to Short et al.'s 2008 and 2010 models which simulate a criminal just vanishing from the scene Short et al. (2010b) further explored these effects). In a 2011 article, Mohler and colleagues assert that their latest development is an improvement, if not superior, to traditional crime mapping techniques. Mainly, the developments in question are directed at expanding the repertoire of applicable theory and practice, primarily crime displacement and/or diffusion; the general phenomenon of crime spreading or moving to different locations, dependent on outside influences (Gabor, 1981; Gross & Hakim, 1982; Johnson et al., 2014; Ratcliffe & Breen, 2011; Telep et al., 2014).

Geolitica/PredPol

In 2010, George Mohler and criminologist-anthropologist Jeff Brantingham, both active contributors to this emerging literature (Brantingham & Tita, 2008; Fonoberova et al., 2010; Mohler et al., 2011; Mohler & Short, 2012; Woodworth et al., 2014), founded PredPol, Inc., the first predictive policing firm explicitly grounded in this mathematical research. By 2012, PredPol had, in the words of one account, become a market leader in crime prediction. Intended to bring to operational scale what the founders and their compatriots had been developing, PredPol, by 2012, "...quickly became one of the market leaders in the nascent field of crime prediction..." (Winston & Burrington, 2018, para. 2). Having secured large funding contracts, PredPol was using preconceived knowledge about criminal behavior to predict how crime would play out in the future.

PredPol attracted considerable early attention, and the research field expanded rapidly, including internationally (Cruz-García et al., 2021; Martínez-Farías et al., 2022; Tang et al., 2019). As PredPol scaled through the 2010s, it attracted sustained critical scrutiny. Despite early recognition from popular press, independent examiners prior, independent research by media started to look closer into what PredPol was doing; the results were not pleasing.

Winston and Burrington (2018) documented that despite substantial government funding, data-driven protocols, and accomplished leadership, PredPol was nonetheless headed toward a grim outcome. Residents of the cities where PredPol was being executed, along with experts in the field, warned that PredPol, given its nature of being based on prior crime data, just like that of any procedural generation program, can be subject to bias. As with any research of this kind, dependent on the who, what, when, where, why, and how of the data, trends often do not tell the whole story. As evinced, for example, by the dark figure of crime (Baumer & Lauritsen, 2010), the well-documented problem of underreporting. Measurement error introduced by the dark figure of crime propagates directly into any algorithm trained on police-recorded data. Lum and Isaac (2016) had warned precisely this: even marginal bias in police data propagates into and is amplified by the algorithm's outputs.

Furthermore, in Winston and Burrington's (2018) piece, experts emphasize the complex nature of crime. As a professor of computer science featured in the article stated:

> If I train a model to predict people's height, we know how to interpret the output and gauge its accuracy.' But, [Christo] Wilson noted, 'gang-related' is a complex, subjective determination. 'So the algorithm is accurate at predicting what? Whether LAPD officers would label a crime as gang-related.
>
> (paras 17–18)

Should the preconceived data upon which the algorithm is trained be 100% accurate, then there should be no problem. Of course, that is unlikely to be the case.

In 2021, investigative journalists Sankin and colleagues found on an unsecured server a repository of PredPol's outcomes across the country. Just as Lum and Isaac (2016) had anticipated, PredPol's outputs showed systematic racial disparities. Between 2018 and 2021, the system generated nearly 6 million crime forecasts, the majority directed at minority neighborhoods, a pattern consistent across all jurisdictions in the data. Beyond documenting disparity, these outcomes are more than concerning, in the face of the most modern developments in artificial intelligence (AI), prejudiced outcomes are not uncommon. With the massive growth of AI usage, explicitly large language models (LLMs) such as ChatGPT, researchers have continued to uncover such effects as those in PredPol. LLMs have been found on multiple accounts to consistently produce bigoted content dependent upon the training data and user input (Blodgett & Talat, 2024; Hofmann et al., 2024). The PredPol context is in some respects more troubling than LLM bias: a system explicitly designed to inform enforcement decisions operating at scale on minority communities carries consequences far more direct than biased text generation. One must also consider how substantially AI capabilities have advanced since PredPol's early 2010s deployment. In retrospect, PredPol exemplified premature deployment: a technically plausible idea pushed to operational scale before its epistemic foundations had been examined (Kuhn, 1962). PredPol was not conceived to produce racially disparate outcomes; its core concept retains merit. But the conditions for responsible deployment did not yet exist.

Independent evaluations found forecast accuracy often below 1%, with significant and consistent bias toward minority neighborhoods. A rebrand to "Geolitica" did not stem criticism. Critics of the technology continued to pinpoint its failures, still citing racially biased and overall disparate outcomes (Ballantyne, 2023; Bhuiyan, 2021; Browne et al., 2023; Degeling & Berendt, 2018; Purves, 2023; Sankin et al., 2021; Thomas, 2024). Some researchers, such as Lally (2022), argue that predictive policing fails in part because algorithmic systems cannot simply be inserted into the institutionally complex, culturally embedded practice of policing. Purves (2023) raises the additional concern of the dehumanizing logic of machine-driven enforcement, noting both persistent bias and the regulatory momentum already building in Europe. Geolitica could not survive the compounding pressures.

With a decade preceding of promising research and development, Lum and Isaac (2016) were vindicated. In late 2023, Geolitica was absorbed by SoundThinking, the makers of ShotSpotter, a gunfire detection technology used in many American cities (Mehrotra & Cameron, 2023). SoundThinking, a company with similar goals to that of Geolitica, although using different technology, has shown great successes where their ShotSpotter systems are placed (Doucette et al., 2021; Goldenberg et al., 2019). The acquisition signals continued commercial interest in algorithmic crime forecasting, now consolidated under an operator with an established record in acoustic detection technology.

The Current and Next

Geolitica's trajectory illustrates the limits of technical expertise alone as a solution to crime. Its founders were accomplished mathematicians who applied rigorous methods to a genuine social problem. The lesson is not that their methods lacked sophistication or analytical validity, but rather that expertise in mathematical abstraction does not necessarily translate into expertise in the social, political, and human realities that crime data represents. Epistemologically, the approach of applying complex mathematics to structure, analyze, and execute a real-world solution to crime is valid. The associated processes can define to us the basest makeup of the physical world, but data about human behavior is never truly separable from the human conditions that produced it.

The fundamental problem is not that crime is unpredictable in principle, but that the data used to predict it is irreducibly human. It carries within it the weight of historical inequity, institutional bias, and the countless social forces that shape who gets policed, who gets reported, and whose behavior gets recorded. An algorithm trained on such data does not transcend these distortions; it codifies and amplifies them. The absence of bias in such a system is not a technical problem awaiting a technical solution; it is, in the current state of the world, a utopia. And it is precisely here that the mathematician's toolkit, however sophisticated, requires the criminologist's: not to question whether crime can be modelled, but to interrogate what the data actually represents and whose reality it reflects.

The mathematical literature on crime hotspots is marked by a conspicuous absence of substantive criminological grounding. Broken windows theory and repeat victimization are typically acknowledged in a single sentence, not integrated into model logic or interpretation. The data are treated as numbers, 0 and 1, without the context that criminologists have spent decades constructing. This is a failure on both sides of the disciplinary divide: mathematicians did not reach across, and criminologists did not sufficiently engage the technical limitations; this is usually reserved to just one sentence. The methodology used relies on real crime data, but entirely lacks context and meaning when it relies solely on numbers, 0 and 1, yes and no. This is a significant oversight, both on the part of mathematicians and criminologists, though it must be acknowledged that criminological scholarship has not been silent on these risks. Works precisely like the present one exist to sound the alarm, to identify the biases inherent in algorithmic systems, and demand better. The problem is not a lack of critical voices, but a failure of those voices to reach, or be heeded by, those building and deploying the technology. It is stated (Sankin & Mattu, 2023) in reporting that Geolitica's creators had been warned by David Weisburd, a leading criminologist, about precisely these risks, and that the company did not respond when contacted (Angwin, 2021). This is precisely the dynamic that must change. The academic and professional community bears a responsibility not only to publish critique, but to demand accountability from those deploying these systems. That this chapter arrives after Geolitica's collapse, rather than before it, is symptomatic of the problem. Predictive policing has not ended; the obligation to get it right rests on both sides of the disciplinary divide.

Ethical and Metaphysical Implications of Predictive Policing

The practical failures of PredPol/Geolitica raise a prior question: what normative framework should govern predictive policing at all? The technology was deployed without one. "Reducing crime" is a loose mandate rather than a coherent normative framework. Crime reduction is multidimensional and transcends prediction alone; no algorithm can remedy the socioeconomic conditions, developmental pathways, and structural realities that produce criminality. Predictive policing will do little to remedy the socioeconomic factors that spawn criminality, the abusive and traumatic factors that sustain it, or the natural elements that we cannot grasp.

None of this forecloses the pursuit of predictive policing. Consider, however, what a genuinely capable system would imply. If police could "...discover from a book of sonnets that a crime will be committed" (Chesterton, 1908, p. 75), the evidentiary foundations of criminal prosecution collapse. Prevention before commission forecloses the actus reus; without a completed act, there is no legally cognizable crime. This produces two entangled problems. First, offenders could never be prosecuted to the extent of their anticipated conduct because no completed actus reus exists. Second, absent a completed offense, evidentiary standards sufficient for prosecution would collapse.

A capable predictive system would also generate its own countermeasures. If offenders cannot be prosecuted for crimes that never occur, the incentive structure shifts: deviant behavior adapts to evade the system's predictive logic. Offenders would account for the predictive powers, attempting to keep them down and invent new avenues to carrying out their conduct. A system that reliably predicts offending would implicitly support a deterministic conception of criminality, complicating the criminological consensus that crime is principally a product of social conditions rather than individual propensity. A system that reliably predicts who will offend muddies the waters in the argument against nature. Is it, at such a point, a matter of the justice system sustaining the conditions which would drive an individual toward criminality, or, if a predictive system could forecast crime perfectly, is criminality baked into the minds of those who tend toward deviance?

These questions ultimately leave empirical criminology and enter moral philosophy. If a predictive system can reliably anticipate criminal acts, the question of free will becomes unavoidable. Either answer is destabilizing—if offenders lack free will, the justice system's premise of moral culpability collapses. If they possess it, then any predictive system is necessarily fallible and its authority to justify pre-emptive intervention is undermined. The implications extend beyond policing and into the foundations of human agency itself.

The ethical terrain is equally fraught and would wholly violate the social contract. The modern justice system is fallible, but its imperfections operate within a compatibilist framework of due process, crime control, and the presumption of innocence. A fully realized predictive policing system would, on the other hand, require comprehensive real-time surveillance of the general population, which would constitute not merely a privacy violation but a structural transformation of the relationship between citizen and state. Such a system would not only entail a monumental breach of privacy but would also amount to "might makes right". It entirely lacks consent, which would make such a system sustainable, ignoring the conventions set out by thinkers over the past 2000 years. Such a powerful system of prediction would be so demoralizing, so destructive, that it would render the very concept of justice meaningless, replacing the presumption of innocence with the presumption of guilt, and transforming governance from a system of laws and deterrence into one of surveillance and coercion.

Conclusion

Geolitica's rise and fall is not simply a cautionary tale about premature deployment; it is a structural indictment of disciplinary insularity. The mathematicians had the tools; the criminologists had the context. Neither was able to meet the other halfway, and the consequences were borne by the communities subjected to the technology's failures. The ethical and metaphysical dilemmas outlined earlier are not hypothetical concerns for a distant future. They are live questions that any renewed effort at predictive policing must confront before deployment, not after.

Predictive policing has not disappeared. Research in the field continues, and the appetite for technological solutions to crime is unlikely to wane. However, the next iteration of this technology must be built on a foundation that the last one lacked: a normative argument, a criminological backbone, and a frank reckoning with what it means to govern human behavior through prediction. The future of predictive policing, if it is to have one worth pursuing, lies not in more sophisticated algorithms alone, but in honest collaboration between criminologists and mathematicians, and in a willingness to ask not only whether something can be predicted, but whether predicting it is just.

Acknowledgements: I extend my heartfelt thanks to my parents, my dedicated faculty mentors, and Cecilia, without whom this work would not have been possible.

References

Amin, R. (2019). Mathematical model of burglary: A review. *International Journal of Engineering Research & Technology*, *8*(10). https://doi.org/10.17577/IJERTV8IS100114

Angwin, J. (2021, December 4). *The disparate impact of predictive policing software – the markup*. https://themarkup.org/newsletter/hello-world/the-disparate-impact-of-predictive-policing-software

Ballantyne, N. (2023, August 7). *The harm that data do: The case of PredPol*. Medium. https://medium.com/@neilballantyne/the-harm-that-data-do-the-case-of-predpol-17603c59a1e2

Baumer, E. P., & Lauritsen, J. L. (2010). Reporting crime to the police, 1973–2005: A multivariate analysis of long-term trends in the national crime survey (NCS) and national crime victimization survey (NCVS). *Criminology: An Interdisciplinary Journal*, *48*(1), 131–185. https://doi.org/10.1111/j.1745-9125.2010.00182.x

Beccaria, C. (1765). *Dei delitti e delle pene*. https://preserver.beic.it/delivery/DeliveryManagerServlet?dps_pid=IE3645594

Beccaria, C. (2016). *On crimes and punishments*. Transaction Publishers.

Bendel, O. (2023). Robots in policing. In *Social Robots in Social Institutions* (pp. 135–144). IOS Press. https://doi.org/10.3233/FAIA220612

Bhuiyan, J. (2021, November 8). LAPD ended predictive policing programs amid public outcry. A new effort shares many of their flaws. *The Guardian*. https://www.theguardian.com/us-news/2021/nov/07/lapd-predictive-policing-surveillance-reform

Blodgett, S. L., & Talat, Z. (2024). LLMs produce racist output when prompted in African American English. *Nature*, *633*(8028), 40–41. https://doi.org/10.1038/d41586-024-02527-x

Bond, B. J., & Nehmens, A. J. (2015). CompStat. In *The encyclopedia of crime and punishment* (pp. 1–4). John Wiley & Sons, Ltd. https://doi.org/10.1002/9781118519639.wbecpx174

Braga, A. A., & Schnell, C. (2017). Beyond putting "cops on dots": Applying theory to advance police responses to crime places. In *Unraveling the crime-place connection, Volume 22* (pp. 261–288). Routledge.

Brantingham, P., & Tita, G. (2008). Offender mobility and crime pattern formation from first principles. *Artificial Crime Analysis Systems: Using Computer Simulations and Geographic Information Systems*, 193–208. https://doi.org/10.4018/978-1-59904-591-7.ch010

Browne, J., Cave, S., Drage, E., & McInerney, K. (2023). *Feminist AI: Critical perspectives on algorithms, data, and intelligent machines*. Oxford University Press.

Chainey, S. P., Curtis-Ham, S. J., Evans, R. M., & Burns, G. J. (2018). Examining the extent to which repeat and near repeat patterns can prevent crime. *Policing: An International Journal*, *41*(5), 608–622. (world). https://doi.org/10.1108/PIJPSM-12-2016-0172

Chaturapruek, S., Breslau, J., Yazdi, D., Kolokolnikov, T., & McCalla, S. G. (2013). Crime modeling with lévy flights. *SIAM Journal on Applied Mathematics*, *73*(4), 1703–1720. https://doi.org/10.1137/120895408

Chesterton, G. K. (1908). *The man who was Thursday: A nightmare*. Modern Library.

Crime stats—COMPStat—NYPD. (n.d.). Retrieved April 4, 2025, from https://www.nyc.gov/site/nypd/stats/crime-statistics/compstat.page

Cruz-García, S., Martínez-Farías, F., Santillán-Hernández, A. S., & Rangel, E. (2021). Mathematical home burglary model with stochastic long crime trips and patrolling: Applied to Mexico City. *Applied Mathematics and Computation*, *396*, 125865. https://doi.org/10.1016/j.amc.2020.125865

Degeling, M., & Berendt, B. (2018). What is wrong about robocops as consultants? A technology-centric critique of predictive policing. *AI and Society*, *33*(3), 347–356. https://doi.org/10.1007/s00146-017-0730-7

Doucette, M. L., Green, C., Necci Dineen, J., Shapiro, D., & Raissian, K. M. (2021). Impact of ShotSpotter technology on firearm homicides and arrests among large metropolitan counties: A longitudinal analysis, 1999–2016. *Journal of Urban Health*, *98*(5), 609–621. https://doi.org/10.1007/s11524-021-00515-4

Engberts, B., & Gillissen, E. (2016). Policing from above: Drone use by the police. In B. Custers (Ed.), *The future of drone use: Opportunities and threats from ethical and legal perspectives* (pp. 93–113). T.M.C. Asser Press. https://doi.org/10.1007/978-94-6265-132-6_5

Fonoberova, M., Fonoberov, V. A., Mezic, I., Mezic, J., & Brantingham, P. J. (2010). Nonlinear dynamics of crime and violence in urban settings. *Journal of Artificial Societies and Social Simulation*, *15*(1), 2.

Gabor, T. (1981). The crime displacement hypothesis: An empirical examination. *Crime & Delinquency*, *27*(3), 390–404. https://doi.org/10.1177/001112878102700306

Gaines, L. K., & Cain, T. J. (1981). Controlling the police organization: Contingency management, program planning, implementation and evaluation. *Police Studies: The International Review of Police Development*, *4*(1), 16–26.

Garland, D., & Sparks, R. (2000). Criminology, social theory and the challenge of our times. *British Journal of Criminology*, *40*(2), 189–204.

Gau, J. M., & Pratt, T. C. (2010). Revisiting broken windows theory: Examining the sources of the discriminant validity of perceived disorder and crime. *Journal of Criminal Justice*, *38*(4), 758–766. https://doi.org/10.1016/j.jcrimjus.2010.05.002

Goldenberg, A., Rattigan, D., Dalton, M., Gaughan, J. P., Thomson, J. S., Remick, K., Butts, C., & Hazelton, J. P. (2019). Use of ShotSpotter detection technology decreases prehospital time for patients sustaining gunshot wounds. *Journal of Trauma and Acute Care Surgery*, *87*(6), 1253. https://doi.org/10.1097/TA.0000000000002483

Goldstein, H. (1979). Improving policing: A problem-oriented approach. *Crime & Delinquency*, *25*(2), 236–258. https://doi.org/10.1177/001112877902500207

Gross, M., & Hakim, S. (1982). The diffusion of crime in the metropolis: A step-by-step analysis. *Journal of Environmental Systems*, *12*(1), 45–60. https://doi.org/10.2190/Q92G-RKCB-AJN9-5CWA

Guo, Z., & Kennedy, L. (2023). Policing based on automatic facial recognition. *Artificial Intelligence and Law*, *31*(2), 397–443. https://doi.org/10.1007/s10506-022-09330-x

Haberman, C. P., Hatten, D., Carter, J. G., & Piza, E. L. (2021). The sensitivity of repeat and near repeat analysis to geocoding algorithms. *Journal of Criminal Justice*, *73*, 101721. https://doi.org/10.1016/j.jcrimjus.2020.101721

Hofmann, V., Kalluri, P. R., Jurafsky, D., & King, S. (2024). AI generates covertly racist decisions about people based on their dialect. *Nature*, *633*(8028), 147–154. https://doi.org/10.1038/s41586-024-07856-5

Johnson, S. D., Guerette, R. T., & Bowers, K. (2014). Crime displacement: What we know, what we don't know, and what it means for crime reduction. *Journal of Experimental Criminology*, *10*(4), 549–571. https://doi.org/10.1007/s11292-014-9209-4

Jones, P. A., Brantingham, P. J., & Chayes, L. R. (2010). Statistical models of criminal behavior: The effects of law enforcement actions. *Mathematical Models and Methods in Applied Sciences*, *20*(supp01), 1397–1423. https://doi.org/10.1142/S0218202510004647

Katz, C. M., & Walker, S. (2017). *The police in America: An introduction*. McGraw-Hill Education.

Kelly, K. (2016). *The inevitable: Understanding the 12 technological forces that will shape our future*. Penguin.

Kolokolnikov, T., Ward, M., & Wei, J. (2012). *The stability of steady-state hot-spot patterns for a reaction-diffusion model of urban crime* (arXiv:1201.3090). arXiv. https://doi.org/10.48550/arXiv.1201.3090

Kuhn, T. S. (1962). *The structure of scientific revolutions*. University of Chicago Press.

Lally, N. (2022). "It makes almost no difference which algorithm you use": On the modularity of predictive policing. *Urban Geography*, *43*(9), 1437–1455. https://doi.org/10.1080/02723638.2021.1949142

Laplace, P. S. (with New York Public Library). (1814). *Essai philosophique sur les probabilités*. Courcier. http://archive.org/details/essaiphilosophi00laplgoo

Laplace, P. S. (with University of California Libraries). (1902). *A philosophical essay on probabilities*. J. Wiley; Chapman & Hall. http://archive.org/details/philosophicaless00lapliala

Lombroso, C. (1876). *L' homme criminel*.

Lombroso, C. (2006). *Criminal man*. Duke University Press.

Lum, K., & Isaac, W. (2016). To predict and serve? *Significance*, *13*(5), 14–19. https://doi.org/10.1111/j.1740-9713.2016.00960.x

Martínez-Farías, F. J., Alvarado-sánchez, A., Rangel-cortes, E., & Hernández-hernández, A. (2022). Bi-dimensional crime model based on anomalous diffusion with law enforcement effect. *Mathematical Modelling and Numerical Simulation with Applications*, *2*(1), Article 1. https://doi.org/10.53391/mmnsa.2022.01.003

Maskaly, J., & Boggess, L. N. (2014). Broken windows theory. In *The Encyclopedia of Theoretical Criminology* (pp. 1–4). John Wiley & Sons, Ltd. https://doi.org/10.1002/9781118517390.wbetc127

Mehrotra, D., & Cameron, D. (2023, September 27). The maker of ShotSpotter is buying the world's most infamous predictive policing tech. *Wired*. https://www.wired.com/story/soundthinking-geolitica-acquisition-predictive-policing/

MIT Technology Review. (n.d.). MIT Technology Review. Retrieved April 4, 2025, from https://www.technologyreview.com/

Mohler, G. O., & Short, M. B. (2012). Geographic profiling from kinetic models of criminal behavior. *SIAM Journal on Applied Mathematics*, *72*(1), 163–180. https://doi.org/10.1137/100794080

Mohler, G., Short, M., Brantingham, P., Schoenberg, F., & Tita, G. (2011). Self-exciting point process modeling of crime. *Journal of the American Statistical Association*, *106*, 100–108. https://doi.org/10.1198/jasa.2011.ap09546

O'Brien, D. T., Farrell, C., & Welsh, B. C. (2019). Broken (windows) theory: A meta-analysis of the evidence for the pathways from neighborhood disorder to resident health outcomes and behaviors. *Social Science & Medicine*, *228*, 272–292. https://doi.org/10.1016/j.socscimed.2018.11.015

Pandey, T., & Pathak, A. R. (2021). The broken windows theory. *International Journal of Law Management & Humanities*, *4 Issue 5*, 1722.

Piza, E. L., & Carter, J. G. (2018). Predicting initiator and near repeat events in spatiotemporal crime patterns: An analysis of residential burglary and motor vehicle theft. *Justice Quarterly*. (world). https://www.tandfonline.com/doi/abs/10.1080/07418825.2017.1342854

Purves, D. (2023, June 13). *What's wrong with predictive policing?* Public Ethics. https://www.publicethics.org/post/what-s-wrong-with-predictive-policing

Ratcliffe, J. H., & and Breen, C. (2011). Crime diffusion and displacement: Measuring the side effects of police operations. *The Professional Geographer*, *63*(2), 230–243. https://doi.org/10.1080/00330124.2010.547154

Ratcliffe, J. H., & Rengert, G. F. (2008). Near-repeat patterns in Philadelphia shootings. *Security Journal*, *21*(1), 58–76. https://doi.org/10.1057/palgrave.sj.8350068

Ross, J. D. (1980). Determination of the predictive validity of the assessment center approach to selecting police managers. *Journal of Criminal Justice*, *8*(2), 89–96. https://doi.org/10.1016/0047-2352(80)90084-7

Sankin, A., Gizmodo, D. M. for, Mattu, S., & Gilbertson, A. (2021, December 2). *Crime prediction software promised to be free of biases. New data shows it perpetuates them – The Markup*. https://themarkup.org/prediction-bias/2021/12/02/crime-prediction-software-promised-to-be-free-of-biases-new-data-shows-it-perpetuates-them

Sankin, A., & Mattu, S. (2023, October 2). *How we assessed the accuracy of predictive policing software*. The Markup. https://themarkup.org/show-your-work/2023/10/02/how-we-assessed-the-accuracy-of-predictive-policing-software

Semple, J. (1993). *Bentham's prison: A study of the panopticon penitentiary: a study of the panopticon penitentiary*. Clarendon Press.

Short, M. B., Bertozzi, A. L., & Brantingham, P. J. (2010a). Nonlinear patterns in urban crime: Hotspots, bifurcations, and suppression. *SIAM Journal on Applied Dynamical Systems*, *9*(2), 462–483. https://doi.org/10.1137/090759069

Short, M. B., Brantingham, P. J., Bertozzi, A. L., & Tita, G. E. (2010b). Dissipation and displacement of hotspots in reaction-diffusion models of crime. *Proceedings of the National Academy of Sciences*, *107*(9), 3961–3965. https://doi.org/10.1073/pnas.0910921107

Short, M. B., D'orsogna, M. R., Pasour, V. B., Tita, G. E., Brantingham, P. J., Bertozzi, A. L., & Chayes, L. B. (2008). A statistical model of criminal behavior. *Mathematical Models and Methods in Applied Sciences*, *18*(supp01), 1249–1267. https://doi.org/10.1142/S0218202508003029

Spaulding, J. S., & Morris, K. B. (2022). An optimised approach to near repeat analysis for intelligence driven crime linkage. *Journal of Policing, Intelligence and Counter Terrorism*, *17*(1), 24–47. https://doi.org/10.1080/18335330.2021.1945663

Tang, Y., Zhu, X., Guo, W., Wu, L., & Fan, Y. (2019). Anisotropic diffusion for improved crime prediction in urban China. *ISPRS International Journal of Geo-Information*, *8*(5), Article 5. https://doi.org/10.3390/ijgi8050234

Telep, C. W., Weisburd, D., Gill, C. E., Vitter, Z., & Teichman, D. (2014). Displacement of crime and diffusion of crime control benefits in large-scale geographic areas: A systematic review. *Journal of Experimental Criminology*, *10*(4), 515–548. https://doi.org/10.1007/s11292-014-9208-5

Thomas, G. (2024, October 15). *Politicians move to limit predictive policing after years of controversial failures*. Tech Policy Press. https://techpolicy.press/politicians-move-to-limit-predictive-policing-after-years-of-controversial-failures

Votey, H. L. Jr., & Phillips, L. (1972). Police effectiveness and the production function for law enforcement. *Journal of Legal Studies*, *1*(2), 423–436.

Winston, A., & Burrington, I. (2018, April 26). *A pioneer in predictive policing is starting a troubling new project*. The Verge. https://www.theverge.com/2018/4/26/17285058/predictive-policing-predpol-pentagon-ai-racial-bias

Woodworth, J. T., Mohler, G. O., Bertozzi, A. L., & Brantingham, P. J. (2014). Non-local crime density estimation incorporating housing information. *Philosophical Transactions. Series A, Mathematical, Physical, and Engineering Sciences*, *372*(2028), 20130403. https://doi.org/10.1098/rsta.2013.0403

Youstin, T. J., Nobles, M. R., Ward, J. T., & Cook, C. L. (2011). Assessing the generalizability of the near repeat phenomenon. *Criminal Justice and Behavior*, *38*(10), 1042–1063. https://doi.org/10.1177/0093854811417551

11

ARTIFICIAL INTELLIGENCE AND SUSPECT IDENTIFICATION

Cassidy B. Haigh and Eric Dlugolenski

Introduction

> Technological change is not additive; it is ecological. A new technology does not merely add something; it changes everything.
>
> —Postman (1992, p. 18)

Anyone who has recently wandered through the exposition hall at the International Association of Chiefs of Police's annual conference will recognize that artificial intelligence (AI) has flooded the zone. The scene resembles the trading floor of a pre-digital stock exchange: vendors pitch their products with the urgency of traders closing a deal, and booths are emblazoned with AI slogans. The commodity on display is not steel or oil, but algorithmic prowess. Policing, thus far, is not immune to the broader AI revolution. The conference floor is only one manifestation of the current AI fervour. Although enthusiasm has reached a fever pitch, some of the excitement is warranted. AI has become an increasingly important investigative tool, significantly expanding law enforcement's capacity for suspect identification. Yet even setting aside the hype, optimism is far from universal. Civil libertarians and civil rights groups are raising their own *hue and cry*—forecasting the last breaths of public and personal privacy.

Despite its contemporary ubiquity, the term *artificial intelligence* was coined more than 70 years ago (Sharma, 2024). Given the proliferation of definitions and the global audience for this text, we adopt the terminology established by the International Organization for Standardization (ISO) and the International Electrotechnical Commission (IEC). Accordingly, when we refer to AI in this chapter, we are referring specifically to AI systems—each as an "engineered

DOI: 10.4324/9781003671312-11

system that generates outputs such as content, forecasts, recommendations or decisions for a given set of human-defined objectives" (ISO & IEC, 2022, p. 1).

The AI tidal wave will fluvially reshape every aspect of modern policing. We do not attempt to chart the entire surge; instead, we focus our examination on one stretch of shoreline where its force is most visible—the ways AI has and continues to revolutionize *the suspect identification process*—specifically through facial recognition technology (FRT) and AI-supplemented eyewitness identification. Drawing on the concepts of surveillant assemblage and surveillantization (Haggerty, 2025; Haggerty & Ericson, 2000), this chapter synthesizes research across four areas: the development and deployment of FRT in policing; the potential of AI to assist in eyewitness procedures; comparative evidence on human and algorithmic performance, including hybrid "fusion" models; and the risks associated with AI-assisted identification, including demographic disparities, governance gaps, and wrongful arrests. We situate these developments within contrasting regulatory frameworks in the European Union, the United States (US), and Canada, and conclude with policy recommendations addressing standards, oversight, and human-in-the-loop safeguards.

Conceptual Framework

From its inception through most of the 19th century, sleuthing was fieldwork. The eyes of governmental and private surveillance were *human*, constrained by the boundaries of human sensorium and atomized presence. The early detective mystique was contextual; their cunning was a requisite feature of epistemic scarcity at a time when citizen observers were an indispensable feature of intelligence. The pre-database era epitomized what Jane Jacobs (1961) would later put into words.

> The sidewalk and street peace of cities is not kept primarily by the police, necessary as police are. It is kept primarily by an intricate, almost unconscious, network of voluntary controls and standards among the people themselves, and enforced by the people themselves.
>
> (pp. 31–32)

In 1857, the New York City Police Department initiated a "rogues' gallery"—the Mulberry Street photo gallery displayed offenders arranged by crimes committed and height (Richardson, 1961). In archival rogues' gallery photographs, it is not uncommon to observe offenders making facial expressions to pervert their actual appearance (Swanson et al., 2023). Despite global diffusion, early rogues' galleries "ha[d] more in common with browsing through a family photo album than with sophisticated attempts to track down an alleged offender" (Jäger, 2001, p. 16). Looking back, rogues' galleries foreshadowed a significant shift in the nature of surveillance, despite osmotically arriving much later in the form of dataveillance, "the systematic use of personal data systems in the investigation or monitoring of the actions of communications of one or more persons" (Clarke, 1988, p. 499).

Photographs, in silo, are but one *discrete* form of surveillance. Building on the works of Gilles Deleuze and Félix Guattari, Haggerty and Ericson (2000) perceive surveillance as focal to the postmodern world and argue that formerly discrete surveillance measures are now coalesced as a *surveillant assemblage.* A key feature of the assemblage is the fragmentation and reconstitution of the body into information flows. Surveillance technologies break down individuals into discrete data points, such as biometric data, which can then be recombined, compared, and circulated across institutions.

> These flows are then reassembled into distinct 'data doubles' which can be scrutinized and targeted for intervention. In the process, we are witnessing a rhizomatic leveling of the hierarchy of surveillance, such that groups which were previously exempt from routine surveillance are now increasingly being monitored.
>
> (Haggerty & Ericson, 2000, p. 606)

Surveillant assemblage far extends the confines of public service institutions like the police. Instead, it recognizes the roles of state and non-state actors, as well as technical, bureaucratic, and commercial infrastructures.

The concept of *surveillantization* builds on this idea by shifting the focus from the structure of surveillance systems to the broader process through which surveillance expands and transforms society (Haggerty, 2025). Surveillantization refers to the "historical and ongoing proliferation, integration, and normalization of systems for observing, categorizing, and managing human life and social organization" (Haggerty, 2025, p. 530). Through surveillantization, systems of monitoring expand and come to be seen as routine features of governance and everyday life.

Together, the concepts of surveillant assemblage and surveillantization provide a framework for understanding the growing integration of AI into policing practices, particularly in suspect identification. Facial recognition systems link together databases, cameras, and analytical algorithms, exemplifying the networked infrastructure described by the surveillant assemblage. At the same time, the increasing adoption of AI-driven identification tools by law enforcement reflects surveillantization, the gradual expansion and normalization of automated surveillance capabilities within policing and broader systems of social control.

We extend our discussions outward given the expansive nature of the surveillant assemblage while maintaining our central claim—artificially intelligent identification is not a single technology, but rather it represents an infrastructural convergence that fundamentally reshapes the dynamics of policing and power, as police become increasingly subordinated to privatized systems of dataveillance. Viewed through the lens of surveillantization, these developments signal more than technological innovation; they reflect a broader social process through which surveillance capacities proliferate, integrate, and become normalized within systems of governance and everyday life. We then turn to the most troubling feature of this trajectory: the risk that civil liberties become casualties in the race to scale and monetize surveillance infrastructures. At the same time, we weigh known and speculative risks against the technologies' promises and societal appetite for efficient crime control. To be clear, our purpose is not to advance a neo-Luddite critique of technological change, but rather to establish guiding sensibilities as police and society navigate this emerging surveillance landscape.

Facial Recognition Technology and Suspect Identification

When we enter a crowded room, we instinctively scan faces, instantly recognizing loved ones, friends, or even foes. We *know* them, or we simply find familiarity in their face and ask, "Do I know you from somewhere? You look so familiar." In a way, we are masterfully skilled facial recognizers. FRT is, in some ways, the computational analogue of our human knack for deciphering "who is who," which just so happens to be of great interest to law enforcement. It is no surprise then that FRT is taking its seat as a significant feature of modern investigative practice. In this section, we examine the foundations of human facial recognition and trace the evolution of computational FRT in law enforcement. We outline the roles and standards governing human examiners, explain the operational principles of FRT, and assess how its expanding use in investigative and surveillance contexts reshapes both identification practices and regulatory challenges.

Human Facial Recognition and the Development of FRT

Facial recognition is a central component of suspect identification; however, individuals differ in their ability to recognize faces, and this variation extends to police officers (White & Burton, 2022). While many people demonstrate average recognition abilities, others are classified as super-recognizers, those who have innate facial identification abilities and generally outperform the average on validated assessments, even without formal training (White et al., 2021).

In law enforcement settings, two types of professionals engage in facial identification: facial reviewers and facial examiners. Facial reviewers receive limited training and are responsible for large numbers of facial identification decisions, such as airport security personnel. In contrast, facial examiners are experts on forensic facial identification and perform in-depth analysis using standardized and defensible procedures (White et al., 2021). Specifically, they conduct "a comparison of image(s)-to-image(s) using a rigorous morphological analysis to compare and evaluate controlled/uncontrolled images for the purpose of effecting an opinion, often used in a forensic application" (Facial Identification Scientific Working Group, 2022, p. 1). Morphological analysis involves the manual, feature-by-feature comparison of facial morphology. Although human facial recognition serves many law enforcement purposes, it is not conducive to scale, and its reliability and validity remain uncertain (see e.g., Bacci et al., 2021; Heyer & Semmler, 2013; Lee et al., 2009). The advent and evolution of computational FRT afforded a solution to the scalability problem, promising exponential increases in the efficiency of law enforcement operations. That promise has been realized and is the primary advantage of law enforcement adoption (Hodge, 2020).

The birth of computational facial recognition is owed to Woodrow Bledsoe (1966), who matched mugshots by measuring unique facial feature distances. Fortunately, computational science has advanced dramatically since Bledsoe's pioneering work. Several pivotal developments paved the way for modern facial recognition technologies, including the 1966 development of the Facial Recognition Technology database (the first known dataset subject to empirical study), the 2007 Labeled Faces in the Wild dataset (the first "web-sourced and unconstrained" dataset), and the 2014 development of DeepFace (the first model to outperform human facial recognition leveraging deep learning; Raji and Fried, 2021). As computational facial recognition advances, its intersection with law enforcement, public safety, and civil liberties reaches a critical mass. The law enforcement field is experimenting with facial recognition in the absence of well-promulgated safeguards and contours for its ethical use.

Operational Principles of FRT and "Data Doubling"

FRT is a form of biometric authentication. As a science, *biometrics* involves the measurement and analysis of individuals' unique physiological or behavioural characteristics, with a primary application in automated human identification and authentication (Bolle et al., 2013). FRT is an umbrella term that refers to various software capable of identifying human facial features in digital images or video frames and matching those features against a database of known faces (Selwyn et al., 2024).

FRT and biometrics more broadly are hallmark examples of the surveillant assemblage's treatment of the human body.

> The observed body is of a distinctively hybrid composition. First, it is broken down by being abstracted from its territorial setting. It is then reassembled in different settings through a series of data flows. The result is a decorporealized body, a 'data double' of pure virtuality.
>
> (Haggerty & Ericson, 2000, p. 611)

FRT is made possible by AI, specifically the subfield of computer vision, which leverages computational techniques to mimic human vision (Szeliski, 2022). FRTs provide *biometric signatures* of individuals that are algorithmically "normalized" for comparison with a full or subset of preidentified signatures. Matching is then accomplished via similarity score thresholds (Tolba et al., 2005). El Fadel (2025) outlined the process of "computer-aided person identification" as follows: 1.) Biometric data is captured via sensors (e.g., surveillance cameras), 2.) unique features or signatures are extracted from the biometric data, 3.) features or signatures are normalized to allow for "apples to apples" comparisons, 4.) biometric samples are compared to those from known individuals to identify potential matches based on similarity, 5.) matches are verified or authenticated based on a predefined process, and finally 6.) a decision is rendered to confirm or deny identification based on the predefined threshold (see Figure 11.1).

FRTs are subclassified based on technical approach (e.g., 2d, 3d, infrared/thermal), matching method (e.g., one-to-one [1:1], one-to-many [1:N], many-to-many [N:N]), and by implementation (e.g., real-time, passive, active; Li et al., 2020; Purshouse & Campbell, 2022; Qinjun et al., 2023; Wanyonyi & Celik, 2022).

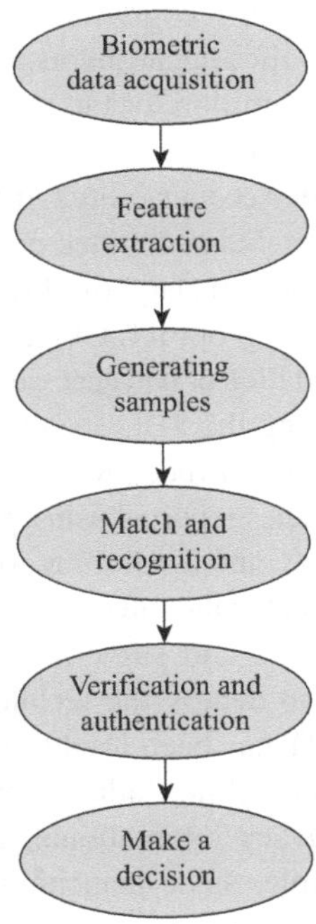

FIGURE 11.1 The General Process of Biometric Identification

Note: Based on the process described by El Fadel (2025).

The Use of FRT in Law Enforcement Contexts

> [Data] doubles ostensibly refer back to particular individuals, they transcend a purely representational idiom. Rather than being accurate or inaccurate portrayals of real individuals, they are a form of pragmatics: *differentiated according to how useful they are in allowing institutions to make discriminations among populations* (emphasis added).
>
> (Haggerty & Ericson, 2000, p. 614)

Law enforcement use of FRT takes two general forms: facial verification (1:1), which aims to validate claimed identity, and facial identification (1:N), which takes an unknown face and attempts to provide a valid match or identification (Garvie et al., 2016). In terms of deployment, FRT is used by law enforcement for identification at checkpoints and during seizures, to supplement and automate video searches for investigations, to locate missing persons, and to conduct real-time surveillance (Boucher, 2025; Johnson et al., 2024).

A decade-old analysis of public records requests estimated that "one in two American adults is in a law enforcement face recognition network" (Garvie et al., 2016, p. 1), suggesting that this estimate is now a severe underrepresentation. As of 2016, the FBI's facial recognition use exceeded that of traditional wiretaps, and five major US. police departments were actively using or formally exploring automatic facial recognition, or the real-time facial recognition from public cameras (Garvie et al., 2016).

In 2021, the US Government Accountability Office (GAO) published testimony to the House of Representatives' Subcommittee on Crime, Terrorism, and Homeland Security, Committee on the Judiciary, disclosing the results of its survey of federal agencies' use and ownership of FRT. Of the 42 federal agencies queried, 20 disclosed that they either owned FRT or had accessed another agency's state-owned system. Eight agencies (including the FBI, Secret Service, and US Customs and Border Protection) reported agency-owned FRT, 17 agencies reported the use of another entity's FRT, and 11 agencies reported using private, non-governmental FRT (e.g., Clearview AI). Importantly, the disclosures were limited to nonsensitive information and thus underrepresented the full scope of federal use (US GAO, 2021).

While criminal investigations and surveillance remain the most common uses of FRT, governments also deploy the technology during periods of civil unrest (Zalnieriute, 2024). FRT has been used to identify, arrest, and prosecute protesters globally, including in Chile, India, Serbia, Russia, Uganda, the US, and the United Kingdom (Privacy International, 2023, 2024; US GAO, 2021; Zalnieriute, 2024). For example, since launching its facial recognition video surveillance network in 2017, Russia has used FRT-equipped cameras to identify, arrest, and detain hundreds of protesters at anti-government demonstrations (Masri, 2023). In the US, law enforcement used FRT to identify suspects responsible for criminal acts during nationwide protests following the killing of

George Floyd by a Minneapolis police officer and in investigations related to the January 6, 2021, US Capitol attack (US GAO, 2021).

The widespread adoption of FRT creates a new challenge; end-users of this software require adequate training to interpret analyses and matches for the ethical and transparent use of this technology. Although law enforcement agencies are navigating a new intersection of public safety and civil liberties, some axiomatic words apply—FRT is an investigative tool with broad applications; however, it shall not be used independently as a means of identification, only as a supplement to a complete investigation (Sims & Johnson, 2024).

AI and Eyewitness Identification

While FRTs abstract the body into biometric data flows, emerging AI applications in the eyewitness domain extend this logic into the cognitive realm. Here, memory, confidence, and linguistic expression are rendered computationally tractable and incorporated into investigative decision systems. In both cases, AI functions as a node within a broader biometric surveillant assemblage that reorganizes how suspicion is generated, evaluated, and acted upon.

A growing body of research examines how AI might assist law enforcement in handling eyewitness identification evidence. Eyewitness misidentification is a leading cause of wrongful conviction (National Registry of Exonerations, n.d.), and biased lineup construction is a common source of error (Wells et al., 2020). Ideally, a photo lineup includes one suspect and at least five fillers who resemble the suspect in appearance and contextual features (Wells et al., 2020). Because officers usually locate fillers manually from image databases, constructing fair lineups can be time-consuming, especially when suspects have distinctive features. Generative AI may help streamline this process by creating appropriate fillers, potentially improving efficiency without compromising fairness (Bell et al., 2024; Greenspan & Bergold, 2025).

Within this field, a key focus is the potential of AI to assess eyewitness accuracy. Smith et al. (2024) identify three primary roles for AI in this context. First, AI may function as an independent evaluator of eyewitness identification accuracy. Techniques such as natural language processing and machine learning have shown promise in analyzing the accuracy of identification decisions (Greenspan et al., 2024; Gustafsson et al., 2025; Seale-Carlisle et al., 2022, 2025). For example, Gustafsson et al. (2025) found that support vector machines can classify correct and incorrect eyewitness statements above chance levels, performing comparably to human judgments. Second, AI may assist investigators as a decision aid when evaluating eyewitness identification evidence (Smith et al., 2024; Kelso et al., 2025a, 2025b). In this role, AI tools may help reduce cognitive biases in human assessments of eyewitness accuracy (Kelso et al., 2025b). Finally, AI may serve as a model for how human evaluators, such as law enforcement personnel, should assess eyewitness evidence (Smith et al., 2024; Gamoran et al., 2024).

In sum, the nascent research on AI in the eyewitness domain is promising, suggesting new ways to enhance efficiency and accuracy in the management of identification evidence. However, further research is needed to inform thoughtful adoption. From the standpoint of the surveillant assemblage, performance metrics are but one discrete concern. Integrating AI into eyewitness procedures is one form of *rhizomatic expansion*, incorporating memory, credibility, and judgment into a broader informational infrastructure that renders persons knowable through circulating data profiles. Improvements in efficiencies are to be celebrated, but they should not distract us from asking whether incorporation fundamentally alters evidentiary authority and the institutional conditions under which suspicion is produced and acted upon.

Human versus Computer

Measuring AI performance against humans strengthens our understanding of its capabilities. Both human eyewitnesses and AI are affected by biases, environmental factors, and occlusions, circumstances where facial features are at least partially obstructed, such as a burglar wearing a mask or a shooter wearing sunglasses in surveillance imagery (Noyes et al., 2021). The general face recognition problem refers to the numerous obstacles that algorithmic systems must overcome to perform on par with or better than humans (e.g., poor lighting, low resolution, varying angles, occlusions, etc.). Phillips and O'Toole (2014) found that while computers outperformed humans in matching (frontal) faces from images, humans maintained their edge for video and still matching with increased complexity, leading them to affirm that "overall, humans are the most accurate face recognition systems" (p. 74). However, the gap has all but closed. Advancements in deep learning (e.g., a type of machine learning that mimics the way the human brain functions using a neural network), specifically, deep convolutional neural networks (DCNNs), "perform nearly as well as humans, on face recognition tasks that have stymied computational modelers for decades… There is a difference, of course, between working and working like humans (O'Toole & Castillo, 2021, p. 20).

Deep learning models are rapidly advancing, achieving human-level performance under constrained conditions, and making significant progress towards solving the general facial recognition problem (Phillips & White, 2025; Phillips et al., 2018; Towler et al., 2023). However, this does not mean human expertise is any less important. Recent research advances the importance of leveraging the strengths of automation and human expertise via fusion models (i.e., combining human expertise with machine learning for facial identification tasks).

Phillips et al. (2018) compared the accuracy of forensic facial examiners, facial reviewers, super-recognizers, and four DCNNs on a complex facial identification test. Forensic examiners paired with the most recent and accurate algorithm performed better on average than pairs of forensic examiners. Forensic facial examiners, super-recognizers, and DCNNs each have their strengths and weaknesses. Super-recognizers are fast and efficient; however, they are more prone to errors and often exhibit false confidence in their identifications. Forensic examiners are slow and methodical. They outscore super-recognizers when comparing faces at different ages and make fewer errors. Furthermore, they tend to (accurately) disagree with DCNNs in some instances (Sexton et al., 2024; Towler et al., 2023). Statistical fusion improves accuracy overall.

The emerging body of fusion research supports the human-in-the-loop model, preserving the strengths of DCNNs while maintaining the balance between human discernment and machine learning. Nevertheless, the exponential advancements in AI will continue to bridge the gap, enhancing the accuracy of identifications and helping to explain how humans achieve facial identification accuracies (Phillips & White, 2025).

Many studies comparing AI and human facial recognition performance rely on still, front-facing images. Extending this work, Kleider-Offutt et al. (2024) compared FRT and human performance in a photo lineup task using surveillance footage from real crimes. Although the FRT was not error-free, it demonstrated greater discriminability than human participants, meaning it more effectively distinguished between guilty and innocent suspects. To evaluate reliability, the researchers compared FRT similarity scores with identification accuracy. Higher similarity scores were associated with greater accuracy, similar to the relationship between eyewitness confidence and identification accuracy. These findings suggest that similarity scores could help investigators interpret FRT matches during suspect identification (Kleider-Offutt et al., 2024).

While the cognitive processes underlying AI and human identifications differ, such comparisons provide insight into AI's potential to assist in the suspect identification process. Despite significant improvements in AI, it is by no means error-proof. As we discuss next, police use of AI to identify suspects is widely criticized and carries significant risks.

Potential Harms of AI Assistance in Suspect Identification

> Technology is neither good nor bad; nor is it neutral.
> —Melvin Kranzberg's First Law of Technology (Kranzberg, 1986)

Kranzberg's (1986) first law of technology is hyper relevant to ethical and policy discussions surrounding the use of AI for suspect identification. Kranzberg effectively foreshadowed emergent technology's potential consequences:

> [T]echnology's interaction with the social ecology is such that technical developments frequently have environmental, social, and human consequences

> that go far beyond the immediate purposes of the technical devices and practices themselves, and technology can have quite different results when introduced into different contexts or under different circumstances.
>
> (p. 545)

In surveillant assemblage terms, indefatigable rhizomatic expansion "derive [in part] from efforts to seek out new target populations that ostensibly require a greater degree of monitoring" (Haggerty & Ericson, 2000, p. 615).

Bragias et al.'s (2021) analysis of public perceptions of police use of AI locates three primary concerns regarding the use of FRT by law enforcement agencies: technology, authority and power, and rights and freedoms. We use these findings as a framework for our discussion of the risks and potential harms of AI assistance in suspect identification. We conclude this section by highlighting an example of how FRT may produce erroneous outcomes.

Concerns About Technology

Key technological concerns surrounding police use of FRT include the "weaponization of technology," referring to the risk that it may disproportionately impact certain groups and communities, and operational issues such as algorithmic bias and inaccuracy (Bragias et al., 2021).

Evaluations show demographic disparities in error rates, with false positives more common among American Indians, African Americans, Asians, women, and younger and older individuals, and false negatives varying by race and image quality (Grother et al., 2019). Although one large-scale study found FRT associated with reductions in violent crime and no observed racial disparities in arrests (Johnson et al., 2024), concerns persist.

As Kranzberg (1986) posited in his sixth law of technology, "Technology is a very human activity" (p. 557). In investigative settings, algorithms often return fixed candidate lists, guaranteeing false positives and shifting decisive authority to human reviewers, thereby introducing additional risks of human error and bias (Grother et al., 2019). Because AI systems reflect the data and societies that produce them, meaningful safeguards, oversight, and continual evaluation are essential to mitigate harm.

Additional technological concerns include the rapid, exponential evolution of FRT and growing apprehension that its capabilities will drive increasingly expansive deployments in policing contexts (Bragias et al., 2021). While FRT is not a novel concept, its maturation and evolving law enforcement use cases exhibit hallmarks of function creep (i.e., FRT use extending into contexts and purposes beyond its initial intention), leading Guo and Kennedy (2023) to lament that FRT "further fundamentally endangers society as a whole – nurturing a culture of authoritarian control of objects and eroding the culture of policing by consent of autonomous, dignified subjects" (p. 411).

Concerns About Authority and Power

Concerns about authority and power focus on the potential overreach of law enforcement, public mistrust, state control, and the absence of legal guardrails (Bragias et al., 2021). Public acceptance of FRT, particularly live facial recognition, appears closely tied to privacy concerns, though perceptions of police legitimacy and shared values can mitigate those fears (Bradford et al., 2020).

As we discuss later, police FRT use is underregulated. In the absence of a mature jurisprudence, Garvie et al. (2016) propose key constitutional and normative questions to guide deployment, including whether searches are targeted or dragnet-style, transparent or invisible, limited or expansive in database scope, real-time or retrospective, and consistent with traditional biometric practices (e.g., fingerprints) or novel. Their framework categorizes searches that are discrete, transparent, and query limited databases as moderate risk. Conversely, real-time, dragnet, and invisible searches using unconstrained databases are considered very high risk (Garvie et al., 2016). From this framework, retrospective and real-time video surveillance stand out as the highest risk and thus most subversive to countervailing civil liberty interests.

Concerns About Rights and Freedoms

Police use of FRT also generates concerns related to rights and freedoms, including restrictions on freedom of movement, privacy erosion, and risks to biometric data protection (Bragias et al., 2021). Large-scale databases, such as Clearview AI's reported 60 billion-image law enforcement repository (www.clearview.ai), illustrate the unprecedented scope of modern facial recognition surveillance, prompting comparisons to Orwellian notions of pervasive monitoring. Police use of platforms like Clearview's enables retrospective identification, representing a seismic shift from traditional law enforcement practices in which narrowly scoped personal data is disclosed through legal compulsion. Instead, some private companies now proactively scrape and compile vast quantities of personal data for law enforcement use (Rezende, 2020). As Haggerty and Ericson (2000) write, "The public is slowly awakening to the profits that are being made from the sale of their data doubles" (p. 616).

Digital investigations involving FRT implicate privacy and data protection rights at every stage—collection, analysis, and use (Simmler & Canova, 2025). Scholars argue that such deployments may interfere with nations' legal frameworks, including provisions of the European Convention on Human Rights and the Charter of Fundamental Rights of the EU (Simmler & Canova, 2025), the Canadian Charter of Rights and Freedoms (West, 2025), and the US Constitution (Rogez, 2025).

The Case of Robert Williams

In 2020, the Detroit Police Department wrongfully arrested Robert Williams, a Black man, after an FRT system matched his expired driver's license photo to low-resolution surveillance footage of a theft (Morioka, 2024). The image was run through state and federal databases, generating hundreds of potential matches. Although Williams was not consistently identified across systems, and the FBI returned no matches, an analyst selected his photo based on visual inspection. His image was then placed in a photo array shown to a loss prevention employee who had only viewed the surveillance footage and was not an actual eyewitness. The employee's identification led to Williams's arrest.

Expert witness Dr. Michael King later explained that the probe image was of such poor quality that it should have been rejected, noting that standard systems typically include safeguards to filter unreliable images. He concluded that investigators failed to appreciate the technology's limitations and did not independently scrutinize the lead (King, 2023, as cited in *Williams v. City of Detroit*, No. 21-cv-10827). The Williams case highlights broader procedural risks in law enforcement's reliance on FRT, concerns echoed in similar incidents around the globe (Booth & Wilding, 2026; Hill, 2020).

The Role of the Private Sector

The New York Times recently uncovered an internal memorandum from Meta (formerly Facebook) discussing the company's plans to incorporate FRT into its "Smart Glasses." Disturbingly, the memorandum acknowledged that the move was likely to draw the ire of civil liberties groups, suggesting FRT launch under the cover of an ensuing political tempest, hoping that the media frenzy would distract from the move. This was also on the heels of Meta settling billion-dollar lawsuits for collecting facial recognition data from Facebook's users without their consent (Hill et al., 2026).

FRT has also been a defining feature of the United States' Immigration and Customs Enforcement (ICE) crackdowns and occupations under President Trump. During "Operation Metro Surge," ICE contracted with Clearview AI and Mobile Fortify to leverage FRT. Soon after, videos spread of agents using mobile devices to conduct FRT in the field. In some of the recordings, agents explicitly inform individuals that their faces are being scanned and added to a database. On the backend, the Department of Homeland Security (DHS) is working with Palantir to build a location-tracking system for immigration enforcement, as well as with Paragon to remotely infiltrate individuals' cell phones, and with Penlink to build profiles of individuals via web scraping (Frenkel & Krolik, 2026).

A recent lawsuit filed against the DHS claims that from the company's launch in June of 2025 through January of 2026, Mobile Fortify processed over 100,000 biometric field identifications using FRT. The lawsuit also accentuates a key shift in law enforcement usage from defined entry points to field deployments, citing internal DHS policy that allows Mobile Fortify use for field identifications—even while acknowledging that the biometric application will inevitably collect photos of citizens, adding them to a database with a 15-year retention period (*State of Illinois & City of Chicago v. Department of Homeland Security et al.*, 2026).

While field-level generation of *body doubles* by law enforcement is one form of *rhizomatic expansion*, it is but a snapshot of the broader surveillant assemblage. When we open the aperture, we recognize that surveillance is now fully co-produced through the rhizomatic expansion and convergence of state and non-state actors. "[T]he surveillant assemblage transcends institutional boundaries, systems intended to serve one purpose find other uses" (Haggerty & Ericson, p. 616).

A thought experiment follows. If Meta was to green-light FRT in smart glasses, *sidewalk peace* could become a function of citizen observers generating digital *body doubles*—synthesized by private firms and routed back to law enforcement—the convergence of the surveillant assemblage in which the watchmen dissolve into the watched.

The Regulatory Landscape of FRT

Considering the significant risks posed by AI-assisted identifications, there are growing calls to regulate the use of biometric data, particularly FRT (Wang et al., 2024). Arguably, a government has a duty to protect its people from the potential harm of AI (Qandeel, 2024), and some nations have done more than others to meet this obligation. This section offers a broad overview of approaches to oversight of police use of FRT.

Before examining the regulatory landscape, it is necessary to clarify a few points. First, although FRT is not the only AI tool that can assist police in identifying suspects, it is the focus of this section given its increasingly controversial and expanding role in police work. Second, it bears noting that few provisions directly govern the use of AI tools in the context of eyewitness identification. However, to the extent that regulations address police applications of FRT, they may be interpreted to encompass the use of FRT with human eyewitnesses. Finally, we focus on the regulation of FRT use by public organizations (law enforcement) rather than private entities (see Chen and Wang, 2023, for a comparative analysis of FRT regulation in the private sector).

European Union

In August 2024, the European Union Artificial Intelligence Act took effect. The Act distinguishes between real-time and ex-post FRT and regulates AI systems based on their level of risk (unacceptable, high, limited, or minimal) to fundamental rights (European Parliament & Council of the European Union [EP & Council], 2024). The use of FRT is restricted or prohibited based on the type of system involved and the context in which it is used. For example, real-time FRT use by law enforcement has unacceptable risk and is therefore prohibited, though there are exceptions. The Act permits use of high-risk AI systems, including those used for biometric identification, but mandates the implementation of risk-management and quality-management systems, along with other regulatory safeguards (EP & Council, 2024). Despite the progress this Act makes in regulating AI use, its overall effectiveness may be constrained by the exceptions it permits and by uncertainties regarding the Union's authority to regulate Member States' criminal proceedings (Simmler & Canova, 2025).

Canada and United States

In contrast to the EU, both Canada and the United States lack federal legislation that expressly governs law enforcement use of FRT (West, 2025). In the absence of a comprehensive national framework, regulation instead depends on an amalgam of existing federal privacy law, agency-issued guidance, and subnational laws and policies.

In Canada, the legal framework governing police use of FRT "comprises a patchwork of statutes and the common law," including federal and provincial privacy legislation, statutes regulating police powers, and Charter jurisprudence (Office of the Privacy Commissioner of Canada [OPC], 2022). For instance, the *Privacy Act* regulates the collection, use, and disclosure of personal information by federal institutions but does not explicitly address FRT (OPC, 2024). As a result, much of the regulation surrounding FRT occurs at subnational levels of government. In Quebec, for example, use of biometric data is governed by a 2001 law; however, no comparable legislation exists in other Canadian provinces (OPC, 2022; West, 2025). At the municipal level, the Toronto Police Services Board introduced a policy regulating the deployment of new or enhanced AI technologies, including FRT, which requires evaluation of new systems as well as ongoing monitoring, reporting, and review (Toronto Police Services Board, 2024).

In the United States, regulations governing police use of FRT also vary widely across jurisdictions. In 2023, the Department of Homeland Security (DHS) issued a directive regulating the use of FRT across its components; however, the directive was removed from the DHS website in 2025 without explanation, leaving it unclear whether it continues to govern DHS agencies (Privacy and Civil Liberties Oversight Board, 2025). At the state and local levels, some jurisdictions initially enacted bans and moratoria on police use of FRT (e.g., Vermont and San Francisco, California; Rogez, 2025). Over time, however, outright bans have become less common than more targeted regulatory approaches that specify when FRT may be used, who is authorized to use it, and the individuals who may be subject to it (Fidler & Hurwitz, 2024; Rogez, 2025). Vermont, for instance, now permits the use of FRT by law enforcement in cases involving sexual exploitation of children. Other states, such as Alabama and Colorado, permit police use of FRT but specify that it cannot be used as the sole basis to establish probable cause (Laperruque, 2025). In Detroit, regulation of FRT emerged through the settlement of Robert Williams's case, which imposed extensive policy and procedural reforms on the Detroit Police Department. Among these changes, officers are prohibited from making an arrest based solely on a facial recognition match or relying exclusively on a photo lineup generated immediately following a facial recognition search (American Civil Liberties Union, 2024).

Policy Recommendations

Despite calls to completely prohibit police use of FRT (e.g., Barrett, 2020; Hartzog et al., 2025), it appears that the technology is here to stay. The rapid expansion of FRT use among law enforcement has outpaced governance and thoughtful regulation. Nevertheless, guidance and best practices are taking shape. In 2016, the Georgetown Law Center on Privacy & Technology released a model policy, informed by the risks identified through its comprehensive study of state and local law enforcement use of FRT. The policy recommendations include, but are not limited to, prohibiting real-time searches, requiring that searches be conducted by trained examiners with built-in peer review, and establishing penalties to deter misuse (for the full model policy, see Garvie et al., 2016). Following Georgetown's work to establish policy, New York University's (NYU) School of Law, Policing Project has released a suite of materials and checklists for national, state, and local legislature (Policing Project, 2025), and the National League of Cities has released a comprehensive list of recommendations for local and municipal consideration (Geraghty, 2021).

Given the severity of concerns for personal privacy and polarization surrounding law enforcement deployment of FRT, public buy-in is the fulcrum on which the entire issue turns. Hill et al. (2022) call on law enforcement executives and decision makers to go beyond public consultation and make public engagement, which they define as "having the public actively co-construct policy through a two-way dialogue with policy-makers" (p. 330), a guiding principle of FRT programming.

The black box of deep learning inhibits oversight that focuses on the learning process itself and the biases it may hold. Nevertheless, human monitoring of outputs is paramount. Installing accountability systems is prudent to illuminate the broader outcomes of algorithms. One way of establishing transparency and accountability is using algorithmic audits (see e.g., Buolamwini & Gebru, 2018; Radiya-Dixit & Neff, 2023). Audits evaluate algorithmic systems to identify harmful behaviour and are usually conducted after a system has been deployed.

Algorithmic audits can evaluate various elements of a system, such as user experience, impact, reliability, or compliance (Radiya-Dixit & Neff, 2023).

Algorithmic audits have the potential to regulate and provide oversight for the fair and impartial use of AI for suspect identification. As the GAO's reporting makes evident, at a minimum, agencies need to maintain administrative records tracking employee use of agency and external FRT (US GAO, 2021). Legislators, policymakers, advocates, and police leaders can, and should, adopt these systems of accountability before deploying an AI technology in the field and as an ongoing check and balance of the program to ensure continuous calibration. With thoughtful placement of guardrails, FRT appears central to realizing a more evolved model of public safety through deterrence and retroactive investigation.

Conclusion

As E.O. Wilson famously asserted, "The real problem of humanity is the following: we have palaeolithic emotions, medieval institutions and God-like technology. And it is terrifically dangerous, and it is now approaching a point of crisis overall" (Watson & Wilson, 2009, 51:00). The use of AI assistance, particularly computational facial recognition, for suspect identification touches on each of Wilson's points: 1.) human forensic facial recognition is based on limited and immature science, 2.) AI involves god-like computations beyond human faculties to fully understand, and 3.) the pace of formal oversight systems and institutions is aptly described as slothful, constrained by their bureaucratic nature, and at least in many western societies, by the decentralized nature of governance and law enforcement.

More importantly, while police *exist* within Haggerty and Ericson's surveillant assemblage, and *ergo* are equally the subject of such surveillance, their expanse far exceeds the police institution. Naturally, civil rights observers engage in a process of reduction, seeking to ban certain AI deployments and police use cases in the hopes of circumventing their chilling effects on society writ large, but this inclination operates under the false assumption that we can ward off the assemblage by attending to its *component parts* and *discrete* technologies. As Haggerty and Ericson (2000) lament:

> [T]he surveillant assemblage cannot be dismantled by prohibiting a particularly unpalatable technology. Nor can it be attacked by focusing criticism on a single bureaucracy or institution. In the face of multiple connections across myriad technologies and practices, struggles against particular manifestations of surveillance, as important as they might be, are akin to efforts to keep the ocean's tide back with a broom – a frantic focus on a particular unpalatable technology or practice while the general tide of surveillance washes over us all. (p. 609)

The tide's erosive capacity is progressive in nature, steadily drawing down on personal anonymity, which Haggerty and Ericson (2000) refer to as the disappearance of disappearance. A paradox unfolds—while AI advances police capacity for suspect identification, it does so at the cost of anonymity, and the complete extinction of anonymity renders the sleuth's raison d'être obsolete.

Police and their constituents (we) have two choices. We can view the surveillant assemblage framework as an intractable problem and accept an outlook of nihilism, or we can recognize that assemblage is diagnostic and not fatalistic. If we accept the latter, then the question becomes how policing navigates its position within a surveillance infrastructure that is already diffuse, privatized, and persistent.

FRT abstracts the body into biometric data flows, rendering faces searchable across vast repositories through 1:1 verification, 1:N identification, and increasingly real-time deployments. AI-assisted eyewitness tools extend this logic into the cognitive domain by converting memory, confidence, and testimony into probabilistic classifications and algorithmically standardized lineups. In concert, these systems transcend investigative efficiency; they embed policing within a broader data infrastructure in which both suspects and witnesses become "data doubles" circulating across institutional networks. In this sense, contemporary suspect identification reflects what Haggerty (2025) describes as surveillantization, the broader societal process through which surveillance capacities proliferate and become normalized within systems of governance.

Within this environment, suspicion is no longer bounded by direct observation but from database queries, match scores, and model outputs generated upstream from officer discretion. Investigative trajectories may begin with biometric similarity thresholds or machine-learning credibility assessments rather than human tips or eyewitness accounts. Officers still exercise judgment, but within parameters shaped by algorithmic systems—deciding when to initiate a search, how to interpret confidence scores, and whether to pursue tentative matches. Supervisors must likewise oversee not only personnel but also search practices, algorithmic performance disparities, and vendor-mediated infrastructures. AI thus becomes embedded in chains of command, training protocols, documentation practices, and risk management frameworks, restructuring what counts as investigative expertise.

Viewed through Packer's (1964) crime control-due process framework, these developments intensify longstanding tensions within policing. FRT and AI-supported eyewitness tools expand the capacity for rapid suspect identification, reinforcing the efficiency aims of the crime control model. Simultaneously, they raise due process concerns by normalizing probabilistic suspicion, diffusing accountability across proprietary systems, and embedding opaque decision-support tools within coercive processes. The diffuse incorporation of AI into the suspect identification process is upon us; how policing institutions self-regulate its integration has yet to mature. Whether surveillance infrastructures will consolidate into opaque systems of algorithmic suspicion or instead be constrained by transparency, oversight, and democratic safeguards will depend on those efforts.

References

American Civil Liberties Union. (2024, June 28). *Civil rights advocates achieve the nation's strongest police department policy on facial recognition technology*. https://www.aclu.org/press-releases/civil-rights-advocates-achieve-the-nations-strongest-police-department-policy-on-facial-recognition-technology

Bacci, N., Davimes, J. G., Steyn, M., & Briers, N. (2021). Forensic facial comparison: Current status, limitations, and future directions. *Biology*, *10*(12), 1269. https://doi.org/10.3390/biology10121269

Barrett, L. (2020). Ban facial recognition technologies for children–and for everyone else. *Journal of Science & Technology Law*, *26*(2), 223–285. https://www.bu.edu/jostl/files/2020/08/1-Barrett.pdf

Bell, R., Menne, N. M., Mayer, C., & Buchner, A. (2024). On the advantages of using AI-generated images of filler faces for creating fair lineups. *Scientific Reports*, *14*, Article 12304. https://doi.org/10.1038/s41598-024-63004-z

Bledsoe, W. W. (1966). The model method in facial recognition. *Panoramic Research Inc.*, Palo Alto, CA, Rep. PR1, *15*(47), 2.

Bolle, R. M., Connell, J. H., Pankanti, S., Ratha, N. K., & Senior, A. W. (2013). *Guide to biometrics*. Springer Science & Business Media.

Booth, R., & Wilding, M. (2026, February 25). Facial recognition error prompts police to arrest Asian man for burglary 100 miles away. *The Guardian*. https://www.theguardian.com/technology/2026/feb/25/facial-recognition-error-prompts-police-to-arrest-asian-man-for-burglary-100-miles-away?utm_source=chatgpt.com

Boucher, H. (2025, November 15). Drones, DNA and AI: How technology is transforming the search for missing people. *The Independent*. https://www.independent.co.uk/news/uk/home-news/missing-people-charity-police-ai-tech-drones-b2863591.html

Bradford, B., Yesberg, J. A., Jackson, J., & Dawson, P. (2020). Live facial recognition: Trust and legitimacy as predictors of public support for police use of new technology. *The British Journal of Criminology*, *60*(6), 1502–1522. https://doi.org/10.1093/bjc/azaa032

Bragias, A., Hine, K., & Fleet, R. (2021). 'Only in our best interest, right?' Public perceptions of police use of facial recognition technology. *Police Practice and Research*, *22*(6), 1637–1654. https://doi.org/10.1080/15614263.2021.1942873

Buolamwini, J., & Gebru, T. (2018). Gender shades: Intersectional accuracy disparities in commercial gender classification. *Proceedings of Machine Learning Research*, *81*, 1–15.

Chen, W., & Wang, M. (2023). Regulating the use of facial recognition technology across borders: A comparative case analysis of the European Union, the United States, and China. *Telecommunications Policy*, *47*(2), Article 102482. https://doi.org/10.1016/j.telpol.2022.102482

Clarke, R. (1988). Information technology and dataveillance. *Communications of the ACM*, *31*(5), 498–512.

El Fadel, N. (2025). Facial recognition algorithms: A systematic literature review. *Journal of Imaging*, *11*(2), Article 58. https://doi.org/10.3390/jimaging11020058

European Parliament and Council of the European Union. (2024). Regulation (EU) 2024/1689 of the European Parliament and of the Council of 13 June 2024 laying down harmonised rules on artificial intelligence (Artificial Intelligence Act). Official Journal of the European Union, L 1689. https://eur-lex.europa.eu/legal-content/EN/TXT/?uri=CELEX:32024R1689

Facial Identification Scientific Working Group. (2022, November 4). *Guide for facial comparison training of examiners to competency*. https://fiswg.org/fiswg_guide_for_facial_comp_trng_of_exmrs_to_competency_v1.0_2022.11.04.pdf

Fidler, M., & Hurwitz, J. (2024). An overview of facial recognition technology regulation in the United States. In R. Matulionyte & M. Zalnieriute (Eds.), *The Cambridge handbook of facial recognition in the modern state* (pp. 214–227). Cambridge University Press.

Frenkel, S., & Krolik, A. (2026, January 30). How ICE already knows who Minneapolis protesters are. *The New York Times*. https://www.nytimes.com/2026/01/30/technology/tech-ice-facial-recognition-palantir.html

Gamoran, A., Lieberman, L., Gilead, M., Dobbins, I. G., & Sadeh, T. (2024). Detecting recollection: Human evaluators can successfully assess the veracity of others' memories, *Proc. Proceedings of the National Academy of Sciences of the U.S.A*, *121*(22), Article e2310979121. https://doi.org/10.1073/pnas.2310979121

Garvie, C., Bedoya, A., & Frankle, J. (2016, October 18). *The perpetual line-up. Unregulated police face recognition in America*. Georgetown Law Center on Privacy & Technology. https://www.perpetuallineup.org/

Geraghty, L. (2021). *Facial recognition report*. National League of Cities. https://www.nlc.org/wp-content/uploads/2021/04/NLC-Facial-Recognition-Report.pdf

Greenspan, R. L., & Bergold, A. N. (2025). Can AI-generated faces serve as fillers in eyewitness lineups? *Memory*, *33*(4), 416–429. https://doi.org/10.1080/09658211.2025.2467134

Greenspan, R. L., Lyman, A., & Heaton, P. (2024). Assessing verbal eyewitness confidence statements using natural language processing. *Psychological Science*, *35*(3), 277–287. https://doi.org/10.1177/09567976241229028

Grother, P., Ngan, M., & Hanaoka, K. (2019). *Face recognition vendor test (FVRT) Part 3: Demographic effects*. National Institute of Standards and Technology. Gaithersburg, MD.

Guo, Z., & Kennedy, L. (2023). Policing based on automatic facial recognition. *Artificial Intelligence and Law*, *31*(2), 397–443. https://doi.org/10.1007/s10506-022-09330-x

Gustafsson, P. U., Lachmann, T., & Laukka, P. (2025). Machine learning predicts accuracy in eyewitnesses' voices. *Journal of Nonverbal Behavior*, *49*(1), 155–169. https://psycnet.apa.org/doi/10.1007/s10919-024-00474-9

Haggerty, K. D. (2025). On assemblages and surveillantization: Thinking and rethinking surveillance theory. *Surveillance and Society*, *23*(4), 529–544. https://doi.org/10.24908/ss.v23i4.20081

Haggerty, K. D., & Ericson, R. V. (2000). The surveillant assemblage. *British Journal of Sociology*, *51*(4), 605–622. https://doi.org/10.1080/00071310020015280

Hartzog, W., Selinger, E., & Rhee, J. H. (2025). Normalizing facial recognition technology and the end of obscurity. *European Review of Digital Administration & Law*, *6*(1), 163–176. https://scholarship.law.bu.edu/cgi/viewcontent.cgi?params=/context/faculty_scholarship/article/5073/&path_info=Normalizing_Facial_Recognition_Technology_and_The_End_of_Obscurity.pdf

Heyer, R., & Semmler, C. (2013). Forensic confirmation bias: The case of facial image comparison. *Journal of Applied Research in Memory and Cognition*, *2*(1), 68–70. https://psycnet.apa.org/doi/10.1016/j.jarmac.2013.01.008

Hill, D., O'Connor, C. D., & Slane, A. (2022). Police use of facial recognition technology: The potential for engaging the public through co-constructed policy-making. *International Journal of Police Science & Management*, *24*(3), 325–335. https://doi.org/10.1177/14613557221089558

Hill, K. (2020, December 29). Another arrest, and jail time, due to a bad facial recognition match. *The New York Times*. https://www.nytimes.com/2020/12/29/technology/facial-recognition-misidentify-jail.html

Hill, K., Huang, K., & Isaac, M. (2026, February 13). Meta plans to add facial recognition to its smart glasses. *The New York Times*. https://www.nytimes.com/2026/02/13/technology/meta-facial-recognition-smart-glasses.html

Hodge, S. D., Jr. (2020). Big Brother is watching: Law enforcement's use of digital technology in the twenty-first century. *University of Cincinnati Law Review*, *89*(1), 30–83. https://scholarship.law.uc.edu/uclr/vol89/iss1/2

International Organization for Standardization, & International Electrotechnical Commission. (2022). *Information technology — Artificial intelligence — Artificial intelligence concepts and terminology (ISO/IEC 22989:2022)*. https://www.iso.org/obp/ui/en/#iso:std:iso-iec:22989:ed-1:v1:en.

Jacobs, J. (1961). *The death and life of great American cities*. Random House.

Jäger, J. (2001). Photography: A means of surveillance? Judicial photography, 1850 to 1900. *Crime, Histoire & Sociétés/Crime, History & Societies*, *5*(1), 27–51.

Johnson, T. L., Johnson, N. N., Topalli, V., McCurdy, D., & Wallace, A. (2024). Police facial recognition applications and violent crime control in U.S. cities. *Cities*, *155*, Article 105472. https://doi.org/10.1016/j.cities.2024.105472

Kelso, L. E., Dobolyi, D. G., Grabman, J. H., & Dodson, C. S. (2025a). AI assistance improves people's ability to distinguish correct from incorrect eyewitness lineup identifications. *Proceedings of the National Academy of Sciences of the U.S.A*, *122*(21), Article e2503971122. https://doi.org/10.1073/pnas.2503971122

Kelso, L. E., Grabman, J. H., Dobolyi, D. G., & Dodson, C. S. (2025b). Does artificial intelligence (AI) assistance mitigate biased evaluations of eyewitness identifications? *Journal of Applied Research in Memory and Cognition*, *14*(1), 130–139. https://psycnet.apa.org/doi/10.1037/mac0000192

King, M. C. (2023). *Expert witness report of Dr. Michael C. King regarding automatied facial recognition technology*, May. Case No. 21-cv-10827, U.S. District Court for the Eastern District of Michigan [Expert report].

Kleider-Offutt, H., Stevens, B., Mickes, L., & Boogert, S. (2024). Application of artificial intelligence to eyewitness identification. *Cognitive Research: Principles and Implications*, *9*, Article 19. https://doi.org/10.1186/s41235-024-00542-0

Kranzberg, M. (1986). Technology and history: "Kranzberg's Laws". *Technology and Culture*, *27*(3), 544–560. https://muse.jhu.edu/article/889531

Laperruque, J. (2025, January 6). *Status of state laws on facial recognition surveillance: Continued progress and smart innovations*. Tech Policy Press. https://www.techpolicy.press/status-of-state-laws-on-facial-recognition-surveillance-continued-progress-and-smart-innovations/

Lee, W.-J., Wilkinson, C., Memon, A., & Houston, K. (2009). Matching unfamiliar faces from poor quality closed-circuit television (CCTV) footage: An evaluation of the effect of training on facial identification ability. *AXIS*, *1*(1), 19–28.

Li, L., Mu, X., Li, S., & Peng, H. (2020). A review of face recognition technology. *IEEE Access*, *8*, 139110–139120. DOI: 10.1109/ACCESS.2020.3011028

Masri, L. (2023, March 28). *Facial recognition is helping Putin curb dissent with the aid of U.S. tech*. Reuters. https://www.reuters.com/investigates/special-report/ukraine-crisis-russia-detentions/

Morioka, S. (2024). *Flawed facial recognition technology leads to wrongful arrest and historic settlement*. Law Quadrangle. https://quadrangle.michigan.law.umich.edu/issues/winter-2024-2025/flawed-facial-recognition-technology-leads-wrongful-arrest-and-historic

National Registry of Exonerations. (n.d.). *% exonerations by contributing factor*. Retrieved November 10, 2025, from https://exonerationregistry.org/exonerations-contributing-factor

Noyes, E., Davis, J. P., Petrov, N., Gray, K. L., & Ritchie, K. L. (2021). The effect of face masks and sunglasses on identity and expression recognition with super-recognizers and typical observers. *Royal Society Open Science*, *8*, Article 201169. https://doi.org/10.1098/rsos.201169

O'Toole, A. J., & Castillo, C. D. (2021). Face recognition by humans and machines: Three fundamental advances from deep learning. *Annual Review of Vision Science*, *7*, 543–570. https://doi.org/10.1146/annurev-vision-093019-111701

Office of the Privacy Commissioner of Canada. (2022, May 2). *Privacy guidance on facial recognition for police agencies*. https://www.priv.gc.ca/en/privacy-topics/surveillance/police-and-public-safety/gd_fr_202205/

Office of the Privacy Commissioner of Canada. (2024, April 8). *About the OPC*. https://www.priv.gc.ca/en/about-the-opc/

Packer, H. L. (1964). Two models of the criminal process. *University of Pennsylvania Law Review*, *113*(1), 1–68.

Phillips, P. J., & O'Toole, A. J. (2014). Comparison of human and computer performance across face recognition experiments. *Image and Vision Computing*, *32*(1), 74–85. https://doi.org/10.1016/j.imavis.2013.12.002

Phillips, P. J., & White, D. (2025). The state of modelling face processing in humans with deep learning. *British Journal of Psychology* [Advance online publication]. https://doi.org/10.1111/bjop.12794

Phillips, P. J., Yates, A. N., Hu, Y., Hahn, C. A., Noyes, E., Jackson, K., Cavazos, J. G., Jeckeln, G., Ranjan, R., Sankaranarayanan, S., Chen, J.-C., Castillo, C. D., Chellapa, R., White, D., & O'Toole, A. J. (2018). Face recognition accuracy of forensic examiners, superrecognizers, and face recognition algorithms. *Proceedings of the National Academy of Sciences*, *115*(24), 6171–6176. https://doi.org/10.1073/pnas.1721355115

Policing Project. (2025). *Regulating police use of face recognition technology – resources for legislators*. https://www.policingproject.org/regulating-police-use-of-face-recognition-technology

Postman, N. (1992). *Technopoly: The surrender of culture to technology*. Knopf.

Privacy and Civil Liberties Oversight Board. (2025, May 9). *Use of facial recognition technology by the Transportation Security Administration*. https://www.pclob.gov/Oversight

Privacy International. (2023, November 7). *UK MPs asleep at the wheel as facial recognition technology spells the end of privacy in public*. https://privacyinternational.org/long-read/5155/uk-mps-asleep-wheel-facial-recognition-technology-spells-end-privacy-public

Privacy International. (2024, December). *Protest surveillance into courts*. https://privacyinternational.org/sites/default/files/2025-01/Protest-surveillance-into-courts.pdf

Purshouse, J., & Campbell, L. (2022). Automated facial recognition and policing: A bridge too far?. *Legal Studies*, *42*(2), 209–227. DOI:10.1017/lst.2021.22

Qandeel, M. (2024). Facial recognition technology: Regulations, rights and the rule of law. *Frontiers in Big Data*, *7*, Article 1354659. https://doi.org/10.3389/fdata.2024.1354659

Qinjun, L., Tianwei, C., Yan, Z., & Yuying, W. (2023). Facial recognition technology: A comprehensive overview. *Academic Journal of Computing & Information Science*, *6*(7), 15–26. DOI: 10.25236/AJCIS.2023.060703

Radiya-Dixit, E., & Neff, G. (2023). A sociotechnical audit: Assessing police use of facial recognition. *Proceedings of the 2023 ACM Conference on Fairness, Accountability, and Transparency*, 1334–1346. https://doi.org/10.1145/3593013.3594084

Raji, I. D., & Fried, G. (2021). About face: A survey of facial recognition evaluation. arXiv preprint arXiv:2102.00813.

Rezende, I. N. (2020). Facial recognition in police hands: Assessing the 'Clearview case' from a European perspective. *New Journal of European Criminal Law*, *11*(3), 375–389. https://doi.org/10.1177/2032284420948161

Richardson, J. F. (1961). *The history of police protection in New York City, 1800-1870.* New York University.

Rogez, Y.-M. (2025). From identification to mass surveillance: FRT use and regulation in the United States of America. *European Review of Digital Administration & Law, 6*(1), 145–153. https://www.erdalreview.eu/free-download/97912218211615.pdf

Seale-Carlisle, T. M., Grabman, J. H., Dobolyi, D. G., & Dodson, C. S. (2025). A comparison between numeric confidence ratings and verbal confidence statements. *Journal of Experimental Psychology: Applied, 31*(1), 12–39. https://psycnet.apa.org/doi/10.1037/xap0000525

Seale-Carlisle, T. M., Grabman, J. H., & Dodson, C. S. (2022). The language of accurate and inaccurate eyewitnesses. *Journal of Experimental Psychology: General, 151*(6), 1283–1305. https://psycnet.apa.org/doi/10.1037/xge0001152

Selwyn, N., Andrejevic, M., O'Neill, C., Gu, X., & Smith, G. (2024). Facial recognition technology: Key issues and emerging concerns. In R. Matulionyte & M. Zalnieriute (Eds.), *The Cambridge handbook of facial recognition in the modern state* (pp. 11–28). Cambridge University Press.

Sexton, L., Moreton, R., Noyes, E., Martinez, S. C., & Laurence, S. (2024). The effect of facial ageing on forensic facial image comparison. *Applied Cognitive Psychology, 38*(1), Article e4153. https://doi.org/10.1002/acp.4153

Sharma, S. (2024). Benefits or concerns of AI: A multistakeholder responsibility. *Futures, 157*, Article 103328. https://doi.org/10.1016/j.futures.2024.103328

Simmler, M., & Canova, G. (2025). Facial recognition technology in law enforcement: Regulating data analysis of another kind. *Computer Law & Security Review, 56*, Article 106092. https://doi.org/10.1016/j.clsr.2024.106092

Sims, L., & Johnson, S. (2024). The effectiveness of quality training on facial examination and identification. In T. Bourlai (Ed.), *Face recognition across the imaging spectrum* (pp. 115–132). Springer.

Smith, A. M., Ayala, N. T., & Ying, R. C. (2024). Using artificial intelligence to assess eyewitness identification accuracy. *Journal of Applied Research in Memory and Cognition, 13*(4), 500–504. https://psycnet.apa.org/doi/10.1037/mac0000206

State of Illinois & City of Chicago v. Department of Homeland Security et al. (2026). No. 1:26-cv-00321 (N.D. Ill.).

Swanson, C. R., Taylor, R. W., Territo, L., & Fox, B. (2022). *Criminal investigation* (13th ed.). McGraw Hill.

Szeliski, R. (2022). *Computer vision: algorithms and applications* (2nd ed.). Springer.

Tolba, A., El-Baz, A., & El-Harby, A. (2005). Face recognition: A literature review. *International Journal of Signal Processing, 2*(2), 88–103.

Toronto Police Services Board. (2024, January 11). *Use of artificial intelligence technology.* https://tpsb.ca/policies-by-laws/board-policies/195-use-of-artificial-intelligence-technology

Towler, A., Dunn, J. D., Castro Martínez, S., Moreton, R., Eklöf, F., Ruifrok, A., Kemp, R. I., & White, D. (2023). Diverse types of expertise in facial recognition. *Scientific Reports, 13*, Article 11396. https://doi.org/10.1038/s41598-023-28632-x

U.S. Department of Homeland Security. (2025, September 29). *Ensuring AI is used responsibly.* https://www.dhs.gov/ai/ensuring-ai-is-used-responsibly

U.S. Government Accountability Office. (2021, July 13). *Facial recognition technology: Federal law enforcement agencies should have better awareness of systems used by employees.* https://www.gao.gov/products/gao-21-105309

Wanyonyi, D., & Celik, T. (2022). Open-source face recognition frameworks: A review of the landscape. *IEEE Access, 10*, 50601–50623. https://ieeexplore.ieee.org/abstract/document/9762647

Wang, X., Wu, Y. C., Zhou, M., & Fu, Hongpeng. (2024). Beyond surveillance: Privacy, ethics, and regulations in face recognition technology. *Frontiers in Big Data*, *7*, Article 1337465. https://doi.org/10.3389/fdata.2024.1337465

Watson, J. D., & Wilson, E. O. (2009, September 9). *Looking back, looking forward: A conversation with James D. Watson and Edward O. Wilson* [Video]. Harvard Museum of Natural History.

Wells, G. L., Kovera, M. B., Douglass, A. B., Brewer, N., Meissner, C. A., & Wixted, J. T. (2020). Policy and procedure recommendations for the collection and preservation of eyewitness identification evidence. *Law and Human Behavior*, *44*(1), 3–36. https://doi.org/10.1037/lhb0000359

West, L. (2025). Facial recognition through the lens of national legislations – Canada. *European Review of Digital Administration & Law*, *6*(1), 199–125. https://www.erdalreview.eu/free-download/979122182111612.pdf

White, D., & Burton, A. M. (2022). Individual differences and the multidimensional nature of face perception. *Nature Reviews Psychology*, *1*(5), 287–300. https://doi.org/10.1038/s44159-022-00041-3

White, D., Towler, A., & Kemp, R. (2021). Understanding professional expertise in unfamiliar face matching. In M. Bindemann (Ed.), *Forensic face matching* (pp. 62–88). Oxford University Press.

Zalnieriute, M. (2024). Power and protest: Facial recognition and public space surveillance. In R. Matulionyte & M. Zalnieriute (Eds.), *The Cambridge handbook of facial recognition in the modern state* (pp. 96–111). Cambridge University Press. https://doi.org/10.1017/9781009321211.009

12

"THE RCMP TRAINED KILLER HORSES"

Misinformation in Public Policing

Laura Huey, Cole Heffren, and Lorna Ferguson

Introduction

In response to growing frustration with the Provincial and Federal COVID-19 vaccine and mask mandates, patchwork and contradictory isolation regulations, and lockdowns that left many at the brink of financial bankruptcy, large groups of disaffected Canadians came together to protest in ways not previously seen before. The most significant of these events occurred in the nation's capital city, Ottawa, Ontario. For three weeks, local citizens experienced chaos in their downtown core, as the narrow streets in and around Parliament Hill were jammed with semi-trucks and other vehicles that had converged around the Hill with the intention of not only demanding acknowledgement of protestors' concerns, but to make sweeping changes in different areas of government unrelated to COVID-19, including a quasi-coup attempt by the protest organizers. The culmination of the event occurred with the invocation of the Emergency Measures Act on February 14, 2022, by Prime Minister Justin Trudeau, which initiated the deployment of a joint police task force on February 18, 2022, to dismantle the protest and facilitate the removal of the vehicles and their owners (Public Safety Canada, 2022).

Of the various news stories arising from the removal of protestors, one in particular caught significant mainstream and social media attention: the claim that an Indigenous elder had been killed by a Royal Canadian Mounted Police (RCMP) horse. Video and still shots of the horse purportedly trampling the woman to death were widely shared. The corresponding public outrage was palpable. It was also global.

Fairly quickly, the story morphed. In some versions, the woman was not an 'elder,' a term of respect in Indigenous communities, but rather 'elderly.' In

DOI: 10.4324/9781003671312-12

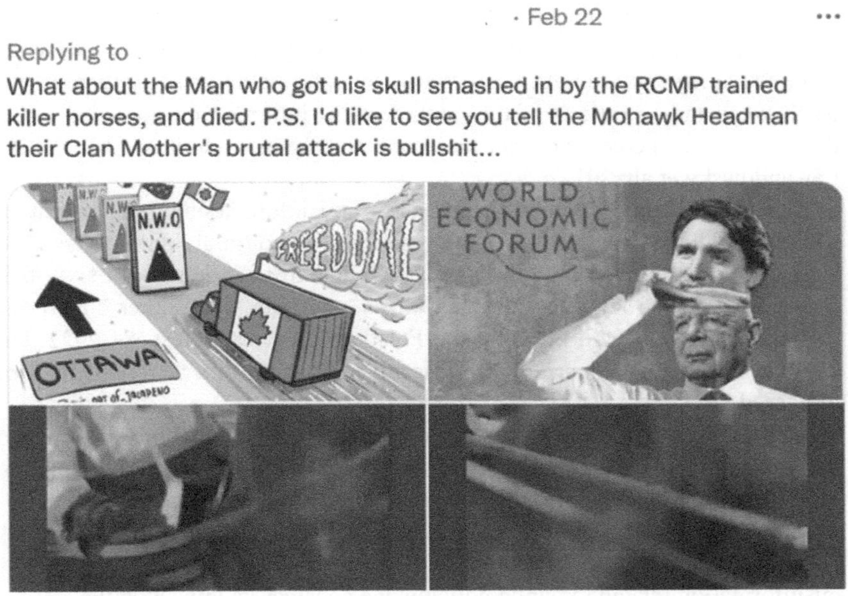

FIGURE 12.1 Killer Horses

Source: Twitter

other versions, she was not killed, but 'seriously injured.' A man who was with her, and also reportedly 'trampled,' was described as having also died as a result of his injuries (see Figure 12.1).

Mainstream news media picked up the story and ran with the different versions. Among other outlets, the RCMP's 'killer horses' became a featured story on the United States (US) Fox News (2022) and in reports by the United Kingdom's (UK) *Daily Mail* (2022). The latter described the event as "An elderly woman was trampled over by police horses during a peaceful protest in Ottawa, Canada" (*Daily Mail*, 2022).

While each of the versions carried a kernel of truth – two protesters did come into contact with police horses after being repeatedly told to leave the area over several hours, receiving minor injuries from the incident (CBC News, 2022; Raymond, 2022b) – the most compelling aspects of the stories shared and re-shared across mainstream, alternative, and social media platforms were fundamentally untrue. They were forms of 'misinformation'[1] – that is, false information spread unintentionally, by error or mistake (Johnson & Marcellino, 2021; Scheufele & Krause, 2019). While some individuals may have intentionally created or shared a false or potentially inaccurate story to stoke the police state rhetoric circling the police deployment that day, most of those who shared, re-tweeted, and/or commented on these stories with friends, family, and various audiences probably did so in good faith, likely believing what they were communicating was true. And that is why misinformation is so dangerous. Indeed, when large portions of the public are misinformed on the same topic, these shared misperceptions can bias collective opinion (Jerit & Zhao, 2020; Lewandowsky et al., 2012).

The present study examines the impacts of misinformation on the institution of public policing, as well as on the emotional toll on individual officers. To explore this topic, we draw on in-depth qualitative interviews with sixty-five police personnel from across Canada, many of whom were either directly or indirectly involved with not only the Freedom Convoy protests of 2022, but also had direct knowledge and experience of some of the other erroneous stories discussed here.

In the pages that follow, we explore the concept of misinformation and demonstrate how the creation and dissemination of false stories about policing events can easily spread through social media networks, cascading into mainstream media outlets, and reflect on the consequences of these inaccurate reports. By highlighting the RCMP's story earlier, and other recent examples of misinformation related to public policing, we consider its impact on the institution of policing, as well as some of the steps taken by agencies to combat the dissemination of false stories. These stories are about real people, accused of horrific things. Thus, we also consider how such untruths affect individuals and their families. Finally, we conclude by reviewing our major findings, highlighting some key points drawn from the data presented, and discussing both the practical and theoretical implications of our findings.

Misinformation

It is not uncommon to see confusion surrounding terms such as fake news, propaganda, and misinformation, and to observe individuals using these terms interchangeably (Scheufele & Krause, 2019). Our interest here is specifically on misinformation, and for the purposes of the present study, we draw on definitions provided by Scheufele and Krause (2019, p. 7662): "Misinformation: False or misleading information that is spread unintentionally, by error or mistake."

Although Kuklinski and colleagues (2000) provide a definition that does not attribute intentionality (confidently held beliefs based on incorrect factual information), we believe that the previous definition more succinctly captures the 'viral' spreading of internet-enabled communication. We also note that it is important to distinguish misinformation from disinformation, both of which rest on an understanding of the sharer's intent. Disinformation is a form of deliberate falsehood intended to manipulate an audience and may include 'fake news,' opinion pieces impersonating journalism, and 'false balance' stories (Kuklinski et al., 2000; Johnson & Marcellino, 2021). Misinformation, by way of contrast, is a false story shared in good faith by the poster (Johnson & Marcellino, 2021; Kuklinski et al., 2000).

Regardless of intent, what makes both forms of communication equally problematic is their contribution to truth decay – the blurring of the line between opinion and objective facts (Kavanagh & Rich, 2018). Authors point to the creation of the 24-hour news cycle as one of the most significant antecedents of truth decay (Johnson & Marcellino, 2021; Kavanagh & Rich, 2018). "Quality news and information are more available than ever before, but in greater amounts so are the trivial, the one-sided and the false" (Pew Research, 2004, p. 1). This drowning out of objectifiable facts can have consequences, especially those with policy-level implications. Indeed, social psychologists need only point to two well-researched phenomena to explain why this is the case: the confirmation bias and the disconfirmation bias. With confirmation bias, media consumers who hold pre-existing beliefs will unconsciously accept uncritical 'evidence,' reinforcing their worldview (Kahneman, 2011). Conversely, with disconfirmation bias, when consumers are presented with information that has the potential to alter their currently held beliefs (i.e. the release of objectifiable facts from trusted news sources or police services), consumers will search through their memories to locate information that will undermine the discrepant material presented (Edwards & Smith, 1996). So, in essence, if a story aligns with one's beliefs, values, and/or ideological lens, a consumer is more likely to accept it on face value (Druckman, 2022; Flynn et al., 2017; Jerit & Zhao, 2020). Conversely, exposure to information that does not conform to one's pre-existing beliefs is likely to be rejected out of hand (Nickerson, 1998).

One potential method for avoiding the inculcation of false beliefs is to employ critical thinking skills to carefully scrutinize and fact-check incoming information. There are, however, two reasons why many people fail to do so. One reason is, again, our hard-wired biases. Not only do we fail to recognize the twin traps of confirmation and disconfirmation biases, but we also tend to incorrectly perceive ourselves as discerning consumers of information – that is, labouring under a delusion psychologists refer to as a bias blind spot (Pronin & Kugler, 2007). A bias blind spot occurs when we fail to recognize how our own biases shape how we view the world. This phenomenon was observed in a study of American students' media literacy by a department of Stanford University, where a large majority of the students were unable to distinguish a news story from a 'sponsored' news advertisement as well as being unable to recognize biases in politically charged tweets (Wineburg et al., 2016).

When it comes to limiting the potential for misinformation to influence our thinking, communication technology offers little help. As a result of the various tools available on social media platforms, we are increasingly seeing individuals narrow their exposure to contradictory opinions and narratives (Coscia & Rossi,

2020). The result is "people on systems like Facebook are increasingly forming into 'echo chambers' of those who think alike. They will keep unfriending those who don't, and passing on rumours and fake news that agrees with their point of view" (Hiltz cited in Anderson & Rainie, 2017, p. 1; see also Del Vicario et al., 2016). Technology not only enables us to make these deliberate choices, but it also helps us narrow our exposure to alternative content further through the use of algorithms that push content to us based on our previous choices.

Our desire to screen our content based on our pre-existing biases leaves us vulnerable to manipulation. In a study of expert opinion on the rise of misinformation, Anderson and Rainie (2017, p. 1) found a subset of participants who believed that "humans mostly shape technology advances to their own, not-fully-noble purposes and that bad actors with bad motives will thwart the best efforts of technology innovators to remedy today's problems." Ill-intentioned actors are aided in their ability to manipulate media consumers through a phenomenon known as the 'firehose effect.' Simply put, the second reason why critical analysis of stories is not a *de facto* response to reading information in social or mainstream media is that even the most reasoned of consumers is likely to be over-saturated with information. The term 'firehose effect' originates from medical researchers, who, in an attempt to combat medical misinformation, likened the volume of content in spaces like Twitter and Facebook to "drinking from the firehose" (Choo et al., 2015, p. 413). Not surprisingly, few individuals have the time or energy to evaluate each piece of shared content for accuracy. Those who do want to assess the accuracy of a piece of content are frequently forced to rely on online fact-checking services, such as Snopes and FactCheck.org. While these services provide an extremely useful function for navigating an otherwise treacherous information landscape, the reality is that misinformation spreads so quickly that by the time information is fact-checked, a falsehood could have been seen by thousands or hundreds of thousands of individuals. And therein lies another problem to which we will return very shortly.

The ability to manipulate portions of a populace into political and other behaviours through the dissemination of false information represents a significant global threat and, as we have seen in the US, a potential danger to democracy and democratic institutions (Hochschild & Einstein, 2015; Schiff et al., 2025). While we can easily point to Russian interference in the 2016 US Presidential election as representing a paradigmatic test case of this point, we prefer to draw from another foreboding example: the spread of erroneous and, in some instances, deliberately false information about the COVID-19 virus and governmental vaccine programs and quarantine policies. Writing in 2017, Flynn and colleagues (2017, p. 127) raised the spectre of misinformation distorting "people's views about some of the most consequential issues in politics, science and medicine." In 2020, we saw this firsthand with the promulgation of conspiracy theories about vaccines killing people, the promotion of useless and potentially deadly homegrown cures, which spread like wildfire through Facebook, Twitter, and other sites. A significant portion of the Canadian population refused to quarantine, some deliberately courting the transmission of the disease through participation in viral challenges on TikTok (Tierney, 2020). One of the worst examples of this behaviour was a challenge aimed at teenagers that saw a TikTok 'influencer' film herself licking an airplane toilet seat (Merrett, 2020). Some viewers who followed this example tested positive for COVID-19 (Merrett, 2020). Even when false information is of a more innocuous nature, it can leave consumers uninformed or misinformed about what is happening in their neighbourhood, their city, or their world. Worryingly, one study conducted in 2018 found that 64% of Americans surveyed "say that fake news has left them with a great deal of confusion about current events" (Shao et al., 2018, p. 1), and a further 23% admitted to sharing a false news story (Barthel et al., 2016).

Aside from encouraging problematic behaviours, misinformation represents a significant threat because of its relative 'stickiness.' As other scholars have put it, such content tends to be 'resilient' – that is, once out in the public domain, it is often impervious to correction (Lewandowsky et al., 2012). The myth of the RCMP's killer horses provides just one such example. An American news reporter who shared false information from reports 'on the ground' about the Ottawa convoy protests had to subsequently retract her comments. However, by the time that happened, her posts had received millions of views, been retweeted approximately 14,000 times, and garnered around 15,000 likes (Raymond, 2022a). Furthermore, misinformation persists in the public domain long after it has been posted. Writing in April 2023, we typed in "RCMP killer horse" on Twitter and went to the 'latest' tab to see the results. The most recent tweet on this topic was posted on February 23, 2022. Not only did the tweet contain erroneous content about someone supposedly being killed at the Ottawa convoy protests, but the name of one of the victims of this alleged trampling was incorrect (see also Figure 12.2).

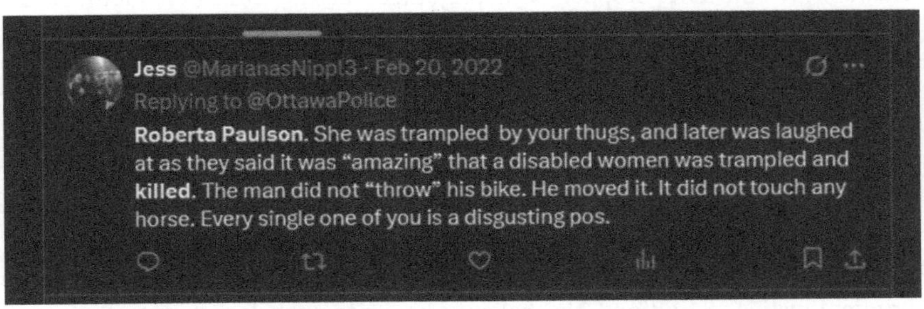

FIGURE 12.2 Erroneous Tweet

Source: Twitter

In combination with misinformation's 'stickiness' and resiliency in the face of new information or corrections, Pronin and Kugler (2007) also found that individuals are more likely to accept the first information they receive on a topic and then subsequently favour that information when faced with conflicting messages (i.e. corrections to a story). This is terribly problematic for public police services, who are handicapped with gag orders from civilian oversight bodies that investigate officer-involved shootings and serious injury incidents (as well as being limited in what information can be provided to the public so as not to harm any future court proceedings). As the police are often unable to be the first to communicate all the objective facts to the public in the initial stages of an incident, misinformation can create a false narrative that is impervious to correction.

Despite the rise of misinformation online and its obvious detrimental impacts on various social institutions, there is a notable lack of academic research on the institutional and personal costs of these activities to police services and personnel. In fact, we could locate only one such study, a paper by Scott Mourtgos and colleagues (2022). Their article utilizes the Jacob Blake interaction with the Kenosha Police Department as a case study, using it as a backdrop to determine whether there was a premature increase in retirements and resignations resulting from the aftermath of the incident in the community. On August 23, 2020, Blake was shot by police during an armed confrontation. During the initial stages of the occurrence, inaccurate information regarding Blake being unarmed was proclaimed on both social and mainstream media sources. In the immediate aftermath of this event, a false story was spread that an unarmed Blake had been shot in the back by police because he was a Black male. The result was protests and rioting, resulting in some $50 million in damages (Mourtgos et al., 2022). Blake later admitted he had been armed with a knife, and an independent investigation subsequently cleared the officer involved, some four months post-event. That was not the only investigation to which this officer was subject. The Department of Justice also initiated an investigation, which was not concluded until October 2021 (Morales, 2021). The officer also faced a civil rights lawsuit launched by Blake, which the latter dropped 'with prejudice'[2] in May 2022 (Vielmetti, 2022). In the months following his encounter with Blake, the officer, Rusten Sheskey, had also received death threats, demands that he lose his job (Mintz, 2022), and been subject to an internal investigation (Madani, 2021). A news report filed in August 2022 stated that, while he retained his employment with the Kenosha Police Department, Sheskey had yet to return to active patrol (Madani, 2021).

Although there has been some recent interest in misinformation and its impacts on policing among academics, to date, there has been little sustained effort at exploring how 'cheap fakes,' 'deep fakes,' lies, and propaganda can undermine criminal justice institutions. Nor have we begun to unpack how misinformation and disinformation can potentially influence public policy, criminal justice practices, and/or negatively affect individuals working within the criminal justice system. With that end in mind, we set out to better understand this phenomenon through an exploratory study of misinformation and its potential impacts on policing within the context of the convoy protests in Ottawa.

Method of Inquiry

The present study is based on an analysis of sixty-five (n=65) in-depth qualitative interviews conducted with police personnel from across Canada, who either had direct empirical experience on the frontlines at the convoy protests staged in Ottawa and other cities and/or had been involved in similar types of political events. Interviewees included police leaders, critical incident commanders, public order unit personnel, emergency response team members, and frontline officers, among others (see Table 12.1).

The data is comprised of interviews drawn from a non-probability sample. The data were collected as part of an ongoing study of public policing of political events. This project began as an oral history of the policing of the Convoy protests, and then subsequently expanded to include police involvement in other controversial political events. Participants were located through one of two methods: the first was through previous connections within the policing community, and the second involved self-selecting responses to social media posts seeking participants on LinkedIn and Twitter. Our semi-structured approach to interviews involved creating a loosely followed interview guide, which asked open-ended questions and allowed participants to guide the direction of the discussion. To ensure diversity in our sample beyond occupation, we deliberately sought participants from as many provinces (excluding territories, as protests occurred in urban metropolises) as possible, including reaching out to previous contacts from ten provinces. Due to the geographic spread of participants, all interviews were conducted on the telephone and lasted approximately 45–90 minutes.

All interviews were conducted with the approval of a university Research Ethics Board and in compliance with TriCouncil guidelines on the ethical treatment

TABLE 12.1 Interviewees by Occupation Type

Category	*n*
Patrol Officer	20
Public Order	19
Incident Commander	13
Police Leader	4
Intelligence Officer	3
Investigator/Special Operations	2
Police Association Representative	4
Total	65

of research participants. All research participants agreed to participate, agreed to review the transcripts of their interviews, and to read (should they choose) a copy of this chapter to ensure we did not misquote them or unintentionally alter their content or the context in which it was said. Taking this step also afforded a greater degree of reliability in the work. It also allowed us to confirm that participants were comfortable with the level of anonymity provided.

The data presented here has also been supplemented by information gleaned from the relevant research literature and from public policy documents, such as the federal inquiry into the use of the Emergencies Act. We also draw on relevant posts from social media (Twitter, Facebook, TikTok, and YouTube) that were collected during and immediately after specific events discussed here.

To begin coding our data, an exploratory analysis of the interview, document, and social media data was first conducted using inductive thematic coding. We employed an inductive approach to allow for greater flexibility in identifying themes and sub-themes, which we wanted to emerge from the data rather than pre-existing theories and concepts (Braun & Clarke, 2006). The first iteration of coding entailed having the first author conduct open coding by engaging in manual line-by-line readings of each transcript to develop a series of major themes. Once these themes were identified, the second author, who had also been involved in data collection, verified the results. To illustrate our approach, for the theme 'misinformation,' obviously relevant codes for the interview data included terms such as 'lie,' 'not true,' and 'false.' When examining potential examples of misinformation online – including the RCMP Killer Horse story – we had to become more creative in identifying it as an instance of misinformation and thus categorizing it as a relevant sub-theme. To do that, we used reputable sources to ascertain the veracity of a story, including investigative reports published by the Ontario Special Investigation Unit and other government agencies. Focused coding then permitted us to identify relevant clusters of sub-themes. For example, two sub-themes of 'misinformation' that emerged in the data were 'impacts of misinformation on the police institution' and 'impacts upon individual officers.'

Results

In the aftermath of the truck convoy protests in Ottawa, the Canadian federal government commissioned an inquiry into its use of the *Emergency Powers Act* to deal with the crisis. In testimony before the inquiry, RCMP Deputy Commissioner Michael Duheme (2022) offered the following comments:

> We know the IMVE [ideologically motivated violent extremism] threat environment is rapidly evolving and complex, and is increasingly fuelled by misinformation and hostile rhetoric surrounding a host of grievances, many of

> which focus on the government's response to COVID-19 and other matters. This has sown distrust in government institutions, including law enforcement, and has augmented the ability for extremist groups to both recruit new members and increasingly foster hostility.

One aspect of that rhetoric that Duheme spoke to in his subsequent remarks is the targeting of the police. It is concerning that this targeting "has manifested itself in all too real confrontation" between police and protestors in Ottawa and at cross-border blockades (Duheme, 2022). What Duheme was referring to in relation to the latter was a series of arrests of individuals in Coutts, Alberta, who had allegedly stockpiled weapons and body armour to be used against police, who were attempting to dismantle the blockade there (Grant, 2022).

Given what we perceive as the potential for serious political and social consequences arising from misinformation – both to the police institution itself and to individual officers – we asked research participants to identify the threats they associate with misinformation. Perhaps not surprisingly, the single biggest concern expressed was the ability of those spreading misinformation to undermine public confidence in policing. An officer we interviewed with an extensive history of working in media relations observed that misinformation "undermines public confidence [in the police] and [police] legitimacy." What he took exception to was not that police are routinely questioned about their activities, but rather that "you're questioning what the institution of policing is doing, but not based on good information." The result, he felt, was "destabilizing" public policing. An intelligence officer in another province agreed. He stated it was difficult for police to "remain accountable when to whom we're being accountable and what we're being accountable about is in flux because of misinformation."

Interviewees also addressed the need for police and governments to react more quickly and decisively against misinformation. "We have to be aware of it," a veteran officer stated, "and be prepared for it." This participant, who has extensive experience with the media, added,

> Facts are very, very important, and we think there are many, many cases over the last quite a few years when the facts aren't actually getting out there, especially in the initial stages when a story or an incident first appears.

Such actions are slowly starting to happen, wherein police leaders or their media personnel are addressing erroneous stories more directly. One such example occurred in 2020, when, in response to complaints over police removal of protestors from a government building, the Chief of the Victoria Police Department, Del Manak, posted a YouTube video to respond to what he termed misinformation online (Harnet, 2020). Other examples include the swift responses of the Vancouver Police Department and its executive to various stories posted on social media. However, as one senior leader observed, even attempts to counter misinformation by police are limited in terms of the ability to correct a narrative once it has been put out on a platform: "[misinformation] that lives out in the world, the wacky world of social media as being the truth, and it sits there forever, which is problematic because that's where people go." He noted that if such false information remains unchallenged, then audiences think, "Well, this must be the truth because nobody came out to correct it." Speaking specifically to the 'killer horse' example, another said:

> We actually had people in our communications section that were doing nothing but monitoring those feeds. We immediately got on and corrected the record. But in a thread of tweets, or in a tweet, it's not easy just to actually capture what you want and send it out.

He then added, "right now, there's no latitude nor ability for us to manage that, other than to, as much as we can, continue to push out actual factual information to the public." However, as we noted before, even attempts to correct false information do not necessarily change the discourse around an event. Individuals who are ideologically committed often readily dismiss factual corrections to the record as 'copaganda,' or the police deliberately framing the narrative in a positive light.

Given the possibility that misinformation might lead to specific targeting and harassment of individual officers, we also asked interviewees what they thought of this potential. Our decision to ask questions concerning individual impacts sprang from misinformation arising from the convoy protests that targeted Ottawa's Deputy Police Chief, Steve Bell. Bell's response to a media question at a press conference after the end of the demonstrations was misconstrued as that he would 'hunt down protestors' to 'charge them' and/or 'financially destroy' them. This story, repeated across social media, then formed the basis of a headline on an alternative media site: "Ottawa Police Chief: 'Every Single Canadian Who Supported Truckers Will be Hunted Down and Ruined'" (Adl-Tabatabai, 2022). The claim was subsequently fact-checked by Reuters (2022) and shown to be false. However, a few months after Reuters debunked the story, the claim was still making the rounds on social media (see Figure 12.3).

FIGURE 12.3 Lawton

Source: Twitter.

Several of those interviewed for this project are or were former members of the Ottawa police. In discussing this case with one, he noted,

> We just had no ability to corral or stop or rectify that [story] because there was a group of people that actually just didn't want to hear it. They wanted that mirror. And we don't know how you can combat that.

Indeed, these interviewees are referring to the 'stickiness' problem described earlier (Pronin & Kugler, 2007). Confirmation and primacy bias are powerful heuristics that make attempts at correcting the record with factually correct information nearly impervious to change.

While officers interviewed recognized the importance of external oversight on police issues, they were also concerned that stories containing misinformation would lead to increases in unfounded complaints against officers. This is not an entirely baseless concern: we were informed, for example, that the false claim concerning the Deputy Chief of Ottawa resulted in approximately 50 complaints lodged against him with external oversight agencies. Discussing this issue with a senior leader in British Columbia, he referenced the stresses false allegations can have on police members:

> when we tell our people to do X, Y, and Z and then they get a complaint about that, even if the complaint is so frivolous that it's just completely out to lunch, it is still a very stressful process for these members. And it takes forever, forever and ever and ever [to resolve].

Depending on the nature of the complaint, even internal investigations by professional standards can take up to two years to complete. During this time, officers cannot apply for promotions, have promotions paused, or transfer between services/departments. These costs are well documented in policing literature (De Angelis, 2009; De Angelis & Kupchik, 2017; Huey et al., 2025; Schaible et al., 2012). When talking about the personal toll that such investigations can take, a police officer in another province spoke from personal experience:

> Your own organization is putting you under scrutiny and investigating everything that you've been doing. And you fall apart. Some people go to a very, very dark place. I went to a dark place, but I got myself out of it.

Although spurious complaints based on misinformation promoted online are one potential issue that individual officers involved in public controversies as a result of their occupation may face, more often than not, participants were concerned about the impact of false stories on their families. As one explained in relation to his participation in the Convoy protests,

> When officers are thrust into the spotlight, it ends up being very, very difficult for the officer, very difficult for the officer's spouse, and particularly

> their children. And I've had many, many instances where a family has been impacted, the spouse and the children, as a result of a media piece, which can go out quite far and wide.

Several related stories of how misinformation online about police actions during the occupation impacted their personal life, from awkward exchanges at junior league hockey to themselves or their significant others losing long-term friendships. It's especially difficult, one noted,

> when a protestor will post on their site inaccurate information … and people read it and then are like '[name deleted] was that you? You actually said that to that person?' … You're like, 'Of course, we didn't say that.' But they've already created a narrative that you can't counter.

Some officers also found the online commentary spawned by misinformation personally difficult. Discussing the aftermath of the convoy protests, a police officer who had been involved remembered:

> Seeing videos and pictures of my teams and myself online after, and the comments people were making about us in those videos and pictures … It was an awkward, hard pill to follow, right down to the comments being made from people when we're on the ground and the stuff coming out of their mouths about being on the wrong side of history and your families and your wife and children must be disgusted by you.

Drawing on the work of Eisenberg (1975), who found that inaccurate media portrayals tarnished police service reputations and decreased officer morale, an inference can be made that in our modern media landscape, where there is an overwhelming amount of information and misinformation competing for paramountcy, that officer stress could be exacerbated by the visceral level of hateful messaging. More research in this area is warranted, however.

Conclusions

On February 18, 2022, as police attempted to clear the roads of downtown Ottawa of trucks and protestors, thousands of social media users remained transfixed by the story of 'Roberta Paulsen,' the purported victim of a horse trampling. As stated in the introduction to this chapter, the story, in various iterations, contained misinformation that was widely shared, shaping global perceptions of what was happening on the ground in Ottawa. Across multiple versions of the story, Paulsen was described as Indigenous, elderly with a walker, an Indigenous elder, dead, seriously injured, injured by a RCMP horse, and/or deliberately trampled. The reality is that Roberta Paulsen was a fictitious name. The woman was 49-year-old Candice Sero, who had stumbled in front of one of the horses belonging to the Toronto Police Mounted Unit as they were walking their horses forward. She was neither killed nor seriously injured. Indeed, according to multiple sources interviewed for this project, she returned to the protest site the very next day. Further, an initial investigation by an independent civilian oversight body, the Special Investigations Unit (2022), found Sero had 'strained' her shoulder, and therefore declined to launch a full investigation (CBC News, 2022; Hudson, 2022).

The misinformation that resulted from this story spread rapidly across social media and even found its way onto international media outlets. This spread of misinformation has significant potential for repercussions, as when large portions of the public have shared misperceptions of events in the same direction, collective bias can occur (Jerit & Zhao, 2020; Lewandowsky et al., 2012). This collective bias can shape the legitimacy of the police actions during the event, and has the potential to shape protestors' response. As noted by several authors, once a person becomes misinformed on a topic, they can stubbornly cling to their inaccurate beliefs (Flynn et al., 2017; Jerit & Zhao, 2020; Kuklinski et al., 2000), and offer resistance when attempts are made to correct them (Flynn et al., 2017; Kuklinski et al., 2000; Pronin and Kugler, 2007).

The present study makes a novel contribution to the policing research literature by addressing an emerging threat to police legitimacy: the spread of misinformation regarding policing actions (see Ellis, 2021). As we documented in the preceding pages, stories containing erroneous information about policing activities are easily circulated, and once a false narrative takes hold (i.e. 'goes viral'), it can be very difficult, if not impossible, to refute. Furthermore, those who create and/or share misinformation rarely incur a transactional cost for doing so, as, to date, no police services or their members have initiated legal action against stories containing false allegations. Compounding the situation, we would argue, is the fact that among individuals who share misinformation online, we must include provincial and federal politicians, who likely do so because the content of the misinformation advances their own political agendas by speaking to concerns of their base. We must also include another worrisome development: the mainstream media's increasing reliance on unverified social media stories. As we saw in relation to the 'killer horse' story, one version of the false narrative surrounding this event was picked up by a mainstream news outlet in the UK (*Daily Mail*, 2022). By attracting extra attention to websites or social media posts that have outrageous tag lines, the mainstream media is contributing to the rise of click-bait material online (Chatterjee & Panmand, 2022; Munger et al., 2020), potentially to increase advertising revenues while at the same time contributing to the spread of misinformation and a lowering of the epistemic value of mainstream content (Fallis, 2021).

This research is not without limitations. This work may have also benefited from a greater number of interviewers and, particularly, from interviewers with diverse language and other skills. One of the recruitment problems we faced was in locating officers from the province of Quebec with English language facility, as neither of the two interviewers is sufficiently fluent in French to conduct and transcribe the interviews. We would also encourage future researchers to supplement our efforts here by considering diverse research methodologies, as well as theoretical frameworks for understanding this phenomenon. Again, our intent here was to present an exploratory analysis of an emergent public policy issue, and thus, there is much that we have not examined and that requires significantly more analysis to potentially inform policy and practice in this area.

Despite the limitations noted earlier, our study raises much-needed awareness of the rise of technology-mediated misinformation in public policing and its potential to undermine police legitimacy (see Russell & Giwa, 2023). In the post-truth era, "facts are increasingly being trumped by existing beliefs and prejudices" (Lewandowsky et al., 2017, p. 361). So, if facts do not have the normative effect they once did, social media companies must make facts more recognizable (Scheufele & Krause, 2019). As well, our study raises interesting questions concerning officer well-being among those who become the targets of misinformation. From a public policy and/or police practice standpoint, we are not in a position to make concrete recommendations at this time; however, what our work does do is highlight potential avenues of further study and consideration for both researchers and policymakers alike. Further, police and policymakers need to begin exploring how best to identify and combat misinformation online. As police often release objective information long after social media has created the discourse around an incident, Nyhan and Reifler (2015) found that providing an alternate, causal account of the event has led to more effective corrections to the dialogue than by a straight refutation of the misinformation (Flynn et al., 2017). Police services and police associations must also start to think about the human toll of misinformation-based social media campaigns on individual officers and their families, as well as how best to mitigate negative impacts on serving personnel. Police agencies must develop a greater understanding of the media ecosphere. Arriving late to the information exchange arena will almost certainly result in decreasing levels of police legitimacy that will require increasing police efforts to maintain. While the present study represents a starting point in that process, we are cognizant of the need for more empirical work in this area and will be using this study as a launching pad towards addressing some of the questions remaining.

Notes

1 We choose this definition of misinformation as it relates more directly to the age of social media over that posited by Kuklinski et al. (2000). We clarify this distinction in greater detail in the literature review.

2 Meaning that Blake could not refile the suit.

References

Adl-Tabatabai, S. (2022). Ottawa Police Chief: 'Every single Canadian who supported truckers will be hunted down and ruined'. *The People's Voice*. Retrieved from https://thepeoplesvoice.tv/ottawa-police-chief-every-single-canadian-who-supported-truckers-will-be-hunted-down-and-ruined/

Anderson, J., & Rainie, L. (2017). The future of truth and misinformation online. Retrieved from https://apo.org.au/node/115741

Barthel, M., Mitchell, A., & Holcomb, J. (2016). Many Americans believe fake news is sowing confusion. *Pew Research.* Retrieved from https://www.pewresearch.org/journalism/2016/12/15/many-americans-believe-fake-news-is-sowing-confusion/

Braun, V., & Clarke, V. (2006). Using thematic analysis in psychology. *Qualitative Research in Psychology*, *3*(2), 77–101. https://doi.org/10.1191/1478088706qp063oa

CBC News. (2022). Injury from police horse during convoy protest too minor to investigate, SIU says. *CBC News*. Retrieved from https://www.cbc.ca/news/canada/ottawa/woman-police-horse-truck-protest-ottawa-siu-1.6408118

Chatterjee, S., & Panmand, M. (2022). Explaining and predicting click-baitiness and click-bait virality. *Industrial Management + Data Systems*, *122*(11), 2485–2507. https://doi.org/10.1108/IMDS-01-2022-0003

Choo, E., Ramney, M., Chan, T., Trueger, S., Walsh, A., Tegtmeyer, K., McNamara, S., Choi, R., & Carroll, C. (2015). Twitter as a tool for communication and knowledge exchange in academic medicine: A guide for skeptics and novices. *Medical Teacher*, *37*(5), 411–416.

Coscia, M., & Rossi, L. (2020). Distortions of political bias in crowdsourced misinformation flagging. *Journal of Royal Society: Interface*, *17*, 20200020, 1–11.

Daily Mail (UK). (2022). Woman is trampled over by police horses during protest in Ottawa. Retrieved from https://www.dailymail.co.uk/video/news/video-2620377/Video-Woman-trampled-police-horses-protest-Ottawa.html

De Angelis, J. (2009). Assessing the impact of oversight and procedural justice on the attitudes of individuals who file police complaints. *Police Quarterly*, *12*(2), 214–236. https://doi.org/10.1177/1098611109332425

De Angelis, J., & Kupchik, A. (2007). Citizen oversight, procedural justice, and officer perceptions of the complaint investigation process. *Policing: An International Journal of Police Strategies & Management*, *30*(4), 651–671. https://doi.org/10.1108/13639510710833929

Del Vicario, M., Bessi, A., Zollo, F., Petroni, F., Scala, A., Caldarelli, G., Stanley, H., & Quattrociocchi, W. (2016). The spreading of misinformation online. *PNAS Proceedings of the National Academy of Sciences of the United States of America*, *113*(3), 554–559.

Druckman, J. (2022). Threats to science: Politicization, misinformation, and inequalities. *The Annals of the American Academy of Political and Social Science*, *700*(1), 8–24.

Duheme, M. (2022). Testimony before Emergencies Act Inquiry. Retrieved from https://www.cpac.ca/articles/emergency-commission

Edwards, K., & Smith, E. E. (1996). A disconfirmation bias in the evaluation of arguments. *Journal of Personality and Social Psychology*, *71*(1), 5–24. https://doi.org/10.1037/0022-3514.71.1.5

Eisenberg, T. (1975). Job stress and the police officer: Identifying stress reduction techniques. In W. H. Kroes & J. J. Hurrell, Jr. (Eds.), *Job stress and the police officer: Identifying stress reduction techniques* (Proceedings of a symposium, Cincinnati, Ohio, May 8–9, 1975, pp. 26–34). US Department of Health, Education, and Welfare, National Institute for Occupational Safety and Health.

Ellis, J. R. (2021). *Policing legitimacy: Social media, scandal and sexual citizenship*. Springer Nature.

Fallis, D. (2021). The epistemic threat of deepfakes: The epistemic threat of deepfakes. *Philosophy & Technology*, *34*(4), 623–643. https://doi.org/10.1007/s13347-020-00419-2

Flynn, D., Nyhan, B., & Reifler, J. (2017). The nature and origins of misperceptions: Understanding false and unsupported beliefs about politics. *Advances in Political Psychology*, *38*(1), 127–150.

Fox News. (2022). *Incident of woman allegedly trampled by Canadian police horse under investigation*. Retrieved from https://www.youtube.com/watch?v=TT6eLv-OC5M

Grant, M. (2022). Coutts arrests: New details on the men and women charged in border blockade. *CBC News*. Retrieved from https://www.cbc.ca/news/canada/calgary/coutts-arrests-charges-border-protest-1.6354587

Harnett, C. (2020). Victoria police chief goes on social media to defend officers after sit-in arrests. *Victoria Times-Colonist*. Retrieved from https://www.timescolonist.com/local-news/victoria-police-chief-goes-on-social-media-to-defend-officers-after-sit-in-arrests-4678821

Hochschild, J., & Einstein, K. (2015). Do facts matter? Information and misinformation in American politics. *Political Science Quarterly*, *130*(4), 585–624.

Huey, L., Ferguson, L., & Towns, Z. (2025). "Cops need doxxed": Releasing personal information of police officers as a tool of political harassment. *Crime and Delinquency*, *71*(3), 714–739. https://doi.org/10.1177/00111287241271069

Jerit, J., & Zhao, Y. (2020). Political misinformation. *Annual Review of Political Science*, *23*(1), 77–94.

Johnson, C., & Marcellino, W. (2021). *Bad actors in news reporting: Tracking news manipulation by state actors*. Retrieved from https://www.rand.org/content/dam/rand/pubs/research_reports/RRA100/RRA112-21/RAND_RRA112-21.pdf.

Kahneman, D. (2011). *Thinking fast and slow*. Anchor Canada.

Kavanagh, J., & Rich, M. D. (2018). *Truth decay: An initial exploration of the diminishing role of facts and analysis in American public life*. Retrieved from chttps://www.rand.org/pubs/research_reports/RR2314.html

Kuklinski, J. H., Quirk, P. J., Jerit, J., Schwieder, D., & Rich, R. F. (2000). Misinformation and the currency of democratic citizenship. *The Journal of Politics*, *62*(3), 790–816.

Lewandowsky, S., Ecker, U. K. H., & Cook, J. (2017). Beyond misinformation: Understanding and coping with the "post-truth" era. *Journal of Applied Research in Memory and Cognition*, *6*(4), 353–369.

Lewandowsky, S., Ecker, U., Seifert, C., Schwarz, N., & Cook, J. (2012). Misinformation and its correction: Continued influence and successful debiasing *Psychological Science in the Public Interest*, *13*(3), 106–131.

Madani, D. (2021). Kenosha officer who shot Jacob Blake won't face discipline, police chief says. *NBC News*. Retrieved from https://www.nbcnews.com/news/nbcblk/no-discipline-kenosha-police-officer-who-shot-jacob-blake-chief-n1263986.

Merrett, R. (2020). The challenge gained popularity earlier this month after TikTok user Ava Louise filmed herself licking an airplane toilet seat. *People Magazine*. Retrieved from https://people.com/human-interest/influencer-who-participated-in-toilet-licking-challenge-says-he-tested-positive-for-coronavirus/

Mintz, H. (2022). All Kenosha officers now wear body cameras. *WISN News*. Retrieved from https://www.wisn.com/article/its-been-two-years-since-kenosha-police-officer-shot-jacob-blake-seven-times-sparking-unrest/40971646#

Morales, C. (2021). What we know about the shooting of Jacob Blake. *The New York Times*. Retrieved from https://www.nytimes.com/article/jacob-blake-shooting-kenosha.html

Mourtgos, S., Adams, I., & Nix, J. (2022). Elevated police turnover following the summer of George Floyd protests: A synthetic control study. *Criminology & Public Policy*, *21*(1), 9–33.

Munger, K., Luca, M., Nagler, J., & Tucker, J. (2020). The (null) effects of clickbait headlines on polarization, trust, and learning. *Public Opinion Quarterly, 84*(1), 49–73. https://doi.org/10.1093/poq/nfaa008

Nickerson, R. (1998). Confirmation bias: A ubiquitous phenomenon in many guises. *Review of General Psychology, 2*(2), 175–220.

Nyhan, B., & Reifler, J. (2015). Displacing misinformation about events: An experimental test of causal corrections. *Journal of Experimental Political Science, 2*(1), 81–93. https://doi.org/10.1017/XPS.2014.22

Pew Research. (2004). *Project for excellence in journalism: The state of the news media report: 2004.* Retrieved from https://www.pewresearch.org/wp-content/uploads/sites/8/2017/05/State-of-the-News-Media-Report-2004-FINAL.pdf

Pronin, E., & Kugler, N. (2007). Valuing thoughts, ignoring behavior: The introspection illusion as a source of the bias blind spot. *Journal of Experimental Social Psychology, 43*(4), 565–578.

Public Safety Canada. (2022). Parliamentary committee notes: Overview – Freedom Convoy 2022. https://www.publicsafety.gc.ca/cnt/trnsprnc/brfng-mtrls/prlmntry-bndrs/20221013/03-en.aspx

Raymond, T. (2022a). Ottawa police dealing with threats, fake calls tying up resources. *CTV News.* Retrieved from https://ottawa.ctvnews.ca/ottawa-police-dealing-with-threats-fake-calls-tying-up-resources-1.5771623

Raymond, T. (2022b). *Ontario police watchdog closes investigation into mounted officers at 'Freedom Convoy'.* Retrieved from https://www.ctvnews.ca/ottawa/article/ontario-police-watchdog-closes-investigation-into-mounted-officers-at-freedom-convoy/

Reuters. (2022). *Fact check: Fabricated quote about trucker protests falsely attributed to Ottawa police chief.* Retrieved from https://www.reuters.com/article/fact-check/fabricated-quote-about-trucker-protests-falsely-attributed-to-ottawa-police-chie-idUSL1N2XP1XM/

Russell, H. C., & Giwa, S. (2023). *Transforming community policing: Mobilization, engagement, and collaboration.* Emond Montgomery Publications Limited.

Schaible, L. M., Angelis, J. D., Wolf, B., & Rosenthal, R. (2012). Denver's citizen/police complaint mediation program: Officer and complainant satisfaction. *Criminal Justice Policy Review, 24*(5), 626–650. https://doi.org/10.1177/0887403412455327

Scheufele, D., & Krause, N. (2019). Science audiences, misinformation, and fake news. *PNAS Proceedings of the National Academy of Sciences of the United States of America, 116*(6), 7662–7669.

Schiff, K. J., Schiff, D. S., & Bueno, N. S. (2025). The liar's dividend: Can politicians claim misinformation to evade accountability? *American Political Science Review, 119*(1), 71–90. doi:10.1017/S0003055423001454

Shao, C., Hui, P., Wang, L., Jiang, X., & Flammini, A. (2018). Anatomy of an online misinformation network. *PLOS ONE*, 13(4), e0196087.

Special Investigations Unit (SIU) (Ontario). (2022). SIU closes investigation into reported serious injury of woman at Ottawa protests; Woman not seriously injured. Retrieved from https://www.siu.on.ca/en/news_template.php?nrid=7650

Tierney, B. (2020). *Social media challenge has teens trying to get COVID-19.* Retrieved from https://www.wsaz.com/content/news/Social-media-challenge-has-teens-trying-to-get-COVID-19-569109331.html

Vielmetti, B. (2022). Jacob Blake withdraws his lawsuit against the Kenosha officer who shot him in the back. *USA Today.* Retrieved from https://www.usatoday.com/story/news/nation/2022/05/10/jacob-blake-drops-lawsuit-against-kenosha-officer-who-shot-him/9715601002/

Wineburg, S., McGrew, S., Breakstone, J., & Ortega, T. (2016). *Evaluating information: The cornerstone of civic online reasoning.* Retrieved from https://stacks.stanford.edu/file/druid:fv751yt5934/SHEG%20Evaluating%20Information%20Online.pdf

13

THE ENEMY WITHIN—POLICE COUNTERINTELLIGENCE AND INSIDER PREVENTION

Ardavan M. Khoshnood

Introduction

Counterintelligence refers to actions taken by states and their agencies to safeguard sensitive information, plans, and operations from hostile intelligence collection. Traditionally associated with specialized intelligence directorates tasked with defending national secrets from foreign penetration, it involves detecting and disrupting espionage, subversion, and other adversarial activities. In some cases, it also extends to covert action—operations designed to secretly influence events abroad or manage threats to state stability (Carlisle, 2015; Nelson, 2015).

A particularly acute risk to counterintelligence efforts is the insider threat: individuals with authorized access to sensitive systems, institutional knowledge, and operational privileges. Unlike external adversaries, insiders know where critical information is stored, how to exploit it, and how to avoid detection. They can cause serious harm through data leaks, sabotage, or the erosion of institutional trust—and are often employees who are induced, manipulated, or coerced into disclosing protected assets (Bunn & Sagan, 2016).

While cyberattacks dominate public discourse, human intelligence (HUMINT) remains a primary method used by both state and non-state actors to access confidential law enforcement data. This includes overt and covert techniques, from casual inquiries to relationship-building and manipulation. In this ecosystem, criminals act as case handlers, while compromised police personnel become their sources (Gay, 2015).

This is not merely a theoretical concern. In Sweden, a country grappling with escalating organized crime and coordinated influence operations targeting public institutions, insider threats have become a national security issue (Khoshnood,

DOI: 10.4324/9781003671312-13

2018; Khoshnood & Gerell, 2019; Khoshnood et al., 2023; Brottsförebyggande rådet, 2025). In April 2025, the Swedish Police Authority publicly acknowledged the problem and committed to new measures aimed at reducing the risk of internal compromise and unlawful influence (Polisen, 2025).

To better understand and prevent insider compromise, this chapter examines the phenomenon through four parts. First, it defines insider threats, distinguishing them from external infiltration and exploring their relevance to law enforcement organizations. Second, it analyzes how insiders are recruited, with attention to both interpersonal manipulation and the technological tools adversaries use to identify and exploit vulnerabilities. A case study from Sweden illustrates how these tactics play out in practice. Third, it explores counterintelligence countermeasures. Finally, the conclusion reflects on the continued importance of prevention-oriented counterintelligence and calls for greater research and reform.

Insider Threats

Defining Insider Threats

An insider is commonly defined as an individual with authorized access to assets that an organization seeks to protect, such as sensitive information, personnel, facilities, or equipment (Bunn & Sagan, 2016). While often employees, insiders may also include contractors or consultants. Insider threats are generally divided into two categories: malicious insiders, who deliberately exploit their position to inflict damage driven by diverse motives; and non-malicious insiders, who may expose the organization to harm through carelessness, ignorance, or manipulation, even without harmful intent (Nurse et al., 2014).

Whereas insider threats originate from individuals already embedded in the organization, infiltration involves the deliberate placement of external actors who obtain access through deception (Colwill, 2009; Cybersecurity and Infrastructure Security Agency, 2020). Infiltrators may pose as legitimate applicants or exploit the social networks of personnel to gain trust and entry. In this sense, infiltration is the process by which an outsider becomes an insider over time, while insider threats begin with a legitimate actor becoming adversarial. Though these categories can overlap, the distinction remains analytically and operationally significant, as they require different countermeasures.

Understanding insider threats also requires attention to institutional context. In military and intelligence agencies, counterintelligence structures are typically formalized and divided between defensive functions like deterrence and detection, and offensive operations such as deception and neutralization (Prunckun, 2019). These frameworks are embedded within agency doctrine, understood here as the set of formally articulated principles and operational logics that guide responses, and allow for proactive interventions under conditions of uncertainty, without necessarily requiring conclusive evidence.

By contrast, counterintelligence in law enforcement has historically received less emphasis and remains comparatively fragmented. Law enforcement operates under strict legal mandates that require evidentiary thresholds for investigative or prosecutorial action, which can constrain anticipatory counterintelligence functions (Manget, 2010). This tension has long distinguished law enforcement from traditional intelligence agencies. For instance, US intelligence services historically worked in analytical isolation, with the FBI—despite its law enforcement mandate—viewed as external to the intelligence community (Cline, 2015). These boundaries have since blurred, as law enforcement increasingly intersects with national security efforts (O'Brien, 2009).

Within law enforcement, counterintelligence responsibilities are often dispersed across internal affairs, anti-corruption units, and professional standards offices. Functions such as building security, digital network protection, and personnel vetting may fall outside police command structures, handled by general government services or external vendors (Prunckun, 2019). This fragmentation creates vulnerabilities, especially where counterintelligence roles are poorly defined or institutionally deprioritized.

That said, not all police organizations operate under fragmented models. Some agencies maintain dedicated counterintelligence units with a unified mandate and centralized oversight. These structures mirror those found in intelligence services and are often better equipped to address insider risks. Still, in many jurisdictions—particularly at the local or municipal level—counterintelligence remains underdeveloped or loosely distributed across functional silos.

Motivations for Becoming an Insider

The decision to betray an organization from within rarely stems from a single moment of ideological awakening or financial desperation. Rather, insider activity typically results from an accumulation of personal vulnerabilities, environmental pressures, and concerning behaviours that often go unaddressed, what Shaw (2023) refers to as the Critical Pathway to Insider Risk (CPIR).

Insider threats may stem from a complex mix of voluntary and involuntary motives. Voluntary drivers include financial gain, ideological alignment, ego gratification, or revenge against perceived injustices. Involuntary ones arise from external pressures such as coercion, blackmail, addiction, psychological disorders, or intense personal stress (Wilder, 2017). The MICE framework—Money, Ideology, Compromise/Coercion, and Ego—remains one of the most widely used models in counterintelligence to categorize these drivers. While MICE helps illuminate why individuals become insiders, the process of how they are influenced or recruited often draws on psychological principles of persuasion, a topic examined in the next section through the RASCLS framework (Burkett, 2013).

Motivation, however, is only one component of insider risk. As Colwill (2009) notes, insider attacks emerge from a confluence of motivation, opportunity, and capability. Motivation is internal; opportunity and capability are either granted through official access or acquired once inside the system. Insider threats are therefore best understood as a transformation from trusted actor to malicious threat that unfolds over time (Cybersecurity and Infrastructure Security Agency, 2020). This transformation is rarely random. Certain individuals, due to psychological, ideological, or situational predispositions such as grievance, divided loyalties, or financial vulnerability, are more likely to engage in insider misconduct, including unauthorized access, information leakage, sabotage, or collaboration with external entities, particularly in environments that tolerate or fail to detect escalating warning signs (Wilder, 2017).

Shaw's (2023) CPIR outlines several stages in the evolution of insider threats. At its foundation are *personal predispositions*—psychological, behavioural, or social vulnerabilities present before the individual joins the organization. These include medical or psychiatric disorders (e.g., substance abuse), personality issues such as narcissism, a history of rule violations, and affiliations with risky social networks (e.g., criminal ties). These vulnerabilities may remain dormant until activated by stressors or negative experiences.

Stressors form the second layer in Shaw's model and include a range of personal, professional, financial, organizational, and even community-level pressures. Personal stressors might include divorce, bereavement, or family illness; professional stressors range from failed promotions to termination or perceived humiliation at work. Financial burdens such as debt, bankruptcy, or unmet expectations (e.g., bonuses or severance) also feature prominently in insider cases.

Over time, individuals with high levels of personal predispositions and cumulative stress are more likely to exhibit *concerning behaviours*; that is, observable actions that breach organizational norms, such as insubordination, chronic grievances, misuse of resources, or interpersonal aggression. These behaviours often act as red flags, but in many cases, they go unaddressed. *Problematic organizational responses*, such as managerial avoidance, procedural delays, or even well-intended accommodations, may unintentionally embolden the individual and accelerate their descent down the risk pathway.

The final stage before the insider act is what Shaw (2023) terms the insider *crime script*. This refers to a period in which the individual engages in operational planning, such as gathering resources or testing security boundaries.

While Shaw's (2023) original CPIR focuses on general organizational misconduct, the model can be adapted to law enforcement contexts where digital access, institutional culture, and HUMINT exploitation play a central role.

In addition to the CPIR model, behavioural science sheds light on insider predispositions. Furnham and Taylor (2022) outline six shaping dimensions: Culture and Clan, Biography and Family, Personal Intelligence, Personality, The Dark Side, and Motivation. These influence how individuals respond to stress, pressure, and opportunity. For instance, close ties to criminal networks may normalize disloyalty to the institution, while narcissistic or antisocial traits—common in insider cases—can foster rationalizations based on entitlement or victimhood. Shaw (2023) highlights related warning signs: hypersensitivity to criticism, interpersonal conflict, and a belief in being "above the rules." Though not always pathological, such traits often appear in workplace behaviour—over-reactions, outbursts, or chronic avoidance of accountability. Over time, these patterns can fuel grievance accumulation and justify harmful actions.

Importantly, insider risk is not always linear or inevitable. Shaw (2023) emphasizes mitigating factors that can halt or reverse the descent down the critical pathway. These include personal resilience, social support systems, successful self-care (e.g., therapy, financial counselling), and proactive, enlightened management. Many individuals who display insider risk factors never proceed to betrayal, either because they seek help, exit the organization, or are supported through institutional interventions. This underlines the importance of not only identifying high-risk individuals but also ensuring that organizations are equipped to respond in ways that de-escalate rather than inflame potential threats.

Finally, it is crucial to note that while behaviour is central to risk identification, the motivation itself is often unknowable. As the Cybersecurity and Infrastructure Security Agency (2020) report cautions, "Behavior is what matters most, not the motivation, whether it is political, religious, ideological, financial gain, or revenge." In practice, what distinguishes those who commit insider acts is not only their internal drive but the presence of enabling conditions that allow those motivations to translate into action.

Recruitment Methods

The recruitment of insiders follows a patterned process rooted in psychology, trust, and manipulation. While conventional counterintelligence doctrine often refers to the MICE model as the key drivers for insider betrayal, this framework has been criticized as overly simplistic (Burkett, 2013). Studies suggest that motivation alone does not explain how insiders are cultivated. As Burkett (2013) argues, recruitment is not a moment, but a six-stage cycle: spotting, assessing, developing, recruiting, handling, and terminating. Though developed to describe the recruitment of spies, the same logic applies to the criminal infiltration of police organizations.

Criminal networks often begin by *spotting* potential insiders; those with access to valuable information or operational influence. This is followed by *assessment*, where vulnerabilities are evaluated: financial distress, social marginality, or psychological fragility. In the *development* phase, the recruiter builds rapport, often via personal relationships. It is here that techniques grounded in Cialdini's (1984) six principles of influence—Reciprocation, Authority, Scarcity, Commitment, Liking, and Social Proof (RASCLS)—become relevant. These principles offer insight into how recruiters create pressure without overt coercion, using small favours, appeals to loyalty or status, and social cues to cultivate complicity.

The *recruitment* moment itself may be implicit: an officer asked to "just check a name" or provide "off the record" updates. Once the line is crossed, *handling* involves reinforcing dependency, concealing the relationship, and tasking the insider for increasingly sensitive operations. If exposure looms or trust breaks down, the relationship is *terminated*—sometimes abruptly, other times by letting the insider fade away.

These dynamics are visible in real-world law enforcement contexts. The Swedish case, as documented by the Swedish National Council for Crime Prevention, provides detailed evidence of how—even if relatively rare—efforts to groom police personnel by organized crime are serious and consequential (Skinnari et al., 2014, 2016). In a survey of 9,813 police officers, 4% (n = 365) reported receiving improper offers—money, gifts, meals—intended to establish reciprocal obligations (Skinnari et al., 2016). These exchanges, while seemingly innocuous, mimic the early stages of the "development" phase in agent recruitment.

Notably, recruiters tend to rely on pre-existing social relationships. The previously mentioned Swedish study reports that among the 99 police officers who had experienced harassment in the preceding 18 months, 81% indicated that the harasser was the client themself (Skinnari et al., 2016). The study further reveals that actors such as suburban youth gangs and criminal networks strategically select individuals perceived as more susceptible, often based on temperament, personal problems, or social isolation. Some researchers distinguish between symbolic influence, where police are targeted as representatives of state authority, and instrumental influence, which aims to achieve specific operational objectives, such as gaining access to case data or disrupting investigations (Baard et al., 2009).

Interviews in these studies also show that recruitment often escalates gradually. Some insiders began with minor unauthorized queries in police databases, later progressing to alerting suspects to raids or even deleting reports (Skinnari et al., 2014). In one rare but alarming case, an individual with physical access to police premises, though not formally employed, was able to destroy incoming reports before they were logged. This operational behaviour closely mirrors Burkett's model of insider handling.

Recruiters may also exploit emotional or financial vulnerabilities. Divorce, addiction, debt, or perceived professional mistreatment all appear as factors in insider profiles, echoing Burkett's critique of MICE as overly simplistic. In place of coercion, many recruiters prefer to elicit voluntary compliance through "liking" and "commitment," making the insider feel seen, supported, and protected, until they are too deeply entangled to withdraw.

Technology and Social Engineering in Recruitment

Platforms and Digital Vectors of Recruitment

Technology has radically altered the landscape of insider recruitment, not only by enabling new forms of access to sensitive information but by transforming how targets are identified, approached, and manipulated. Recruiters increasingly exploit open-source intelligence (OSINT), social media, encrypted messaging platforms, and online relationship tools to identify and assess potential insiders. This reflects the "spotting" and "assessing" phases of Burkett's (2013) recruitment cycle, now supercharged by digital surveillance and profiling. Social media platforms, for instance, offer real-time insight into personal struggles, lifestyle aspirations, romantic availability, and professional affiliations, all of which can inform a tailored approach to recruitment.

Evidence from Sweden confirms how these technologies are being deployed in criminal recruitment efforts. Researchers describe how actors in criminal networks engage in deliberate digital reconnaissance—Googling potential targets, browsing their social media to discover interests or vulnerabilities, and waiting for a moment of increased personal stress before initiating contact. Encrypted chat messages show that phrases like "do you know someone who works at X?" or "we need a bank employee" precede the targeting of specific individuals within extended personal networks (Skinnari et al., 2024).

In some cases, recruitment may even begin via dating apps or social media platforms, where searches are filtered by profession or location. While this is explored further in the Swedish case study, it is clear that some individuals use these platforms not to seek romance, but to identify vulnerable targets with access to restricted systems or sensitive processes (Skinnari et al., 2024).

Looking ahead, advances in artificial intelligence (AI) are likely to automate many of these recruitment processes. AI-driven systems could aggregate publicly available data across platforms to identify individuals whose professional roles, grievances, financial stress, or social affiliations align with recruitment objectives. Rather than relying on manual browsing, such tools would flag potential targets based on criteria like employment sector, proximity to sensitive institutions, or behavioural indicators. On dating applications and social media platforms, the same technologies could filter for specific occupations, generate tailored personas, and initiate highly personalized engagement at scale.

In addition, advances in generative AI enhance the effectiveness of social engineering. Large language models can craft context-specific messages that mimic shared interests, professional jargon, or emotional tone, increasing the credibility of initial contact. Deepfake technologies further expand this capability by enabling the fabrication of convincing audio or video content, potentially simulating trusted colleagues, supervisors, or romantic partners. Such techniques reduce the need for physical proximity and allow adversaries to create synthetic trust relationships that would previously have required sustained human effort. In combination, AI-driven profiling and synthetic media tools may significantly lower the cost and increase the speed of identifying, approaching, and manipulating potential insiders.

Regardless of whether initial contact occurs through manual browsing, dating platforms, or AI-assisted profiling, what follows is often a gradual process of entanglement. Rather than immediate threats, recruiters exploit vulnerability and affinity: shared backgrounds, aspirational lifestyles, or personal crises that create emotional openings. Common tactics include spending time with the target, presenting oneself as trustworthy or sympathetic, and then drawing the individual into small, seemingly innocuous favours that escalate over time. This methodical psychological approach aligns with Cialdini's (1984) RASCLS principles—particularly liking, reciprocation, and commitment—which are equally applicable to the covert world of criminal recruitment as they are to espionage (Burkett, 2013).

Technology also plays a central role in sustaining manipulation. Individuals from criminal networks use digital platforms to harass, dox, and intimidate police officers; publishing private information, threatening family members, and tracking movements online. Such tactics allow for persistent, asynchronous pressure, often with no immediate traceable source (Skinnari et al., 2016; Baard et al., 2009). As Hershkovitz (2022) notes, most existing theories on organizational vulnerability either over-emphasize technology or social structure, but rarely both. Yet it is precisely in the intersection between technological affordance and social engineering that recruitment becomes most effective.

Moreover, technology facilitates information exfiltration once an insider has been compromised. Skinnari et al. (2024) shows how compromised insiders often begin by performing small database queries—retrieving addresses, names, or case statuses. Over time, these leaks grow in sensitivity and frequency, suggesting that digital systems allow for gradual escalation without detection, especially where oversight is fragmented or nonexistent. In some cases, insiders have deleted or failed to register case information, approved payments without creating a corresponding digital case file, or performed unauthorized searches in sensitive databases—examples include welfare administrators who allowed benefits to be paid out without any digital documentation in the case management system, police staff conducting prohibited system queries to warn network members, and social services employees who "parked" or delayed digital registrations to influence outcomes.

It is also worth noting that not all insider activity requires hacking or advanced cyber intrusion. In many law enforcement and administrative organizations, access to strategic information is broad and loosely governed. In some agencies, multiple staff categories have access to sensitive operational data, whether directly via information systems or indirectly through procedural familiarity. This expands the pool of potential insiders and lowers the threshold for criminal targeting (Skinnari et al., 2024).

Finally, the underreporting of digital harassment further compounds institutional risk. In law enforcement agencies such as the Swedish police and judiciary, only a minority of personnel subjected to harassment or improper digital contact choose to report it to security departments (Skinnari et al., 2016). This silence not only impedes early intervention but also emboldens adversaries who understand that the threat of exposure alone can produce compliance.

A Case from Sweden

A 2024 investigative report by one of Sweden's largest newspapers, *Dagens Nyheter* (DN), uncovered a disturbing pattern of insider recruitment within the Swedish Police Authority, revealing how organized criminal networks have systematically exploited vulnerabilities in both personnel and digital infrastructure (Erlandsson & Örstadius, 2024). The findings highlighted the convergence of coercive tactics and technological platforms, particularly dating apps, to penetrate law enforcement and gain unauthorized access to sensitive police information.

One of the cases involved a police academy student, pseudonymously referred to as Elin, who was romantically targeted by a well-known, high-risk offender affiliated with a criminal network, called Jonas in the report. Jonas initiated contact via the dating site *Happy Pancake*[1], masking his intent under the guise of a romantic relationship. As the relationship developed, he manipulated Elin into conducting unauthorized searches in multiple police registers, including the suspected persons database, surveillance records, and warrant lists, to obtain confidential information about himself, his associates, and his rivals.

Once Elin graduated and began working at a police station, her privileged access enabled the network to stay ahead of police operations. Coordinated raids and surveillance operations were compromised, with suspects vanishing shortly before police action. Colleagues noticed an unusual pattern of failed operations and growing signs of criminal foreknowledge, yet the source remained initially undetected. According to DN, the criminal network not only accessed intelligence through Elin's searches but also appeared to gain insights into police routines, shift schedules, and personal details of individual officers.

Elin used several operational techniques to evade detection by internal monitoring systems. These included staging false emergency calls to create plausible justifications for register queries and drafting meaningless internal memos to simulate investigative legitimacy. These strategies allowed Elin to fabricate a plausible operational context for each query. For example, a fake emergency call could be used to justify an urgent database check, while an internal memo—even if content-free—would create a paper trail that made the action appear legitimate during audits. Because system logs focus on action rather than intent, these procedural artifacts helped her mask malicious activity as standard protocol.

The consequences were severe. DN's investigation links Elin's unauthorized data searches to at least two violent incidents. In one, an individual with a protected identity was located and brutally assaulted. In another, a man targeted by the network disappeared and remains missing. Although these connections could not be legally proven in court, the correlation between Elin's activity and the timing of the incidents was strong enough to raise serious institutional concerns.

Elin was ultimately convicted of unauthorized access to official records and received a fine. The charges were limited to the unlawful data searches, and despite the serious implications, no formal legal connection could be established between her actions and the subsequent violent incidents.

The recruitment strategy extended beyond Elin. DN reported that the same offender claimed to have recruited multiple law enforcement insiders, including one with extensive professional experience. The strategy was systematic: targeting individuals on dating platforms like *Tinder*, *Happy Pancake*, and *BodyContact*[2], often setting proximity filters to locate police academy students. Recruits were typically identified through their social media activities or class affiliations. Pride in the policing profession, expressed online, became a vulnerability exploited by criminal actors.

Prevention and Countermeasures

The management of insider threats requires more than *ad hoc* investigation or technical barriers. It demands an institutional shift toward prevention-oriented counterintelligence. Effective mitigation requires systematic efforts to identify, monitor, and reduce the risks posed by individuals with privileged access (Steele & Wargo, 2007). While traditional information security often focuses on external threats and perimeter defenses such as firewalls and intrusion detection systems, insiders operate behind those defenses (Colwill, 2009). Prevention must therefore combine technical, organizational, and cultural strategies, anchored in both defensive and offensive counterintelligence logic. Table 13.1 provides a consolidated overview of these strategies and their core functions.

Detection alone is insufficient if it comes too late. As Prunckun (2019) outlines, detection follows five key premises: identifying an event, the actors involved, their organizational position, their current status, and the facts that support an actionable conclusion. However, without a strong cultural foundation and adequate monitoring systems, many of these steps become reactive rather than preventive.

TABLE 13.1 Counterintelligence (CI) Measures for Preventing Insider Threats

Category	*Recommended Measure*	*Purpose*
Culture	Integrate CI awareness into daily police work culture	Normalize vigilance, reduce stigma
Education	Use RASCLS-based examples and insider case briefings	Recognize social engineering tactics
Preparedness	Develop standardized CI checklists	Ensure consistency, reduce oversight
Awareness	Democratize CI knowledge across ranks and roles	Close gaps between sworn and civilian staff
Monitoring	Implement continuous lifestyle vetting	Detect shifts in risk profile
Behavioral Detection	Track anomalies in access/use patterns	Identify hidden abuse of digital systems
Support	Provide wellness and mental health checks	Prevent crises from becoming breaches
Reporting	Establish anonymous, stigma-free channels	Encourage early self-reporting or alerts
Response	Offer reassignment, protection, counseling	Support vulnerable or compromised staff
Investigation	Use risk-based, surgical inquiries	Minimize morale damage
Legal Reform*	Introduce insider-specific legislation	Strengthen deterrence and procedural clarity

*Legal reforms—such as the creation of dedicated insider threat legislation—require national-level legislative action and cannot be implemented solely by law enforcement agencies.

Building an Institutional Culture of Counterintelligence

One of the most effective, non-technical defenses against insider threats is education. As Colwill (2009) emphasizes, protecting an organization's information is the responsibility of all staff, not just IT or security departments. Security awareness, counterintelligence literacy, and routine briefings should become integrated into the professional culture of law enforcement agencies. This includes regular discussion of risk behaviours, how to handle undue influence, and how to report early warning signs without stigma. These discussions may also incorporate examples aligned with Cialdini's RASCLS principles, which are known to precede behavioural shifts in insider recruitment (Cialdini, 1984; Burkett, 2013).

Swedish studies reinforce the point. In some police districts, dealing with undue influence from organized crime is part of the professional routine. These workplaces often have written protocols and practiced responses, not only for life-threatening scenarios but also for more subtle forms of coercion such as harassment or social pressure. Other districts lack any structured approach, often because influence attempts are infrequent or not recognized as serious (Baard et al., 2009). This inconsistency reveals a broader cultural problem: the normalization or denial of threat exposure depending on local experience, rather than on standardized institutional preparedness.

Furthermore, civilian staff, who may be more vulnerable to influence, are often not mentally prepared in the same way as sworn officers (Baard et al., 2009). This asymmetry in preparedness can create systemic weak points. Security departments often hold the greatest awareness of the risks posed by enablers, but this knowledge does not always reach the broader workforce (Skinnari et al., 2024). Awareness must therefore be democratized. Drawing on insights from aviation and healthcare, where checklists are used to enhance crew-wide situational awareness and reduce human error (Clay-Williams & Colligan, 2015), law enforcement and counterintelligence units should develop similar tools to standardize internal procedures, strengthen institutional memory, and ensure consistent threat response. In a law enforcement context, such tools could take the form of standardized counterintelligence checklists designed to guide both proactive monitoring and responsive investigations. These checklists can enhance preparedness, ensure continuity during personnel changes, and prevent critical oversights by formalizing institutional knowledge. For example, when no specific threat is known, checklists might help CI officers document known vulnerabilities in units handling sensitive cases, verify the rotation of digital access rights, or confirm that no personnel are under undue stress or coercion. In cases where suspicion arises, checklists can support systematic steps—such as verifying alibis for flagged database queries, mapping social relationships, or reviewing recent lifestyle changes. Much like aviation or surgical checklists, these tools do not replace judgment but reduce reliance on memory and help CI units maintain discipline and consistency without rigidity.

Indeed, the importance of reducing systemic vulnerabilities cannot be overstated. As Söderlund and von Zeipel (2024) argue, the ability of criminal actors to disrupt security-sensitive institutions indicates that hostile state actors can likely do the same. Counterintelligence cannot remain siloed in isolated units, it must become an integrated mindset across the entire organization.

At the same time, agencies must recognize that lack of intervention is itself a vulnerability. Shaw (2023) points to a critical gap: even when risk awareness exists, failures to investigate or act are common. This inaction may result from legal ambiguity, unclear internal policies, or unspoken institutional norms that discourage escalation. Such barriers must be addressed if counterintelligence is to shift from reactive to truly preventive.

Vetting and Monitoring

Detecting insider risk requires not only attention to individual behaviour, but also to lifestyle patterns that may change over time. This necessitates continuous vetting, rather than one-time background checks. Individuals who were stable at hiring may become vulnerable due to personal crises, financial instability, or professional grievances. Prunckun's (2019) distinction between *defensive* and *offensive* counterintelligence is instructive here: continuous vetting is a defensive posture, but if integrated with behavioural analysis and lifestyle monitoring, it becomes a proactive, even offensive, countermeasure. Routine monitoring of personnel should include:

- Regular security interviews
- Peer and supervisory assessments
- Flagging sudden lifestyle changes
- Behavioural anomalies

These monitoring efforts should be supported by technological tools such as audit trails, access control logs, and behavioural anomaly detection systems, provided they are implemented with respect for ethical and privacy considerations.

However, as demonstrated in the Swedish case study, technical monitoring tools alone are not foolproof. Although systems logged Elin's unauthorized database queries, she successfully masked her behaviour by generating false justifications such as staging 112 emergency calls or creating bogus internal memos. These actions allowed her to exploit the appearance of legitimacy while evading internal alarms. This illustrates the limits of purely digital detection systems and underscores the need to interpret access behaviour within its broader human and operational context.

Insider threats can follow multiple developmental pathways. Individuals may enter through different routes: self-motivated, recruited, infiltrated, inadvertent, or coerced (Bunn & Sagan, 2016). Each path presents unique challenges for detection. Some individuals may exhibit warning signs such as disgruntlement or financial distress; others may maintain a professional demeanour until placed under external pressure. Coerced insiders, in particular, may evade standard screening entirely, as their loyalty appears intact until a family member is threatened.

One solution is to incorporate routine mental health and wellness checks into personnel monitoring, not as surveillance, but as institutional care. These checks can help detect latent vulnerabilities, identify behavioural changes, and signal to staff that their well-being is central to the agency's integrity.

Internal Reporting and Support Mechanisms

A robust insider prevention strategy must include secure, anonymous, and stigma-free reporting systems. The earlier personnel feel safe to report concerns, about themselves or others, the greater the chance of early intervention. But reporting is not only about channels; it is about trust. Personnel must believe that raising an issue will lead to help, not punishment.

As Baard et al. (2009) note, increasing the sense of safety for the targeted individual is of high importance in managing undue influence. In many police units, fear of reprisal or being perceived as disloyal suppresses internal reporting. Those who have been pressured or compromised must be offered support structures and not just disciplinary procedures. This may include temporary reassignment, counselling, financial review, or, where necessary, protection.

Investigating suspected insider activity presents a separate but related challenge. Investigations can be discreet and surgical, or broad and morale-damaging (Bunn & Sagan, 2016). In high-trust environments, sweeping suspicion may lead to dysfunction. A more precise, risk-based approach, possibly drawing on red-teaming or behavioural auditing, can reduce collateral harm while still identifying real threats.

A final dimension concerns the legal framework, which is typically a national rather than local responsibility. Where such legislation is lacking—as in Sweden—insider violations are often prosecuted under general statutes like unauthorized access or breach of confidentiality. As seen in the Elin case, this can result in limited legal consequences and hinder effective deterrence. A dedicated insider law could clarify thresholds, expand investigative authority, and signal institutional resolve.

Conclusion

The modern landscape of insider threats is increasingly shaped by the integration of digital platforms into everyday professional life. Technology has revolutionized not only how information is stored and accessed, but also how adversaries recruit, manipulate, and manage insiders. Criminal actors now use encrypted communication, social media, and OSINT to conduct surveillance, establish contact, and sustain influence with a degree of precision and persistence once limited to state intelligence services. The Swedish case illustrates just how seamlessly this digital toolkit can be adapted for compromising insiders, transforming dating platforms and social networks into vectors of recruitment.

Yet despite this digital sophistication, the core mechanisms of insider recruitment remain fundamentally human. Trust, dependency, ego, vulnerability, and psychological manipulation are still the levers by which individuals are turned. Technology enhances these dynamics, but it does not replace them. As this chapter has shown, HUMINT, the cultivation and exploitation of human relationships, remains the most effective method of accessing restricted law enforcement information, particularly for non-state actors like organized crime.

This duality presents a profound challenge for police counterintelligence. Digital systems require continuous refinement through access logs, behavioural analytics, and anomaly detection, but they are only as effective as the cultural and operational context in which they are embedded. As the case of Elin in Sweden demonstrates, even well-designed digital safeguards can be circumvented by insiders who understand how to simulate legitimacy. Register queries were logged. Memos were filed. Justifications were fabricated. Only when broader patterns became visible, patterns difficult to detect through automated means alone, was the breach exposed.

As policing becomes more digitized, insider threats are not fading—they are adapting. Criminal actors no longer need physical proximity or shared social space to identify and manipulate targets. Encrypted messaging, social media reconnaissance, and access to digitized personnel records make it easier than ever to assess vulnerabilities remotely.

In the coming decade, this adaptive dynamic is likely to intensify. Advances in artificial intelligence will not replace human recruitment mechanisms, but they may automate and scale them. Automated profiling systems, synthetic digital personas, and AI-assisted social engineering techniques could significantly lower the cost and increase the speed of identifying and engaging potential insiders. Deepfake technologies may further blur the boundary between authentic and fabricated trust, complicating verification processes within law enforcement environments. The convergence between algorithmic targeting and human vulnerability is therefore poised to become a defining feature of future insider risk.

But the real danger is institutional: many police organizations are modernizing their infrastructure without modernizing their counterintelligence mindset. Without clear mandates, trained CI personnel, and responsive protocols, digital systems become not just tools, but weaknesses. The future of policing will be shaped not only by what technology is added, but by what human oversight is missing.

Thus, a successful insider prevention strategy must blend technological vigilance with a deep understanding of human behaviour. The ultimate goal of counterintelligence, however, is not merely detection. As Olson (2019) argues, it is to prevent recruitment in the first place. This requires more than surveillance. It requires education, foresight, and institutional courage; to intervene early, to support vulnerable personnel, and to cultivate a culture where compromise is not only rare, but unthinkable.

Acknowledgements: The author acknowledges the use of ChatGPT (GPT-4, OpenAI) during the preparation of this chapter. The tool was used to support language refinement, structural suggestions, editing, and synthesis of author-provided content, with the aim of enhancing clarity, coherence, and readability. It was not used to generate original research ideas or theoretical frameworks. All outputs were critically reviewed, edited, and verified by the author, who takes full responsibility for the final content. This use complies with the Taylor & Francis policy on the responsible use of generative AI in scholarly publishing: https://taylorandfrancis.com/our-policies/ai-policy/.

Notes

1 Happy Pancake (often abbreviated HP) is a popular Swedish dating website known for being entirely free. Users have full access to each other's profiles, though profile images can be hidden and selectively revealed.
2 BodyContact is a Swedish adult-oriented dating and contact platform focused on casual encounters, BDSM, and kink. It allows pseudonymous profiles and is popular among users seeking alternative sexual lifestyles, with many profiles offering selective visibility of photos and preferences.

References

Baard, P., Skinnari, J., Korsell, L., Weding, L., & Heber, A. (2009). *Polisens möte med organiserad brottslighet: En undersökning om otillåten påverkan*. Brottsförebyggande rådet. https://bra.se/rapporter/arkiv/2009-04-02-polisens-mote-med-organiserad-brottslighet
Brottsförebyggande rådet. (2025, April 29). Otillåten Påverkan. Retrieved June 12, 2025, from https://bra.se/amnen/otillaten-paverkan
Bunn, M., & Sagan, S. D. (Eds.) (2016). Introduction: Inside the insider threat. *Insider Threats* (pp. 1–9). Cornell University Press.
Burkett, R. (2013). An alternative framework for agent recruitment: From MICE to RASCLS. *Studies in Intelligence*, *57*(1), 7–17.
Carlisle, R. P. (Ed.). (2015). Introduction. In *Encyclopedia of intelligence and counterintelligence, Volume One–Two* (pp. vii–ix). Routledge.
Cialdini, R. (1984). *Influence: The psychology of persuasion*. Quill/William Morrow.
Clay-Williams, R., & Colligan, L. (2015). Back to basics: Checklists in aviation and healthcare. *BMJ Quality & Safety*, *24*(7), 428–431.
Cline, L. E. (2015). Interagency cooperation. In R. P. Carlisle (Ed.), *Encyclopedia of intelligence and counterintelligence, Volume One–Two* (pp. 322–324). Routledge.
Colwill, C. (2009). Human factors in information security: The insider threat–Who can you trust these days? *Information Security Technical Report*, *14*(4), 186–196.
Cybersecurity and Infrastructure Security Agency. (2020). *Insider threat mitigation guide*. US Department of Homeland Security.
Erlandsson, Å., & Örstadius, K. (2024). *Polisläckorna*. Dagens Nyheter. https://www.dn.se/polislackorna/
Furnham, A., & Taylor, J. (2022). *The psychology of spies and spying: Trust, treason, treachery*. Matador.
Gay, R. A. (2015). Collection. In R. P. Carlisle (Ed.), *Encyclopedia of intelligence and counterintelligence, Volume One–Two* (pp. 152–154). Routledge.
Hershkovitz, S. (2022). *The future of national intelligence: How emerging technologies reshape intelligence communities*. Rowman & Littlefield.
Khoshnood, A. (2018). Firearm-related violence in Sweden – A systematic review. *Aggression and Violent Behavior*, *42*, 43–51.
Khoshnood, A., & Gerell, M. (2019). Gun and explosive violence. In M. Väfors Fritz & A. Khoshnood (Eds.), *Crime, victimization and vulnerability in Malmö* (pp. 19–32). Studentlitteratur.
Khoshnood, A., Ohlsson, H., Sundquist, J., & Sundquist, K. (2023). Firearm-related homicide in Sweden: A latent class analysis of suspected offenders. *Crime & Delinquency*, *69*(1), 88–104.
Manget, F. F. (2010). Intelligence and law enforcement. In L. K. Johnson (Ed.), *The Oxford handbook of national security intelligence* (pp. 189–211). Oxford University Press.
Nelson, G. H. (2015). Counterintelligence. In R. P. Carlisle (Ed.), *Encyclopedia of intelligence and counterintelligence, Volume One–Two* (pp. 172–173). Routledge.

Nurse, J. R., Buckley, O., Legg, P. A., Goldsmith, M., Creese, S., Wright, G. R., & Whitty, M. (2014). Understanding insider threat: A framework for characterising attacks. In *2014 IEEE security and privacy workshops* (pp. 214–228). IEEE.

O'Brien, K. A. (2009). Managing national security and law enforcement intelligence in a globalised world. *Review of International Studies*, *35*(4), 903–915.

Olson, J. M. (2019). *To catch a spy: The art of counterintelligence*. Georgetown University Press.

Polisen. (2025, April 10). *Polisen arbetar intensivt för att upptäcka och förebygga påverkansförsök. Retrieved Juny* 12, 2025, from https://polisen.se/om-polisen/pressrum/debattartiklar-och-kommentarer/om-insiderproblematik/

Prunckun, H. (2019). *Counterintelligence theory and practice*. Rowman & Littlefield.

Shaw, E. D. (2023). *The psychology of insider risk: Detection, investigation and case management*. CRC Press.

Skinnari, J., Ekdahl, E., & Korsell, L. (2014). *Korruption i Myndighetssverige: Otillåten påverkan mot insider*. Brottsförebyggande rådet. https://bra.se/rapporter/arkiv/2014-01-24-korruption-i-myndighetssverige

Skinnari, J., Hurve, K., & Jonsson, A. (2016). *Otillåten påverkan mot myndighetspersoner: En uppföljning*. Brottsförebyggande rådet. https://bra.se/rapporter/arkiv/2016-09-08-otillaten-paverkan-mot-myndighetspersoner

Skinnari, J., Hurve, K., & Monti, A. (2024). *Möjliggörare för kriminella nätverk: Om möjliggörare i kommunal, statlig och privat sektor*. Brottsförebyggande rådet. https://bra.se/rapporter/arkiv/2024-03-01-mojliggorare-for-kriminella-natverk

Steele, S., & Wargo, C. (2007). An introduction to insider threat management. *Information Systems Security*, *16*(1), 23–33.

Söderlund, Y., & von Zeipel, P. (2024). *Säkerhetsskyddsanalys i teori och praktik*. Norstedts Juridik.

Wilder, M. U. (2017). Why spy? The psychology of espionage. *Studies in Intelligence*, *61*(2), 19–36.

14

AI IN POLICING

Capturing Police Performance (Good and Bad) in Routine, Rare, and Novel Events

Seth Watts, Michael D. White, and Aili Malm

Introduction

Policing in the United States generates an abundance of data. In the US there are about 18,000 law enforcement agencies that generate approximately 50 million police–civilian interactions a year (Tapp & Davis, 2024). Add to the situation that nearly two-thirds of all agencies and approximately 80% of large police agencies have body-worn cameras (BWCs) (Hyland, 2018), resulting in an inordinate amount of police–civilian encounter-level video and audio data. Unfortunately, the vast majority of the footage (~95%) is never reviewed by anyone, internally or externally (Uchida et al., 2022). The footage that is reviewed is primarily done so for evidentiary purposes and enhancing transparency for specific encounters (e.g., use of force). The inability to review BWC footage at scale likely limits the value that BWCs add to a police department. Thus, there are two important questions: 1) How can BWC video data be efficiently synthesized? 2) How can BWC video data be utilized to provide important insights about police work? Artificial intelligence (AI) offers the potential to address both these questions by cutting down labor costs and enhancing the value of BWC data.

The substantial amount of BWC footage, and the handling of that footage, present a new challenge for police departments. Because of this emerging problem, there are a few market competitors including Axon, Polis Solutions, and Truleo that have specifically targeted the issue with an AI-based solution. One of the main selling points of these platforms and other AI-based platforms more generally is the purported efficiency gains. Outside of policing there have been reports suggesting that the use of large language models (LLMs) is associated with time savings and productivity gains (Brynjolfsson et al., 2023). However,

DOI: 10.4324/9781003671312-14

there are also a handful of studies that suggest the time savings claims should be tempered (Adams et al., 2024; Becker et al., 2025). Despite this, given the amount of footage police departments generate on a daily basis, it is clear why an AI-based platform is an appealing alternative. A chief of police can confidently report 100% of the BWC footage is being reviewed, the BWC review process for sergeants can be expedited, and footage can be turned into actionable data.

In addition to potential efficiency gains, AI in policing offers the ability to capture outcomes that are either not found in administrative data or are too costly to observe via systematic social observation (SSO) or video-based SSO (e.g., BWC footage coding; VBSSO) methods. Historically, rich qualitative data on the nature of police work was derived from SSO (Bittner, 1967; Muir, 1979). This method, while informative, is resource intensive. More recent qualitative (and quantitative) endeavors have focused on VBSSO to capture police behavior (Makin et al., 2021; McLean et al., 2025; White et al., 2022). Similarly, sergeants' BWC review duties tend to include randomly reviewing a certain number of videos for each officer in a given time frame (e.g., monthly, quarterly; see White et al., 2017). This process is limited in the information it can provide given most encounters are mundane and some are hours long (Chillar et al., 2021). The advent of LLMs and natural language processing provide a method for synthesizing BWC footage in a repeatable, resource-efficient way, and has the potential to be insightful to both researchers and practitioners.

In this chapter, we explore the role of AI in harnessing the value of BWC footage. First, we will discuss the goal of efficiency in policing describing both historical and contemporary examples of technological advancements that were adopted to achieve this end. Second, focusing specifically on AI, we will discuss this technology's potential to transform how police practitioners and researchers systematically measure and assess police behavior. Next, we outline methodological considerations focusing on data structure, power, and the validity of AI-generated data. Fourth, we review concerns surrounding the use of AI-based platforms within police departments. Lastly, we will look forward and propose how the use of AI in policing can balance the goals of efficiency and measurement and what this means for policy and practice.

Efficiency in Policing

Historical and Contemporary Efficiency Tools

As the function and structure of the police have evolved over the last 150 years, its relationship with technology has as well. Over the course of the 20th century, there was an intimate relationship between the evolution of policing and technology. There was constant technological innovation and shifts in how the police deliver services and control crime (Seaskate, Inc., 1998). Indeed, many of the technologies adopted by the police were done so as an attempt to improve their efficiency. In the latter part of the 20th century the advent of the computer revolutionized key aspects of policework. Following recommendations from the President's 1967 Crime Commission (President's Commission on Law Enforcement and Administration of Justice, 1967), the Law Enforcement Assistance Administration (LEAA) pushed to expand the police capabilities through computerization (Seaskate, Inc., 1998). Computerization led to a host of downstream innovations and improvements such as computer-aided dispatch (CAD) systems, seamless information sharing between agencies (e.g., National Crime Information Center), automated fingerprint identification systems (AFIS), improved records management, and resource allocation (e.g., deployment to higher crime areas) (see Colton, 1979; Seaskate, Inc., 1998).

The relationship between technology and evolving practices reigns true today with a host of technological advancements occurring within policing in the 21st century. Examples include BWCs, gunshot detection systems, and automated license plate readers. While this is not an exhaustive list of technological innovations within policing that plausibly improved efficiency, it nonetheless demonstrates the close relationship between innovation and efficiency (Lum et al., 2017). The same is true for one of the most recent technological advancements in policing: artificial intelligence.

AI in Policing

AI as an Efficiency Enhancer

Artificial intelligence (AI) broadly refers to the ability of computers to mimic human reasoning and learning (Stryker & Kavlakoglu, 2024). AI has evolved over time to include machine learning, deep learning, and generative AI. Many applications of AI within policing focus squarely on machine learning models, particularly natural language processing (NLP) and large language models (LLMs). For instance, LLMs have been applied to aid in police report writing (*Get Started—Draft One*, n.d.; TRULEO Introduces AI Generated Police Reports Powered by Amazon Bedrock, 2024) and NLP has been used to help triage 911 calls for service (Atherley, 2025).

AI in policing is broadly appealing due to the sheer volume of data that is produced by the police. There are approximately 240 million calls for service per year in the United States (National Emergency Number Association, 2021) and around 50 million police–civilian contacts (Tapp & Davis, 2024), which together generate an abundance of administrative and BWC footage data. As an example, Axon hosts around 100 petabytes of BWC footage which is approximately equivalent to a cloud-based platform hosting 25 million copies of the 2023 film *Barbie* (Farooq, 2024). For perspective, with *Barbie* being 1 hour and

54 minutes long, the time it would take to watch all 25 million copies is around 3.6 billion minutes, or 6,849 years. Notably, this is not a fixed quantity: new BWC footage is being produced each minute of each day. Indeed, there is not enough human labor nor time to handle the amount of data—particularly BWC footage—ingested by police departments.

Moreover, this is not an issue in the aggregate or for large agencies only. Consider a smaller agency with 20 patrol officers. If each officer is outfitted with a BWC and is working 4 × 10-hour shifts, at a maximum, there would be 800 hours of BWC footage produced each week by those 20 officers. If there are 4 sergeants each responsible for 5 officers, there would be 200 hours of footage for each sergeant to review. Even if we consider a lower bound estimate of 2 hours worth of footage per shift per officer, each sergeant still has 40 hours of footage to review each week. Of course, sergeants are not expected to review all the footage. Usually they are expected to review—at random—a few videos per officer per month/quarter (White et al., 2017). Nonetheless, this demonstrates that the issue permeates through policing irrespective of department size—hence the appeal of AI.

In addition to reviewing the BWC footage that is produced in near-real time, AI integration has the potential to provide efficiency gains in other areas as well. For instance, applying natural language processing to the audio of BWC footage can produce text-based transcripts. Then, algorithms can be trained on the text to provide generative summaries of each incident and label certain events that occur throughout the encounter. In turn, this could yield a useful template for officers to then use to expedite the report writing process. Moreover, the summaries and event labeling could lend themselves useful for supervisory BWC review processes as well.

Identifying Rare and Hard to Capture Outcomes

In addition to the potential efficiency gains provided by AI, the technology also serves as a tool to potentially enhance the ability of police departments to capture outcomes that are hard to systematically observe. For example, de-escalation is not easy to define and thus it is hard to measure. Indeed, despite a focus on de-escalation training in the President's Task Force on 21st Century Policing (2015), and the quick diffusion of various de-escalation training programs (Engel et al., 2020; McLean et al., 2025; Orosco et al., 2025), there is no accepted uniform definition of de-escalation (Todak & James, 2018). However, if a definition is identified and specific verbal utterances can be agreed upon as being integral to a de-escalation attempt, an AI algorithm can be trained on those particular words to help systematically capture de-escalation attempts.

Going beyond de-escalation, good policing is largely invisible (Fyfe, 1988). Good policing can manifest in many ways that do not show up in administrative data nor in mandatory BWC review processes. Alternatively, bad policing can be hard to identify as well. Derogatory language, for instance, is not present in administrative data and may not appear in supervisory random BWC review duties. While not all profanities are inherently problematic (Adams, 2024a; Adams, Olson, et al., 2025), it is important to consider the deleterious effects of directed profanity towards the public on police legitimacy. AI has the ability to capture profanities in BWC footage via natural language processing. Given the need for contextual nuance, this process would likely require a "human-in-the-loop" to determine the veracity of the label. Nonetheless, a behavior that was largely unobservable can now be surfaced for review with the use of AI. The same can be said for an unreported use of force, or an officer's failure to take action (e.g., duty to intervene, failure to arrest, etc.)

Together, the integration of AI into BWC footage can aid in identifying good and bad policing. Capturing outcomes such as officer respect, level of explanation, and profanities are now much more feasible than ever before. These outcomes are not captured in administrative data and are quite time-intensive to observe through SSO or VBSSO. Moreover, there is the risk of a Hawthorne effect and observer bias when using SSO and VBSSO, which can lead to imprecisely measured police behavior. Though AI does have downsides, as we will discuss later, it does provide a systematic way of capturing unique outcomes.

Analyzing Complex Police–Civilian Interactions

In addition to capturing rare and hard to measure outcomes, the integration of AI into BWC footage can help elucidate the complexity of police–civilian encounters. Encounters between civilians and police officers are transactional with various decision points that influence subsequent behavior and ultimately determine the outcome of the encounter (Binder & Scharf, 1980; Terrill, 2005). The multi-stage "give-and-take" between an officer and civilian, which was invisible prior to the advent of BWCs, is essential to capture to have a granular understanding of the nature of police encounters. However, systematically capturing the stages of police–civilian encounters to deconstruct its temporal nature is resource intensive, particularly the coding process of BWC footage (Makin et al., 2021; McCluskey & Uchida, 2023).

One of the notable upsides to using AI to analyze BWC footage of police–civilian encounters is the ability to capture the events sequentially that occur throughout an encounter. This process can yield a storyboard-like interpretation of the events (Camp et al., 2024; Prabhakaran et al., 2018). Not only does this open up a variety of new methodological approaches for researchers but it also provides a detailed account of the events that transpired within an incident. An AI-based examination of decision points in a specific set of encounters, such as community members in a mental health crisis, has enormous value to a law enforcement agency in terms of training, policy, and practice.

Take for instance a use of force incident. Given the importance of situational characteristics (Piza et al., 2022), it is critical to accurately capture not only the temporal ordering of events but also the proximate event that led to the use of force. Piza et al.'s study uses a unique dataset of coded use of force incidents from BWC footage that explicitly demarcates the temporal ordering of events within each encounter. Specifically, they generate a dataset that has the variables of interest for each 5-second interval throughout the encounter. Their findings highlight how behavior (e.g., civilian physical antagonism, officer commands) is related to subsequent use of force.

Supervision, Training, and Evaluation

Because the use of AI can capture rare and hard to identify outcomes and can highlight the complexity of police–civilian encounters, it may be able to help facilitate improved supervision, training, and performance evaluation. Specifically, a sergeant's ability to monitor, mentor, and evaluate the performance of their officers will likely improve given the granularity of the new and detailed insights into their officer's encounters. AI can act as a buffer in this scenario, scaling down supervisory workload when reviewing officer behavior via BWC footage. Further, officers may access their data to review their own performance allowing for self-reflection. This may be potentially useful to review certain encounters and consider alternative methods or approaches that may have been more useful.

Second, the use of AI could be incorporated into early intervention systems to allow for officers who are at risk to be identified more efficiently. Consider an example where an officer has increasingly been flagged for directed profanity towards citizens. Further, this trend is accompanied by an increase in flags for threatening force. It is possible that this could cascade into more problematic behavior and may be worth a discussion at the direction of a sergeant. Related, the AI-based platform could capture traumatic events that officers experience such as responding to a death, or specifically, the death of a child. Exposure to traumatic events may lead to coping strategies that negatively impact subsequent performance. Being able to identify instances when an officer has come across a traumatic event (or multiple over the course of a short time frame), will allow sergeants to develop a course of action for that officer.

Methodological Implications

Data Structure and Power

The integration of AI auditing of BWC footage in police departments creates a plethora of opportunities to analyze and breakdown the complexity of police–civilian encounters. This goes for crime analysts, training units, and researchers alike. For researchers, AI completely alters data structure and analysis options. Instead of relying on aggregated data at the incident- or officer-level, within officer and encounter data are available. This effectively transforms the data into both multilevel and micro-longitudinal data, which opens up a whole new set of potential research questions with more appropriate modeling techniques.

In conjunction with the transformation in data structure also comes a shift in the ways in which researchers can model the data. Much of the criminological literature is under-powered (Barnes et al., 2020) since many of the outcomes of interest are generally rare. When dealing with rare outcomes, many observations of the outcome of interest are required to be able to correctly reject the null hypothesis (Adams, 2024b), In policing research, this is a particularly looming issue given the outcomes of interest are usually quite infrequent, such as use of force (Tapp & Davis, 2024). AI cannot fix the issue of infrequent observations of specific outcomes, but it can help with the issue of power by improving the signal to noise ratio.

For example, the impact of de-escalation training is often measured through the prevalence of use of force. Did use of force decline after officers received de-escalation training? However, most evaluations of de-escalation training have not consistently documented a reduction in use of force. One explanation for this is that the training "did not work." But it may also be that a) methodologically, the effect cannot be detected due to insufficient power or b) it is such a rare event it primarily occurs within the bounds with which it is prescribed and thus may not be as amenable to training curricula. If either of these are true, it may be important to think of other outcomes that are of interest (White et al., 2023), potentially outcomes that can be observed more frequently with the help of AI. Other outcomes, such as officer respect (Camp & Voigt, 2025) or use of procedural justice, can be more precisely captured via natural language processing. Looking at Figure 14.1, NLP could recognize the speech of the officer and

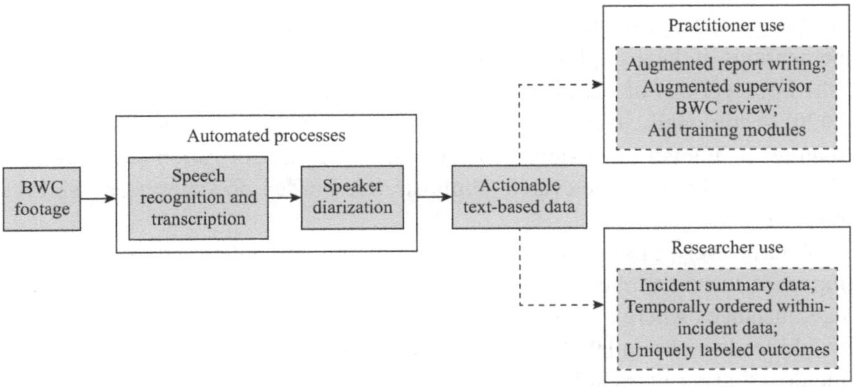

FIGURE 14.1 Automated Actionable BWC Footage Data

others on scene, categorize the speakers to identify the officer, and then label instances of respect or even generate a "respect score." Importantly, officer respect could be captured in each encounter (overcoming the issue of rarity) and, in research terms, the data would be nested at the officer-encounter level (ability to control for officer propensities; see Adams, McLean, et al., 2025). Together, this could help facilitate a more precise evaluation of the effects of a de-escalation training program on officer respect because it would be well powered. There are, of course, limitations to this specific example as de-escalation also entails nonverbal cues, but presumably if automated video processing is the next step in this space, it could potentially be integrated in some capacity in the future.

Concerns

Over- and Under-Surveillance

AI-auditing of BWC footage is not without concerns. Broadly speaking, there are concerns that AI may contribute to a loss of privacy and exacerbate racial and ethnic disparities in police activities (Ferguson, 2017). There have been a few accounts of both civil libertarians and police unions expressing concern over AI being a tool for excessive surveillance of both officers and community members (Carter, 2023; Porter & Ogdon, 2023; Sault, 2023). In fact, the Seattle police union considered the adoption of Truleo—an AI-based platform—as a tool for "spying" on officers (Carter, 2023). Moreover, at least one study found that algorithmically generated feedback is viewed as patently unfair among police officers (Adams, 2025).

Another concern is the false positive and false negative rates of the algorithms, both of which have potential consequences. If the algorithm has an elevated false positive rate, there is the risk that an officer may face some form of coaching, training, or punishment based on false pretenses. This not only has the potential to generate a negative view of the technology but also negative perceptions of the disciplinary process within the organization leading to diminished perceptions of organizational justice among officers (Wolfe & Lawson, 2020). Additionally, if the elevated false positive rate is for a specific label that requires a "human-in-the-loop" to verify the AI's categorization (e.g., profanities), it could place an elevated administrative burden on supervisors who are reviewing the flags.

Alternatively, false negatives could miss important police actions. Considering most current applications of this technology audits the audio of BWC footage, instances where audio is muffled or no verbalization of actions are made would lead to certain labels being missed. For example, consider a use of force incident that escalates quickly, requires an officer to go hands on, and is in close quarters; the AI algorithm may fail to capture the use of force label and thus a flag would not be generated. Of course, the use of force would appear in administrative data and would trigger an internal review but over-reliance on the algorithm's output could be problematic in some cases.

Generative Suspicion

The use of AI-generated police reports provides some cause for concern as well. Police reports are critical to criminal justice processes because they frequently contain information that justifies police intervention (e.g., reasonable suspicion). Importantly, this information is supposed to be capturing the officer's perspective and rationale for their actions. With the use of automated report writing software, there is a risk that the transcription process of audio to text may lead to "generative suspicion," that is, AI-generated suspicion (Ferguson, 2024). It is possible that the algorithm picks up on audio that did not necessarily influence an officer's decision making in a given encounter.

Other concerns include blatant errors in reporting. Axon's Draft One platform can be configured to contain purposeful errors to ensure officers are reviewing the report. If there are algorithmically generated errors or hallucinations that provide information that are unrelated to a given encounter, the report and evidence could be thrown out of court. Moreover, the officer could face disciplinary action. Because of these concerns, some states have considered pieces of legislation that require officers to indicate when a report was written using generative AI. For instance, California recently passed HB 524 which requires disclosures of AI usage and a clear audit trail of officer reports (Putman, 2025).

Normative Disagreements

One concern over the use of AI in police departments may revolve around the privatization of such algorithms. Proprietary algorithms and unknown rates of false positives and false negatives may cast a cloud of doubt over such platforms. However, the development of technology within the private sector is not new to policing (e.g., dash-cameras, BWCs, drones, less than lethal weapons [Conducted Energy Devices]).

Also, there will likely be disagreements over how specific behaviors are conceptualized and measured using AI. For instance, Truleo has an outcome that is labeled "Officer Professionalism." It is a tripartite measure where high professionalism is indicated when an officer a) uses at least 25 words of explanation before an official action, b) there is no threat of force, c) no use of force, and d) no impolite language. Substandard professionalism is when an officer uses impolite language and a sergeant confirms that it was the officer and that what was said was impolite. Standard professionalism lies in-between these two categories and reflects an officer adhering to department policy.[1]

Professionalism could be captured in a variety of ways. It is plausible that in some scenarios, a use of force is professional. Additionally, maybe 25 words of explanation is a conservative threshold. Not all impolite language is "unprofessional" (Adams, 2024a). Further, nonverbal cues play an important part in determining officer professionalism as well. These are just a few ways in which disagreements may arise over the measurement of an AI-generated outcome.

Looking Ahead

Implications for Police Practitioners

The integration of AI into police practices will undoubtedly take the profession into uncharted waters. As we have discussed earlier, the potential benefits are significant. The use of AI could fully transform how BWC footage is used, moving beyond evidentiary value and transparency, to a more thorough way of evaluating police performance. Innovation in this direction to realize the full potential of BWC footage will be an important endeavor. But there are concerns, and there may also be unintended consequences that are not yet clear. The Police Executive Research Forum (PERF; 2023, p. 36) recognizes the challenges around the use of AI, noting:

> AI raises multiple serious concerns related to privacy, civil liberties, and government misuse. Thus, it is essential for law enforcement agencies to include community members, academics, civil libertarians, and technology experts, among others, in all phases of program development, from software acquisition and policy writing to outcome evaluation and data transparency.

Though AI is a unique innovation, we can draw on lessons learned from the integration of other technologies in policing to provide guidance for the adoption of AI. For example, the Bureau of Justice Assistance, US Department of Justice developed a detailed *Law Enforcement Implementation Checklist* to serve as a best-practices guide for planning and implementing a BWC program (Bureau of Justice Assistance, 2015). White et al. (2018, p. 651) discussed seven key principles for effective program implementation: learn the fundamentals, develop a plan, form a working group, develop policy, define technology solution (procurement), communicate [with] and educate stakeholders, and execute phased rollout/implementation.

Similarly, Orosco et al. (2025) developed a "De-escalation Training Checklist" that provides a series of guidelines and considerations for agencies to plan, deliver, and evaluate de-escalation training. Though they address other innovations, the principles from these tools can inform the planning and implementation of an AI program, as demonstrated next.

Learn the fundamentals of AI and develop a plan: Agency leadership should first identify one or more goals they seek to achieve with AI. The organizational goals of deploying AI should shape the parameters of its use. Moreover, agency leaders should have a clear understanding of the perceived advantages and disadvantages of using AI. The agency must do their homework on AI by engaging with others who already use it (via peer networks, conferences such as International Association of Chiefs of Police [IACP], etc.), accessing available resources on the topic, and scouring the available research literature. Last, the leadership should develop a project plan with a specific timeline and milestones. The plan should be flexible and subject to change as needed.

Create an AI working group: The agency should create an "AI working group" that guides the planning and implementation process. All relevant units should have membership in the group to provide open lines of communication through all levels of the organization. The working group can take the lead on staying apprised of changes in local, state, and federal law that may affect the use of AI in law enforcement. It can also be a resource for officers who have questions or concerns about AI.

Develop an AI administrative policy: The working group can take the lead in developing an AI administrative policy that will govern all aspects of its use by the agency. The policy should adhere to relevant local, state, and federal law, and it should be vetted with department leadership, department unions, and city leadership (e.g., city attorney's office). Police leadership groups such as IACP and PERF have begun to compile information on AI use that can guide policy development. For example, IACP has created an "Artificial Intelligence Resource Hub" that includes a use-case collection and policy guidance (https://www.theiacp.org/working-group/artificial-intelligence-resource-hub). Moreover, the AI policy can serve as the centerpiece of AI training for officers.

Communicate [with] and educate stakeholders: AI is a topic that often generates strong reactions, from concerns about "big brother," surveillance, and privacy to algorithm accuracy and fairness. Within the organization, the working group can play a primary role in internal messaging before AI deployment to communicate the goals to the rank and file, assuage concerns, and answer questions. In their review of the US DOJ BWC Checklist, White et al. (2018, p. 656) note "A similar campaign to external stakeholders can reduce concerns/questions among citizens, advocacy groups, and other criminal justice actors." The same applies with AI.

Execute phased rollout/implementation: It may be wise for agencies to engage in a phased deployment of AI, rather than going agencywide. For example, the Arizona Department of Public Safety (AZ DPS) deployed Truleo to 40 troopers in two districts in Phoenix before rolling out the AI-based BWC analytics program statewide approximately five months later. The phased rollout is more measured and allows for "real time learning" about implementation that can guide the larger agencywide deployment. Such an approach can also serve to short circuit internal resistance by providing an early snapshot of the technology in operation.

Overall, a law enforcement agency that decides to deploy AI, whether through BWC analytics or another form, will need to balance sometimes competing goals including enhanced efficiency, accountability, organizational justice, and fairness (Council on Criminal Justice, 2025). At the same time, the use of AI in criminal justice contexts demands careful attention to potential risks and unintended consequences. The stakes in criminal justice require that we pay attention to how AI systems can malfunction or even undermine democratic control (***https://counciloncj.org/principles-for-the-use-of-ai-in-criminal-justice/***).

Implications for Researchers

The diffusion of AI in policing has implications for researchers as well. First, it will likely be difficult for many researchers to gain access to AI platforms and/or department data that is subjected to AI (e.g., BWC footage). The most viable avenue is to develop researcher–practitioner partnerships that are grounded in trust, shared understanding, and clear expectations (see Sullivan et al. [2013] for guidelines on developing such partnerships).

Researchers can also play an important advisory role for law enforcement agencies in terms of planning and implementing the use of AI. Researchers can help agency leaders think about the challenges, benefits, and consequences of AI use. They can also assist in finding emerging resources on the topic. For example, Arizona State University hosts an AI webpage that includes access to experts, an evaluation and research team, an ethics committee, and a suite of AI tools (https://ai.asu.edu/).

Last, there is very little empirical research examining the use of AI in policing. Much like with the diffusion of BWCs, researchers need to move quickly to build an evidence base that can guide practitioner decision making regarding AI. This evidence base should, at a minimum, explore how AI can be used in policing, the challenges surrounding its use, unintended consequences, and the benefits it can deliver. The dialogue on AI in policing is currently grounded in speculation and anecdotes. An emerging research base will ground that dialogue in evidence.

Conflicts of interest: None to declare.

Funding: The research on which this chapter draws from was supported by Arnold Ventures under grant #74377. Any opinions, findings, and conclusions or recommendations expressed here are those of the authors and do not necessarily reflect those of Arnold Ventures.

Note

1 See https://help.truleo.co/how-truleo-recognizes-professionalism

References

Adams, I. T. (2024a). Fuck: The police. *Police Quarterly*, *28*(1), 3–44. https://doi.org/10.1177/10986111241241750

Adams, I. T. (2024b). Power simulations of rare event counts and introduction to the 'power lift' metric. *CrimRxiv.* https://doi.org/10.21428/cb6ab371.dfc6b8fa

Adams, I. T. (2025). Automation and artificial intelligence in police body-worn cameras: Experimental evidence of impact on perceptions of fairness among officers. *Journal of Criminal Justice*, *97*, 102373. https://doi.org/10.1016/j.jcrimjus.2025.102373

Adams, I. T., Barter, M., McLean, K., Boehme, H. M., & Geary, I. A. (2024). No man's hand: Artificial intelligence does not improve police report writing speed. *Journal of Experimental Criminology*. https://doi.org/10.1007/s11292-024-09644-7

Adams, I. T., McLean, K., & Alpert, G. P. (2025). Improving police behavior through artificial intelligence: Pre-registered experimental results in two large US agencies. *Criminology*. https://doi.org/10.1111/1745-9125.70028

Adams, I. T., Olson, M., James, L., Tregle, B., & Boehme, H. M. (2025). Fuck: Public opinion. *Police Quarterly*. 10986111251357508. https://doi.org/10.1177/10986111251357508

Atherley, L. T. (2025). Intelligent risk management: Natural language processing real-time triage of police calls for service. *Police Practice and Research*, *26*(6), 654–672. https://doi.org/10.1080/15614263.2024.2388210

Barnes, J. C., TenEyck, M. F., Pratt, T. C., & Cullen, F. T. (2020). How powerful is the evidence in criminology? On whether we should fear a coming crisis of confidence. *JQ: Justice Quarterly*, *37*(3), 383–409. https://doi.org/10.1080/07418825.2018.1495252

Becker, J., Rush, N., Barnes, E., & Rein, D. (2025). *Measuring the impact of early-2025 AI on experienced open-source developer productivity* (No. arXiv:2507.09089). arXiv. https://doi.org/10.48550/arXiv.2507.09089

Binder, A., & Scharf, P. (1980). The violent police-citizen encounter. *The ANNALS of the American Academy of Political and Social Science*, *452*(1), 111–121. https://doi.org/10.1177/000271628045200111

Bittner, E. (1967). *Police discretion in emergency apprehension of mentally ill persons.*

Brynjolfsson, E., Li, D., & Raymond, L. R. (2023). *Generative AI at work* (Working Paper No. 31161). National Bureau of Economic Research. https://doi.org/10.3386/w31161

Bureau of Justice Assistance. (2015). *Body-worn camera partnership program.* https://bja.ojp.gov/program/bwc-partnership-program/overview

Camp, N. P., & Voigt, R. (2025). Body camera footage as data: Using natural language processing to monitor policing at scale & in depth. *Behavioral Science & Policy*, 23794607241308636. https://doi.org/10.1177/23794607241308636

Camp, N. P., Voigt, R., Hamedani, M. G., Jurafsky, D., & Eberhardt, J. L. (2024). Leveraging body-worn camera footage to assess the effects of training on officer communication during traffic stops. *PNAS Nexus*, *3*(9), pgae359.

Carter, M. (2023, September 27). Decision to halt program analyzing Seattle police bodycam video under scrutiny. *The Seattle Times*. https://www.seattletimes.com/seattle-news/law-justice/decision-to-halt-program-analyzing-seattle-police-bodycam-video-under-scrutiny/

Chillar, V., Piza, E., & Sytsma, V. (2021). Conducting a systematic social observation of body-camera footage: Methodological and practical insights. *Journal of Qualitative Criminal Justice & Criminology.* https://doi.org/10.21428/88de04a1.6642b3cd

Colton, K. W. (1979). The impact and use of computer technology by the police. *Communications of the ACM*, *22*(1), 10–20. https://doi.org/10.1145/359046.359049

Council on Criminal Justice. (2025, October 30). *Principles for the use of AI in criminal justice—Council on criminal justice*. https://counciloncj.org/principles-for-the-use-of-ai-in-criminal-justice/

Engel, R. S., McManus, H. D., & Herold, T. D. (2020). Does de-escalation training work? A systematic review and call for evidence in police use-of-force reform. *Criminology & Public Policy*, *19*(3), 721–759. https://doi.org/10.1111/1745-9133.12467

Farooq, U. (2024, February 2). *Police departments are turning to AI to sift through millions of hours of unreviewed body-cam footage*. ProPublica. https://www.propublica.org/article/police-body-cameras-video-ai-law-enforcement

Ferguson, A. G. (2017). *The rise of big data policing: Surveillance, race, and the future of law enforcement.* New York University Press. https://doi.org/10.18574/nyu/9781479854608.001.0001

Ferguson, A. G. (2024). *AI-assisted police reports and the challenge of generative suspicion* (SSRN Scholarly Paper No. 4897632). https://papers.ssrn.com/abstract=4897632

Fyfe, J. J. (1988). Police use of deadly force: Research and reform. *Justice Quarterly*, *5*(2), 165–202. https://doi.org/10.1080/07418828800089691

Get Started—Draft One. (n.d.). Axon.Com. Retrieved November 1, 2025, from https://www.axon.com/getstarted/draft-one

Hyland, S. (2018). *Body-worn cameras in law enforcement agencies, 2016*. US Department of Justice, Office of Justice Programs, Bureau of Justice https://bjs.ojp.gov/content/pub/pdf/bwclea16.pdf

Lum, C., Koper, C. S., & Willis, J. (2017). Understanding the limits of technology's impact on police effectiveness. *Police Quarterly*, *20*(2), 135–163. https://doi.org/10.1177/1098611116667279

Makin, D. A., Willits, D. W., & Brooks, R. (2021). Systematic social event modeling: A methodology for analyzing body-worn camera footage. *International Journal of Social Research Methodology*, *24*(2), 163–176. https://doi.org/10.1080/13645579.2020.1766775

McCluskey, J. D., & Uchida, C. D. (2023). Video data analysis and police body-worn camera footage. *Sociological Methods & Research*, *52*(3), 1120–1154. https://doi.org/10.1177/00491241231156968

McLean, K., Bussey, T., Nix, J., Rojek, J., & Alpert, G. P. (2025). Police de-escalation training and its effects on communication: Evidence from an experimental evaluation. *In CrimRxiv*. https://doi.org/10.21428/cb6ab371.fe9287ce

Muir, W. K. (1979). *Police: Streetcorner politicians*. University of Chicago Press.

National Emergency Number Association. (2021). *9-1-1 statistics—National Emergency Number Association*. https://www.nena.org/page/911Statistics

Orosco, C., White, M. D., & Sorensen, D. (2025). A primer on the design, delivery, and evaluation of de-escalation training: Explaining the impactful findings from the Tempe Smart Policing Initiative. *Justice Evaluation Journal*, 1–20. https://doi.org/10.1080/24751979.2025.2475516

Piza, E. L., Connealy, N. T., Sytsma, V. A., & Chillar, V. F. (2022). Situational factors and police use of force across micro-time intervals: A video systematic social observation and panel regression analysis. *Criminology*, *61*(1), 74–102. https://doi.org/10.1111/1745-9125.12323

Police Executive Research Forum. (2023). *Body-worn cameras a decade later: What we know*. Police Executive Research Forum.

Porter, J., & Ogdon, S. (Directors). (2023, March 29). *ACLU Colorado opposes AI review of Aurora PD body camera video* [Video recording]. https://www.youtube.com/watch?v=IfzZcYV45oo

Prabhakaran, V., Griffiths, C., Su, H., Verma, P., Morgan, N., Eberhardt, J. L., & Jurafsky, D. (2018). Detecting institutional dialog acts in police traffic stops. *Transactions of the Association for Computational Linguistics*, *6*, 467–481. https://doi.org/10.1162/tacl_a_00031

President's Commission on Law Enforcement and Administration of Justice. (1967). *The challenge of crime in a free society*. https://clecpc.org/wp-content/uploads/1967-The-Presidents-Commission-on-Law-Enforcement-and-Administration-of-Justice-The-Challenge-of-Crime-in-a-Free-Society.pdf

President's Task Force on 21st Century Policing. (2015). *Final report of the President's Task Force on 21st Century Policing*. Office of Community Oriented Policing Services. https://www.govinfo.gov/content/pkg/GOVPUB-J36-PURL-gpo64136/pdf/GOVPUB-J36-PURL-gpo64136.pdf

Putman, J. (2025, October 27). *Calif. Passes transparency requirements for police use of generative AI report writing*. https://www.police1.com/artificial-intelligence/calif-passes-transparency-requirements-for-police-use-of-generative-ai-report-writing

Sault, L. D. (2023, July 9). *Under union pressure, Vallejo police chief ends body camera analysis*. Open Vallejo. https://openvallejo.org/2023/07/09/under-union-pressure-vallejo-police-chief-ends-body-camera-analysis/

Seaskate, Inc. (1998). *The evolution and development of police technology*. National Institute of Justice. https://www.ojp.gov/pdffiles1/Digitization/173179NCJRS.pdf

Stryker, C., & Kavlakoglu, E. (2024, August 9). *What is artificial intelligence (AI)?* IBM. https://www.ibm.com/think/topics/artificial-intelligence

Sullivan, T. P., McPartland, T., & Fisher, B. S. (2013). *Guidelines for successful researcher-practitioner partnerships in the criminal justice system, findings from the Researcher-Practitioner Partnerships Study (RPPS)* (pp. 1–26). https://www.ojp.gov/pdffiles1/nij/grants/243918.pdf

Tapp, S. N., & Davis, E. J. (2024). *Contacts between police and the public, 2022*. Bureau of Justice Statistics. https://bjs.ojp.gov/document/cbpp22.pdf

Terrill, W. (2005). Police use of force: A transactional approach. *Justice Quarterly*, *22*(1), 107–138. https://doi.org/10.1080/0741882042000333663

Todak, N., & James, L. (2018). A systematic social observation study of police de-escalation tactics. *Police Quarterly*, *21*(4), 509–543. https://doi.org/10.1177/1098611118784007

TRULEO introduces AI generated police reports powered by Amazon Bedrock. (2024, October 22). Police1. https://www.police1.com/police-products/police-technology/software/video-analysis/truleo-introduces-ai-generated-police-reports-powered-by-amazon-bedrock

Uchida, C. D., Solomon, S. E., Connor, C., McClusky, J., Markovic, J., Katz, C. K., White, M. D., Patterson, Q., & Land, A. (2022). *Managing digital evidence from body-worn cameras: Case studies in seven sites*. Justice & Security Strategies, Inc. https://bwctta.com/sites/default/files/2022-03/1%20DEM%20Final%20Report%2003%2001%2022_CONTENT_0.pdf

White, M. D., Flippin, M., & Katz, C. M. (2017). *Key trends in body-worn camera policy and practice: A two-year policy analysis of US Department of Justice-funded law enforcement agencies*. Arizona State University. https://cvpcs.asu.edu/sites/default/files/content/pages/Policy%20Analysis%20Year%202%20FINAL.pdf

White, M. D., Orosco, C., & Watts, S. (2023). Beyond force and injuries: Examining alternative (and important) outcomes for police de-escalation training. *Journal of Criminal Justice*, *89*, 102129. https://doi.org/10.1016/j.jcrimjus.2023.102129

White, M. D., Todak, N., & Gaub, J. E. (2018). Examining body-worn camera integration and acceptance among police officers, citizens, and external stakeholders. *Criminology & Public Policy*, *17*(3), 649–677. https://doi.org/10.1111/1745-9133.12376

White, M. D., Watts, S., Orosco, C., Perrone, D., & Malm, A. (2022). Leveraging body-worn camera footage to better understand opioid overdoses and the impact of police-administered naloxone. *American Journal of Public Health*, *112*(9), 1326–1332. https://doi.org/10.2105/AJPH.2022.306918

Wolfe, S. E., & Lawson, S. G. (2020). The organizational justice effect among criminal justice employees: A meta-analysis. *Criminology*, *58*(4), 619–644. https://doi.org/10.1111/1745-9125.12251

15

THE HEART OF THE MATTER

Integrating Physiological Stress Measurement in High-Intensity Virtual Reality Police Scenario Simulations

John E. Muñoz, Jennifer Lavoie, Lisanne Kleygrewe, Lisa Whittingham, and Alan T. Pope

Introduction: Training Police to Effectively Respond to High-Intensity Calls for Service

Police officers routinely encounter situations in the line of duty that are high-intensity, dynamic, and present a danger to themselves or the public they are sworn to protect. High-stress policing incidents often feature ambiguous information, time pressure, and threats to safety that may require split-second decisions that bear significant consequences. These calls generate a heavy cognitive load under which officers must rapidly assess risk, make accurate decisions, and perform procedural tasks, such as precisely deploying weapons or equipment. Some of the most stressful incidents police officers attend involve use-of-force encounters, like active shooters or armed suspects, or high emotionality of the person involved, like domestic violence calls, and suicidal or agitated persons in mental health crisis (Regehr et al., 2021). These high-intensity situations reliably elicit strong physiological stress responses among officers that can impact their perception, memory, judgment, and performance. High-stress operational conditions may compromise police performance, thereby elevating the likelihood of serious harm or death and undermining community trust.

To ensure officers are operationally prepared to meet real-world demands, scenario-based training has been recognized as the gold standard in police training (See & Davies, 2024). Scenario-based training relies on staging carefully designed simulations of police encounters, which closely replicate the environmental, situational, physical, and psychological demands of real-world incidents. Scenario-based training enables officers to safely rehearse

DOI: 10.4324/9781003671312-15

procedural knowledge, ethical decision-making, communication, and performance while being evaluated and receiving instructor feedback. While such training can provide a realistic environment for officers to repeatedly practice techniques, there are limitations in scalability, consistency, and cost, given the resources needed to mount simulation (Martaindale et al., 2024). Virtual Reality (VR) has been proposed as a viable medium to address many of the limitations in scenario-based training. VR describes computer-generated, three-dimensional environments that users can experience from a first-person perspective through head-mounted displays and motion-tracked controllers or body sensors, enabling a realistic perception of space, presence, and interaction with virtual characters and objects in real time (Jerald, 2015). Some of the benefits of using VR for scenario-based training include access to difficult-to-replicate environments (e.g., natural disasters), standardized scenarios to ensure training consistency, and authentic character portrayals (Slater & Sanchez-Vives, 2016). By adopting VR in police training, officers have the opportunity to rehearse skills in highly immersive simulated environments that feature realistic high-pressure situations (e.g., violence, crisis situations) to increase their field operational preparedness for the real world, where stakes are high (Podoletz et al., 2024)

In recent years, scenario-based police training using VR has been combined with physiological sensors to assess bodily stress responses among officers undergoing simulations. Research integrating physiological measurement into scenario-based training applications has confirmed that these simulations consistently invoke stress arousal levels comparable to the real world (Baldwin et al., 2019). Moreover, research by Andersen and colleagues (2016) has directly examined how integrating stress modulation techniques (such as tactical breathing techniques) into scenario-based police training can reduce officers' stress reactivity and improve decision-making and performance in critical incident simulations. As VR technology continues to develop for first responders, it can be strengthened by integrating physiological sensing technologies (e.g., heart rate variability, eye tracking). These modalities can provide objective, moment-to-moment indicators of stress, cognitive load, and emotional regulation during simulated encounters, some of which may pose ethical issues or be difficult to replicate, and allow trainers to move beyond purely behavioural observation and subjective impressions (Fairclough, 2009). When VR and physiological monitoring are combined, they can provide a more precise assessment of how officers respond under pressure, support biofeedback-based coaching and practice of self-regulation, and allow the trainer to adjust the scenario difficulty or provide feedback based on an officer's internal state. Therefore, the purpose of this chapter is to describe how VR and physiological monitoring have jointly been used to transform police training in teaching de-escalation and self-regulation skills during stressful simulated scenarios.

VR as a Training Tool for Law Enforcement: Benefits and Current State

VR training has gained traction in law enforcement as an effective, immersive medium for scenario-based learning. VR systems enable officers to practice decision-making in realistic simulations that replicate field conditions with high fidelity, but in a safe, data-driven and repeatable setting (Podoletz et al., 2024). Police departments across North America, Europe, the Middle East, and Australasia have begun piloting VR training systems to improve decision-making and reduce use-of-force incidents. Early evidence suggests VR-based training can lead to better-prepared officers (Scott et al., 2025) and, ultimately, safer outcomes for both police and the public during mental health crises.

Identified key benefits of VR in police training include:

- Immersive Realism: Modern VR scenarios can incorporate life-sized environments, interactive characters (including live actors via motion capture), and authentic sound, creating stress and complexity comparable to real incidents. This realism enhances situational awareness and stress inoculation in trainees (Zechner et al., 2023a).
- Safe, Controlled Environments: Officers can experience volatile situations (e.g., a person wielding a weapon in a crisis) without actually endangering themselves, meaning mistakes become learning opportunities instead of life-threatening events. VR allows repeatable practice of rare critical incidents that officers might otherwise seldom encounter but need to be operationally prepared for (Kleygrewe et al., 2023b; Liu et al., 2023).
- Performance Tracking: Unlike traditional training, VR can log every action and decision. It also enables after-action review, with replay and objective data (e.g., timing of decisions, where the officer was looking, etc.). Trainers can pinpoint specific moments for feedback, improving the debriefing process (Kleygrewe et al., 2023a).
- Adaptability and Range of Scenarios: VR training scenarios can be easily modified or scaled. Trainees can be exposed to a wide variety of situations (different environments, subjects, or incident types) to broaden their experience. This flexibility is valuable globally – scenarios can be tailored to local cultural contexts and common incident types for each region (See & Davies, 2024).

Despite these advantages, VR-based training also has limitations. Current systems offer limited physical realism and haptic feedback, which can lead to officers learning movement patterns or tactics that do not fully transfer to real-world physical constraints (e.g., lack of recoil, reduced proprioceptive load, simplified weapon handling), otherwise known as "training scars." In addition, issues such as simulator sickness (also called cybersickness), equipment failures, and the need for technical support can disrupt training flow and may reduce acceptance among some users (Podoletz et al., 2024). That said, active duty officers and cadets have expressed a general acceptance of VR as a training tool, a critical factor for adoption (Lavoie et al., 2023).

Physiological Sensing Technologies in VR Training

Incorporating physiological sensing into VR training means outfitting trainees with wearable devices that capture real-time data on their bodily responses. These biosignals provide an objective window into an officer's stress, arousal, and emotional state during a training scenario. By combining VR scenarios with sensors like heart rate, breathing, chest straps, and motion capture, it becomes possible to objectively assess how officers regulate stress, how their body language evolves, and even infer aspects of decision-making under pressure. Figure 15.1 showcases a conventional setup of physiological sensing devices, VR equipment, and researcher/subject configuration for experiments involving training with physiological recording.

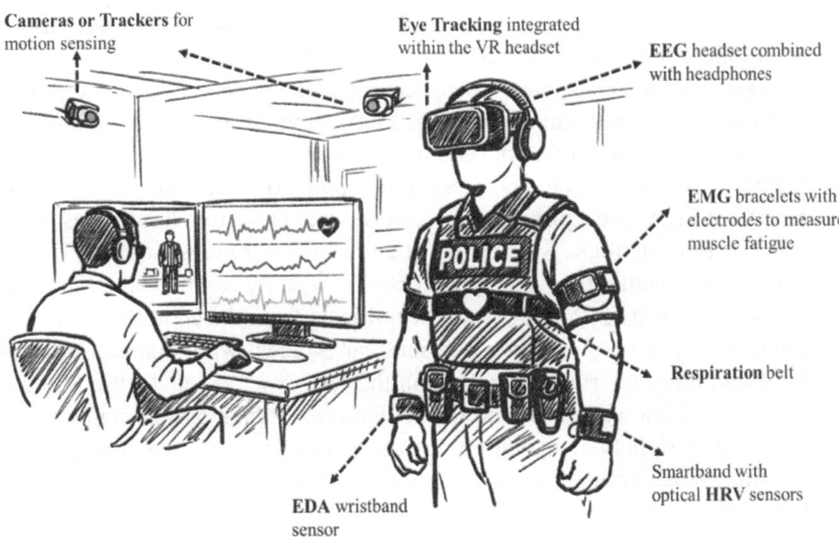

FIGURE 15.1 VR Setup with Physiological Monitoring Used in Scenario-Based Training. Wearable Physiological Sensors are Located Around the Officer or Embedded into the VR/Tracking System

Source: The authors

This section introduces the key sensing modalities relevant to police training and what they offer:

- Heart Rate and Heart Rate Variability (HR & HRV): Heart rate (HR; in beats per minute) and heart rate variability (HRV; the fluctuation in time between heartbeats) are core measures of physiological arousal and stress regulation. A chest strap sensor or other heart monitor (e.g., smartwatch that uses photoplethismography – PPG) is typically used. HRV tends to fluctuate with adrenaline and stress. Lower HRV generally indicates stress and less flexibility in physiological regulation, whereas higher HRV suggests more effective coping (Ernst, 2014). Tracking HRV can thus indicate an officer's ability to self-regulate under pressure. These cardiovascular metrics are valuable for feedback: they objectively show how an officer's body responds in a scenario, and over time, improved control (e.g., smaller HR spikes, quicker calm-down) can be a measurable training outcome. A study tested a closed-loop HRV system embedded in an intense VR action game with 109 police trainers and found that officers learned to significantly increase their HRV in action (about 32% on average), indicating better physiological self-control under high arousal (Michela et al., 2025).
- Electrodermal Activity (EDA): EDA measures changes in skin conductance caused by sweat gland activity, an autonomic response closely tied to emotional arousal. Even subtle stress or excitement can produce detectable changes in skin conductance (often recorded via wristband sensors or finger electrodes). In a VR training setting, EDA provides a moment-by-moment indicator of arousal. Spikes or rises in EDA often accompany startling events or intense moments. Conversely, a calming phase or successful de-escalation might see EDA levels plateau or drop as the officer's stress diminishes. EDA data can thus highlight which parts of a scenario were most stressful for the trainee and whether they managed to physiologically calm down by the end. A study exposed 63 Portuguese police officers from different divisions to a single VR scenario simulating a serious car accident while monitoring their EDA and other metrics. Officers from the less-experienced Traffic Surveillance Squad showed higher arousal (significantly higher skin conductance and lower peripheral temperature) than both the traffic-accident investigators and the control group, indicating they reacted more strongly to the stressful VR scene (Gamito et al., 2024).
- Electromyography (EMG): EMG measures the electrical activity produced by skeletal muscles, providing a window into how the body recruits muscular effort under stress or during fine motor control. In VR-based police training, EMG can be applied at the limbs and torso to quantify effort, tension, or tremor during tasks such as weapon handling, reaching, or maintaining defensive postures. Surface EMG sensors are typically placed on the skin using

small electrodes, and signals are then amplified, filtered, and converted into features such as root mean square (RMS) amplitude or activation patterns over time. These metrics allow researchers and trainers to detect moments of heightened muscular tension that may indicate stress, frustration, or deteriorating motor control, and to link them to specific events in the scenario. Facial EMG (fEMG) uses electrodes (often embedded in a VR-compatible mask or attachment) to measure electrical activity from facial muscles. Certain muscle groups correspond to emotional expressions – e.g., the corrugator supercilii (brow) tenses during stress or frustration, while zygomaticus (cheek) activity relates to positive affect or smiles (Gnacek et al., 2022). In a training context, fEMG can reveal subconscious emotional reactions. For instance, a spike in corrugator muscle activity might indicate the officer is frowning or feeling increased stress, even if they maintain a calm verbal demeanor. Although studies of fEMG using VR in police officers are scarce, a study tested 24 police officers on a working-memory task, then exposed them to a threatening video to induce negative emotionality before they completed a computerized shoot/do-not-shoot task while measuring their affective responses using fEMG. Officers with lower working-memory capacity made more shooting errors; they were more likely to shoot unarmed targets and fail to shoot armed ones, but this effect only appeared in those who showed strong negative emotional reactions to the threat video. In other words, limited working memory becomes particularly risky for accurate shoot decisions when officers are emotionally aroused, suggesting that both cognitive capacity and emotion regulation are critical to preventing shooting errors (Kleider et al., 2010).

- Electroencephalography (EEG): EEG records electrical activity from the scalp generated by synchronized neuronal populations in the cortex, offering insight into cognitive and attentional states during complex tasks. In VR police training, lightweight EEG headsets or headbands can be worn under or integrated with the VR headset to track oscillatory activity in frequency bands associated with vigilance, mental workload, and cognitive control (e.g., frontal midline theta, alpha suppression). By deriving indices such as "engagement," "workload," or "vigilance" from these patterns, EEG enables real-time estimation of whether an officer is under-focused (bored, distracted), optimally engaged, or overloaded during critical moments in a scenario. Although EEG is more sensitive to motion artifacts than other modalities, careful sensor design, robust signal processing, and targeted use of a small number of channels make it feasible to deploy as part of operationally realistic VR training. For instance, significant correlations between performance metrics and neural activations were found in a study involving 58 cadets exposed to simulated scenarios, demonstrating the use of EEG to reveal important evaluation metrics applied in law enforcement settings (AlSabah et al., 2025).

- Respiration rate: Breathing patterns are key indicators of autonomic arousal and are also a primary lever for deliberate self-regulation. In training environments, respiration is typically measured using a thoracic or abdominal respiratory belt, a stretch sensor integrated into a vest, or, less commonly, airflow or acoustic sensors close to the mouth. These devices provide continuous measures of breathing frequency, depth, and variability, which tend to change systematically with stress, for instance, rapid, shallow breathing during high threat versus slower, deeper breathing during calm states. Because controlled breathing is a well-established technique for down-regulating physiological arousal, respiration data can serve both as an assessment signal and as a direct target for self-regulation training. Trainees can be prompted to slow their breathing when their respiratory rate exceeds a threshold, and they can immediately see or feel the impact on their overall physiological profile (e.g., biofeedback). Integrating respiration into VR police training thus supports the development of practical, embodied self-regulation skills that officers can transfer to real-world crisis encounters. A study investigating psychophysiological responses associated with controlled self-regulation training using respiration during firearms training proposes a potential framework for automatic adaptations of VR simulations using breathing patterns (Brammer et al., 2021).
- Eye tracking: Eye tracking measures where, how long, and in what sequence a person looks, providing a direct window into visual attention and situational awareness. In VR-based police training, eye tracking is typically implemented with infrared cameras integrated into the headset that continuously estimate gaze direction, fixations, saccades, and sometimes pupil diameter. From these data, trainers can derive metrics such as dwell time on critical cues (e.g., a subject's hands, bystanders, escape routes), breadth of visual scanning, and the presence of "tunnel vision" under stress. Heatmaps and scan-path visualizations allow instructors to see whether an officer systematically checks key areas or fixates too narrowly on a weapon or the subject's face. Pupil dilation and changes in blink rate can also serve as indirect indicators of arousal and cognitive load. One study used VR and integrated eye tracking in a 360° crime scene to compare visual attention patterns of students from two institutions, generating over 2.6M gaze samples. Eye-tracking metrics, especially temporal sequence features like scan-path similarity and fixation regularity, successfully distinguished visual behaviour patterns between groups (clustering accuracy ≈78%) and predicted proficiency with good performance (random forest R^2 ≈0.70) (Yang et al., 2025).
- Motion Capture (MoCap), body tracking, and kinematics: MoCap technology uses trackers or cameras to record the trainee's physical movements, posture, and gestures in VR. Kinematic parameters such as position, speed, acceleration, and movement smoothness can be computed to explore movement patterns associated with specific behaviours. For police training, motion data can

reveal, for example, tactical movements (Did the officer adopt a defensive stance? Draw their weapon? Maintain an open, non-threatening posture?) and communication gestures (e.g., hand movements, maintaining distance). The benefit of MoCap is twofold: (1) it enhances training realism (the officer sees their avatar's body move naturally in VR, and can interact physically), and (2) it provides an objective log of performance. For example, motion data can show whether an officer approached too quickly or if they resorted to drawing a firearm. Combined with physiological data, this helps connect internal state with external action. Such insights come from aligning motion events with physiological signals. Overall, all modern VR systems contain movement sensors such as optical markers, cameras, or inertial measurement units (e.g., VR controllers or trackers placed on police equipment) that are used to track movement and can be used to log important kinematic parameters. A study showed how a full-body MoCap suit combined with the biomechanic analysis can be used to analyze police arrest techniques in training. Using ergonomic risk analysis on 11 officers performing "Basic Technique 1" of Operational Tactical Procedures, the authors found mainly medium–high (but not maximal) risk levels and showed that this core technique is relatively well designed to limit musculoskeletal injury, while also differentiating novice, intermediate, and expert officers (Vera-Jiménez et al., 2025).

Each of these technologies contributes a piece to the puzzle of understanding and improving police performance under stress. By integrating multiple sensors, trainers can obtain a rich, multi-modal picture of an officer's experience in VR – what they did, how they felt (inside), and how their body reacted (see Appendix I for a broader description). The following section will review findings from four studies that have been recently conducted by our team using VR with physiological measurements, demonstrating the feasibility and benefits of this approach.

Empirical Findings: Integrating Physiological Sensing and VR in Police Training

Study One: Psychophysiological Insights and User Experience Perspectives

The first study, entitled "*Psychophysiological insights and user perspectives: enhancing police de-escalation skills through full-body VR training*" (Muñoz et al., n.d.), examined how a group of active police officers in the USA responded to a full-body VR de-escalation training scenario while wearing multiple physiological sensors. Ten SWAT-trained officers participated in an immersive mental health crisis simulation involving a live-acted character in VR. The simulation used is part of a wider program for Mental Health Crisis

Response in Ontario, Canada. Regarding *stress Responses*, officers experienced significant cardiovascular stress during the VR scenario. HR analysis showed a clear increase from baseline to the peak of the scenario (group average HR ~105 bpm under VR stress vs ~89 bpm at rest, $p < 0.05$). Additionally, HRV (e.g., time-sensitive parameters) was significantly higher during the scenario than at baseline, indicating dynamic engagement of sympathetic nervous system activity during the training. Elevated HRV in this context suggests officers were experiencing and modulating stress in real time – a sign that VR can effectively simulate high-stakes encounters that tax an officer's self-regulation capacity. Moreover, in terms of *user experience and acceptance*, the study also gauged officers' perspectives on the training through questionnaires. Results were encouraging; overall, user experience was rated positively, with minimal VR-induced symptoms (e.g., nausea was low). Notably, a custom "Perceived Usefulness" survey showed strong agreement among officers that integrating physiological monitoring into VR training is beneficial. Officers saw these technologies as valuable for stress management and for recognizing their own bodily responses linked to effective conflict de-escalation. In other words, the participants believed that seeing and using their physiological signals could help them improve how they handle stress in the field. This study's findings underscored both the feasibility of multi-sensor VR training and the buy-in from end-users: officers found the combined VR + physiological sensing approaches not only acceptable but useful for building skills.

As part of our efforts in theory building, we explore a concept called "Defensive Dynamics Dichotomy," by exploring the de-escalation patterns, as coded by an expert after revising the video of the VR scenario of all participants, and the cardiovascular responses. Officers who escalated (drew their weapon during the scenario) showed stronger sympathetic activation (higher HRs and other stress indicators) compared to those who kept their weapon holstered. Conversely, officers who de-escalated without drawing their weapon tended to have more balanced physiological responses (better stress regulation) and scored slightly higher on de-escalation performance metrics. This dichotomy suggests that physiological data can reflect not only stress levels but potentially the quality of decision-making and tactics. Those who remained calmer physiologically were more likely to use communication and patience rather than force, aligning with effective crisis intervention strategies (Muñoz et al., n.d.).

Study Two: Virtual Reality Training for Police Officers: A Comparison of Training Responses in VR and Real-Life Training

The second study, "*Virtual reality training for police officers: a comparison of training responses in VR and real-life training*" (Kleygrewe et al., 2023b), examined how police officers respond physically and psychologically to VR scenario-based training (VR SBT) compared with traditional real-life scenario-based training (RL SBT). Using a within-subject design embedded in operational training days of the Dutch National Police, 237 officers completed both training modalities. RL SBT involved one extended live scenario using role-players, realistic props, and training weapons, whereas VR SBT comprised three shorter immersive scenarios delivered through a full-body VR system with head-mounted display, motion tracking, and tactical replica equipment. Training responses assessed included physical indicators (average and maximum HR, activity level), psychological responses (perceived stress, mental effort), and VR-specific experience factors (engagement, sense of presence, negative effects), alongside participant characteristics such as prior VR use and gaming frequency. Considering *stress responses*, average HR did not differ between VR and RL, indicating comparable sustained cardiovascular activation. However, peak HR and overall physical activity were significantly higher during real-life training (Max HR: M = 136.96 bpm in RL vs 126.28 bpm in VR; $p < 0.001$). These findings likely relate to the physical constraints of VR training (e.g., no running due to equipment and safety considerations), while RL SBT allowed natural movement, rapid mobilization, and more intense engagement. Both modalities nonetheless produced responses aligned with the relatively stationary nature of the training objectives (e.g., protection and observation tasks). Moreover, regarding *user experience and sense of presence*, officers reported similar levels of perceived stress in VR and RL, suggesting that VR can provide psychologically demanding environments comparable to real-life scenarios. However, mental effort was significantly higher during VR SBT (M = 52.64 vs 46.11; $p < 0.01$), likely reflecting the additional cognitive demands of adapting to virtual environments and managing VR interfaces alongside tactical decision-making. Regression analyses revealed that VR engagement and the experience of negative effects (e.g., cybersickness) predicted higher mental effort and perceived stress, whereas frequent gaming experience reduced cognitive load. Participant demographics had minimal influence relative to moment-to-moment VR experience quality.

These findings point toward a functional complementarity between training modes. RL SBT elicited higher peaks in physical activation, reinforcing its suitability for scenarios requiring unrestricted movement and high-intensity physical engagement (e.g., pursuit, arrest). VR SBT, while more cognitively demanding, matched RL in sustained cardiovascular engagement and stress responses, suggesting its value for training decision-making, situational awareness, and stress regulation in controlled, repeatable conditions. Importantly, the psychological impact of VR appears to depend not on officer characteristics but on the quality of immersion and management of adverse effects. In essence, VR SBT should not be viewed as a replacement for RL SBT but as a complementary modality. When engagement is high and adverse effects are minimized, VR offers an effective platform to train cognitive, perceptual, and stress management skills, while RL remains essential for physically intensive tasks.

Study Three: Affective Responses and Perceived Usefulness of VR-Based Crisis Training (Preliminary Unpublished Data, 2025)

Building on the previous efforts, a recent (under review) pilot study explored integrating facial EMG into a VR mental health crisis response training for police officers. In this ongoing work, 11 active-duty Canadian police officers experienced an immersive VR scenario of a person in crisis while wearing an Emteq Pro mask that recorded fEMG signals from various facial muscles (Gjoreski et al., 2021). The study's focus was twofold: assess how fEMG can provide insight into officers' emotional states during de-escalation and gauge officers' perceptions of this tech-assisted training. Notable early findings include measurements of *affective state responses* via facial EMG, which provided a proof-of-concept that emotional cues can be quantitatively captured during a training scenario. Electrodes positioned over key muscles such as the corrugator (associated with frowning/negative affect), zygomaticus (smiling/positive affect), frontalis (brow, surprise/attention), and orbicularis oculi (around eyes, arousal), showed distinct activation patterns aligning with scenario events. For instance, as soon as the scenario began and the virtual person in crisis appeared ("Start"), muscle activation levels (measured by EMG amplitude) jumped and stayed elevated, indicating an immediate stress/anxiety response. A particularly large EMG spike was observed at the moment a virtual door burst open unexpectedly, a high-stress trigger in the scenario. Toward the resolution, the EMG patterns diverged depending on the outcome: most officers succeeded in de-escalating (the subject dropped their weapon), while two officers experienced an escalated outcome requiring the use of a taser. Those who had to resort to force tended to show different EMG dynamics (though sample size was small) – suggesting that facial tension was higher during escalated confrontations. While quantitative analysis is ongoing, these preliminary results demonstrate that fEMG can sensitively detect micro-expressions and stress reactions during training, even when officers maintain a professional demeanour externally. Furthermore, officers' *acceptance and perceived usefulness* were also measured before experiencing the VR scenario. Officers filled out a questionnaire about the idea of combining VR with physiological sensing for training. The feedback was overwhelmingly positive. Officers strongly agreed that using these technologies would help them learn about their own bodily responses, manage stress better, and understand the "ideal" physiological reactions for conflict de-escalation. The highest-rated perceived benefits were in areas of self-awareness: "learning about my own body responses" and "stress management skills" were top-ranked, closely followed by seeing how proper physiological regulation aids de-escalation. Conversely, the statement "I do not think this solution could help" received very low (strongly disagree) ratings. These results indicate a very high acceptance of VR+biofeedback training among the officers; they clearly recognize the potential value of the approach. In fact, the data suggests officers especially value how such training could unveil their internal triggers and teach them self-regulation techniques – critical skills for handling real crises. After actually undergoing the VR scenario, participants also completed the VR Neuroscience Questionnaire: scores reflected strong immersion and comfort (very mild simulator sickness), reinforcing that the addition of fEMG gear did not impede the experience. In summary, wearing the fEMG sensor was well-tolerated, and officers remained enthusiastic about the system's usefulness for training.

Study Four: A Psychophysiological Model of Firearms Training

Another study explored the role of psychophysiological responses during firearms training involving active police officers and a VR simulation. This preliminary study introduced the concept of a biocybernetic adaptation loop in police training (Muñoz et al., 2020). In this experiment, 10 police officers went through shooting drills in VR while their brain activity (using EEG) and heart data were recorded. The aim was to develop a psychophysiological model that could drive real-time adjustments in the training environment based on the officer's stress and cognitive state. After completing a controlled experiment, a computational bioadaptive model where simulation difficulty could be modulated in real time using physiological inputs was proposed. The study characterized how officers' EEG (frontal theta waves related to focus) and HR responses changed under different difficulty levels (easy, medium, hard scenarios). Based on these empirical patterns, the target physiological ranges for optimal training were identified: for example, a moderate increase in HR to 100–115 bpm was considered an ideal "engaged but not overwhelmed" stress level for training shooters. Using these targets, an adaptive rule was created: if an officer's HR and brain focus level stayed below the desired range (meaning the officer is too calm or disengaged), the system would automatically increase scenario difficulty – e.g., making targets move faster or appear more suddenly. This ensures the trainee is sufficiently challenged and stressed to simulate real pressure. Conversely, if the officer's stress was too high or they were struggling, the system could ease up. Although this was a preliminary model, it demonstrated the technical feasibility of closed-loop VR training guided by physiological signals (Pope et al., 2014). Officers also provided *user experience feedback and perceptions of sensor comfort*; despite involving multiple sensors (including EEG headbands and chest straps), the study reported that officers reacted positively to the VR training experience. In post-training interviews, participants described the simulation as immersive and even said it made them consciously focus on breathing and staying calm while operating their weapon. Many officers highlighted the realism of the scenario and were enthusiastic about trying VR for the first time. Importantly, they commented that the wearable sensors were "minimally invasive and comfortable," noting that the simple, wireless setup did not hinder their movement. This feedback speaks to the practicality of adding physiological monitors to training – if designed well, they need not cause discomfort or distraction. In fact, four firearms instructors who observed the study endorsed the potential of the system, praising the scenario's personalization and the integration of the VR headset with physiological sensors. This concept of a responsive training environment lays the groundwork for the broader idea of emotion-aware, adaptive VR police training.

Technical Challenges of Physiological Integration in VR Training

While the integration of VR and physiological sensing offers considerable promise, it also introduces technical challenges that must be addressed to ensure reliable and effective training systems.

Signal quality and temporal alignment: A key issue concerns signal quality and synchronization. Physiological signals, such as HRV, eye tracking, and EDA, are highly susceptible to motion artifacts and wireless interference. Precise temporal alignment between these signals and VR events is essential for meaningful interpretation and real-time adaptation, yet remains difficult in dynamic, interactive environments (Novak, 2014). Recent wearable biosensor research further shows that standardization of signal acquisition and processing across VR applications is still underdeveloped, complicating cross-study comparisons and the integration of adaptive feedback mechanisms (Guillen-Sanz et al., 2024).

Calibration, reliability, and hardware constraints: Beyond signal acquisition, sensor calibration and reliability present closely related challenges. Physiological sensors often require per-user and context-specific calibration (e.g., baseline recordings, signal normalization) to account for variability in anatomy, skin impedance, movement patterns, and even room temperature. Many current setups still depend on research-grade hardware, manual electrode placement, or frequent recalibration to prevent signal drift, which limits scalability and repeatability outside controlled laboratory conditions. Consequently, embedding robust, low-maintenance physiological sensing into everyday VR controllers, head-mounted displays, or duty-equipment form factors remains technically demanding and is a critical bottleneck for widespread deployment (Moinnereau et al., 2022).

Ergonomics, wearability, and cost barriers: Alongside measurement reliability, practical constraints related to equipment comfort, ergonomics, and cost further affect feasibility. Integrating multiple physiological sensors into VR systems can increase physical burden, restrict natural movement, and introduce discomfort, reducing immersion and training effectiveness in police officers. Bulky or intrusive setups may undermine ecological validity and user acceptance, particularly during longer or repeated sessions. Moreover, high-fidelity sensors and adaptive VR systems remain costly, limiting large-scale adoption despite recent advances in more affordable wearable technologies (Podoletz et al., 2024).

Data interpretation, governance, and ethical use: Finally, even when reliable data can be collected, data management and interpretation remain major challenges. Physiological data are complex, high-dimensional, and context-dependent, requiring careful preprocessing and well-grounded analytical approaches. Translating physiological signals into information that is meaningful for trainers or adaptive VR training systems depends on validated models and clear visual representations (Muñoz et al., n.d.; Zechner et al., 2023b). Without these, misinterpretation or overfitting to artefactual patterns is likely. In addition, the collection and use of such sensitive data raise important ethical and privacy considerations as physiologically adaptive VR training systems continue to mature (Nasri, 2025).

Officer Attitudes Toward Wearable Physiological Sensing and Training Adoption

No matter how sophisticated a training system is, its impact ultimately depends on officer and organizational buy-in. Across the empirical work reviewed in this chapter, officers have generally responded positively to VR-based training and to the integration of physiological sensing when the purpose is clearly framed as skill development and wellness, rather than surveillance. In our full-body VR de-escalation study, officers reported high immersion, low simulator sickness, and strong perceived usefulness of physiological monitoring to help them understand and manage their own stress responses (Muñoz et al., n.d.). Similarly, in the preliminary fEMG pilot, officers strongly endorsed statements about learning "how my body responds" and improving "stress management skills," while almost universally rejecting the notion that such systems would not be helpful. These findings echo broader work showing that officers perceive VR as a realistic and valuable addition to conventional scenario-based training when implemented in close collaboration with trainers and subject-matter experts (Gamito et al., 2024; Kleygrewe et al., 2023a; Zechner et al., 2023a).

At the same time, user feedback and emerging literature highlight important reservations that must be acknowledged if adoption is to be sustainable. Officers express concerns about the potential misuse of physiological data for performance evaluation, fear that body traces might be interpreted without context (e.g., equating high arousal with incompetence), and apprehension about comfort, workload, and technical reliability when using multiple sensors during already demanding simulations (Brammer et al., 2021; Podoletz et al., 2024). Therefore, adding qualitative methods, like interpretive phenomenological analysis (Eatough & Smith, 2017), can help provide user insight about the cognitive process, like decision-making, associated with physiological measurements. Further, addressing these concerns requires transparent data-governance policies (e.g., limiting access, focusing data use on learning and wellness rather than discipline), careful ergonomic design of sensing setups, and meaningful involvement of officers and trainers in the co-design of training protocols (Bartkowiak-Théron & Atkinson, 2024; Jerald, 2015; Lavoie et al., 2022). In this context, officer attitudes are not fixed barriers but modifiable outcomes of how VR and physiological sensing are introduced, when systems demonstrably support safer, more competent practice and protect officer dignity, willingness to adopt them appears high.

Future Directions, Scalability, and Ethics

As VR and physiological monitoring technologies mature, a key challenge will be moving from proof-of-concept studies and pilot deployments to scalable, routine integration in police training ecosystems. On the technical side, advances in embedded sensors and consumer-grade wearables are already making it more feasible to integrate HR, HRV, respiration, and eye tracking directly into headsets, vests, or duty belts, reducing setup time and improving comfort, and increasing the accessibility of these technologies (Gnacek et al., 2022; Guillen-Sanz et al., 2024). Future systems are likely to use integrated platforms that can combine multiple types of physiological data in real time and use those signals to adjust training automatically, without requiring complex setup. This approach (sometimes called biocybernetic adaptation) allows training systems to respond directly to how an officer's body is reacting during an exercise (Muñoz et al., 2020; Pope et al., 2014). To justify investment at scale, however, agencies will require longitudinal evidence linking these systems to operational outcomes such as reduced use of force, improved decision-making under pressure, and better officer wellbeing (Gamito et al., 2024; Scott et al., 2025). This calls for multicentre trials, standardized measures, and closer collaboration between researchers, police organizations, and policy-makers.

Adoption of both VR and physiological sensors as training technologies by police will also require serious ethical consideration to promote adoption. First, consideration will need to be made about the collection of fine-grained physiological and behavioural data in training. Consideration and best practices need to be developed and adopted regarding the privacy of this information, consent to collect and store the data, as well as the fairness and the unintended harms to officers of collecting and storing this data. Future work must develop clear guidelines for data minimization, role-based access, retention limits, and the separation of training data from formal performance appraisal. Finally, increased awareness of post-traumatic stress disorder (PTSD) and other stress-related effects on police officers (e.g., changes to blood pressure) suggests the need to better understand the relationship between past experience and current physiological arousal to scenarios. It is important that accurate baseline data is taken to ensure physiological arousal caused by workplace stress is not misinterpreted as a situational response. Further, training for instructors will be necessary to ensure they know how to incorporate biological feedback without pathologizing normal stress responses and how to adopt a trauma-informed response for those who have experienced a similar high-intensity scenario and may or may not be aware of how it impacted them. Ultimately, the future of physiologically informed VR training will depend not only on technological innovation but on robust governance and interdisciplinary collaboration that position these systems as tools for learning, accountability, and care, both for the communities served and for the officers themselves. An additional ethical consideration concerns the portrayal of virtual characters within training scenarios. As VR simulations increasingly depict individuals in mental health crises, domestic disputes, or culturally diverse community contexts, careful attention must be paid to avoiding stereotypical, stigmatizing, or biased representations. Research in immersive media and policing has emphasized that character realism should not come at the expense of fairness, dignity, or cultural sensitivity (Lavoie et al., 2022; Podoletz et al., 2024). Ethical character design requires consultation with community stakeholders, subject-matter experts, and individuals with lived experience to ensure that behaviours, language, and narrative framing reflect complexity rather than caricature. Failure to do so risks reinforcing implicit biases or normalizing problematic response patterns. Therefore, responsible VR training development must include structured review processes for scenario content, aligning technological innovation with principles of equity, procedural justice, and trauma-informed practice.

Acknowledgements: The authors gratefully acknowledge the police services, industry partners, and training organizations that supported and collaborated on the studies described in this chapter. We also thank the officers who generously contributed their time and expertise to participate in the research and advance evidence-based police training.

References

AlSabah, N., Alasfour, A., Marr, C., & Di Nota, P. (2025). Linking psychophysiological markers to situational performance: An EEG study of police cadets during critical incident simulations. *Applied Psychophysiology and Biofeedback*. https://doi.org/10.1007/s10484-025-09736-8

Andersen, J. P., Pitel, M., Weerasinghe, A., & Papazoglou, K. (2016). *Highly realistic scenario based training simulates the psychophysiology of real world use of force encounters: Implications for improved police officer performance*. https://tspace.library.utoronto.ca/handle/1807/73822

Baldwin, S., Bennell, C., Andersen, J. P., Semple, T., & Jenkins, B. (2019). Stress-activity mapping: Physiological responses during general duty police encounters. *Frontiers in Psychology*, *10*, 2216. https://doi.org/10.3389/fpsyg.2019.02216

Bartkowiak-Théron, I., & Atkinson, C. (2024). Foundations of empathy and resilience: Integrating trauma-informed policing from recruit training onward: This article is directly related to the first global Trauma Informed Policing and Law Enforcement Conference held in Melbourne, Australia in February 2024. *Journal of Community Safety and Well-Being*, *9*(3), 135–140.

Brammer, J. C., Van Peer, J. M., Michela, A., Van Rooij, M. M., Oostenveld, R., Klumpers, F., Dorrestijn, W., Granic, I., & Roelofs, K. (2021). Breathing biofeedback for police officers in a stressful virtual environment: Challenges and opportunities. *Frontiers in Psychology*, *12*, 586553.

Eatough, V., & Smith, J. A. (2017). Interpretative phenomenological analysis. In *The Sage handbook of qualitative research in psychology* (pp. 193–209). Sage.

Ernst, G. (2014). *Heart rate variability*. Springer.

Fairclough, S. H. (2009). Fundamentals of physiological computing. *Interacting with Computers*, *21*(1–2), 133–145.

Gamito, P., Oliveira, J., Silva, J., Rosa, J., Mendes, M. L. R., Dias, R., Dias, F., Mansuklal, S. A., Cartaxo, J., António, H., & Salvador, Á. (2024). Stress inoculation in police officers using virtual reality: A controlled study. *Cyberpsychology, Behavior, and Social Networking*, *27*(4), 253–260. https://doi.org/10.1089/cyber.2023.0385

Gjoreski, H., I. Mavridou, I., Fatoorechi, M., Kiprijanovska, I., Gjoreski, M., Cox, G., & Nduka, C. (2021). emteqPRO: Face-mounted mask for emotion recognition and affective computing. *Adjunct Proceedings of the 2021 ACM International Joint Conference on Pervasive and Ubiquitous Computing and Proceedings of the 2021 ACM International Symposium on Wearable Computers*, 23–25. https://doi.org/10.1145/3460418.3479276

Gnacek, M., Broulidakis, J., Mavridou, I., Fatoorechi, M., Seiss, E., Kostoulas, T., Balaguer-Ballester, E., Rosten, C., & Nduka, C. (2022). EmteqPRO-fully integrated biometric sensing array for non-invasive biomedical research in virtual reality. *Frontiers in Virtual Reality*, 3.

Guillen-Sanz, H., Checa, D., Miguel-Alonso, I., & Bustillo, A. (2024). A systematic review of wearable biosensor usage in immersive virtual reality experiences. *Virtual Reality*, *28*(2), 74. https://doi.org/10.1007/s10055-024-00970-9

Jerald, J. (2015). *The VR book: Human-centered design for virtual reality*. Morgan & Claypool.

Kleider, H. M., Parrott, D. J., & King, T. Z. (2010). Shooting behaviour: How working memory and negative emotionality influence police officer shoot decisions. *Applied Cognitive Psychology*, *24*(5), 707–717. https://doi.org/10.1002/acp.1580

Kleygrewe, L., Hutter, R. I. V., Koedijk, M., & Oudejans, R. R. D. (2023a). Changing perspectives: Enhancing learning efficacy with the after-action review in virtual reality training for police. *Ergonomics*, 1–10. https://doi.org/10.1080/00140139.2023.2236819

Kleygrewe, L., Hutter, R. I. V., Koedijk, M., & Oudejans, R. R. D. (2023b). Virtual reality training for police officers: A comparison of training responses in VR and real-life training. *Police Practice and Research*, 1–20. https://doi.org/10.1080/15614263.2023.2176307

Lavoie, J. A. A., Alvarez, N., & Kandil, Y. (2022). Developing community co-designed scenario-based training for police mental health crisis response: A relational policing approach to de-escalation. *Journal of Police and Criminal Psychology*, *37*(3), 587–601. https://doi.org/10.1007/s11896-022-09500-2

Lavoie, J., Álvarez, N., Baker, V., & Kohl, J. (2023). Training police to de-escalate mental health crisis situations: Comparing virtual reality and live-action scenario-based approaches. *Policing: A Journal of Policy and Practice*, *17*, paad069.

Liu, R., Becerik-Gerber, B., & Lucas, G. M. (2023). Effectiveness of VR-based training on improving occupants' response and preparedness for active shooter incidents. *Safety Science*, *164*, 106175. https://doi.org/10.1016/j.ssci.2023.106175

Martaindale, M. H., Sandel, W. L., Duron, A., & McAllister, M. J. (2024). Can a virtual reality training scenario elicit similar stress response as a realistic scenario-based training scenario? *Police Quarterly*, *27*(1), 109–129. https://doi.org/10.1177/10986111231182729

Michela, A., van Peer, J. M., Oostenveld, R., Dorrestijn, W., Smit, A. S., Granic, I., Roelofs, K., & Klumpers, F. (2025). Preparing the heart for duty: Virtual reality biofeedback in an arousing action game improves in-action voluntary heart rate variability control in experienced police. *IEEE Transactions on Affective Computing*, 1–12. https://doi.org/10.1109/TAFFC.2025.3619161

Moinnereau, M.-A., Oliveira, A. A., & Falk, T. H. (2022). Instrumenting a virtual reality headset for at-home gamer experience monitoring and behavioural assessment. *Frontiers in Virtual Reality*, *3*, 971054.

Muñoz, J. E., Lavoie, J. A., & Pope, A. T. (n.d.). Psychophysiological insights and user perspectives: Enhancing police de-escalation skills through full-body VR training. *Frontiers in Psychology*, *15*, 1390677.

Muñoz, J. E., Quintero, L., Stephens, C. L., & Pope, A. T. (2020). A psychophysiological model of firearms training in police officers: A virtual reality experiment for biocybernetic adaptation. *Frontiers in Psychology*, *11*.

Nasri, M. (2025, June). Towards intelligent VR training: A physiological adaptation framework for cognitive load and stress detection. In *Proceedings of the 33rd ACM Conference on User Modeling, Adaptation and Personalization* (pp. 419–423).

Novak, D. (2014). Engineering issues in physiological computing. In S. H. Fairclough & K. Gilleade (Eds.), *Advances in physiological computing* (pp. 17–38). Springer London. http://link.springer.com/chapter/10.1007/978-1-4471-6392-3_2

Podoletz, L., McGill, M., McIlhatton, D., Marshall, J., Healy, N., & Tanczer, L. M. (2024). A critical review of virtual and extended reality immersive police training: Application areas, benefits & vulnerabilities. *30th ACM Symposium on Virtual Reality Software and Technology*, 1–21. https://doi.org/10.1145/3641825.3687707

Pope, A. T., Stephens, C. L., & Gilleade, K. (2014). Biocybernetic adaptation as biofeedback training method. In S. H. Fairclough & K. Gilleade (Eds.), *Advances in physiological computing* (pp. 91–115). Springer London. http://link.springer.com/chapter/10.1007/978-1-4471-6392-3_5

Regehr, C., Carey, M. G., Wagner, S., Alden, L. E., Buys, N., Corneil, W., Fyfe, T., Matthews, L., Randall, C., White, M., Fraess-Phillips, A., Krutop, E., White, N., & Fleischmann, M. (2021). A systematic review of mental health symptoms in police officers following extreme traumatic exposures. *Police Practice and Research*, *22*(1), 225–239. https://doi.org/10.1080/15614263.2019.1689129

Scott, D., Blake, D., & Suss, J. (2025). Examining the use of interactive video-based simulators in law enforcement human performance research: A scoping review. *Journal of Experimental Criminology*, *21*(2), 649–688. https://doi.org/10.1007/s11292-023-09606-5

See, P. J., & Davies, A. (2024). How far have we advanced in simulation-based training for policing and law enforcement? A literature review 2014–24. *Policing: A Journal of Policy and Practice*, *18*, paae116.

Slater, M., & Sanchez-Vives, M. V. (2016). Enhancing our lives with immersive virtual reality. *Frontiers in Robotics and AI*, *3*, 74. https://www.frontiersin.org/journals/robotics-and-ai/articles/10.3389/frobt.2016.00074/full

Vera-Jiménez, J. C., Vera-Jurado, J. C., & Ayuso, J. (2025). Enhancing police training through biomechanical analysis and wearable technology—OTP. *Indian Journal of*

Occupational and Environmental Medicine, *29*(3), 193–198. https://doi.org/10.4103/ijoem.ijoem_123_24
Yang, W.-C., Shih, C.-H., Jiang, J., Pallas Enguita, S., & Chen, C.-H. (2025). Analyzing visual attention in virtual crime scene investigations using eye-tracking and VR: Insights for cognitive modeling. *Electronics*, *14*(16), 3265. https://doi.org/10.3390/electronics14163265
Zechner, O., Kleygrewe, L., Jaspaert, E., Schrom-Feiertag, H., Hutter, R. V., & Tscheligi, M. (2023a). Enhancing operational police training in high stress situations with virtual reality: Experiences, tools and guidelines. *Multimodal Technologies and Interaction*, *7*(2), 14.
Zechner, O., Schrom-Feiertag, H., Uhl, J., Nguyen, Q., Kleygrewe, L., & Tscheligi, M. (2023b). Mind the heart: Designing a stress dashboard based on physiological data for training highly stressful situations in virtual reality. In J. Abdelnour Nocera, M. Kristín Lárusdóttir, H. Petrie, A. Piccinno, & M. Winckler (Eds.), *Human-computer interaction – INTERACT 2023* (pp. 209–230). Springer Nature Switzerland. https://doi.org/10.1007/978-3-031-42293-5_16

Appendix I

TABLE 15.1 Summary of Physiological Modalities and Examples of Research Involving VR in Policing

Modality & Sensor	*What it Measures*	*Training Insight Gained*	*Example in Research*
Heart Rate & Heart Rate Variability (HR & HRV) – chest strap/heart monitor	Beats per minute and beat-to-beat variability, reflecting overall arousal and autonomic balance	Quantifies stress level and quality of physiological self-regulation over time	Closed-loop HRV biofeedback in a VR action game with 109 police trainers increased in-action HRV by ~32% and improved real-world shooting performance (Michela et al., 2025)
Electrodermal Activity (EDA) – wristband/finger electrodes	Skin conductance changes driven by sweat gland activity (sympathetic arousal)	Pinpoints peak arousal moments and recovery across a scenario	Sixty-three Portuguese officers in a VR car-accident scenario; less-experienced traffic squad showed higher skin conductance and lower peripheral temperature, indicating stronger stress responses (Gamito et al., 2024)

(*Continued*)

TABLE 15.1 (Continued)

Modality & Sensor	*What it Measures*	*Training Insight Gained*	*Example in Research*
Electromyography (EMG & fEMG) – surface electrodes, VR-compatible facial mask	Electrical activity in skeletal muscles (limbs, torso, face)	Detects muscular tension and subtle emotional reactions linked to task events	fEMG study showed that officers with lower working memory and stronger negative emotional responses made more shoot/no-shoot errors (Kleider et al., 2010)
Electroencephalography (EEG) – lightweight headbands/ HMD-integrated sensors	Scalp electrical activity; oscillations related to vigilance, workload, and control	Indexes engagement and cognitive load during critical decision points	EEG in 58 cadets exposed to simulated scenarios correlated neural activity with performance metrics for evaluation in law-enforcement settings (AlSabah et al., 2025)
Respiration Rate – respiratory belt, vest-integrated stretch sensor	Breathing frequency, depth, and variability	Tracks arousal and provides a direct target for breathing-based self-regulation	Controlled respiration during firearms training informed a framework for automatic VR adaptation using breathing patterns (Brammer et al., 2021)
Eye Tracking – infrared cameras in VR headset	Gaze direction, fixations, saccades, scan paths, pupil diameter	Reveals attention allocation, tunnel vision, and search strategy quality	VR crime-scene study with >2.6M gaze samples used gaze metrics to cluster groups (~78% accuracy) and predict proficiency ($R^2 \approx 0.70$) (Yang et al., 2025)
Motion Capture (MoCap), Body Tracking & Kinematics – optical/IMU-based trackers, VR controllers	Whole-body kinematics and posture/ gesture patterns	Objectively logs tactical movement and ergonomic risk across skill levels	Full-body MoCap plus biomechanical analysis of 11 officers' arrest technique showed mainly medium–high ergonomic risk and differentiated novice, intermediate, and expert performance (Vera-Jiménez et al., 2025)

16

ABOUT FACE

Why the Police May Have Fewer Surveillance Cameras in the Future

Fraser Sampson

Introduction

> By comparison with that existing today, all the tyrannies of the past were half-hearted and inefficient.
>
> —Orwell (1949)

When people talk of police surveillance, they invariably have in mind an increasing number of networked CCTV cameras focused unblinking on the citizen, looking paternalistically over the population of a street or city from above. Journalists, academics and politicians tend to follow this default model by directly referencing the 'Orwellian' characterization of a 'dystopian' world in which the surveillance machinery of the state becomes an increasingly prominent and inescapable feature of the physical landscape. In this seemingly indelible image, the evolution of state surveillance emerges as a patriarchal proliferation of visible capability and envisages ever greater intrusion by state-operated technology. This fictional pastiche is often depicted as a panopticon world of high-definition cameras, transmitting thousands of images to central control rooms where screen walls are intently monitored by an army of uniformed law enforcement officials.

The reality of surveillance ecology is, however, very different and has taken a direction not prophesied even by the adjectival Orwell and his seminal novel *Nineteen Eighty-Four*, which still colours public discourse on the subject after 75 years. The emerging direction of surveillance evolution is the focus of this chapter, together with the several reasons behind it and what that might mean for the future of policing and law enforcement.

DOI: 10.4324/9781003671312-16

Cooperative Surveillance

While the Orwellian dystopia is impelled by technological hegemony and nostalgic paranoia about state surveillance, the world emerging before our eyes is materializing from a different direction, in a combination of cooperative evolution and cultural shift.

The recent development of surveillance can be tracked from three key perspectives or vantage points that help reveal the interplay between the driving forces. The three principal (and overlapping) factors shaping the direction of surveillance are the technologically possible (what can be done), the legally permissible (what must/must not be done), and the societally acceptable (what people support/expect to be done). These areas overlap considerably, and there is a dynamic interplay between them. Alternatively summarized as innovation, regulation and expectation, the interface between the first and the third – availability of advanced technology and societal influence – has probably received the least attention in the development of remote biometric capability such as Facial Recognition Technology (FRT) being used in policing, but the future is being shaped by them.

It is undeniable that the technology of surveillance has changed, but rather than being directed by its adoption and legitimization by the state, surveillance *practice* appears to be following the application of that technology by the private citizen. Cultural changes unforetold by the storytellers are now shaping the future of an equally worrying society, but one in which the police will have less need to own and operate the surveillance technology and therefore fewer cameras of their own – because society itself has become the surveillance machinery watching it. Whether it is badged as the third (Gordon, 2016), fourth (Wang Chao, 2018) or fifth (Nosta, 2023) in the surveillance context, the 'industrial revolution' presaged by Artificial Intelligence (AI) is looking more like an introspective, techno-sociological evolution.

Before examining why this is an important departure from prophesied surveillance futures, it is necessary to understand a central fact: public surveillance is no longer about where the police put their cameras; it is about what they do with the images from *everyone's* cameras. Live facial recognition cameras have dominated the AI-enabled surveillance debate, but uploads from privately owned and operated phones, dashcams, doorbells and other devices are changing the surveillance landscape.

Changes in self-surveillance and remotely accessible private devices have made global surveillance rankings loved by journalists (Minardi, 2020), researchers (Bandara, 2025) and politicians (Hafiz, 2023) all but meaningless. Counting street cameras reveals nothing about the nature, depth and consequences of state surveillance. Whether a visible camera is operating its latent functions, such as the ability to record sound or read vehicle licence plates, is not evident from looking up at it. Dividing the number of publicly operated cameras by recorded population may provide mathematical comfort, but it cannot begin to indicate how many people were under state surveillance in that country at any given moment. A rough estimation of *visible and working cameras* covering public spaces over square miles would be possible, but no more accurate. Much 'public' commercial space – retail, transport, entertainment – is privately owned and monitored. In the UK, most visible street cameras covering 'pure' public space like streets and parks are operated by local authorities rather than the police; many do not work, have poor image quality, variable retention periods and/or are unmonitored.

If it were possible, combining social media analytics with other mass surveillance capabilities like call record metadata, biometrics-based financial services, mobile driver's licences and digital identity wallets would produce another figure but would still be a long way from anything resembling a ballpark. Internet scraping might give a vague idea of how many pictures were snapped of the Eiffel Tower or in front of the Sydney Opera House, but that will not account for sound files, Automated Number Plate Readers (ANPRs) or phone mast 'pings', let alone how many were subsequently searched for, edited, matched and shared on how many occasions.

Land, water and airborne vehicles contain multiple recording devices capturing data as they navigate in, around, above and below our cities: the amount of data they hold about people and places is incalculable. Once vehicles become self-driving, the automated total data capture of their surroundings will become a functional necessity, and the extent of 'surveillance' will shift further out of sight.

Spatially, camera counting in streets and shopping malls assumes that surveillance of a location and its inhabitants needs to be conducted from that location or visible from it. With satellite-based surveillance like global positioning, everywhere can be watched from somewhere. Claiming a position as the 'world's most surveilled city' is like claiming to be the world's least dreamed about person – there is no reliable way of measuring either.

But the main reason why using the mathematics of countable camera infrastructure is a flawed method of assessing surveillance of a population is the population itself.

Citizens' Access to Surveillance Technology

We are undergoing a socio-technological evolution within which there are two principal factors at play: the *availability* of the technology, not just to the state but to all of us, and the anthropological global *changes in behaviour* that it has caused, or to which it has at least contributed. The reasons behind our compulsion to share images and personal data are a fertile area for sociological research (see e.g. the Why We Post social media project at University College London: Miller et al., 2016), but what this means for the future direction and shape of state surveillance is the focus here.

In terms of availability, I reported to the UK parliament in 2023 (Sampson, 2023) that the citizen now has ready access to technology that, only recently, was the preserve of state intelligence agencies. But, unlike secret intelligence gathering bodies, the citizen is very willing to share the product of their individual, privately operated technology at large, so much so that the supply of shared data is almost unbounded. In addition, I and anyone with whom I share the IP address can monitor the street outside my home from the other side of the planet using a smart doorbell and a mobile phone; it can also be hacked remarkably easily (see e.g. Bandura, 2024). By installing, operating and exposing my technology, I have become part of the public space surveillance infrastructure, whether I intended it or not.

Mechanization and adaptation are acknowledged features of human evolution; in the context of surveillance trends, the importance of this is the voluntary – and ineradicable – sharing of images and associated metadata from which we and others can be identified, located and monitored. Both the ubiquity and utility of this surveillance data are elementally different from previous practices of coercive capture by the state.

State Access to Citizen Surveillance Technology

Lending private technological capability to public purposes is not new, and its formidable impact has been well documented. Donating private computing power has been a popular research tool for nearly 30 years (see e.g. Ma et al., 2024) and has become phenomenally potent. For example, a project at Stanford University in 2020, where individuals donated their computer time to tackle the coronavirus, was reported as showing "a total compute performance of over 1.5 ExaFLOPS (aka 1,500,000,000,000,000,000 floating point operations per second)", dwarfing "the computing ability of even the most powerful mainframe supercomputers on the planet" (Bowman, 2020). Crowdsourcing capabilities have also been well documented (Garrigos-Simon & Narangajavana-Kaosiri, 2024), and lending privately owned surveillance capability to governments is an international phenomenon seen in military and critical infrastructure settings. But the phenomenon under consideration here is not merely the extension of temporary access to a device or capability – it is an irreversible evolution of the praxis of state surveillance.

What is emerging is an increasingly powerful 'aggregated surveillance capability' available to the state, and with it a permanent surrender of data. Any former presumption that it would be the state's deployment of increasingly sophisticated technology that brought the endpoint of privacy and the inevitable rise of intrusive state-controlled surveillance must be re-evaluated in that light.

Self-Surveillance

In terms of behavioural change, one feature of our digital evolution from what one researcher calls "analogue humanity to digital humanity" (Laterza, 2021) is our eagerness to share detailed accounts, searchable images and minutely referenced data points relating to every aspect of our lives. This *folie à tous* obsession with telegraphing our every life event – not just facial images, opinions and preferences, but meals, journeys, haircuts, tattoos, childbirth, death, surgery, crime – has given rise to an 'expository society' (Harcourt, 2015). World leaders have adopted social media as their principal public interface, combining what one Nobel laureate calls a 'reality of polyphonic first-person narratives' (Tokarczuk, 2019) with democratic accountability. In and of itself, this evolutionary phenomenon raises many sociological and psychological questions, but its particular impact on state surveillance has been technology-dependent.

Whatever the longer-term sociological consequences of self-promotion turn out to be, the images produced via our proliferation of dashcams, doorbells, drones, body-worn devices and home security systems would be of no practical use to the police without the capability to process them. Uncounted billions of images and other surveillance data reference points are being captured and shared across the world every second, generating infinitely recurring opportunities for searching, comparing and matching. When it needed a human to do it, combing and comparing these petabytes of data put it beyond any utility for local law enforcement purposes. Until now, collating and analyzing submitted images from security cameras in homes, businesses and government bodies was a critical resourcing decision, balancing input against likely outcome, and the ratio was vastly skewed against investment. But technological developments such as Edge AI and micro data centres (Singh & Gill, 2023) have made mega-matching cheap and fast. AI has alchemized what was once digital chaff into surveillance gold, making public appeals for it de rigueur in law enforcement across the world (Sampson, 2025), and the traditional metaphor of finding a needle in a haystack will make no sense to the next surveillance generation.

Moreover, while most of the attention from both the public and the surveillance community has been on police use of *live* FRT, the capability to match faces retrospectively from this universe of data is far more potent in terms of extending the surveillance reach of the state. Policing is about connecting the dots and, as Steve Jobs said, you can only do that by looking backwards. That is precisely what retrospective facial recognition does, making it a formidable and indispensable investigative tool. Unlike live FRT, retrospective matching is an unseen function, without street camera vans and deliberate public advertisement. The policies of conspicuity that accompany police use of live FRT do not apply to retrospective matching. Whether it is conducted in real time or by poring over decades' worth of photos and videos captured on security systems, class graduation photographs, 'selfies', promotional videos, blogs or communication apps, matching citizen-submitted data takes place behind closed doors with no signs or opt-out provisions. To this extent, live facial recognition has become the surveillance conjuror's left hand: we watch in rapt fascination while the real wizardry is taking place under the table.

Privacy advocates reach for Orwell and his 'dystopian' fiction to corroborate their warnings of the growth in state surveillance, but the reality is more like Bentham's famous panopticon, except the world is the 'building' and we, the people, are its interns. Or perhaps, given its susceptibility to Deepfakery, disinformation or hallucination, our digitally naked world is closer to a "mirrored glass pavilion" (Harcourt, 2015) where everything we do is reflected and refracted.

Whichever simile we employ, the evidence shows that society, enabled by privately operated technology, is fundamentally altering the shape of state surveillance. This phenomenon is not the same as other manifestations of 'crowdsourcing', for example, to raise money or profiles. Attention on the 'expository society' (Harcourt, 2015) and wider concepts like "surveillance capitalism" (Zuboff, 2019) has primarily been on private companies' use of big data and prospect surveillance for commercial purposes, while very little has been paid to the contribution that our 'rampant self-celebration' (Popova, 2024) is making to the surveillance relationship between citizen and the state and between citizen and citizen, both of which are undergoing an evolution which has, so far, gone largely unnoticed.

Changing Surveillance Relationships

Viewed through today's surveillance lens, Sontag's observation, "Like guns and cars, cameras are fantasy-machines whose use is addictive" (Sontag, 1979), was eerily prescient. Addiction to, or fetishization of, image capture technology is not without constraints and, in many jurisdictions, the processing (which includes capturing, storing, editing, sharing and retaining) of data that is sensitive or by which a person can be identified is governed by clear legal and regulatory frameworks. Many countries have independent oversight by regulators and statutory guardrails in place. But these countermeasures have largely evolved within a legal context of data rights and privacy, and the realities of the law enforcement context are challenging.

For example, data sharing agreements, such as those required by the General Data Protection Regulation (GDPR), covering European member states, place strict limits and conditions on the sharing of personal data. Many impose 'purpose limitation', notionally preventing the data from being used for a purpose other than for which it was originally divulged. Such agreements allow parties that intend to share images and other data to delineate in advance the extent to which they are consenting to share it and the purposes for which it can be deployed. However, the practical ability for the surveillance-minded citizen to be selective about the purpose(s) for which they are prepared to share their metadata with the state is very limited.

Policing bodies will have detailed and documented data sharing agreements/ data acceptance policies covering all their activities, and these will apply to uploads and other voluntary acts of sharing. But these can only be broadly descriptive and votive ("we will endeavour to do x/not to do y") and ultimately cannot give guarantees in advance of purposive need. The open-ended obligations of law enforcement agencies to fight crime and protect the public make any conditional 'consent' unlikely to be accepted, let alone honoured, and any data sharing conditions unenforceable, at least to the extent that they conflict with those overarching duties. Once the citizen has handed their data to the state, the original purpose or motive for doing so is arguably irrelevant, as their control over it is lost. While it may have been shared for the express purpose of helping find a specific vulnerable missing person or apprehending a known dangerous person on the loose, the footage shared by the citizen will be available for other 'policing purposes', and those purposes are very wide. The police can readily find a compelling reason for retention and sharing the images under a portmanteau exception of the "investigation or prevention of crime, prosecution of offenders, or to ensure public safety". In recent facial matching for the investigation of crime, the UK government has made no distinction between the primary purpose of citizens uploading formal images of themselves in order to obtain a passport or driver's licence and the subsequent mass matching processes for law enforcement (Burt, 2025).

There are two immediate strategic risks to policing from this infinite purposing reality. First, the lack of certainty around how the police will use shared images and other data makes the prediction of the citizen's continuing support difficult. A recent finding showed that UK voters are now motivated by single-issue subjects such as immigration or the environment, and are less likely to have ideological or more general political convictions (YouGov, 2025). If this new 'consumerism' is applied to the transactional sharing of images and data with the police – perhaps driven by emotional or highly situation-specific reasons – the citizen's expectations as to what wider use will be made of their contributed surveillance product may be less predictable. Second, even though the police and other agencies may have policies requiring audit and scrutiny of retrospective facial matching for 'additional related' purposes, the volume of data shares alone will become a challenge, and the inability to investigate instances of non-compliance or departure from the original permitted purpose(s) may bring its own 'chilling effect' on citizen sharing.

Realistically, if the citizen does try to withdraw or withhold consent, or to apply conditions on their sharing permission, history is on the side of the state (Sampson, 2016); commercial platforms and individual users may try to shield their surveillance product from the state, but the prevention and investigation of crime are high thresholds to clear, while national security trumps everything (Kleinman & McMahon, 2025).

In addition to the shifting surveillance relationship with the state, the relationship between citizens inter se is also changing. As citizen-on-citizen surveillance increases with the use of doorbells, drones and other image capture devices, the surveillance relationship between us has yet to be thoroughly explored. Breaches of expectations of privacy by neighbours installing sophisticated surveillance technology already provide a fertile source of news and commentary (Buccieri, 2025), but we are at the beginning of a new epoch where traditional expectations of privacy are questionable. The surveillance nexus between our nearest neighbours and us has already been transformed by AI-spectacles with integrated always-on functionality like speech recording (Borak, 2025) and lip-reading capability (*Times*, 2025a), but to what effect we do not yet know. We do know that the discovery of micro-surveillance devices in public toilets, hotel bedrooms and private offices revealed by the molka craze in South Korea (Sampson, 2016) has illustrated how fragile enforceable privacy rights have become. Armed with increasingly intrusive and undetectable technology, we literally have the future of state surveillance capability in our own hands. Shrinkworld surveillance technology is expanding, and our use of smaller and less obtrusive objects, like RFID signals in golf balls (Reddy et al., 2019), vehicle telemetry in bicycles (Migue, 2020), satellite tracking of sports watches, trainers, pets (Plaut, 2026) and even children (Murray, 2026) is embedding latent surveillance capability within the fabric of our everyday lives.

The new surveillance relationships and dispersed ownership of such extraordinarily intrusive assets also make the surveillance ecosystem much more porous and exposed, with interference getting harder to detect (Hamilton & Gardham, 2025) and address. In a world where your neighbour's Wi-Fi router can be used to track your movements through walls without the need for cameras or visual contact (Puiu, 2023), traditional expectations of privacy from each other are unstable at best. The prospect that our neighbours can see and capture everything about us remotely and undetected is alarming enough; the fact that they might share the images and information with the state, remotely and undetected, is beyond Orwellian fiction.

From the *molka* experience, it is a reasonable prediction that once nano-technology becomes globally available to the citizen, privacy as we have come to understand it will be extinct.

Extinction of Privacy?

In the UK, there is no free-standing right to privacy (see *Campbell v. MGN*, 2004), rather there is an extension of the concept of confidentiality to incorporate Article 8 of the European Convention on Human Rights (ECHR), which protects a much broader entitlement to the enjoyment of home and family life, etc. Similarly, there is no 'right' to go missing – not even within the ECHR – but neither is there any legal wrong in doing so. As the techno-sociology of surveillance has evolved (see e.g. Lyon, 2017), the wider idea of privacy has changed:

the privacy question for future surveillance will be how far remaining undetected by others is a technological possibility, let alone a reasonable expectation.

For the state, locating people is a basic policing function. Some people must be found, because they are suspected of causing or about to cause harm (to themselves or others), or they are unlawfully at large. In these cases, the police will not just try to find them; they will have a duty to look for them. Once the capability to locate virtually every individual at large is cost-effective and technologically within their reach, why would they not do so? Using the aggregated surveillance capability of their communities, the police now have extraordinary power to look for people who are reported as missing and all the risk to them and the public lies in not looking.

An example of this capability can be seen in a case in 2025 where police in the UK launched an appeal to find a woman who had first been reported as missing in 1972 when she was 16 years old. The BBC reported how posting a photograph on the police website and social media platforms led to a large response from the public sharing information enabling the police to confirm that she was alive and well (Benton, 2025). The aggregated surveillance capability of the community ended a 52-year period of voluntary absence in a matter of hours. The fact that she had disappeared of her own volition was irrelevant.

When people go missing, there are many charities dedicated to finding them and commercial companies with ‘missing persons’ databases containing hundreds of thousands of facial images ready to join in the search (Liang, 2024). At the same time, there are others within the criminal justice system for whom being found would bring significant risk: victims rehabilitating after abusive relationships, protected witnesses and undercover police officers. For them, anonymity is critical, but the ability for the state to guarantee it is being eroded.

While there might be no general legal requirement for the police to look for someone who has chosen to go ‘no contact’, when receiving a report, they must ascertain that the absence is voluntary and benign. What might have started out as a voluntary exercise of freedom may have ended in an accident, crime or illness: experience shows it will be the one the police decide not to look for that will be the one they regret. Obvious vulnerability factors like age, mental and physical health will be relevant, but our ‘expository’ society can often mean that lack of constant contact is itself viewed with suspicion. Traditional ideas of privacy are losing out to our need to be noticed – asserting our freedom to disappear has become proof of our need to be found.

The technological ability to search for and match faces from shared images in backgrounds on shared selfies, social media posts, houses and offices with smart doorbells, passing vehicles and bikes with GoPros, dashcams and drones makes finding us easier for the state to do and not looking for us harder for it to defend.

Using AI to find suspects and vulnerable people represents one form of surveillance challenge, but the technology is also being used in non-criminal incidents. How it will be used for monitoring attendance at protests, industrial disputes or future pandemic lockdowns is not yet known or knowable, while the contribution it will make to the actuarial process of 'predictive' policing is (fittingly) pure conjecture. In a society where we are so readily findable, having a 'right not to be found' would be like a right to privacy where all clothing is see-through, entirely dependent on no one looking.

All the Technologies of the Past

As the state surveillance debate continues to take place against the backdrop of Orwellian fiction, his description of the surveillance 'tyrannies' of the past might be applied instead to the *technologies* of the past. In comparison with emerging surveillance capabilities set out here, all those of the past have been half-hearted and inefficient. Technologies like CCTV have been wholly inefficient when compared to the shared metadata and biometric analytics taking place in a vacuum of regulatory constraint. Biometric capabilities like FRT are transforming security cameras, but the devices are nothing like CCTV; they are not on closed circuit, and they are not on television. CCTV was photography, and facial recognition is biometrics. After 50 years of operation, decades of research and vast sums of public money, CCTV has yet to demonstrate its impact on crime (Chen et al., 2025). However intrusive they may be in terms of numbers of cameras and saturation of metres-squared, even the latest versions of HD PTZ (high-definition pan, tilt, zoom) cameras are a different species from biometric-capable tools. In terms of their impact on crime and criminality, old-school CCTV and in-store cameras have plainly not proved an effective deterrent. This much is clear from the extraordinary surge, not only in retail crime like shop theft and assaults on workers (BRC, 2025), but also fare evasion on the London underground, phone snatches and other street crime. Whether they are supermarkets or convenience stores, every one of the venues behind the statistics will almost certainly have some form of traditional security cameras in place. With over 70,000 public-facing cameras, London Underground has one of the most concentrated surveillance systems in the country, if not the world, while the square metres of camera coverage of streets, bus stations, playgrounds and car parks have never been higher. Forecourt drive-offs have also risen significantly despite the operation of ANPR cameras at filling stations, perhaps a reflection of how astonishingly easy it is to defeat ANPR surveillance with little risk of detection and puny penalties for conviction (Sampson, 2023). While the FBI is developing 'next gen ID' for people (Law Enforcement Resources, n.d.), one look at reliance on vehicle registration plates and ANPR cameras shows that even 'this gen ID' for vehicles is a long way down the road. In sharp contrast to such technologies of the past, retailers using live facial recognition in the UK have reported sustainable reductions of 70% (Das, 2024), making the impact of the new biometric technology on crime a verifiable fact.

The notion of 'mission creep' or scope creep within technology projects has also been a feature of past technologies and a recognized risk within public bodies for decades (see e.g. Larson & Larson, 2009); it has featured in police facial recognition debates (*Times*, 2025b). But with AI-powered image matching and sharing, there is no 'creeping'– it has been expanding at warp speed. Moreover, the classic concept of mission or function creep is anathema to the AI world. The risk from function creep is technological trespass into areas beyond the original mission, whereas AI is in a permanent *beta* state; one of its great strengths is that it will evolve iteratively and therefore be capable of functions beyond those envisaged at the time of its procurement. Like many technological concepts from surveillance history, function creep is anachronistic and needs an upgrade.

The police and security sector may still talk about CCTV and Orwell more out of habit than accurate description (Sampson et al., 2024), but how do you compare a Google Maps camera car upload from a quiet Spanish street, which becomes evidence in a homicide investigation (Greenall, 2024), with the static CCTV staring blankly at a patch of pavement in a capital city? The next generation security systems for mass surveillance will be nothing like the technologies of the past – factual or fictitious – and an early mistake will be to treat them as such.

About Face

The fictional portents were wrong, and the surveillance tyrannies of the future will be self-induced, if not wholly then at least in part. While neighbour spying on neighbour *is* a well-known tyranny (Gershgorn, 2021), the parasitic approach of the state attaching itself to their privately operated technology is a new surveillance phenomenon.

It is possible to imagine a world with no overt police cameras, no CCTV or body cameras – a world with a control room and receiving billions of data feeds from tens of thousands of people, vehicles and privately owned devices. It seems an unlikely future, but renowned 'long view' strategist Peter Schwartz advised that the signs of the future are often all around us if we only knew what to look for (Schwartz, 1996). At the time of writing, some of the signs of a hybrid (citizen-and-police) approach to surveillance are emerging. In August 2024, the government of New South Wales revealed its BluLink tool, which citizens can use to upload data and livestream footage of events directly to the police when calling the national emergency number[1]. The press release described how this capability will allow the citizen to give the police access to the scene before they have even arrived. Such citizen-on-scene capabilities may be the next evolutionary stage in the new surveillance relationship and may be accompanied by other features. For example, the UK government is actively considering brigading citizen volunteers to protect the country's critical infrastructure (Yorke & Wheeler, 2025), and it would be easy to invite such a body to bring their own biometrics and surveillance devices under a BYO policy. Meanwhile, a UK court has recently accepted that recording a motorist allegedly breaking the law and then sharing that data with the police is not a breach of the driver's data protection rights or privacy protection (Reid, 2025).

Reliance on citizen-operated surveillance technology is potentially *more* intrusive than it would be if the police sought to operate it directly themselves. Private surveillance capabilities may exceed those allowable to the police because the legal and regulatory treatment of personal and private data processing is less restrictive than that applicable to the state, with all its powers of investigation, enforcement and sanction. Law enforcement bodies are subject to many additional oversight, scrutiny and regulatory mechanisms than the private citizen. As an example, 'fine' location-sharing apps like Life360[2] are highly intrusive in the detail that they give their users, but they are generally deployed between consenting parties such as family members concerned for each other's safety and wellbeing. It is difficult to envisage the state being permitted to use them in many democratic jurisdictions, but if citizen users choose to make their content available to the state on an *ad hoc* basis, the police and other agencies can access all the benefits for investigation and intelligence gathering without the scrutiny and regulatory safeguards.

The principal policing requirement from surveillance networks is for their *product*. Owning and operating surveillance technology brings the expense of procurement, training, upgrading and obsolescence together with the risk of legal challenge and the burden of procedural compliance for bias and misuse. If the police can access the operational product of our aggregated surveillance capability without surveillance systems of their own, police chiefs may want to reduce the number of cameras they operate in the future.

Regulating this environment will be increasingly difficult – developments in citizen-generated surveillance will, at the very least, bring legal considerations of agency, direction and control, as will personal matters of disclosure and identification of the surveillance 'source' in the prosecutorial process (see *R v Hewitt and Davis* [1992]; *R v Grimes* [1994]). None of these issues is directly covered by the current regulatory regime in the UK, and the government's Surveillance Camera Code for public spaces does not cover citizen-generated data sharing (Gov.uk, 2021). Rapidly evolving technology is being habitually used by the citizen to such an extent that the state will become increasingly reliant upon citizen-generated data captures. However, the regulatory framework, created for and in a pre-AI era when public spaces were watched over by one-dimensional image capture devices from fixed points, continues to focus myopically and inconsistently solely on those systems operated by local policing and government bodies (Gov.uk, 2021).

Dependency equals risk, and the trends highlighted here bring several future hazards for the police. Having moved from a society where the state needed images *of* the people to one where it depends on images *from* them, the police will become more exposed as their dependence on citizen-generated surveillance increases. In such an environment, digital disobedience and resistance found more generally in relation to data reliability (Harcourt, 2015) would have a particularly significant impact on police intelligence and evidence gathering, so too would deliberate subterfuge (uploading deepfakes, etc., to disrupt and distort data flows on which the police rely). Then there are political and sociological responses to the surveillance *zeitgeist* generally (Karpa & Rochlitz, 2024).

There are technological risks, too. For all its ingenuity and accuracy, FRT has a single point of failure: the face. In much the same way as ANPR relies on the availability of a visible, digitally readable licence plate, FRT is entirely dependent on the availability of sufficient unique facial features to allow comparison with a probe image. The covering of faces to defeat security systems has been recognized in, for example, banks for many years and visitors to premises have become used to removing crash helmets and facemasks. In a law enforcement context, primary legislation has given the police express powers to require the removal of facial coverings for the purposes of keeping public order[3] and the UK parliament has introduced a Crime and Policing Bill which will extend those powers to public assemblies and protests, making it a criminal offence to conceal one's face in certain prescribed circumstances. However, these are exceptional situations, and generally, citizens are under no obligation to show their faces when in public. In the other direction, law enforcement personnel are increasingly vulnerable to being identified as such when off duty. The French government attempted to prohibit the publication of pictures of police officers on duty (Brunet, 2020) – a law subsequently withdrawn – while the necessity of some Mexican drug police to conceal their identity at work (against a background of over 30,000 homicides each year since 2018; Al Jazeera, 2022) has created an army of Darth Vaders. In a world with blanket facial recognition capability but no faces left to recognize, the police will need something else, and there are many more things yet to be captured and calibrated. One thing we can be sure of is that state surveillance of the future will not be about face alone. It will be about gait, veins, heartbeat, brainwaves and even breath (*Times*, 2025c) – what I have labelled *zoemetrics*: the comparative measurement of every manifestation of life.

Whether it relies on state security apparatus, the aggregated data feeds of the citizen or a hybrid model, the global impact of AI-driven surveillance in the future will ultimately depend on balancing three things: the technological (what can be done), the legal (what must/must not be done) and the societal (what people will support/expect to be done). That may or may not mean fewer police surveillance cameras, but understanding, framing and regulating the future surveillance landscape will need a wholly different analysis and solution architecture from anything in the past.

Notes

1 https://www.police.nsw.gov.au/safety_and_prevention/policing_in_the_community/blulink
2 www.life360.com/en-gb
3 See s.60AA of the Criminal Justice and Public Order Act 1994.

References

Al Jazeera. (2022, March 26). *Officials killed in one Mexican state up by 300 percent* [Video]. YouTube. www.youtube.com/watch?v=ous9onmOltg

Bandara, P. (2025, August 14). These cities have the most surveillance cameras in the world. *PetaPixel*. https://petapixel.com/2025/08/14/these-cities-have-the-most-surveillance-cameras-in-the-world/

Bandura, I. (2024, April 17). AI is making smart devices – watches, speakers, doorbells – easier to hack. Here's how to stay safe. *The Conversation*.

Benton, C. (2025, January 1). Woman missing for 52 years found alive and well. *BBC News*. www.bbc.co.uk/news/articles/cwyxm7wrk8mo#:~:text=Woman%20missing%20for%2052%20years%20found%20alive%20and%20well&text=Det%20Sgt%20Jenna%20Shaw%20from,find%20a%20photo%20of%20Sheila"

Borak, M. (2025, August 22). Harvard duo behind facial recognition glasses launching always-on speech recording. *Biometric Update*. www.biometricupdate.com/202508/harvard-duo-behind-facial-recognition-glasses-launching-always-on-speech-recording

Bowman, M. W. (2020, March 27). People are contributing unprecedented computing power to fight coronavirus. *Vice*.

BRC. (2025, January 30). *Retail crime 'spiralling out of control'*. https://brc.org.uk/news-and-events/news/corporate-affairs/2025/ungated/retail-crime-spiralling-out-of-control/

Brunet, R. (2020, November 21). French bill banning images of police sparks concern over media freedom. *France 24*.

Buccieri, S-M. (2025, January 23). Doorbell cameras: Peace of mind or paranoia? *BBC News*. www.bbc.co.uk/news/articles/clyzrrrrz3qo

Burt, C. (2025, August 7). Clandestine facial recognition search of civil databases by UK police surge. *Biometric Update*. www.biometricupdate.com/202508/clandestine-facial-recognition-searches-of-civil-databases-by-uk-police-surge

Campbell v. Mirror Group Newspapers Ltd, UKHL 22, 2 AC 457 (2004).

Chen, R., de Melo, S. N., Lan. M., Li, Y., Jiang, S., & Xu, Y. (2025, April 3). "Less is more": How effective is the joint effect on CCTV crime reduction? *Cities*, *162*.

Das, S. (2024, January 27). Facial recognition cameras in supermarkets targeted at poor areas in England. *The Guardian*.

Garrigos-Simon, F. J., & Narangajavana-Kaosiri, Y. (2024). Crowdsourcing: A systematic literature review and future research agenda. *European Journal of Studies in Management and Business*, *30*, 1–6.

Gershgorn, D. (2021, March 2). China's 'sharp eyes' program aims to surveil 100% of public space. *OneZero, Medium*. https://onezero.medium.com/chinas-sharp-eyes-program-aims-to-surveil-100-of-public-space-ddc22d63e015

Gordon, R. J. (2016). *The rise and fall of American growth*. Princeton University Press.

Gov.uk. (2021, November 22). *Update to Surveillance Camera Code of Practice*. www.gov.uk/government/publications/update-to-surveillance-camera-code

Greenall, R. (2024, December 18). Google Street View image helps police unlock murder case. *BBC News*. www.bbc.co.uk/news/articles/clyxdxrm339o

Hafiz, A. (2023, February 27). More CCTC, more crime: India's most-surveilled cities are the least safe. *Rest of World*. https://restofworld.org/2023/cctv-crime-surveillance-india/
Hamilton, F., & Gardham, D. (2025, May 19). Britain needs anti-subversion laws to save democracy from itself. *Times*.
Harcourt, B. (2015). *Exposed: Desire and disobedience in the digital age*. Harvard University Press.
Karpa, D., & Rochlitz, M. (2024). Authoritarian surveillance and public support for digital governance solutions. *Comparative Political Studies*, *58*(10), 2237–2265.
Kleinman, Z., & McMahon, L. (2025, March 12). Secret hearing on Friday in Apple and UK government data row. *BBC News*. www.bbc.co.uk/news/articles/c798xv5qwylo
Larson, R., & Larson, E. (2009). *Top five causes of scope creep ... and what to do about them*. Paper presented at PMI® Global Congress 2009—North America, Orlando, FL. Project Management Institute.
Laterza, V. (2021). Human-technology relations in an age of surveillance capitalism – Towards an anthropological theory of the dialectic between analogue and digital humanity. *EtnoAntropologia*, *9*(2), 59–74.
Law Enforcement Resources. (n.d.). Next Generation Identification (NGI). https://le.fbi.gov/science-and-lab/biometrics-and-fingerprints/biometrics/next-generation-identification-ngi
Liang, L-H. (2024, December 4). Facial recognition search engine claims 50K new photos of missing people. *BiometicUpdate*. www.biometricupdate.com/202412/facial-recognition-search-engine-claims-50k-new-photos-of-missing-people
Lyon, D. (2017). Surveillance culture: Engagement, exposure, and ethics in digital modernity. *The International Journal of Communication*, *11*(2017), 824–842.
Ma, P., Garg, S., & Barika, M. (2024). Research allocation in mobile volunteer computing system: Taxonomy, challenges and future work. *Future Generation Computer Systems*, *154*, 251–265.
Migue, A. (2020, September). BYB telemetry 2.0: cycling telemetry taken to the next level. *Brujulabike*.
Miller, D. et al. (2016). *How the world changed social media*. UCL Press.
Minardi, D. (2020, October 16). The grim fate that could be 'worse than extinction'. *BBC*. www.bbc.co.uk/future/article/20201014-totalitarian-world-in-chains-artificial-intelligence
Murray, A. (2026, February 6). The best GPS trackers and devices for kids you can buy now. *ZDNet*. www.zdnet.com/article/best-gps-trackers-and-devices-for-kids/
Nosta, J. (2023, October 6). The fifth industrial revolution: The dawn of the cognitive age. *Psychology Today*.
Orwell, G. (1949). *Nineteen eighty-four*. Martin Secker & Warburg.
Plaut, M. (2026, May 11). The best GPS dog collars and pet trackers. *Wirecutter*. www.nytimes.com/wirecutter/reviews/best-gps-pet-trackers/
Popova, M. (2024). *Unselfing social, the marginalian*. https://www.themarginalian.org/2022/09/10/unselfing-social/
Puiu, T. (2023, January 20). WiFi routers can see people through walls. Here's how it works. *ZME Science*. www.zmescience.com/feature-post/technology-articles/computer-science/wifi-router-sees-people-through-walls/
R v Grimes, CLR 213 (1994).
R v Hewitt and Davis, 95 Cr.App.R 81 (1992).
Reddy, N., Mathews, I., Bhattacharyya, R., Peters, I. M., Buonassisi, T., & Sarma, S. (2019, April 26). Long range battery-less PV-powered RFID tag sensors. *IEEE Internet of Things Journal*.
Reid, C. (2025, August 13). UK judge affirms legality of public-submitted road crime footage in landmark ruling. *Forbes.com*.

Sampson, F. (2016). Whatever you say…the case of the Boston College tapes and how confidentiality agreements cannot put relevant data beyond the reach of criminal investigation in policing. *A Journal of Policy and Practice*, *10*, 222–231, Oxford University Press.

Sampson, F. (2023) Commissioner for the retention and use of biometric material annual report January 2021–March 2022, and surveillance camera commissioner annual report March 2021–March 2022.

Sampson, F., McBride, N., Wright, S., Sweetland, J., & Jones, J. (2024, August 15). The future of CCTV in the UK: Adapting to new technology while maintaining security, privacy and accountability under a new Labour government. *Public Policy exchange.* www.publicpolicyexchange.co.uk/event.php?eventUID=OH15-PPE

Sampson, F. (2025) Policing, AI and the new surveillance relationship. In Y-F. Ng, & M. Groves (Eds), *Automation in governance: Theory, practice and problems* (chapter 4). Bloomsbury.

Schwartz, P. (1996). *The art of the long view: Planning for the future in an uncertain world.* Bantam Dell.

Singh, R., & Gill, S. (2023). Edge AI: a survey. *The Internet of Things and Cyber-Physical Systems*, *3*, 71–92.

Sontag, S. (1979). *On photography*. Penguin.

Times. (2025a, August 13). *Scientists develop 'superpower' glasses that can read lips.* www.thetimes.com/uk/scotland/article/ai-glasses-that-can-lip-read-for-deaf-people-zx5cwh2rj

Times. (2025b, May 16). *Senior police officer would bring in facial recognition tech 'tomorrow'*. www.thetimes.com/uk/scotland/article/police-scotland-steve-johnson-live-facial-recognition-v5rhhkl57

Times. (2025c, June 12). *How you breath is as unique as your fingerprint, study finds.* www.thetimes.com/uk/science/article/how-you-breathe-is-as-unique-as-your-fingerprint-study-finds-kbp9722fb

Tokarczuk, O. (2019, December 7). Nobel Lecture in Literature, Stockholm.

Wang Chao. (2018, June 25). Interview with Yang Qiang. *UNESCO Courier*.

Yorke, H., & Wheeler, C. (2025, May 18). Home guard to protect UK from attack. *Times*.

YouGov. (2025, May 7). *When politics meet the checkout: How Shopper Activism is shaping FMCG in Europe*. https://yougov.com/articles/52089-when-politics-meet-the-checkout-how-shopper-activism-is-shaping-fmcg-in-europe

Zuboff, S. (2019). Surveillance capitalism and the challenge of collective action. *New Labor Forum*, *28*(1), 10–29. The Murphy Institute, University of New York.

17

CO-CREATION IN PREDICTIVE POLICING

Cross-Stakeholder Collaboration and Community Engagement

Maria Lungu

Introduction

Predictive policing uses data analytics and machine learning to analyze historical crime patterns and forecast where crimes are likely to occur or who might be involved (Perry et al., 2013; Lungu, 2025). Law enforcement agencies have adopted these tools to improve public safety and target resources more precisely, typically alongside problem-oriented and intelligence-led policing rather than as a replacement for them (Meijer & Wessels, 2019; National Institute of Justice, 2014; Ratcliffe, 2004). Proponents contend that this targeting can lower crime rates and make patrol allocation more efficient (Mohler et al., 2015; Ratcliffe, 2004). Those performance claims, however, remain contested, context-dependent, and uneven across jurisdictions (Degeling & Berendt, 2018).

Much of the existing research frames predictive policing as a technical system requiring improved data inputs or refined bias-mitigation techniques, thereby neglecting how these systems operate within broader socio-technical ecosystems (Degeling & Berendt, 2018; Leese, 2021; Lee et al., 2024; Mugari & Obioha, 2021). This technocentric framing narrows the scope of analysis, shifting attention away from governance decisions, such as who defines the problem the system is designed to solve and how success is evaluated. As a result, the structural sources of community mistrust surrounding predictive policing remain insufficiently examined.

This chapter approaches predictive policing as a form of governance. That shift changes what questions matter. Instead of asking whether a model is accurate, we can ask questions about who decided the model was needed, who defined the problem it solves, and who gets to say whether it worked. These are

DOI: 10.4324/9781003671312-17

not solely technical questions, and they rarely have clean answers. This chapter develops a framework for co-creating predictive policing structures with community members, focusing on where engagement occurs and where it stalls. The point is less to offer a blueprint than to map the terrain that any honest attempt at community involvement has to cross. This connects theoretical debates about democratic governance to the practical realities of policing.

Theories of community engagement emphasize participatory decision-making and accountability as foundations for trust between police and the public (Eversole, 2011; Williams, 2005). Community-police research also highlights the importance of trust and reciprocity, but few studies evaluate whether predictive policing can strengthen or erode these relationships (Alikhademi et al., 2022; Egbert & Leese, 2021). This gap motivates a shift toward socio-technical frameworks attentive to both data and democracy.

Procedural justice research has some consistent findings, including that people judge the police less by whether they were treated fairly and had a chance to be heard (Tyler & Fagan, 2008; Tyler, 2025; Williams, 2005). That finding matters here because predictive systems move enforcement decisions into a process most people never see. When the basis for a police stop sits inside a model the public cannot inspect, the sense of fair treatment that procedural justice depends on has little to hold onto.

This chapter examines the literature across three domains. Those domains are the technological foundations, sociopolitical implications, and community engagement. The chapter is structured, first, with a background on predictive policing and community engagement in policing. A classification of existing techno-sociological and community-centric perspectives follows this. The chapter then presents a proposed framework.

Predictive Policing Review

Defining Predictive Policing

Definitions of predictive policing have shifted as data capabilities and analytical tools have advanced, and the literature has worked to keep pace (Lee et al., 2024; Meijer & Wessels, 2019). Predictive policing is "any policing strategy or tactic that develops and uses information and advanced analysis to inform forward-thinking crime prevention" (Uchida, 2010, p. 1). Early conceptualizations emphasized data as the foundation of prediction, describing tools that drew on "data from different sources" (Pearsall, 2010, p. 19) and "a broad variety of sorts of data" (Meijer & Wessels, 2019, p. 1035). The focus highlighted the integration of diverse data streams for prediction.

As predictive technologies matured, scholarly definitions shifted focus from data availability to the analytical processes applied to that data. Accordingly, definitions of predictive policing began to focus on the "application of analytical techniques, particularly quantitative techniques, to identify targets for police intervention and prevent crime or solve past crimes by making statistical predictions" (Perry et al., 2013, p. 1). Terms such as algorithmic technologies and advanced analytics (Egbert & Krasmann, 2020; Sandhu & Fussey, 2021) became more common in definitions, reflecting a focus on quantitative algorithmic techniques to generate actionable insights.

Federal agencies also adopted this framing, defining predictive policing as "harnessing the power of information, geospatial technologies, and evidence-based intervention models to reduce crime and improve public safety" (National Institute of Justice, 2014, p. 4). Despite this variation, the definitions share a common thread. Predictive policing uses computational tools to make policing more efficient, sharpen resource allocation, and intervene before crime occurs (Ariel et al., 2023; Lungu, 2024). Scholars similarly converge on the purpose of predictive policing as the generation of forecasts about "people and places deemed [likely] to be involved in or experience crime" (Sandhu & Fussey, 2021, p. 66) to inform tactical field deployment and strategic planning (Brantingham et al., 2018). That premise is what later debates over fairness and societal impact take up and contest.

Conflicts Between Traditional Techniques and Predictive Tools

Traditional patrolling and algorithmically informed deployment rest on different logics, and the contrast is clearest in how each allocates officers across space. Police patrolling traditionally relies on officers circulating through areas believed to be crime-prone (Weisburd & Eck, 2004). However, empirical studies assessing its effectiveness remain mixed (Braga, 2005; Farrington & Welsh, 2005).

To understand why patrol outcomes vary, it is necessary to clarify the concept of crime risk. Crime risk refers to the probability of criminal events occurring at specific locations and times, influenced by environmental conditions, routine activities, target availability, offender motivation, and levels of guardianship (Mugari & Obioha, 2021). Critically, crime risk is not evenly distributed across urban space. Weisburd's (2015) findings show that approximately 50% of crime in most cities occurs at just 5% of street segments, while another 20–40% of the geography experiences little to no crime. Similar patterns are observed temporally, with crime clustering around repeat-victimization cycles and short-term flare-ups (Johnson et al., 2007).

Given this uneven distribution, random police patrols frequently have minimal measurable impact, as they allocate officer resources to areas with little or no underlying crime risk (Johnson et al., 2007; Sherman et al., 1989). This insight informs the rationale behind algorithmic hotspotting and predictive policing models, which aim to identify the specific micro-places and time windows where the probability of crime is most concentrated.

Real-world applications of these tools reveal limitations and unintended consequences (Perry et al., 2013). Predictive policing is still in its early stages, and its effectiveness remains uncertain; however, it has garnered significant interest from both governments and the public (Lungu, 2025). Contradictions between projected potential and observed outcomes have intensified debate. For instance, Geolitica (formerly PredPol), a prominent predictive policing tool, demonstrated a success rate of less than 0.5% in predicting crime types and locations in an analysis of over 23,000 predictions for the Plainfield Police Department (Perry et al., 2013). Such findings raise questions about the reliability of these tools and their potential to misguide resource allocation. Opponents of predictive policing argue that these qualities must be weighed against ethical concerns, technological biases, and greater transparency in implementation (Head, 2007; Perry et al., 2013). This tension, between innovation and public risk, frames the central debate explored in this chapter.

Crime Concentration

A foundational principle in contemporary criminology is the *Law of Crime Concentration* (Weisburd, 2015), which holds that crime is not randomly distributed across urban environments but rather clusters tightly within a small proportion of spatial units. Weisburd (2015) argues that this concentration is consistent across cities of varying sizes, demographics, and governance systems. Specifically, evidence indicates that a small number of street segments (typically 3–6%) account for 50% or more of recorded crime (Sherman et al., 1989), while the majority of urban space experiences little to no persistent criminal activity (Weisburd, 2015).

Across a 16-year study in Seattle, Weisburd et al. (2004) found that the same micro-places continued to generate disproportionately high crime levels, suggesting that chronic hotspots are stable features of urban life rather than temporary anomalies. Similar findings in Los Angeles, Minneapolis, and London corroborate the idea that places, not broad neighborhoods, are the most accurate units for crime analysis (Braga, 2005).

Understanding crime concentration reshapes how police agencies conceptualize crime risk. Instead of viewing crime as a diffuse neighborhood attribute, this perspective situates risk at micro-locations, such as street corners, business fronts, housing complexes, and transit stops, where routine activity patterns converge. The implication is strategic; interventions targeted at a small set of high-risk areas can yield disproportionate reductions in crime, especially compared with generalized patrols or city-wide resource distribution. This is where hotspotting is considered.

Hotspotting

Hotspotting emerged from problem-oriented policing, which identified recurring crime problems at specific places rather than focusing solely on individual offenders (Goldstein, 1990). Building on this place-based logic, hotspotting is a common estimating technique that utilizes several algorithmic approaches to assess crime risk in areas with disproportionately high crime rates (Bowers et al., 2004; Braga, 2005; Braga & Bond, 2008; Chainey & Ratcliffe, 2013).

Multivariate crime hotspot models incorporate fixed environmental factors such as population demographics (Wang & Brown, 2012), socioeconomic status (Liu & Brown, 2003), and proximity to crime attractors (Kennedy et al., 2011). Combined with crime incident data, these fixed variables help identify persistent, long-term crime patterns by minimizing variance. However, this approach raises an important sociological concern. When specific geographic or demographic characteristics are treated as stable predictors of crime, hotspotting models can inadvertently reproduce forms of geographical or social determinism, in which neighborhoods or populations are defined by their statistical risk profile rather than by dynamic social conditions (Ariel et al., 2023).

Dynamic hotspot mapping focuses on short-term patterns such as repeat victimization (Bowers et al., 2004). These models employ kernel density estimation applied to sliding time windows spanning several weeks, emphasizing temporal volatility rather than stable structural features. Newer hotspotting models have introduced the epidemic-type aftershock sequence (ETAS) model (Mohler et al., 2015), which integrates long-term, fixed environmental risks with dynamic, short-term near-repeat risks. This method is similar to ETAS models used in seismology (Marsan & Lengline, 2008), where a stationary point process captures stable environmental risks, and a short-term triggering kernel accounts for temporal fluctuations. The model uses an expectation-maximization algorithm to estimate both components simultaneously, providing a nuanced approach to predicting crime patterns (Mohler et al., 2015). Municipal applications suggest hotspotting reduces crime not only within targeted areas but also nearby via diffusion of benefits (Bowers et al., 2004), with minimal displacement (Weisburd et al., 2004).

Hotspot policing directs significant resources to areas with high crime rates based on unevenly distributed patterns (Sherman & Weisburd, 1995). This approach reduces crime in the targeted areas and extends its impact to nearby locations through diffusion of benefits (Bowers et al., 2004). Research suggests that the movement of offenders to other areas, referred to as displacement, is only partial in theory and in practice (Weisburd et al., 2004; Ratcliffe et al., 2011).

Research also suggests that the relationship between patrol presence and crime reduction is not linear or deterministic. Koper's (1995) seminal formulation of the "Koper Curve" posits that crime deterrence in hotspots is optimized when officers remain visibly present for approximately 10 to 15 minutes, after which marginal returns diminish. This insight complicates assumptions that longer or more intensive patrols necessarily yield greater crime reductions. For example, the 'Philadelphia Foot Patrol Experiment' consisted of hotspot patrolling for 16 hours a day, five days a week, using newly trained recruits (Ratcliffe et al., 2011). This initiative led to a 23% reduction in crime in treatment areas compared to controlled areas. However, the study noted that it was unclear whether similar results could be achieved with less concentrated patrols (Ratcliffe et al., 2011).

Sherman and Weisburd (1995) previously tested another strategy that assigned small geographic clusters of officers to conduct three-hour daily patrols in high-crime areas. Despite challenges in sustaining this approach, their study found significant reductions in calls for service and disorder. Sustaining such labor-intensive patrols is difficult. The United States allocates substantial funding to policing, often for high-cost tactical equipment, vehicles, and surveillance tools, yet many departments face staffing and patrol labor constraints (Lee et al., 2024; Lungu et al., 2024). This suggests a structural tension in which capital investments may be prioritized over personnel capacity, creating environments in which longer, labor-intensive patrols are challenging to maintain, even when empirically shown to reduce crime (Kennedy et al., 2011).

Race and Predictive Policing

A central concern in comparing traditional and algorithmic techniques is that both can perpetuate bias, particularly along racial lines (Brunson, 2007). While predictive policing is often presented as a data-driven approach to crime prevention, critics argue that it can reinforce existing disparities by relying on historical crime data that disproportionately target marginalized communities (Ariel et al., 2023). The nexus of race and predictive policing has garnered increasing scrutiny, especially given research highlighting racial disparities in traditional policing practices (Brantingham et al., 2018; Lungu, 2025).

Contemporary studies have shown racial bias in aspects of law enforcement, including vehicle stops (Ariel et al., 2023; Lee et al., 2024; Tyler, 2025), pedestrian stops (Gelman et al., 2007), traffic ticketing (Dunn, 2009), drug enforcement and arrests (Lynch et al., 2013), and use of force (Nix et al., 2017). While the mechanisms that underpin these racial disparities, such as racial profiling, stereotyping, cognitive bias, differential deployment, or racial animus, are complex and challenging to separate, these racial disparities in policing are well-documented.

The assumption that predictive policing is inherently neutral has often been challenged by evidence suggesting that these systems reinforce pre-existing racial disparities in policing outcomes (Lee et al., 2024). Critics argue that predictive algorithms, while ostensibly objective, are trained on historical crime data that disproportionately reflects policing practices in communities of color. As a result, these systems risk directing heightened police presence to areas historically over-policed, creating a self-reinforcing cycle of racialized law enforcement (Ariel et al., 2023). Some scholars argue that predictive tools should be trained on victim-reported data rather than on arrest data, thereby reducing discretionary profiling (Mohler et al., 2015).

Place-based crime forecasting is particularly vulnerable to racial amplification (Lee et al., 2024; Lungu, 2025). While crime-focused, these models inherit biases from prior policing patterns. Police dispatched to predictive hotspots are more likely to encounter and engage with residents in those areas, increasing the likelihood of discretionary stops and surveillance of racial minorities (Brunson, 2007). Collaborative governance can moderate these risks by involving community representatives in defining hotspot boundaries, setting operational limits, and monitoring outcomes. If systemic biases remain unaddressed within police culture or broader social structures, co-creation may only partially mitigate racial disparities rather than eliminate them.

Community Engagement in Policing

Historical Evolution of Community-Oriented Policing

According to Blair et al. (2021), societies can effectively reduce crime and improve security by focusing on the relationship between police and the communities they serve. Modern policing, introduced in the early 1800s, was designed to prevent crime, yet it simultaneously produced new challenges, most notably the potential for coercive power to be misused (Eck, 2018). Over time, various non-technological policing strategies, such as stop-and-frisk, saturation policing, and militarized patrol units, have not only eroded public trust but also demonstrated limited effectiveness in achieving sustained crime reduction (Skogan, 2008; Skogan et al., 2000).

One approach to rebuilding trust is community policing, which encourages direct collaboration between law enforcement and the community. The Chicago Alternative Policing Strategy, introduced in the 1990s, demonstrated that this model could reduce crime rates and police–community relations, leading to its adoption in many countries worldwide (Skogan et al., 2000). However, the effectiveness of community policing is highly context-dependent, influenced by factors such as local governance and accountability (Lungu, 2025). To better understand its impact beyond Western contexts, a multisite randomized trial conducted in six sites of the Global South assessed whether community policing reduces crime and fosters trust in these regions (Blair et al., 2021). Variability in implementation, ranging from differences in police training to levels of community participation, makes it challenging to draw universal conclusions about its success, but issues related to trust and transparency must be considered.

Principles of Trust and Transparency in Community Policing

Algorithmic systems shift how police produce knowledge. Decisions that were once rooted in local relationships and officer discretion are now influenced by data processing at a scale, speed, and complexity that individuals alone cannot replicate (Brantingham et al., 2018). A data-driven environment may reduce the role of human judgment, potentially alienating residents who feel seen only as data points rather than as partners in safety (Lee et al., 2024). The issue is whether communities feel protected, respected, and included in how these predictive tools are used and how legitimacy is measured or observed.

Distrust between law enforcement and African American communities is long-standing and well-documented (Brunson, 2007). Research suggests that both direct encounters and vicarious experiences of shared narratives of police misconduct contribute to diminished trust and negative perceptions of law enforcement (Sampson & Bartusch, 1998). This strained relationship has been exacerbated by high-profile police interactions involving Black people, such as George Floyd in Minneapolis, Breonna Taylor in Louisville, and Jacob Blake in Kenosha. Regardless of officer race, African Americans continue to exhibit low trust levels in the police, highlighting systemic concerns rather than individual officer concerns (Brunson & Gau, 2015).

These incidents have reinforced deep-seated skepticism toward law enforcement in communities of color. Fine et al. (2022) examine how adolescents form attitudes toward police through vicarious experience, arguing that people develop their views of police early, often without direct interaction. As Warren (2011) argues, vicarious experiences (stories and narratives of police misconduct shared within social networks) contribute to a broader culture of distrust, further diminishing perceptions of police legitimacy. Additionally, direct firsthand experiences with law enforcement shape public attitudes, with negative encounters disproportionately affecting minority communities (Brunson & Gau, 2015).

Given this crisis of legitimacy, scholars and policymakers have called for police reforms emphasizing procedural justice and legitimacy-building measures (Tyler & Fagan, 2008). The Black Lives Matter movement has intensified calls for structural changes, leading to renewed interest in community-centered approaches to policing. In response to widespread protests and civil unrest following fatal police encounters in Ferguson, Baltimore, and Dallas, President Obama issued an executive order on December 18, 2014, establishing the Task Force on 21st Century Policing (President's Task Force on 21st Century Policing, 2015). This task force identified six key pillars for improving police–community relations: (1) building trust and legitimacy, (2) policy and oversight, (3) technology and social media, (4) community policing and crime reduction, (5) training and education, and (6) officer wellness and safety.

Focusing on pillar four, community policing has become a widely embraced reform strategy for strengthening relationships between law enforcement and local communities through sustained engagement and partnerships (Diphoorn & van Stapele, 2021; Eversole, 2011; Head, 2007). This approach rests on the idea that trust and cooperation grow when communities are treated as active partners rather than passive recipients of policing (Tyler & Fagan, 2008). Evidence suggests that community policing cannot succeed in isolation; its promise depends on meaningful accountability and broader institutional reforms that address structural inequities embedded in policing practices.

Community Engagement in Contemporary Policing

Community policing varies significantly in scope and effectiveness across different regions. One of the main objectives of police reform initiatives is to reestablish confidence in the police and create trusting relationships (Diphoorn & van Stapele, 2021). To achieve this, community policing programs are regularly applied globally, with significant variation in scope, practice, and success.

Two cases illustrate both the promise and the fragility of community policing outside Western contexts. In Kenya, community policing has transformed the state police toward a people-centered approach, aligning with the broader goals of police reform. Over the past several decades, state-driven initiatives and those led by nongovernmental organizations have been introduced to promote community-based security through training programs, partnerships with local leaders, and community policing forums (Diphoorn & van Stapele, 2021). In Colombia, Nilsson and Jonsson (2023) find that, particularly in post-conflict settings, community policing can facilitate short-term cooperation and improve information flows. However, these gains remain unstable in environments marked by ongoing violence and fragmented state authority.

Community policing strategies are sometimes met with pushback from community members and other societal actors (e.g., officers, policymakers, media) (Nillson & Jonsson, 2023). These failures can be attributed to several factors, including the diversity of definitions and practices surrounding community policing (Head, 2007). In some contexts, it is framed as a grassroots, collaborative effort driven by local communities, while in others, it is a top-down, state-imposed model (Diphoorn & van Stapele, 2021). This ambiguity in approach leads to inconsistent implementation, making it challenging to build trust between police and the public when they do not feel that the process is genuinely participatory.

Another significant barrier is the failure to align community policing principles with law enforcement practices. Many officers continue to operate within traditional, hierarchical structures that emphasize control over community engagement (Tyler & Fagan, 2008). As a result, the promise of community policing as a transformative tool for police reform remains unfulfilled, and it is sometimes only symbolic.

Community Framework Development

Co-Creation in Public Administration Literature

Co-creation in public administration has been discussed as a collaborative approach to achieving public value (Khan & Krishnan, 2021). It emphasizes shared decision-making and the joint production of strategies, policies, and outcomes between internal and external stakeholders, guided by principles of open innovation (Khayyat & Bannister, 2017). While co-creation occurs in both the public and private sectors, its application in public governance extends beyond efficiency to considerations of legitimacy, accountability, and citizen-centered service delivery (Dunleavy & Hood, 1994; Lungu, 2024).

Ideally, co-creation enables governments and citizens to jointly shape policy, allocate resources, and design services, positioning communities as active participants rather than passive recipients (Khan & Krishnan, 2021; Khayyat & Bannister, 2017; Nilsson & Jonsson, 2023). Accordingly, participatory governance and open innovation operate as mutually reinforcing mechanisms that enhance e-government inclusivity and responsiveness (Baka, 2017; Lungu, 2024).

Despite the growth of co-creation scholarship, the adoption of predictive policing remains technocratic rather than collaborative. Power asymmetries can constrain meaningful participation when dominant voices in the department or community overshadow marginalized perspectives (Sargsyan & Prox, 2019). Engagement efforts may also fall prey to tokenism, appearing inclusive while lacking genuine influence, thereby reinforcing mistrust rather than building legitimacy (Lungu, 2025; Lee et al., 2024). In some circumstances, co-creation may even produce counterproductive effects, creating confusion over decision-making authority or unrealistic community expectations that cannot be met due to legal or operational constraints (Kearney et al., 2024). These gaps inform the development of a qualitative framework to consider before introducing or reintroducing digital technology into a police agency (Lungu, 2022).

Lack of Inclusive Stakeholder Engagement During Technology Adoption

A central challenge in adopting predictive policing technologies is the lack of inclusive stakeholder engagement (Sargsyan & Prox, 2019). Many agencies introduce these tools without consulting the communities most affected, generating perceptions of intrusion and over-surveillance, particularly in historically marginalized neighborhoods (Kearney et al., 2024; Ariel et al., 2023). Co-creation can mitigate some of these risks, but its feasibility depends on organizational culture and leadership commitment (Khan & Krishnan, 2021). Involving community members in priority setting or reviewing predictive output requires sustained time, training, and institutional buy-in, conditions that are not always present. Without these elements, engagement risks being superficial, performative, or even counterproductive.

In a co-creation model, engagement is proactive rather than reactive. Stakeholder engagement actively involves diverse individuals and groups in decision-making, ensuring that those directly affected by predictive policing technologies have a voice in shaping their implementation (Braga & Bond, 2008; Brantingham et al., 2018). These stakeholders include community leaders, local advocacy organizations, civil rights groups, marginalized communities, and residents who may face the brunt of the surveillance and enforcement policies associated with predictive policing (Kearney et al., 2024). Without such input, the resulting systems are likely to be perceived as intrusive and oppressive, particularly in historically marginalized communities that have been over-policed or subjected to discriminatory practices (Ariel et al., 2023; Bennett Moses & Chan, 2018; Khan & Krishnan, 2021).

Limited Continuous Feedback Loops

Limited continuous feedback mechanisms further constrain co-creation. Predictive policing systems that do not integrate structured, ongoing community input risk reinforcing bias and eroding trust (Alikhademi et al., 2022; Meijer & Wessels, 2019). Feedback loops are essential for ensuring predictive policing systems remain responsive to community needs and concerns.

Feedback channels such as forums, surveys, and advisory boards let residents shape implementation and hold agencies accountable (Akbar et al., 2018; Gigler & Bailur, 2014). Sustaining them is difficult, as staff workloads, competing priorities, and institutional hierarchies limit their effectiveness, and forums without clear decision-making authority or follow-up can heighten frustration rather than build trust. Without functioning feedback, predictive systems risk perpetuating over-policing in already marginalized communities based on historical data (Akbar et al., 2018; Lee et al., 2024). Recognizing these constraints frames co-creation as a deliberate practice that demands attention to organizational resistance and structural inequity.

Table 17.1 outlines the proposed co-creation framework for predictive policing adoption, with examples of how to achieve it.

TABLE 17.1 Community-Centered Framework for Co-Creation in Predictive Policing

Theoretical Foundation	*Standard*	*Co-Creation Actions*
Collaborative governance theory Collaborative governance is rooted in deliberative democracy theories (Ansell & Gash, 2008). Collaborative governance is often associated with intergovernmental and interagency cooperation (Agranoff & McGuire, 2003) and the management of common-pool resources (Ostrom, 1990). This multi-actor perspective illustrates that collaborative governance is not a single type of interaction and operates on a spectrum of cooperative arrangements, each with its own unique mechanisms and challenges (Ostrom, 1990).	**Inclusive stakeholder engagement and co-governance structures**	- Establish a standardized consultation process and framework. - Before deployment, public hearings and feedback sessions with community leaders, civil rights organizations, and residents should be held to gather input, address concerns, and incorporate diverse perspectives in the decision-making process. - Implement community advisory boards for oversight. - Form AI ethics committees with diverse and interdisciplinary representation. - Foster partnerships between law enforcement, academia, and civic organizations.
Public value management Moore (1995) developed the concept of public value management and proposed that public organizations focus on producing value for the citizenry through public interventions that may address societal problems and social needs.	**Transparency and accountability mechanisms**	- Ensure AI decision-making is explainable and accessible to the public. - Mandate regular audits to assess algorithmic fairness and bias. - Develop public reporting mechanisms for oversight and redress. - Conduct longitudinal studies on the impact of predictive policing. - Analyze effects on community trust and policing strategies. - Establish review cycles for policy adjustments based on findings.
Digital era governance Digital-era governance focuses on how digitization transforms public sector public service delivery (Dunleavy et al., 2006). The focus is on structures and systems that assist this change.	**Ethical and standardized implementation**	- Create standardized guidelines for ethical AI use in policing. - Require human oversight in AI-driven decisions. - Establish precise data collection, retention, and consent policies. - Mechanisms for feedback and continuous evaluation are critical to assess the impact of predictive policing technologies on the community and make necessary adjustments based on community input and evolving needs.
Deliberative Democracy Theory Deliberative democracy emphasizes public engagement and informed participatory decision-making (Habermas, 1996). There is a focus on developing administrative structures that incorporate reasoned feedback to promote public engagement (Ackerman & Fishkin, 2004).	**Public perception management**	- Engage in community outreach and public education before securing predictive policing contracts. - Correct misleading media narratives about management decisions, data privacy, data storage, etc. - Publicize and procure regular audits of algorithms within these tools. - Allow interdisciplinary deliberation about developing explainable AI systems.

Conclusion

This chapter shows why community input matters. When police rely on predictive technologies, they make choices that carry real consequences for public safety and civil liberties, and those choices *cannot and should not* rest on technical authority alone (Kearney et al., 2024). Community engagement mechanisms, such as advisory boards, public reporting, and structured feedback processes, provide communities with a way to ask how a model works, who it targets, and whether it is doing what was promised. These mechanisms turn predictive policing from a decision made about a community into one made with it. These processes transform predictive policing from a technical decision into a hopefully democratically accountable choice. Over time, these exchanges can help build community trust by making it clear that policing is shaped through deliberate responsibility.

That shift is where trust is built or lost. A community that can question a system, see how it performs, and press for changes has reason to regard policing as a shared undertaking rather than something done to it. The framework offered here does not resolve the tension between algorithmic efficiency and democratic participation, nor does it pretend that consultation can erase the histories of over policing that shape how these tools are received. What it offers is a way to keep that tension visible and contestable. Predictive policing will continue to spread. Whether it earns public trust depends less on the accuracy of its forecasts than on whether the communities subject to it have a genuine voice in how it is used.

References

Ackerman, B., & Fishkin, J. (2004). *Deliberation day*. New Haven, CT: Yale University Press.

Agranoff, R., & McGuire, M. (2003). *Collaborative public management: New strategies for local governments*. Georgetown University Press.

Akbar, H., Baruch, Y., & Tzokas, N. (2018). Feedback loops are dynamic organizational knowledge-creation processes in the context of the innovations' front-end. *British Journal of Management*, *29*(3), 445–463.

Alikhademi, K., Drobina, E., Prioleau, D., Richardson, B., Purves, D., & Gilbert, J. E. (2022). A review of predictive policing from the perspective of fairness. *Artificial Intelligence and Law*, 1–17.

Ansell, C., & Gash, A. (2008). Collaborative governance in theory and practice. *Journal of Public Administration Research and Theory*, *18*(4), 543–571.

Ariel, B., Sutherland, A., Weisburd, D., Ilan, Y., & Bland, M. (2023). Can the police cool down quality-of-life hotspots? A double-blind national randomized control trial of policing low-harm hotspots. *Policing: A Journal of Policy and Practice*, *17*, paad040.

Baka, V. (2017). Co-creating an open platform at the local governance level: How openness is enacted in Zambia. *Government Information Quarterly*, *34*(1), 140–152.

Bennett Moses, L., & Chan, J. (2018). Algorithmic prediction in policing: Assumptions, evaluation, and accountability. *Policing and Society*, *28*(7), 806–822. https://doi.org/10.1080/10439463.2016.1253695

Blair, G., Weinstein, J. M., Christia, F., Arias, E., Badran, E., Blair, R. A., … & Wilke, A. M. (2021). Community policing does not build citizen trust in police or reduce crime in the Global South. *Science*, *374*(6571), eabd3446.

Bowers, K. J., Johnson, S. D., & Pease, K. (2004). Prospective hot-spotting: the future of crime mapping? *British Journal of Criminology*, *44*(5), 641–658.
Braga, A. A. (2005). Hot spots policing and crime prevention: A systematic review of randomized controlled trials. *Journal of Experimental Criminology*, *1*, 317–342.
Braga, A. A., & Bond, B. J. (2008). Policing crime and disorder hot spots: A randomized controlled trial. *Criminology*, *46*(3), 577–607.
Brantingham, P. J., Valasik, M., & Mohler, G. O. (2018). Does predictive policing lead to biased arrests? Results from a randomized controlled trial. *Statistics and Public Policy*, *5*(1), 1–6.
Brunson, R. K. (2007). "Police don't like black people": African-American young men's accumulated police experiences. *Criminology & Public Policy*, *6*(1), 71–101.
Brunson, R. K., & Gau, J. M. (2015). Officer race versus macro-level context: A test of competing hypotheses about black citizens' experiences with and perceptions of black police officers. *Crime & Delinquency*, *61*(2), 213–242.
Chainey, S., & Ratcliffe, J. (2013). *GIS and crime mapping*. John Wiley & Sons.
Degeling, M., & Berendt, B. (2018). What is wrong about Robocops as consultants? A technology-centric critique of predictive policing. *Ai & Society*, *33*(3), 347–356.
Diphoorn, T., & van Stapele, N. (2021). What is community policing?: Divergent agendas, practices, and experiences of transforming the police in Kenya. *Policing: A Journal of Policy and Practice*, *15*(1), 399–411
Dunleavy, P., & Hood, C. (1994). From old public administration to new public management. *Public Money & Management*, *14*(3), 9–16.
Dunleavy, P., Margetts, H., Bastow, S., & Tinkler, J. (2006). New public management is dead—long live digital-era governance. *Journal of Public Administration Research and Theory*, *16*(3), 467–494.
Dunn, R. A. (2009). Measuring racial disparities in traffic ticketing within large urban jurisdictions. *Public Performance & Management Review*, *32*(4), 537–561.
Eck, K. (2018). The origins of policing institutions: Legacies of colonial insurgency. *Journal of Peace Research*, *55*(2), 147–160.
Egbert, S., & Krasmann, S. (2020). Predictive policing: not yet, but soon preemptive?. *Policing and Society*, *30*(8), 905–919.
Egbert, S., & Leese, M. (2021). *Criminal futures: Predictive policing and everyday police work* (p. 242). Taylor & Francis.
Eversole, R. (2011). Community agency and community engagement: Re-theorizing participation in governance. *Journal of Public Policy*, *31*(1), 51–71.
Farrington, D. P., & Welsh, B. C. (2005). Randomized experiments in criminology: What have we learned in the last two decades? *Journal of Experimental Criminology*, *1*, 9–38.
Fine, A. D., Del Toro, J., & Orosco, C. (2022). Consequences of fearing police: Associations with youths' mental health and felt obligation to obey both the law and school rules. *Journal of Criminal Justice*, *83*, 101934.
Gelman, A., Fagan, J., & Kiss, A. (2007). An analysis of the New York City police department's "stop-and-frisk" policy in the context of claims of racial bias. *Journal of the American Statistical Association*, *102*(479), 813–823.
Gigler, B. S., & Bailur, S. (Eds.). (2014). *Closing the feedback loop: Can technology bridge the accountability gap?* World Bank Publications.
Goldstein, H. (1990). Excellence in problem-oriented policing. *In New York, NY: Police Executive Research Forum*.
Habermas, J. (1996). Between facts and norms: Contributions to a discourse theory of law and democracy (W. Rehg, Trans.). MIT Press. (Original work published 1992)
Head, B. W. (2007). Community engagement: Participation on whose terms? *Australian Journal of Political Science*, *42*(3), 441–454.

Johnson, S. D., Bernasco, W., Bowers, K. J., Elffers, H., Ratcliffe, J., Rengert, G., & Townsley, M. (2007). Space–time patterns of risk: A cross-national assessment of residential burglary victimization. *Journal of Quantitative Criminology*, *23*, 201–219.

Kearney, C., Hron, J., Kosc, H., & Zilka, M. (2024, June). Beyond Use-Cases: A Participatory Approach to Envisioning Data Science in Law Enforcement. In *The 2024 ACM Conference on Fairness, Accountability, and Transparency* (pp. 1809–1826).

Kennedy, L. W., Caplan, J. M., & Piza, E. (2011). Risk clusters, hotspots, and spatial intelligence: Risk terrain modeling as an algorithm for police resource allocation strategies. *Journal of Quantitative Criminology*, *27*, 339–362.

Khan, A., & Krishnan, S. (2021). Citizen engagement in co-creation of e-government services: A process theory view from a meta-synthesis approach. *Internet Research*, *31*(4), 1318–1375.

Khayyat, M., & Bannister, F. (2017). Towards a model for facilitating and enabling co-creation using open government data. *Information Polity*, *22*(4), 211–231.

Koper, C. S. (1995). Just enough police presence: Reducing crime and disorderly behavior by optimizing patrol time in crime hot spots. *Justice Quarterly*, *12*(4), 649–672.

Lee, Y., Bradford, B., & Posch, K. (2024). The effectiveness of big data-driven predictive policing: systematic review. *Justice Evaluation Journal*, *7*(2), 127–160.

Leese, M. (2021). Security as socio-technical practice: Predictive policing and (non-) automation. *Swiss Political Science Review*, *27*(1), 150–157.

Liu, H., & Brown, D. E. (2003). Criminal incident prediction using a point-pattern-based density model. *International Journal of Forecasting*, *19*(4), 603–622.

Lungu, M. (2022). The coding manual for qualitative researchers. *American Journal of Qualitative Research*, *6*(1), 232–237.

Lungu, M. (2024). Artificial intelligence, procurement, and public service delivery: Exploring efficiency, innovation, and designs. *Handbook of Public Service Delivery*, 188–204.

Lungu, M. (2025). *Predictive policing AI is on the rise: Making it accountable to the public could curb its harmful effects*. The Conversation. https://theconversation.com/predictive-policing-ai-is-on-the-rise-making-it-accountable-to-the-public-could-curb-its-harmful-effects-254185

Lungu, M., Atkinson, C., McCue, C., & Saginor, J. (2024). Disparity studies: Isomorphic discrimination? *The Review of Black Political Economy*, *51*(3), 479–502.

Lynch, M., Omori, M., Roussell, A., & Valasik, M. (2013). Policing the 'progressive' city: The racialized geography of drug law enforcement. *Theoretical Criminology*, *17*(3), 335–357.

Marsan, D., & Lengline, O. (2008). Extending earthquakes' reach through cascading. *Science*, *319*(5866), 1076–1079.

Meijer, A., & Wessels, M. (2019). Predictive policing: Review of benefits and drawbacks. *International Journal of Public Administration*, *42*(12), 1031–1039. https://doi.org/10.1080/01900692.2019.1575664

Mohler, G. O., Short, M. B., Malinowski, S., Johnson, M., Tita, G. E., Bertozzi, A. L., & Brantingham, P. J. (2015). Randomized controlled field trials of predictive policing. *Journal of the American Statistical Association*, *110*(512), 1399–1411.

Moore, M. H. (1995). *Creating public value: Strategic management in government*. Harvard University Press.

Mugari, I., & Obioha, E. E. (2021). Predictive policing and crime control in the United States of America and Europe: Trends in a decade of research and the future of predictive policing. *Social Sciences*, *10*(6), 234.

National Institute of Justice. (2014). *Predictive policing*. https://www.nij.gov/topics/law-enforcement/strategies/predictive-policing/Pages/welcome.aspx.

Nilsson, M., & Jonsson, C. (2023). Building relational peace: Police-community relations in post-accord Colombia. *Policing and Society*, *33*(5), 518–536.

Nix, J., Campbell, B. A., Byers, E. H., & Alpert, G. P. (2017). A bird's eye view of civilians killed by police in 2015: Further evidence of implicit bias. *Criminology & Public Policy*, *16*(1), 309–340.
Ostrom, E. (1990). *Governing the commons: The evolution of institutions for collective action*. Cambridge University Press.
Pearsall, B. (2010). Predictive policing: The future of law enforcement. *National Institute of Justice Journal*, *266*(1), 16–19.
Perry, W. L., McInnis, B., Price, C. C., Smith, S. C., & Hollywood, J. S. (2013). *Predictive policing: The role of crime forecasting in law enforcement operations* (RR-233-NIJ). RAND Corporation. https://www.rand.org/pubs/research_reports/RR233.html
President's Task Force on 21st Century Policing. (2015). *Final report of the President's Task Force on 21st Century Policing*. Office of Community Oriented Policing Services.
Ratcliffe, J. H. (2004). The hotspot matrix: A framework for the spatio-temporal targeting of crime reduction. *Police Practice and Research*, *5*(1), 5–23. doi:10.1080/1561426042000191305
Ratcliffe, J. H., Taniguchi, T., Groff, E. R., & Wood, J. D. (2011). The Philadelphia foot patrol experiment: A randomized controlled trial of police patrol effectiveness in violent crime hotspots. *Criminology*, *49*(3), 795–831.
Sandhu, A., & Fussey, P. (2021). The 'uberization of policing'? How police negotiate and operationalise predictive policing technology. *Policing and Society*, *31*(1), 66–81.
Sankin, A., & Mattu, S. (2023, October 2). Predictive policing software terrible at predicting crimes. *The Markup*. https://themarkup.org/prediction-bias/2023/10/02/predictive-policing-software-terrible-at-predicting-crimes
Sampson, R. J., & Bartusch, D. J. (1998). Legal cynicism and (subcultural?) tolerance of deviance: The neighborhood context of racial differences. *Law & Society Review*, *32*(4), 777–804.
Sargsyan, G., & Prox, R. (2019). Augmenting crime predictions with engagement: Synergy of predictive policing and community policing paradigms. *Synergy of Community Policing and Technology: A Comparative Approach*, 31–40.
Sherman, L. W., & Weisburd, D. (1995). General deterrent effects of police patrol in crime? Hot Spots?: A randomized, controlled trial. *Justice Quarterly*, 12, 625–648.
Sherman, L. W., Gartin, P. R., & Buerger, M. E. (1989). HotSpots of predatory crime: Routine activities and the criminology of place. *Criminology*, *27*, 27–56.
Skogan, W. G. (2008). An overview of community policing: Origins, concepts, and implementation. *The Handbook of Knowledge-Based Policing: Current Conceptions and Future Directions*, 43–57.
Skogan, W. G., Steiner, L., DuBois, J., Gudell, J. E., & Fagan, A. (2000). *Taking stock: Community policing in Chicago* (NCJ 189909). U.S. Department of Justice, Office of Justice Programs, National Institute of Justice. https://www.ojp.gov/pdffiles1/nij/189909.pdf
Tyler, T. R. (2025). Legitimacy-based policing. *Criminology & Public Policy*, *24*(2), 165–187.
Tyler, T. R., & Fagan, J. (2008). Legitimacy and cooperation: Why do people help the police fight crime in their communities? *Ohio St. J. Crim. L.*, *6*, 231.
Uchida, C. D. (2010). *A national discussion on predictive policing: Defining our terms and mapping successful implementation strategies*. National Institute of Justice. Justice & Security Strategies, Inc. https://www.ojp.gov/pdffiles1/nij/grants/230404.pdf
Wang, X., & Brown, D. E. (2012). The spatio-temporal modeling for criminal incidents. *Security Informatics*, *1*, 1–17.
Warren, P. Y. (2011). Perceptions of police disrespect during vehicle stops: A race-based analysis. *Crime & Delinquency*, *57*(3), 356–376.

Weisburd, D. (2015). The law of crime concentration and the criminology of place. *Criminology*, *53*(2), 133–157.
Weisburd, D., & Eck, J. E. (2004). What can police do to reduce crime, disorder, and fear? *The Annals of the American Academy of Political and Social Science*, *593*, 42–65.
Weisburd, D., Bushway, S., Lum, C., & Yang, S. M. (2004). Trajectories of crime at places: A longitudinal study of street segments in the city of Seattle. *Criminology*, *42*(2), 283–322.
Williams, C. (2005). Fostering community engagement and tackling undeclared work: The case for an evidence-based 'joined-up' public policy approach. *Regional Studies*, *39*(8), 1145–1155.

18

LARGE LANGUAGE MODEL TECHNOLOGIES IN POLICING

Early Lessons in Artificial Intelligence from Research and Practice

Alexis R. Fabila, Ian T. Adams, and Kyle McLean

The Newest "Revolution"? AI Steps into Policing

The history of policing in the United States (US) is marked by incremental technological advancements. In the mid-1890s, future President Theodore Roosevelt created one of the early bicycle squads as Commissioner of the New York Police Department (NYPD) in an effort to use the latest technology to improve response times for the NYPD. August Vollmer would go on to make Berkeley the first department where every patrol officer was equipped with a bicycle for efficiency (Oliver, 2017). Over the next century, departments incorporated cars, telephones, and two-way radios into routine operations. In 1968, the President's Crime Commission recommended a universal emergency number, and the Federal Communications Commission established the 911 system (Stroshine, 2021). In 1994, CompStat was introduced as a performance management framework intended to reduce crime and sharpen organizational focus through frequent data reporting, managerial accountability, and structured problem solving. It has been described as "perhaps the single most important organizational innovation in policing during the latter half of the 20th century" (United States Bureau of Justice Assistance, 2013, p. 2). It spread quickly. Later developments, including crime mapping, hot-spot policing, and other predictive tools, were promoted as scientific methods for allocating officers more efficiently by highlighting locations where crime was expected to cluster (Stroshine, 2021). Each innovation promised to make policing faster, smarter, or more objective. Each reshaped expectations about what technology could deliver.

By the late-2010s, body-worn cameras had diffused widely, particularly after the President's Task Force on 21st Century Policing endorsed them in 2015

DOI: 10.4324/9781003671312-18

as mechanisms to increase transparency, reduce citizen complaints, and create an ostensibly objective record of police–citizen encounters (Lum et al., 2019; Tregle & McLean, 2021). Across these episodes, technology has been framed as a way to streamline decision-making, lighten administrative burdens, and inject greater objectivity into a domain frequently criticized for opacity. The pattern is remarkably consistent: each generation of technology arrives with bold claims, faces institutional friction, and ultimately reshapes policing in ways its promoters did not anticipate.

Artificial intelligence (AI) now occupies the same rhetorical space. Vendors, police agencies, and many researchers describe AI as the next major advance in police technology (Council on Criminal Justice, 2025), one that can automate paperwork (Adams, 2024), summarize hours of body-worn camera footage (Adams et al., 2025; Watts et al., 2025), and flag potential misconduct for supervisory review (Adams, 2025). Agencies piloting these tools often proceed under the assumption that AI will free officers for more "productive" patrol work by reducing time spent on report writing, transcription, and video review (Axon, 2024). Public discourse reinforces this view, frequently presenting AI as a transformative "revolution" in how policing is organized and delivered.

The evidence to date, however, does not support a simple story of technological acceleration. Axon marketed its Draft One tool with the claim that it could reduce report-writing time by 82 percent. In the first randomized trial to test that claim, it delivered no measurable time savings at all (Adams et al., 2024). Across experiments, agency pilots, and evaluations in adjacent professions, the pattern holds: AI-assisted report writing has not produced the efficiency gains claimed in marketing materials. Officers in Anchorage and other departments report that AI-generated narratives require substantial verification and editing to address omissions, sequencing errors, and factual inaccuracies (Adams et al., 2024; Guariglia, 2025). At the same time, other strands of evidence point to different forms of value. Transcript-based feedback systems like Truleo can shift communication patterns and reduce instances of substandard professionalism when embedded in existing supervisory structures (Adams et al., 2025). Citizens also tend to interpret AI adoption as a signal of modernization and objectivity, increasing public confidence and adoption pressure even when performance gains are modest or absent (Schiff et al., 2023; Senadheera et al., 2024). If AI does not save time, why are departments continuing to adopt it?

The evidence splits along two dimensions of value: efficiency (time and workload) and behaviour and professionalism (how officers interact with citizens and supervisors and how their work is documented and reviewed). The empirical record so far is asymmetric across these dimensions. Efficiency gains are scarce and often illusory, while effects related to behaviour and professionalism are measurable but highly context-dependent and contingent on organizational capacity.

This chapter advances a central claim: while AI is unlikely to revolutionize policing by dramatically increasing administrative efficiency, it can reshape the governance and meaning of police work by altering documentation practices, supervisory review, and feedback structures. That is a more modest claim than vendors have promised. It is also a more defensible one.

The sections that follow use that distinction as an organizing framework. They describe the development of large language models (LLMs) and their integration with body-worn camera systems, review emerging evidence on AI's measurable effects on report writing, examine the gap between perceived and actual performance gains, assess AI's impact on supervision and professionalism, and identify four structural challenges—disruption of established workflows, legal and evidentiary complications, uneven digital literacy, and underdeveloped governance—that constrain effective implementation. These challenges help explain why tools that appear transformative in theory often produce modest, uneven, or contested results in practice.

The Rise of AI in Police Work

"Artificial intelligence" is a term of art encompassing a wide range of tools, but this chapter centers on large language models (LLMs) and related systems that process language: GPT-class models, automated transcription tools, and generators that create, summarize, or categorize text. Although AI applications such as computer vision, video-based analytics, and multimodal systems are under active development in policing, most early deployments and empirical evaluations have focused on language- and text-based tools. These models are trained on mixtures of publicly available data and licensed corpora, and they produce outputs that closely resemble human writing (Leon, 2026; OpenAI, 2023). The technology advanced rapidly. The introduction of the Transformer architecture in 2017 allowed substantial gains in machine text generation and comprehension (Vaswani et al., 2017). Between 2018 and 2025, OpenAI released GPT-1 through GPT-5, with each generation producing more coherent and contextually appropriate text (Brown et al., 2020; OpenAI, 2025; Radford et al., 2018, 2019). These systems were soon formalized as "foundation models," general architectures that could be adapted to a wide range of language tasks (Bommasani et al., 2022).

The public release of ChatGPT in late 2022 marked the point at which LLMs entered mainstream use. Within two months, it had reached 100 million users. Subsequent releases and more capable speech-recognition systems (OpenAI, 2023; Radford et al., 2022) enabled real-time transcription and more accurate text generation at scale. By 2023, products such as Axon's Draft One for narrative generation, Truleo's body-worn camera (BWC) transcript analytics, and a host of other vendor offerings drove the incorporation of LLM-based tools into law enforcement settings. In policing, LLMs currently function as language-processing tools: they convert speech to text, draft and revise reports, and summarize interactions captured in audio or BWC footage. Their appeal lies in the claim that AI can convert raw speech or field notes into standardized, coherent documentation—a task that sits at the core of police work. Crucially, these tools do not forecast crime or identify suspects. They automate the language that surrounds police activity: the reports, the transcripts, the summaries.

The Intuitive Appeal of AI and Efficiency

Policing is a paperwork-heavy occupation. Officers routinely describe documentation as frustrating, repetitive, and time-consuming (Howgrave-Graham, 1943; Seawright, 2012). Against that backdrop, the promise that AI can automate report writing or transcription has obvious appeal (May, 2025). New accounts document this directly (Murphy & O'Brien, 2024): officers in several jurisdictions began using ChatGPT and Microsoft Copilot informally, prior to any official policy, to draft reports, summarize statements, and smooth narrative flow. Officers characterized these tools as "a relief from endless paperwork," reported that AI could generate drafts in "seconds," and claimed that it produced "a better report than I could have ever written, and it was 100% accurate" (p. 1). In these accounts, AI is treated as time-saving technology, even though these perceived gains had not been systematically measured.

This intuitive appeal is not specific to policing. LLMs have become a "behavioral signature" of professional communication, shaping how academics, journalists, and other professionals write (Askitas, 2025). Their output is polished, structurally uniform, and smooth in its transitions. It looks efficient. That appearance matters. Users often mistake this reduction in drafting difficulty for an actual reduction in total work. The same mechanism likely operates in police settings. Officers interpret the smoothness and coherence of AI-generated text as evidence of competence and speed, independent of any demonstrated performance gains.

Whether this perceived ease translates into actual efficiency gains is an empirical question—and one with a surprisingly clear answer. The evidence, drawn from randomized experiments, agency pilots, and evaluations in adjacent professions, points consistently in the same direction. The gains are largely illusory.

LLMs in Report Writing: Evidence vs. Expectations

AI-assisted report writing is not a uniform process across vendors, and differences in system design shape how these tools operate in practice. Systems such as Axon's Draft One generate draft narratives by processing BWC audio and reconstructing events from recorded interactions, while other systems, such as Truleo's "Field Notes" feature, center on officer-recorded voice notes captured in real time and later structured into report narratives, sometimes supplemented by automated transcription of BWC audio (Police1, 2024). These design choices do not imply superior performance for any particular system, and independent evaluations remain limited. However, these differences illustrate that AI-assisted drafting varies meaningfully in how much interpretive work is delegated to the model versus retained by the officer, with implications for accuracy, sequencing errors, and the downstream time required for verification and correction. Vendors promoting dictation-centered approaches often frame these workflows as reducing administrative burden by preserving the officer's narrative voice and limiting the model's need to reconstruct events from footage; however, such claims remain largely untested, and the extent to which they reduce verification demands under operational conditions is not yet known.

Despite strong vendor claims and enthusiasm among officers and supervisors, current evidence shows modest to no efficiency gains from AI-assisted report writing across these different system designs. Randomized trials, agency pilots, and evaluations in adjacent sectors converge on a similar pattern: AI-generated reports often feel easier to produce, yet they do not materially reduce the total time spent on documentation. The explanation is straightforward. LLMs reallocate effort from drafting to verifying, correcting, and reorganizing AI-produced text. That verification work frequently offsets any speed gained during initial draft generation.

Why LLMs Feel Fast Even When They Are Not

The mechanics of LLM-assisted work explain the lack of efficiency gains. Draft generation is fast; verification is not. The work that matters for legal, clinical, and organizational purposes still requires human review. Officers, clinicians, and programmers must check each detail for factual accuracy, policy and legal compliance, and internal coherence (Adams et al., 2024; Becker et al., 2025; Guariglia, 2025; Kupferschmidt et al., 2025).

LLMs also tend to omit critical information. Users often have to reinsert legal elements, clinical findings, technical specifications, or other required details that the model either glosses over or excludes (Adams et al., 2024; Kupferschmidt et al., 2025). In addition, AI-generated narratives may read smoothly in tone yet misorder events, misinterpret causality, or conflate key actors (Adams et al., 2024; Guariglia, 2025; Stanley, 2024). Correcting these issues demands the same substantive expertise as writing the document from scratch, and sometimes more, because users must both reconstruct the underlying facts and unwind AI-introduced errors.

In many settings, including policing, AI automates only a single component of a larger workflow. Narrative generation does not remove the need to complete structured fields for victims, suspects, evidence, property, or other mandatory entries (Adams et al., 2024; Guariglia, 2025). The result is that LLMs reduce the mechanical labour of typing sentences but not the substantive labour of producing correct, complete, and procedurally sound documentation. Across sectors, the pattern is consistent: AI speeds up drafting, not the overall task (Adams et al., 2024; Becker et al., 2025; Kupferschmidt et al., 2025; Senadheera et al., 2024; Vaccaro et al., 2024). Figure 18.1 illustrates this dynamic as a production isoquant: AI moves officers from Point A (high drafting, low verification) to Point B (low drafting, high verification), but both points lie on the same output curve—total effort is unchanged.

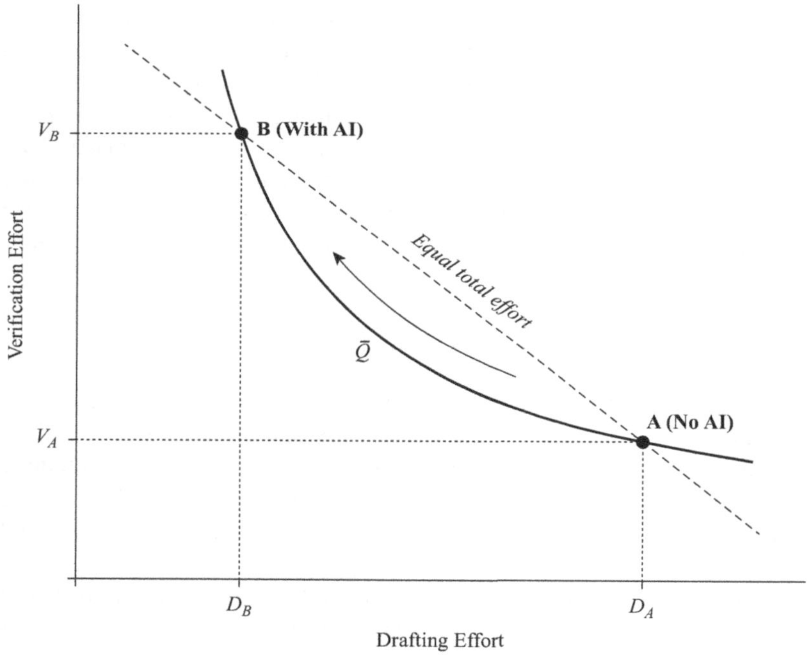

FIGURE 18.1 Report Production Isoquant. AI reallocates effort from drafting to verification without reducing total workload. Point A represents traditional report writing (high drafting, low verification). Point B represents AI-assisted writing with Draft One (low drafting, high verification). Both points lie on the same isoquant ($\bar{Q}$), indicating identical total output cost. The dashed line marks the isocost frontier: because A and B fall on the same line, total effort is unchanged.

Draft One RCT: 82% Promise That Never Arrived

The clearest evidence comes from a randomized controlled trial by Adams et al. (2024), the first study to directly test whether AI assistance reduces police report-writing time. Officers ($n = 85$) were randomly assigned either to business-as-usual report writing or to use Axon's AI-assisted tool "Draft One" (Axon, 2024). Because the agency's records management system captured exact report generation times, the study could measure any time savings with precision. Given random assignment and precise timing data, the estimates can reasonably be interpreted as causal effects of AI assistance on report duration.

Despite the vendor's claim that Draft One would reduce report-writing time by 82 percent, Adams et al. (2024) found no evidence of time savings. None. Officers assigned to use Draft One did not complete reports faster than officers in the control group. Survey responses suggest a plausible mechanism: officers reported spending additional time reviewing, correcting, and restructuring AI-generated narratives. Draft One automates only the narrative portion of the report; officers still must complete structured fields, evidence and property sections, and other mandatory components that the tool does not touch. In addition, AI-generated narratives frequently omitted key facts or introduced timeline inconsistencies that required manual correction, offsetting any speed gained at the initial drafting stage. The authors conclude that Draft One alters the composition of the work (from drafting to reviewing) but does not reduce the total workload. In this sense, a tool marketed as efficiency-enhancing fails to produce measurable time savings under operational conditions.

A similar pattern emerged outside a formal experimental setting when the Anchorage Police Department piloted AI-assisted report writing in 2024–2025. After a three-month trial of generative tools, the department reported no measurable reduction in report-writing time. They stopped using it. Officers described the same basic problems documented by Adams et al. (2024): AI-generated drafts required substantial review, introduced inaccuracies, and often omitted key incident details, which in turn increased the volume of editing (Guariglia, 2025). The Anchorage experience shows that even when agencies experiment on their own terms, outside the structure of a randomized trial, they arrive at a similar conclusion: AI-assisted drafting has not yet delivered the efficiency gains promised in marketing materials.

A qualitative evaluation of Draft One at the Oklahoma City Police Department offers a somewhat more favourable account but reinforces the same underlying dynamics. Brems (2026) interviewed officers who described improvements in report quality and organization, and who perceived reductions in administrative time. However, these perceptions were not verified against time-stamped records, and officers simultaneously reported persistent challenges: ethical concerns about accuracy, policy restrictions limiting which report types could use

AI, and the risk of over-reliance on generated text at the expense of traditional writing skills. Even in a department where officers viewed the tool positively, the need for human oversight, verification, and bias mitigation remained a central theme—consistent with the experimental evidence from other sites.

Lessons from Other Professions

Evidence from other professional domains closely parallels the pattern observed in policing: LLMs often make work feel easier but yield limited, and sometimes negative, effects on efficiency. In a field experiment with experienced software developers, Becker et al. (2025) examined how generative AI tools affected performance. Developers ($n = 16$) completed independent programming tasks ($n = 246$). On average, those using AI assistance were 19 percent slower than those working without it. The core problem was not generation but verification: AI-produced code frequently required debugging, correction, and logic checks, which more than offset the apparent convenience of automated code generation.

Clinical settings show a similar dynamic. In an in-depth qualitative evaluation of AI-assisted clinical documentation, Kupferschmidt et al. (2025) found that physicians spent more time verifying and revising AI-generated notes than drafting them manually. The tools often omitted clinically relevant details or introduced subtle inaccuracies. AI made the writing look better. It did not make the work faster.

The pattern holds at scale. When Vaccaro et al. (2024) aggregated results across more than one hundred studies, human–AI teams performed worse than human workers alone on expert tasks, with an average standardized effect size of $g = -0.23$ (Hedges' g; a small-to-medium negative effect by conventional benchmarks). Efficiency gains, when they appeared at all, were confined largely to simple content-generation tasks.

In government service delivery, where chatbots were adopted in part to speed communication and improve responsiveness, Senadheera et al. (2024) similarly found little evidence of performance improvement and documented substantial organizational costs associated with training, oversight, and technical integration. Across domains, the mechanism is similar: LLMs generate fluent text that looks efficient, but the downstream work of verification, correction, and contextual judgment often cancels any time savings.

The studies reviewed earlier are genuine experiments that found null or negative effects. But they must compete for attention against claims that are not genuine at all. The Toner-Rodgers episode, one of the most widely cited examples of AI "breakthrough hype" in 2024, illustrates the problem. Toner-Rodgers (2024), then a graduate student at MIT, released experimental findings claiming that AI assistance dramatically accelerated scientific discovery among materials scientists ($n = 1{,}018$). The study received substantial media coverage and was quickly cited as evidence that AI was transforming expert work. Some commentators even pointed to it as proof that null findings in policing, such as the Draft One experiment by Adams et al. (2024), were exceptions. Several months later, an investigation at MIT revealed that the paper's data, analyses, and conclusions had been generated entirely by ChatGPT (Massachusetts Institute of Technology, 2025). The datasets were fabricated. The experimental results were invented. The statistical output was machine-produced. The incident illustrates how quickly dramatic claims about AI can diffuse, even when they rest on no empirical foundation, and underscores the need for rigorous, transparent evaluation before treating AI as a genuine performance-improving innovation.

These lessons are particularly consequential for policing, where records, reports, and video are not merely internal organizational artifacts but foundational elements of legal accountability and public trust (Ferguson, 2025). Errors or fabrications in police documentation can directly affect criminal charging decisions, court proceedings, civil liability, and perceptions of legitimacy (Fair and Just Prosecution, 2025; Stanley, 2024). An investigation by the Electronic Frontier Foundation found that Axon's Draft One system appears deliberately designed to resist external audits: it does not retain intermediate drafts, does not disclose model behaviour, and limits the ability of courts or oversight bodies to reconstruct how a final report was produced (Guariglia & Maass, 2025). The Toner-Rodgers episode illustrates how easily fabricated datasets and AI-generated outputs can circulate when technical claims outpace verification. In the policing context, comparable failures, such as AI-generated inaccuracies in incident narratives, use-of-force reports, or BWC documentation, would carry far more serious consequences, inviting legal challenge, undermining evidentiary integrity, and eroding confidence in police institutions (Ferguson, 2025; Stanley, 2024). These risks underscore why lessons from other professions should be treated as warnings with heightened stakes when AI systems are integrated into policing practice. But if AI-assisted report writing produces no measurable time savings, why do officers and supervisors consistently describe it as helpful? That question—the gap between what AI delivers and what users believe it delivers—is the subject of the next section.

The Perception–Performance Gap

Nearly half of the officers who used Draft One reported that it saved them time. Roughly 60 percent of supervisors rated AI-generated narratives as higher quality than officer-written ones. Time-stamped records showed neither was true (Boehme et al., 2025). This disconnect between subjective experience and objective performance—a perception–performance gap—is one of the central dynamics shaping early AI adoption in policing. Understanding why officers perceive efficiency gains in the absence of measurable time savings helps clarify both diffusion and institutional enthusiasm.

Imagined AI vs. Actual AI: What Officers Thought Before Tools Existed

Officers' attitudes toward AI in policing formed before the technology existed. In one of the earliest studies focused on perceptions rather than usage, Adams (2025) fielded an experimental vignette survey to assess how patrol officers would respond to hypothetical BWC systems capable of automated detection, flagging, and transcription. Because such tools were not yet deployed, officers anticipated a range of risks: AI might misinterpret their behaviour, flag routine actions as problematic, or be used punitively in performance evaluations. Many respondents expressed concerns about reduced discretion, heightened oversight, and the prospect that automated systems would "get things wrong" in ways that harmed them. Taken at face value, these expectations suggested that officers would strongly resist AI once it appeared.

When real systems became available, reactions were more muted. Watts et al. (2024) studied baseline attitudes among officers in two Arizona agencies participating in a multi-site randomized trial of Truleo's automated BWC transcript analysis. Contrary to the anticipated resistance in Adams (2025), officers with direct experience described these systems as modest administrative aids rather than major threats. Many noted that automated transcript summaries could help them recall interactions or streamline supervisory reviews. The anticipated resistance largely did not materialize. Concerns about fairness and surveillance remained but were less intense, and few officers described the tools as harmful or intrusive. Crucially, officers' views were shaped by the narrow capabilities of early systems, which focused on categorizing and summarizing interactions rather than evaluating conduct or generating recommendations.

Post-deployment surveys confirmed this trajectory. White et al. (2025) found that after five months of using Truleo, officer attitudes remained mostly neutral—neither enthusiastic nor hostile. Importantly, officers reported a better understanding of the system and became less concerned about how the AI platform was being used. They did not believe it had a significant impact on their work performance, yet they accessed it regularly (1.6–1.8 times per week for officers, 3.6–4.6 times per month for supervisors). Together, these studies suggest that ex ante resistance gives way to pragmatic acceptance once officers encounter the limited, non-punitive scope of early tools. That acceptance created space for a different dynamic: optimism about performance improvements that exceeded what objective measures would later show.

AI Feels Faster Because It Feels Easier

Despite records management system (RMS) data showing no reduction in report-writing time, many officers perceived AI assistance as making them faster. The numbers are striking. In follow-up surveys from the Draft One experiment, Boehme et al. (2025) found that 48 percent of officers in the AI condition reported that the tool saved them time, and a majority (54–57 percent) reported that it made reports easier to write. Supervisors shared this view, with roughly 60 percent rating AI-generated narratives as higher quality. Independent evaluations found no systematic differences in accuracy, completeness, or editing workload. The perception was real. The performance gains were not.

These results are consistent with the broader psychological mechanism described by Askitas (2025): polished, fluent AI-generated text reduces perceived mental effort, and users often misinterpret this reduced cognitive load as a genuine productivity gain. Officers experience fewer "blank page" moments, face smoother prose, and encounter fewer immediate drafting decisions, which creates the subjective impression that work has sped up even when total task duration has not changed. In short, AI reduces the difficulty of initiating and structuring a report. It does not reduce the total labour required to complete it.

This pattern is not unique to policing. As the evidence reviewed in "LLMs in Report Writing: Evidence vs. Expectations" suggests, new technologies are repeatedly predicted to revolutionize or even eliminate labour, yet they more often reorganize where effort is concentrated rather than eliminating it altogether. AI-assisted drafting fits this broader pattern: it shifts effort from composing to reviewing rather than removing effort entirely. In policing, longstanding expectations that technology will enhance efficiency (Stroshine, 2021) amplify this dynamic, making officers particularly receptive to tools that promise administrative relief.

Public Support and Diffusion

The perception–performance gap inside agencies is reinforced by generally optimistic public views of AI in government. In a large survey experiment, Schiff et al. (2023) presented more than 4,000 respondents with randomized vignettes describing different AI adoption scenarios, including uses in local police departments for predictive tasks and internal review functions. The design varied three institutional factors: agency level (local versus national), whether AI targeted the public or officers, and whether the agency had the capacity to implement the technology responsibly. Across conditions, respondents consistently expressed greater trust and support when AI was used by local law enforcement and frequently assumed that these systems would make policing more objective, fair, and efficient—regardless of whether the agency had the institutional capacity to implement AI responsibly.

Public expectations are also shaped by how AI-generated documentation interacts with existing records. Anderson et al. (2025) found across two experiments ($n = 1{,}580$) that when BWC footage and officer reports were inconsistent, public trust and perceived accuracy dropped significantly, and charging decisions increased. Participants also preferred that officers write reports *before* reviewing footage, suggesting that the public values independent recollection over AI-mediated reconstruction. These findings reinforce Ferguson's (2025) concern that AI-generated narratives may contaminate officer memory and complicate evidentiary assessments.

These reinforcing beliefs matter because adoption decisions often follow attitudes and reputational incentives rather than performance data. When officers perceive AI as helpful, supervisors view outputs favourably, and citizens assume technological improvement, agencies face strong pressures to adopt tools even when experimental evaluations show little change in completion times (Adams et al., 2024). Research on government technology adoption similarly shows that innovations are frequently embraced for their reputational appeal, allowing agencies to present themselves as modern and technologically sophisticated (Senadheera et al., 2024). Vendor marketing intensifies this effect by promising dramatic efficiency gains that empirical tests have not substantiated.

The result is a self-reinforcing diffusion dynamic: perceptions of improvement circulate more rapidly than evidence about actual performance. This perception–performance gap does not imply that AI lacks value. Rather, it suggests that AI's influence in policing is driven as much by how it reshapes experience, expectations, and institutional signalling as by measurable gains in speed. In short, perception often precedes proof. But if AI does not make documentation faster, does it do anything that matters? The next sections suggest it does—not by saving time, but by changing how officers behave.

Behaviour and Professionalism

After the Truleo randomized trial concluded at the Aurora Police Department, some personnel stated informally that the system "didn't work" (Adams et al., 2025). The trial had, in fact, produced some of the largest reductions in substandard professionalism in the study. But because the tool did not transform workflow or reduce report-writing time, its behavioural effects were easy to discount. That response captures a recurring pattern: agencies evaluate AI through an efficiency lens, and tools that change behaviour but not perceived workload risk being misclassified as failures.

Efficiency gains, as the previous sections have shown, are minimal. But improvements in behaviour and professionalism show more promise.

Beyond Efficiency: What Truleo Teaches Us About Behaviour Change

LLMs have not produced credible efficiency gains in report writing. But there is evidence that AI can produce measurable effects in a different domain: behaviour change through BWC transcript analysis. Systems such as Truleo automatically transcribe BWC audio, classify officer speech, and generate structured feedback on dimensions such as respect, clarity, profanity, explanation, and de-escalation. Rather than promising speed, these tools aim to reshape how officers communicate.

Adams et al. (2025) evaluated this model using two pre-registered randomized controlled trials in large US agencies. Officers were randomly assigned to receive AI-generated feedback directly (self-assessment), via supervisors (supervisor-mediated), or not at all (control). Randomization at the officer level allows the authors to attribute observed differences in professionalism to the feedback conditions rather than to preexisting differences across officers. The trials were conducted in two very different settings—the Aurora Police Department in Colorado and the Richland County Sheriff's Department in South Carolina—to test whether organizational context shapes the impact of AI-driven professionalism interventions.

The results show that AI-assisted feedback can alter behaviour. At Aurora, both treatment groups experienced significant reductions in substandard professionalism, with the largest effects in the supervisor-mediated condition. The feedback changed how officers spoke. At Richland County, officers with direct access to feedback showed higher rates of high professionalism, and the combined impact across treatment groups produced modest but detectable agency-wide improvements. Across both agencies, the evidence indicates that AI-driven transcript analytics can shift communication patterns and reduce problematic behaviours—not by speeding up paperwork, but by supporting coaching, supervision, and professional development. A parallel evaluation of Truleo deployment in two Arizona agencies further supports these findings. White et al. (2025) found that officers integrated the system into routine practice, accessing it 1.6–1.8 times per week, while supervisors used it 3.6–4.6 times per month. Officers' baseline attitudes, which had been mostly neutral prior to deployment (Watts et al., 2024), remained stable after five months of use, suggesting that AI-driven BWC review can be absorbed into daily operations without generating the resistance that early attitudinal surveys had predicted.

Writing Support, Accessibility, and Documentation Quality

Behavioural feedback is not the only domain where AI's value lies outside efficiency. Documentation quality—how clearly and accessibly reports are written—offers a parallel case. In the Draft One experiment, officers frequently reported that AI-generated narratives were more organized, easier to revise, and offered a cleaner starting point than a blank page (Boehme et al., 2025). The primary benefit in these accounts is qualitative: better baseline text rather than faster completion.

Qualitative evidence from the United Kingdom points in the same direction. Walley and Glasspoole-Bird (2025) evaluated an AI-assisted statement-writing pilot in Hertfordshire Constabulary through interviews with officers and supervisors. Officers who struggled with written documentation, particularly those with dyslexia, reported "huge" perceived time savings and described substantial improvements in the quality and readability of their statements. For them, AI was transformative—not because it was faster, but because it was accessible.

At the same time, the Hertfordshire pilot revealed recurring integration problems: inconsistent accuracy, the need for extensive review, and friction in fitting AI tools into existing workflows (Walley & Glasspoole-Bird, 2025).

Taken together, these findings suggest that AI's main contribution to documentation is not administrative acceleration but accessibility and communication quality. AI can help produce more coherent, standardized narratives and can lower barriers for officers who find writing difficult. The underlying administrative burden, however, remains largely intact.

Challenges to Performance Improvement

In Hertfordshire, an AI writing tool meant to help officers draft statements ended up requiring so much editing that some treated it as one more system to manage rather than a replacement for existing processes (Walley & Glasspoole-Bird, 2025). In Anchorage, officers still had to complete structured fields, correct omissions, and verify facts—on top of reviewing the AI's narrative (Guariglia, 2025). These are not stories of technological failure. The tools worked. The organizations were not ready. Even when AI tools perform well in pilots or controlled studies, implementation inside police agencies is constrained by organizational routines, legal requirements, and institutional capacity.

The most visible challenge is workflow disruption. AI tools disrupt documentation workflows more often than they streamline them. Both the Draft One experiment and the Anchorage Police Department pilot showed that AI-assisted report writing did not reduce total documentation time because AI-generated narratives required extensive review and editing on top of existing tasks (Adams et al., 2024; Guariglia, 2025). Officers still had to complete structured fields, evidence and property entries, and other mandatory sections that AI did not touch, while also correcting omissions and inaccuracies in the narrative. In Hertfordshire Constabulary, Walley and Glasspoole-Bird (2025) found that although some officers, particularly those with dyslexia, experienced AI-assisted drafting as helpful, the tool often produced text that required substantial editing, did not integrate cleanly with records systems, and could not be trusted without close oversight. Workflow friction is annoying, but it is also the most tractable of the four challenges discussed here.

The legal complications are harder to resolve. AI-generated reports and BWC outputs are not merely internal records; they are used in court, disciplinary proceedings, and public scrutiny. Murphy and O'Brien (2024) argue that when AI heavily shapes report narratives, it becomes unclear whether the text reflects the officer's words or the model's reconstruction. Stanley (2024) raises related concerns about accuracy and bias, noting that LLMs can misrecognize speech or distort content, particularly in noisy settings or with nonstandard dialects. Once officers review AI-generated narratives, their own recollections may shift toward the model's version, weakening the independence of their memory as evidence (Ferguson, 2025). A prosecutorial analysis reinforces the stakes: Fair and Just Prosecution (2025) argues that AI-generated reports risk introducing systematic inaccuracies into the evidentiary record, with downstream consequences for charging decisions, plea negotiations, and trial outcomes. Transparency compounds the problem. Vendors rarely disclose model behaviour or retain draft histories, which prevents defendants and courts from examining how the final text was produced. Stanley (2024) notes that failing to preserve earlier drafts may conflict with *Brady* disclosure obligations, which require prosecutors to share exculpatory evidence with the defense. These concerns mean that agencies must not only deploy AI systems, but also construct policies, training, and documentation practices that can withstand legal scrutiny and public review.

Harder still is the question of organizational capacity. Uneven digital literacy conditions both adoption and sustainability. Systems such as Truleo do not operate as stand-alone fixes; they depend on supervisors who can interpret feedback, incorporate it into coaching, and maintain follow-up over time (Adams et al., 2025). A survey of 140 Texas police chiefs confirmed this pattern: Tao et al. (2025) found that transformational leadership, adequate budgets, and chiefs' advanced education predicted generative AI engagement, while prior BWC deployment and the mere presence of a formal AI policy did not. The implication is that organizational capacity and leadership vision matter more than prior technology experience or policy frameworks alone. In lower-capacity environments, AI tools may be introduced without adequate training, technical support, or clear responsibility for oversight, which produces inconsistent use, frustration, and abandonment—a pattern documented across both private-sector and government AI adoption (Challapally et al., 2025; Senadheera et al., 2024). Structural constraints such as high turnover, limited IT support, and competing reform priorities add further barriers. Even within a single department, some units may adapt quickly while others struggle, generating uneven implementation (Walley & Glasspoole-Bird, 2025).

The deepest challenge is governance—not because agencies refuse to act, but because the questions have no established owners. The broader governance and accountability framework remains underdeveloped. Many of the issues raised by the use of AI in report writing and BWC analytics (including privacy, data retention, vendor transparency, and error auditing) do not map neatly onto existing records or evidence policies. Agencies often lack the expertise to independently test vendor claims or conduct technical audits, which leaves them reliant on marketing materials and vendor assurances. Senadheera et al. (2024) show that in local government, AI systems are frequently adopted because they signal modernization and responsiveness, rather than on the basis of validated performance. The US Department of Justice has recognized these gaps, releasing a governance framework that calls for structured oversight, validation requirements, and accountability mechanisms for AI use in criminal justice (US Department of Justice, 2024). Civil liberties organizations, such as the American Civil Liberties Union, have raised concerns about the expansion of AI in documentation and surveillance (Stanley, 2024), and an investigation by the Electronic Frontier Foundation found that Axon's Draft One is structured in ways that resist external auditing (Guariglia & Maass, 2025), adding political and normative pressure to an already complex environment. Unresolved governance questions can delay adoption or produce fragmented, underdeveloped policies (Council on Criminal Justice, 2025; Senadheera et al., 2024).

These challenges are not incidental to AI's performance—they define the conditions under which performance is measured. Tools that show clear benefits in randomized trials or targeted pilots may be judged as failures if they disrupt familiar workflows, generate unresolved legal risks, or exceed an agency's capacity to manage them. Some of these barriers will diminish as tools mature, integration improves, and governance frameworks develop. But the central lesson is already clear: AI's value in policing cannot be evaluated apart from the institutions that deploy it. Success depends as much on institutional preparation and oversight as on the technical properties of the AI systems themselves.

Policy and Research Implications

The growing use of AI in policing raises basic questions about how agencies should evaluate, adopt, and regulate these systems. Across the evidence reviewed here, one pattern stands out: AI has not delivered on efficiency promises in report writing; officer and public perceptions are mixed but generally positive; and improvements in officer professionalism, measured through BWC analytics, are real but context-dependent. That is a humbler finding than vendors promised. It is also a more useful one. These results suggest that AI's primary value in policing is not speed, but its effects on behaviour, documentation quality, and organizational learning. At the same time, the challenges outlined in "Challenges to Performance Improvement"—workflow disruption, legal and evidentiary complications, uneven digital literacy, and underdeveloped governance—remain substantial barriers to realizing even these more modest benefits. Policy and research agendas should adjust to that reality.

The first implication is that evaluation criteria must shift. Vendor marketing emphasizes large reductions in workload—Axon's 82 percent claim is the most prominent example—yet experimental and qualitative work shows that

AI-assisted report writing does not reduce officers' total workload and can increase verification demands (Adams et al., 2024; Becker et al., 2025; Guariglia, 2025; Kupferschmidt et al., 2025). Rather than asking whether a tool "saves time," agencies would be better served by asking whether it produces clearer and more consistent documentation, improves supervisory review, or supports communication and professionalism, as in the Truleo randomized trials (Adams et al., 2025). Anchoring adoption decisions in demonstrated performance rather than optimistic expectations can narrow the gap between vendor claims and observed practice.

But better metrics alone are not enough. Institutional readiness determines whether AI tools stick or get abandoned. Systems such as Truleo are most effective when supervisors can interpret and use the feedback they generate, which presupposes stable supervisory structures, sustained training, and adequate analytic support (Adams et al., 2025). Departments with limited IT capacity, high turnover, or fragmented training may struggle to integrate such systems into routine practice (Challapally et al., 2025; Senadheera et al., 2024). Assessing readiness before deployment can help agencies determine not only whether a tool is potentially useful, but also whether they are equipped to sustain its use over time.

Transparency and documentation policies must evolve alongside AI adoption. Concerns raised by Murphy and O'Brien (2024) and Stanley (2024) illustrate how AI-generated records complicate questions of authorship, accuracy, chain of custody, and discoverability. Agencies should adopt clear rules for preserving intermediate drafts, specifying which version constitutes the "official" report, and documenting how AI was used in drafting or review. Without such safeguards, AI-generated records will remain vulnerable in court and in oversight investigations.

Evaluation practice must also grapple with the perception–performance gap. As this chapter has shown, officers often feel AI tools make them faster or more effective even when time-stamped data show no gains (Boehme et al., 2025), and the strong public support for AI in government documented by Schiff et al. (2023) can reinforce these optimistic beliefs. Evaluations that integrate perception-based measures (such as ease of use and acceptance) with objective indicators (such as report-writing duration, professionalism scores, and error rates) provide a more complete account of how these systems function in practice and help distinguish genuine improvements from the appearance of improvement.

Finally, continued investment in rigorous, real-world research is not optional. The Draft One experiment, the Truleo trials, and the broader cross-sector findings reviewed in this chapter demonstrate that transparent, methodologically strong evaluations can separate warranted from unwarranted claims (Adams et al., 2024; Adams et al., 2025; Becker et al., 2025; Kupferschmidt et al., 2025; Vaccaro et al., 2024). Federal governance frameworks have begun to reflect this priority, with the US Department of Justice calling for structured oversight, validation, and accountability mechanisms to guide AI adoption across criminal justice settings (US Department of Justice, 2024). Without such institutional commitments, vendor assurances fill the void. Going forward, randomized controlled trials, quasi-experimental designs, and structured agency–researcher partnerships will be critical for guiding AI policy in policing in a way that is empirically grounded rather than driven by marketing or intuition.

Conclusion: AI as a Mirror, Not a Motor

Axon promised Draft One would cut report-writing time by 82 percent. A randomized trial found the reduction was zero (Adams et al., 2024). The Anchorage Police Department reached the same conclusion independently and discontinued its AI pilot after three months (Guariglia, 2025). Experienced software developers using AI completed tasks 19 percent slower (Becker et al., 2025). Across randomized experiments, field pilots, and studies in adjacent professions, the evidence converges on a single finding: AI-assisted report writing does not reduce workload. The polished, fluent outputs of LLMs create an impression of speed, but time-stamped data show little to no gain in actual performance. The core problem is not that AI "fails," but that its strengths have been misidentified.

The strongest evidence of value comes from tools that support learning, professionalism, and organizational consistency rather than speed. In Aurora, the Truleo randomized trial produced significant reductions in substandard professionalism—yet agency personnel informally dismissed the system because it did not speed up paperwork (Adams et al., 2025). In Hertfordshire, officers with dyslexia described AI-assisted drafting as transformative for their ability to produce coherent statements (Walley & Glasspoole-Bird, 2025). Neither result involved time savings. Both involved making police work better, not faster. These effects are not transformative at scale, but they are real, measurable, and aligned with longstanding goals of improving officer–citizen encounters.

The future of AI in policing will turn less on automation and more on alignment between technical design and institutional context. The appeal of "magic" AI should not license magical thinking. These systems must work within existing legal standards, organizational routines, and supervisory structures. AI tools will not succeed simply because they are novel or widely promoted as markers of innovation. They will only succeed where agencies have the training, capacity, governance, and supervision needed to translate AI outputs into sustained behavioural change.

The chapter's guiding question was whether AI makes policing more efficient or effective, or whether it merely creates the appearance of improvement. The evidence is clear. The AI report-writing and documentation tools evaluated to date have not made police work more efficient. These tools do not reduce documentation time, and feeling faster is not the same as being faster. But AI can make policing more effective in narrower respects—not as a motor that drives transformation on its own, but as a mirror that reflects communication patterns, structures feedback, and supports consistency across interactions.

These claims rest on a small and still-developing evidence base—a handful of agencies, a narrow set of tools (Draft One and Truleo), and research teams with overlapping membership. LLMs are also beginning to reshape the research tools used to study policing itself: Robinson et al. (2026) demonstrate that AI-generated officer profiles can serve as valid, reproducible visual stimuli for experimental criminology, suggesting that the technology's influence extends beyond operations into the methods used to evaluate them. The studies reviewed here reflect early-generation LLM applications; future tools with improved accuracy, tighter integration with records systems, or multimodal capabilities may produce different results. This chapter also does not address AI applications in crime prediction, video analytics, or investigative support, where the dynamics of adoption and effectiveness may differ substantially. The conclusions here are bounded, not universal.

Even so, the direction of the evidence is consistent. If efficiency is treated as the primary metric, AI will continue to disappoint. If, instead, agencies focus on better documentation, clearer communication, and more professional encounters, AI has a plausible role to play. The policy implication is clear in principle, if difficult in practice: use AI where it demonstrably adds value, and resist adopting it where benefits exist only in vendor claims or in the subjective feeling that work has become easier.

References

Adams, I. T. (2024). Large language models and artificial intelligence for police report writing. *CrimRxiv*. https://doi.org/10.21428/cb6ab371.779603ee

Adams, I. T. (2025). Automation and artificial intelligence in police body-worn cameras: Experimental evidence of impact on perceptions of fairness among officers. *Journal of Criminal Justice*, *97*. https://doi.org/10.1016/j.jcrimjus.2025.102373

Adams, I. T., Barter, M., McLean, K., Boehme, H. M., & Geary, I. A. (2024). No man's hand: Artificial intelligence does not improve police report writing speed. *Journal of Experimental Criminology*. https://doi.org/10.1007/s11292-024-09644-7

Adams, I. T., McLean, K., & Alpert, G. P. (2025). Improving police behavior through artificial intelligence: Pre-registered experimental results in two large U.S. agencies. *Criminology*. https://doi.org/10.1111/1745-9125.70028

Anderson, K.-A. S., Jones, K., & Strange, D. (2025). Body-worn camera versus officer reports: How inconsistencies influence public perceptions of trust, accuracy, and punishment. *Applied Cognitive Psychology*, *39*(5). https://doi.org/10.1002/acp.70113

Askitas, N. (2025). *The behavioral signature of GenAI in scientific communication*. IZA Institute of Labor Economics. https://docs.iza.org/dp18062.pdf

Axon. (2024). *Draft one*. https://www.axon.com/products/draft-one

Becker, J., Rush, N., Barnes, B., & Rein, D. (2025). *Measuring the impact of early-2025 AI on experienced open-source developer productivity*. https://doi.org/10.48550/arXiv.2507.09089

Boehme, H. M., Adams, I. T., Barter, M., Geary, I. A., & McLean, K. (2025). Writing at the speed of hype: Officers' post-experimental perceptions of report writing. *Journal of Experimental Criminology*. https://doi.org/10.1007/s11292-025-09679-4

Bommasani, R., Hudson, D. A., Adeli, E., Altman, R., Arora, S., Arx, S. von, Bernstein, M. S., Bohg, J., Bosselut, A., Brunskill, E., et al. (2022). *On the opportunities and risks of foundation models*. https://arxiv.org/abs/2108.07258

Brems, R. (2026). Transforming police reporting with generative AI: Insights from the Oklahoma City Police Department. *The Police Journal*, *99*(1), 86–102. https://doi.org/10.1177/0032258X251346365

Brown, T. B., Mann, B., Ryder, N., Subbiah, M., Kaplan, J., Dhariwal, P., Neelakantan, A., Shyam, P., Sastry, G., Askell, A., et al. (2020). *Language models are few-shot learners*. https://arxiv.org/abs/2005.14165

Challapally, A., Pease, C., Raskar, R., & Chari, P. (2025). *The GenAI divide: State of AI in business 2025*. https://mlq.ai/media/quarterly_decks/v0.1_State_of_AI_in_Business_2025_Report.pdf

Council on Criminal Justice. (2025). *Principles for the use of AI in criminal justice*. https://counciloncj.org/principles-for-the-use-of-ai-in-criminal-justice/

Fair and Just Prosecution. (2025). *AI-generated police reports: High-tech, low accuracy, big risks*. Fair; Just Prosecution. https://fairandjustprosecution.org/wp-content/uploads/2025/06/AI-Generated-Police-Reports-High-Tech-Low-Accuracy-Big-Risks-June-2025.pdf

Ferguson, A. G. (2025). Generative suspicion and the risks of AI-assisted police reports. *Northwestern University Law Review*, *120*(2). https://ssrn.com/abstract=4897632

Guariglia, M. (2025). *Anchorage police department: AI-generated police reports don't save time*. Electronic Frontier Foundation. https://www.eff.org/deeplinks/2025/03/anchorage-police-department-ai-generated-police-reports-dont-save-time

Guariglia, M., & Maass, D. (2025). *Axon's Draft One is designed to defy transparency*. Electronic Frontier Foundation. https://www.eff.org/deeplinks/2025/07/axons-draft-one-designed-defy-transparency

Howgrave-Graham, H. M. (1943). The writing of reports and minutes. *The Police Journal*, *16*(2), 141–148. https://doi.org/10.1177/0032258X4301600209

Kupferschmidt, K. L., O'Doherty, K., & Skorburg, J. A. (2025). *Write on paper, wrong in practice: Why LLMs still struggle with writing clinical notes*. https://doi.org/10.48550/arXiv.2509.04340

Leon, M. (2026). GPT-5 and open-weight large language models: Advances in reasoning, transparency, and control. *Information Systems*, *136*, 102620. https://doi.org/10.1016/j.is.2025.102620

Lum, C., Stolz, M., Koper, C. S., & Scherer, J. A. (2019). Research on body-worn cameras: What we know, what we need to know. *Criminology & Public Policy*, *18*(1), 93–118. https://doi.org/10.1111/1745-9133.12412

Massachusetts Institute of Technology. (2025). *Assuring an accurate research record*. MIT Economics. https://economics.mit.edu/news/assuring-accurate-research-record

May, B. (2025). Are we DrAIfting? The role of large language models in police investigative interviewing. *Investigative Interviewing: Research & Practice*, *15*(1). https://iiirg.org/wp-content/uploads/2025/09/IIRP_20250506_May_Final.pdf

Murphy, S., & O'Brien, M. (2024). *Police officers are starting to use AI chatbots to write crime reports. Will they hold up in court?* The Associated Press. https://www.ap.org/news-highlights/spotlights/2024/police-officers-are-starting-to-use-ai-chatbots-to-write-crime-reports-will-they-hold-up-in-court/

Oliver, W. M. (2017). *August vollmer: The father of american policing*. Carolina Academic Press.

OpenAI. (2023). *GPT-4 technical report*. https://arxiv.org/pdf/2303.08774

OpenAI. (2025). *GPT-5 system card*. https://cdn.openai.com/gpt-5-system-card.pdf

Police1. (2024). *Truleo introduces AI generated police reports powered by Amazon Bedrock*. https://www.police1.com/police-products/police-technology/software/video-analysis/truleo-introduces-ai-generated-police-reports-powered-by-amazon-bedrock

Radford, A., Kim, J. W., Xu, T., Brockman, G., McLeavey, C., & Sutskever, I. (2022). *Robust speech recognition via large-scale weak supervision*. https://doi.org/10.48550/arXiv.2212.04356

Radford, A., Narasimhan, K., Salimans, T., & Sutskever, I. (2018). *Improving language understanding by generative pre-training*. https://www.mikecaptain.com/resources/pdf/GPT-1.pdf

Radford, A., Wu, J., Child, R., Luan, D., Amodei, D., & Sutskever, I. (2019). *Language models are unsupervised multitask learners*. https://cdn.openai.com/better-language-models/language_models_are_unsupervised_multitask_learners.pdf

Robinson, C. G., Adams, I. T., Logan, M. W., & Blair, J. P. (2026). AI-generated human stimuli for experimental social science. *Journal of Experimental Criminology*. https://doi.org/10.1007/s11292-026-09731-x

Schiff, K. J., Schiff, D. S., Adams, I. T., McCrain, J., & Mourtgos, S. M. (2023). Institutional factors driving citizen perceptions of AI in government: Evidence from a survey experiment on policing. *Public Administration Review*, *82*(2), 451–467. https://doi.org/10.1111/puar.13754

Seawright, L. (2012). *The literacy practices of law enforcement* [PhD thesis, University of Arkansas]. https://www.proquest.com/docview/1010417366/abstra

Senadheera, S., Yigitcanlar, T., Desouza, K., Mossberger, K., Corchado, J., Mehmood, R., Li, R. Y. M., & Cheong, P. H. (2024). Understanding chatbot adoption in local governments: A review and framework. *Journal of Urban Technology*, *32*(3), 35–69. https://doi.org/10.1080/10630732.2023.2297665

Stanley, J. (2024). *Police departments shouldn't allow officers to use AI to draft police reports*. American Civil Liberties Union. https://assets.aclu.org/live/uploads/2024/12/Automated-Police-Reports-1291.pdf

Stroshine, M. S. (2021). Technology in policing: The past, present, and future. In R. G. Dunham, G. P. Alpert, & K. D. McLean (Eds.), *Critical issues in policing: Contemporary readings* (8th ed., pp. 605–620). Waveland Press, Inc.

Tao, J., Chism, K. A., Luo, F., Carmen, A. del, & Bowling, B. (2025). Catalysts of generative AI adoption in policing: The primacy of transformational leadership and organizational capacity. *Policing: An International Journal*, *49*(1), 90–108. https://doi.org/10.1108/PIJPSM-04-2025-0071

Toner-Rodgers, A. (2024). *Artificial intelligence, scientific discovery, and product innovation*. https://doi.org/10.48550/arXiv.2412.17866

Tregle, B., & McLean, K. (2021). Body-worn cameras. In R. G. Dunham, G. P. Alpert, & K. D. McLean (Eds.), *Critical issues in policing: Contemporary readings* (8th ed., pp. 621–640). Waveland Press, Inc.

United States Bureau of Justice Assistance. (2013). *Compstat: Its origins, evolution, and future in law enforcement agencies*. Police Executive Research Forum. https://bja.ojp.gov/sites/g/files/xyckuh186/files/Publications/PERF-Compstat.pdf

US Department of Justice. (2024). *Artificial intelligence and criminal justice: Final report*. US Department of Justice, Office of Legal Policy. https://www.justice.gov/olp/media/1381796/dl

Vaccaro, M., Almaatouq, A., & Malone, T. (2024). When combinations of humans and AI are useful: A systematic review and meta-analysis. *Nature Human Behaviour*, *8*, 2293–2303. https://doi.org/10.1038/s41562-024-02024-1

Vaswani, A., Shazeer, N., Parmar, N., Uszkoreit, J., Jones, L., Gomez, A. N., Kaiser, L., & Polosukhin, I. (2017). *Attention is all you need*. https://doi.org/10.48550/arXiv.1706.03762

Walley, P., & Glasspoole-Bird, H. (2025). *An evaluation of the pilot application of artificial intelligence to witness statement and report generation at Hertfordshire Constabulary*. Centre for Policing Research; Learning. https://university.open.ac.uk/centres/policing/sites/www.open.ac.uk.centres.policing/files/files/Outputs/Herts%20AI%20Report%202025.pdf

Watts, S., Pozo, B. del, White, M. D., & Malm, A. (2025). Does automated feedback impact the acceptability of AI-generated police body worn camera review? An implementation science natural experiment. *Journal of Experimental Criminology*. https://doi.org/10.1007/s11292-025-09711-7

Watts, S., White, M. D., & Malm, A. (2024). Automating body-worn camera footage review through AI: Baseline attitudes from a multisite randomized control trial. *Policing: A Journal of Policy and Practice, 18*. https://doi.org/10.1093/police/paae107

White, M. D., Watts, S., Malm, A., & Navarrete, G. B. (2025). Officer acceptance and use of AI-driven body-worn camera footage review. *American Journal of Criminal Justice*. https://doi.org/10.1007/s12103-025-09857-0

19

THE END OF COLD CASES—AND GENEALOGISTS?

A Primer on the Future of Investigative Genetic Genealogy

Michael Arntfield and Daniel J. Robinson

Introduction

Since first deployed in 2018 as a breakthrough technology in the "Golden State Killer" case in California, Investigative Genetic Genealogy (IGG) has revolutionized police inquiries where offender DNA is available but not found in any law enforcement databases. Since 2018, IGG has solved more than 1400 cold case serious crimes or missing persons in North America and Europe; many involve cases more than 30 years old (Kilgannon, 2025).

In this chapter, we explore critical questions facing IGG at this key inflection point in the development of this new technology, focusing on three main topics. First, police forces today generally limit the use of IGG to "cold cases," prompting questions as to this term's classification and meaning in the context of advancing IGG capabilities. What separates a "cold case," for instance, from one potentially resolved by "traditional investigative methods?" If IGG were to become part of the traditional investigative methods involving "active" cases, what implications would there be for law enforcement, criminal prosecution, and individual civil rights?

Second, we examine racial and ethnocultural representation in IGG investigations. People of western European origin are heavily over-represented in genetic genealogical samples on sites like GEDmatch; those with African American and Asian ancestry are largely underrepresented, meaning that the IGG process is far more effective when the forensic DNA sample involves Caucasian Americans than when it involves other racial groups (Lasyone et al., 2025). How might this disparity affect the legitimacy and public acceptance of IGG? What measures might ameliorate the uneven rates of DNA sharing on genealogy sites among different racial and ethnic groups?

DOI: 10.4324/9781003671312-19

Finally, we explore current and potential future uses of Artificial Intelligence (AI) to automate and accelerate IGG processes, which are time- and labour-intensive and require specialized skill sets related to genealogy. For IGG to expand to more police forces, the process would need to become more scalable and automated, owing to the paucity of skilled genetic genealogists and the time-consuming nature of constructing family trees that often have thousands of members.

How IGG is Used to Identify Offenders

IGG (sometimes known as Forensic Investigative Genealogy, or FIGG) combines DNA genetic science with traditional genealogical work. People who have completed direct-to-consumer (DTC) DNA tests, from companies like Ancestry or 23andMe, can opt to submit their DNA profiles to online databases like GEDmatch and FamilyTreeDNA, in search of genetic matches. When doing so, they can also provide consent to law enforcement to use their DNA data to assist with historical "cold case" investigations involving homicide, sexual assault, or missing persons. By the early 2020s, some three million people had uploaded DNA profiles to law enforcement accessible sites like GEDmatch (Glynn, 2022; Kling et al., 2021).

Investigators and genetic genealogists then compare the forensic DNA sample, say from a crime scene, with the genetic profiles found on these sites. Typically, most "hits" are distant to the forensic sample, at the third cousin level or beyond. (One person can have hundreds of fourth cousins.) Genealogists then take this list of partial DNA matches and, using public records like birth certificates, census data, parish records, and obituaries, construct far-ranging family trees that connect these matches to the Most Recent Common Ancestors (MRCA) of these distant cousins and the forensic sample. This often requires tracing back family lines to the mid-19th century or earlier (Dahlquist et al., 2024; Guerrini et al., 2024).

Once these MRCA couples have been identified, genealogists then build family trees of their descendants, moving towards the present day. Using technical measures like centiMorgan counts, researchers then determine which family lines to focus on to identify closer ancestors to the forensic DNA sample. IGG genealogists, through processes of inclusion and exclusion, narrow down their search to a handful of potential suspects, typically members of a present-day family. Police investigators then secure confirmatory DNA samples from these people until an identical DNA match is made with the original forensic sample. The latter can involve police operations to surreptitiously retrieve DNA traces (beverage containers, cigarette butts, etc.) publicly discarded by the short list of suspects. As well, the police can retrieve the DNA by way of a court order in order to more expeditiously confirm a direct match to the forensic sample. Given the laborious and detailed nature of this genealogical work, investigations often take weeks or months to complete and are not always successful (Glynn, 2022;

Kling et al., 2021). While a complicated and painstaking process, the results, when successful, have proved transformative and sometimes controversial.

"Cold Case" Homicides and Historical Investigations

The term "cold case," while widely used among law enforcement and forensic personnel, is essentially a media construct, first popularized in the late 1990s with television news magazine shows like *Cold Case Files*. It premiered on the A&E network in 1999. The term has no legal or statutory definition. Around the same period, several large police departments began setting up historical crimes task forces, colloquially known as "cold case" squads. These units typically had time-limited resources and investigated unsolved crimes, which were often arbitrarily selected and varied widely by police department in terms of their vintage (Arntfield & Mains, 2016).

Only recently has there been a consistent and streamlined definition of "cold case." A proposed three-point criterion (Arntfield, 2022) renders a violent crime investigation as "cold" and thus suitable for IGG if it satisfies the following points: the case has had no substantive update (new interviews, tips) for at least 12 months; the case no longer has the original lead investigator assigned, breaking file continuity and institutional memory; and all lab work and expert reports are complete, meaning that no further delays are contingent on any third parties. Applying these criteria, an investigation can reasonably be deemed "cold" after about 18 months, inclusive of allowing six months for conventional methods to reach an impasse.

Currently, the only major guidance for law enforcement and genealogists in this area is the 2019 US Department of Justice (DOJ) Interim Policy on IGG (US DOJ, 2019). Although it does not explicitly use the term "cold case," this DOJ decree provides best practices for IGG, which it requires to be used only after conventional investigative methods and "all other available techniques" have been exhausted. The policy also limits IGG use to cases where it is reasonable and necessary in the circumstances in order to avoid the appearance of a police "fishing expedition." However, what exactly these "other available techniques" are and how they must first be exhausted is not specified and will, of course, naturally vary by case (US DOJ, 2019)

As noted at the start of this chapter, the 2018 arrest of Joseph James DeAngelo, the "Golden State Killer," quickly legitimized IGG as a pioneering and effective investigative methodology in cold case homicides (Arntfield, 2022). DeAngelo's crimes had occurred in different cities during the 1970s and 1980s, and investigators had initially attributed the dozens of rapes and murders to multiple suspects. Only later, when investigators determined that the DNA retrieved from multiple crime scenes was identical, did they attribute these crimes to a single but still unidentified serial killer (Arntfield 2022; McNamara, 2018). After years of inactivity and failed leads, IGG was ultimately able to identify

DeAngelo in a matter of months, this after four decades of conventional detective work had yielded no substantive results (McNamara, 2018).

Media coverage of this case and later IGG-solved crimes often stressed the "cold" component of these crimes; many decades old and no longer being actively investigated, the public was told that, were it not for IGG, these crimes, often serial in nature, would never have been solved. Yet academic works on IGG to date have rarely discussed the cold case/active case dyad. This raises the question of whether all major crimes (typically murders and sexual assaults) for which offender DNA is available might be solvable via IGG in the near future, while these cases are still active and not "cold," based on the Arntfield (2022) three-point criteria.

For example, the rapid use of IGG to identify quadruple murderer Bryan Kohberger (responsible for the November 2022 University of Idaho stabbings) inevitably raised concerns about the technique's use when "traditional investigative methods" were still viable. Kohberger's defense team quickly seized on this issue, and it was expected to be the cornerstone of their defense strategy. Kohberger's surprise guilty plea in July 2025, however, rendered the matter moot, preventing the investigation's status and police methods from being scrutinized in open court (Levenson & Casarez, 2025). In light of high-profile cases like Kohberger's, other jurisdictions have since implemented regulatory guardrails to prevent criminal investigations from engaging in what some have called IGG "overreach" (Guerrini et al., 2024).

The 2019 DOJ Interim Policy was, in fact, largely a response to criticism of potential IGG overreach, as was postulated during the technique's first year of existence. Civil and privacy rights groups were immediately concerned about unwarranted police access to sensitive DNA data and genetic information on individuals and families housed on privately owned ancestry sites. Critics highlighted the potential for privacy violations and the "criminalization" of relatives by association when people opted into these databases (DeGroot et al., 2021).

Despite these concerns, IGG has to date been highly effective as a result of significant public opt-in to sites like GEDmatch, which has resulted in the identification of more than 300 perpetrators in historical cold case homicides and sexual assaults (Guerrini et al., 2024). It has also enabled the identification of human remains in North America at an average rate of one case per week. However, the practice is far from standardized; its use in the United States (US) and Canada is informed by a loose and inconsistent set of procedural guidelines. It also remains far less used outside of North America, leaving questions about the future of IGG abroad.

IGG and "Legacy" DNA Technology

One explanation for the limited scholarly and legal discussion of IGG to date is that the extant DNA framework used by police services in North America, sometimes colloquially known as "legacy" DNA databases, is already an abstruse concept for those outside of law enforcement. IGG thus adds the esoteric nature of genealogical research to this already complex system. However, understanding the inherent limitations of these legacy DNA databases is essential for law enforcement personnel and the public writ large in order to comprehend how IGG functions as a force multiplier to these dated systems and not just as an intended substitute.

The use of DNA for investigative purposes, including its collection, preservation, testing, and administration, has from the outset been regulated by federal legislation, even when carried out at state and local levels. This regulatory framework began with the *DNA Identification Act* of 1994. (Canada passed a same-named statute in 1998.) Both laws provided the regulatory framework for the creation of the Combined DNA Index System (CODIS), the shared operating system between the US and Canada, allowing DNA samples to be uploaded to the US National DNA Index System (NDIS) and the Canadian National DNA Data Bank (NDDB). While similar smaller programs exist in the United Kingdom and New Zealand, CODIS holds many times more reference samples in its system (Wickenheiser, 2022).

These national DNA databanks contain separate indexes to distinguish crime scene evidence from known offender samples. These are the Crime Scene Index (DNA from victims and offenders recovered from crime scenes by police) and the Convicted Offender Index (DNA obtained from people convicted of specific violent offences). Offender samples are typically collected by either court officials or, in some cases, police officers. However, since 2013, some US states have also permitted collection by police merely upon arrest and prior to any court-related disposition (Totenberg, 2013).

While the legacy CODIS program has expanded since the late 1990s, its core function remains straightforward: every day, the Crime Scene Index automatically compares samples with the Convicted Offender Index. Any resulting match—colloquially termed a "cold hit" when an offender is linked for the first time to a historical case—is reported to the law enforcement agency responsible for the original investigation and/or the submission of the sample. This automated process is the primary driver of DNA-related arrests; by 2020, CODIS was, for instance, conservatively estimated to have directly or indirectly "assisted with" over 540,000 arrests in North America (Hazel & Clayton, 2021).

Despite such efficiencies, the CODIS system relies on the assumption of repeat offending. It presumes that violent perpetrators who leave DNA at a crime scene will later commit another violent felony of some kind, resulting in their DNA being added to the Convicted Offender Index, and thus matching their prior crime scene profile(s). This assumption is especially strong when the same unknown offender DNA profile is recovered from multiple scenes (thus a Crime Scene Index "scene-to-scene match," as colloquially known), thereby indicating a prolific multi-offender even in the absence of an identified suspect. This scenario unfolded over many years with the DeAngelo case.

When a prolific violent offender's DNA is found at multiple crime scenes but is not in CODIS, police face considerable public pressure to explain how a suspect had evaded arrest for years or decades. Why were there no DNA matches in the Convicted Offender Index, as the system was designed to accomplish? The usual explanations offered by police include the following: the perpetrator is deceased, having died before arrest or adjudication; the perpetrator emigrated outside North America, where CODIS is unavailable; and, in older cold cases, the offender was already in prison for another crime, sentenced before CODIS laws allowed for sample collection, and has since been released without re-offending. However, IGG has repeatedly shown these assumptions to be false. Successful IGG cases, achieved after legacy CODIS methods have failed, often reveal that prolific offenders rarely moved far from the area of their original crimes.

A relevant example here is the Canadian offender Calvin Hoover, who was known to police while investigating the 1984 kidnapping and murder of schoolgirl Christine Jessop. Hoover's role was grossly misinterpreted by investigators at the time, allowing him to evade suspicion and police questioning while another man was arrested and wrongfully convicted for the murder (Johnston, 2021). Despite leaving DNA at the crime scene, Hoover was not identified for another 36 years, and only via the use of early-stage IGG in 2020. This identification came after Hoover's death by suicide, even though he had been convicted of another crime after the implementation of CODIS. This failure was due to a legacy DNA loophole in Canada, where only violent offenders or those convicted of certain crimes were subject to inclusion in the Convicted Offender Index. With an arrest and conviction for impaired driving, Hoover was screened out of this process, making IGG the only viable method for tying him to the Jessop crime scene, as other physical evidence was absent (Johnston, 2021).

The Jessop case, resolved in October 2020, clearly demonstrates the inherent limitations of legacy DNA databanks, which only allow for crime scene DNA comparison against individuals arrested and convicted of specific, qualifying crimes (McNair, 2020). Although neither the FBI, which administers NDIS, nor the Royal Canadian Mounted Police (RCMP), which administers the NDDB, will publicly state how many unmatched DNA samples remain in the Crime Scene Index, IGG has thoroughly disrupted and added on to this sometimes outdated and inadequate legacy model. IGG proved that "playing the waiting game"—by only comparing crime scene DNA to that of select convicted offenders—was an outmoded process replete with failures. In contrast, IGG compares forensic crime scene samples to the DNA profiles of millions of individuals (and their relatives) in the general population through networks of family tree data.

Racial and Ethnic Bias

As noted earlier, the IGG process can be laborious and fragile, subject to interruption or termination at any stage due to various factors. One potential failure point centers on insufficient genetic saturation: if too few relatives of the forensic sample have submitted their DNA to online databases used by law enforcement, then useful kinship matches may not be found. If the closest matches are at the third cousin level or beyond, then the IGG process will have a lower probability of success (Glynn, 2022).

A second possible failure point involves available genealogical resources: even if usable partial genetic matches are found, one must still be able to build far-ranging family trees in order to eventually connect these matches to the suspect or to unidentified human remains. If there are gaps in traceable lineages within family trees due to poor record-keeping, limited civil and demographic records, or historical disruption (e.g. wartime destruction of archives), then the required genealogical searches become difficult or impossible. This requirement for stable and documentable multi-generational ancestry means that the method's success is closely tied to the historical and demographic characteristics of jurisdictions involving the suspect's ancestral population. For certain demographic groups, factors like minimal genetic saturation and limited genealogical resources combine to produce structural barriers to identification. For these reasons, IGG is more effective with certain racial and ethnic groups (people of Northern or western European ancestry) than it is with others (African Americans and those of Asian ancestry) (McEwen et al., 2021).

Such disparities involving race and ethnicity in IGG also mirror lapses in the scientific community to achieve genomic equity. Researchers have consistently observed that the bulk of genetic information housed in academic reference databases (e.g. the Genome-Wide Association Study Catalog) and commercial DTC platforms like Ancestry.com are mostly derived from individuals of European ancestry (Fatumo et al., 2022). Fields like precision medicine have highlighted this underrepresentation of non-European groups in genomic databases, which in turn disadvantages these groups in terms of treatment options and clinical care (Saey, 2021).

While underrepresentation in online DNA databases involves many non-European populations, the case of African American ancestry presents a unique challenge; here, systemic historical oppression weakens the efficacy of IGG beyond the issue of lower participation rates of African Americans uploading their DNA to online genealogy sites. For African Americans, tracing genealogical lineage is disrupted by the Transatlantic Slave Trade and the institution of slavery in the US (and to a lesser extent in Canada). Slavery fractured family structures and destroyed vital records, and often eliminated surnames. It disrupted the institutional continuity necessary for conventional genealogical tracing (David, 2024). For many African Americans, locating ancestors before the Civil War is a fraught undertaking. Census and vital records typically listed slaves as the property of their owners, most often without family names and with only scant identifying demographic information.

Were an IGG genealogist to build out family trees for an African American suspect based on DNA matches, the investigation may well hit a dead-end in the 1860s. The critical stage of IGG, which involves tracing the lineage of distant matches and the forensic sample back to their most recent shared ancestor couple and then moving forward to the generation of the unknown perpetrator, becomes highly challenging due to slavery's disruption of traceable family lines.

One workaround for black people in North America involves genetic genealogy to locate genetic relatives by sharing one's DNA online. This provides a limited means of redressing the structural limitation imposed by slavery on conventional genealogical methods. In this sense, genetic genealogy can act in a reparative manner to help reclaim the history, culture, and sense of place denied to African Americans by slavery (David, 2024). Despite this, African Americans engage in genetic genealogy sharing at lower rates than do Americans of European origin.

The limited ability of IGG to solve cold cases involving African Americans as suspects or missing persons stems from a key structural barrier: the technology's required methodology, dependent on stable, documented, multi-generational lineages, excludes populations whose genealogical trajectory was destroyed by historical systemic violence. Of course, this ironically contrasts with CODIS, discussed earlier, a database in which African Americans comprise 34 percent of entries while representing 13 percent of the US population. (Moore et al., 2023)

Other impediments exist involving genealogical research among non-European populations. For example, Chinese genealogy presents significant difficulties, particularly for Western researchers, stemming from its foundational structures and barriers to access. Transcribing Chinese names is also complicated by the use of different Romanization systems (e.g. Pinyin, Wade-Giles) across various Chinese-speaking regions, leading to inconsistencies in surname spelling. The Chinese genealogical system is centered around the "zupu," a detailed record intrinsically tied to clan systems and culture. These records historically served as semi-closed documents and often remain unavailable to individuals outside of the clan, thereby restricting their use for academic or personal ancestry tracing. The zupu's patriarchal bias means that these records focus mainly on male lineage and systematically exclude women. It is thus very challenging to trace female ancestral lines, as is often needed in IGG work (Chao, 2006; Wang, 2023).

While there have been efforts to digitize records, such as the Chinese Genealogy Knowledge Service Platform by the Shanghai Library, significant barriers remain. The platform is difficult to navigate, and most zupu records are only available as photocopies of archaic scripts, rather than as transcribed text. Accessing these resources often requires a Chinese citizen ID number, effectively excluding non-citizens. Even with the modernization of historical records, the sheer number of dispersed records and the specialized skills required for cataloging them complicate efforts to create a comprehensive database for broader public use, including law enforcement genealogists (Chao, 2006; Wang, 2023).

Thus, it bears repeating: even if one could increase the number of DNA samples from African or Chinese Americans in IGG-related databases, this still would not address the structural problem of insufficient or inaccessible genealogical records involving these groups.

This raises an interesting question: how would public support for IGG be affected if people knew that it worked more effectively with Caucasians than it did with African Americans and other racialized groups? Is this an equity issue for law enforcement? And what about the perspectives of victims and their families? Should African American victims of crimes committed by fellow African Americans not also have the same chance of achieving justice and resolution as exists with white Americans?

To this end, there should be more investment in research activities aimed at recovering and documenting genealogies fractured by historical events. New methods that successfully link living individuals to historically marginalized populations, such as enslaved persons, demonstrate the viability of this approach and can contribute vital data related to both reparative and forensic goals (Dutchen, 2023). This work should be ethically guided, focusing on community trust and mutual respect to overcome historical trauma, in order to encourage voluntary DNA sharing with sites like GEDmatch (David, 2024). As well, advisory or regulatory bodies such as the Scientific Working Group on DNA Analysis Methods should establish mandatory reporting standards for IGG success rates among population groups. This would allow for transparent tracking and external validation of demographic disparities in cold case resolution (McEwen et al., 2021).

Artificial Intelligence and IGG

The IGG work process is two-fold: first, one searches for and then obtains relevant genetic information, often generated from Single Nucleotide Polymorphism (SNP) profiles derived from consumer genetic databases; second, one deploys this genetic information alongside publicly accessible genealogical data (e.g. census records, obituaries, etc.) to construct expansive family trees with the goal of producing a short list of people in close kinship to the forensic sample, often members of a single or extended family (Guerrini et al., 2021).

While the genetic profiling component has seen rapid technological innovation, the genealogical process itself constitutes a practical barrier to the wider use of IGG. This genealogical work requires a range of skills involving historical research and data organization. It is time-consuming, often taking weeks or months to complete, depending on the complexity of the genealogical case; for these reasons, it sometimes fails to produce useful leads (Guerrini et al., 2021). This raises the question as to what extent computational solutions could automate and accelerate this painstaking genealogical work. Artificial Intelligence

(AI), with its subfields of Machine Learning (ML), Natural Language Processing (NLP), and Computer Vision (CV), offers possible tools for transforming this labour-intensive process. To what extent could AI, as it has done in other sectors, increase the speed, accuracy, and reliability of ancestry searching and family tree building involving massive genealogical datasets like those in Ancestry.com?

AI is already used extensively in the genetic phase of IGG, where its capacity to process massive, complex genomic datasets far exceeds human capability. Modern forensic research focuses on emerging markers like microhaplotypes, SNPs, and the application of Massively Parallel Sequencing (MPS). AI techniques—including ML, data mining, and pattern recognition—enable forensic experts to efficiently process the massive body of genomic information, while minimizing risks of misinterpretation (Liu et al., 2024). Here, AI offers more than improved performance; it has become a sine qua non tool to manage and interpret the vast scale of data involved in contemporary genomic science (Sessa et al., 2024).

AI has also boosted operational efficiencies by automating the initial, time-consuming steps of data aggregation. Researchers can now employ AI to rapidly process vast quantities of historical documents, including birth and death certificates, census records, and marriage licenses (Mulcahy, 2024). Natural Language Processing (NLP) is particularly valuable, as it enables machines to understand and interpret human language in historical documents. NLP algorithms are trained to analyze the language used and extract critical structured information, such as names, dates, and locations (Tanner, 2024). Furthermore, machine learning models, often trained on thousands of verified manual matches, can overcome persistent challenges in genealogy research, such as spelling variations in names or date discrepancies common in historical records (Rabideau, 2025).

Computer vision systems also enhance the analysis of non-textual artifacts and the mass digitization and processing of handwritten or visual historical sources (Salazar, 2024). AI, therefore, can automate some of the tedious tasks of data entry and initial correlation, allowing human genealogists to direct their research efforts to more beneficial and challenging areas (Tanner, 2024).

The limits of AI, however, become apparent when research questions transition from simple correlation and extraction to complex synthesis and interpretation. Human genealogists rely on hypothetical-deductive reasoning, individual judgment, and heuristics to resolve conflicts and construct accurate pedigrees. This can be seen with the Board for Certification of Genealogists' Genealogical Standard Proof, which is a set of guidelines for genealogical research to ensure that findings are strongly supported by evidence to a reasonable degree of certainty (Genealogical Proof Standard, n.d.).

While AI is highly productive for data ingestion and simple linking, its utility plateaus quickly when faced with the need for nuanced interpretation of historical contexts (Rabideau, 2025). How does one handle statistical outliers or results defying typical categorization? In genealogy, such outliers might include intricate adoption histories or endogamous cultural practices that complicate genetic relatedness (Salazar, 2024). AI-generated suggestions, even if statistically plausible, would occasionally lead researchers down incorrect paths because the models lack the cultural and historical context necessary for accurate judgment. The central question regarding the extent to which AI can replace human genealogical research hinges on the high cognitive demands of family tree construction. The evidence suggests that AI excels at high-volume data ingestion but far less so when the task requires context-specific interpretation and deductive reasoning.

The adoption of AI in IGG currently reflects more of a model of augmented intelligence, rather than full automation or replacement of the specialized human investigator. As such, human genealogists remain the critical gatekeepers and the final authorities on resolving complexity and ensuring the historical accuracy of ancestral relations (Salazar, 2024).

Conclusion

The rapid adoption of IGG since 2018 has fundamentally disrupted the "legacy" DNA model and the very notion of the "cold case." IGG's success, as evidenced by the resolution of many hundreds of cases, has exposed the core limitation of the CODIS system and its reliance on the presumption of repeat offending coupled with inevitable arrest and conviction. As the DeAngelo and Hoover cases (among many) demonstrate, waiting for an offender to enter the Convicted Offender Index can fail when suspects avoid conviction or benefit from regulatory loopholes. Future police investigations of serious crimes will therefore no doubt benefit from a proactive, IGG-informed methodology. Such a shift, however, requires updated legal frameworks and industry standardization. The controversy surrounding the rapid use of IGG to identify Bryan Kohberger, for example, highlights the legal vulnerability of applying the technique to "active" cases before traditional methods are fully exhausted. The current regulatory environment, relying heavily on the 2019 DOJ Interim Policy, is also inadequate. Jurisdictions in the US and Canada must define clear trigger points for IGG use and establish regulatory guardrails to prevent "overreach," ensuring that this powerful investigative tool operates reasonably and responsibly within legal and ethical limits.

The long-term legitimacy and effectiveness of IGG are, however, compromised by current structural inequities in genealogical data. IGG's reliance on stable, multi-generational ancestral records creates a systemic barrier for populations whose lineages were historically disrupted, most notably African Americans affected by slavery. Consequently, IGG is demonstrably more effective in resolving cases involving suspects of western/northern European descent. This disparity raises critical questions of forensic equity and public trust, as police technology must not be allowed to systematically favour one demographic group in the pursuit of justice. To address this inherent racial bias in the data, a two-pronged approach is needed: first, implementing mandatory reporting standards for IGG success rates related to genetic ancestry to ensure full transparency; and second, making significant investments in research and community-led initiatives focused on ethically recovering and documenting genealogies damaged by historical oppression.

Finally, while the complex synthesis required for constructing accurate family trees still necessitates the specialized skills of human genetic genealogists, AI may represent a viable path to scaling IGG practice in the future. The genealogical process remains labour-intensive, making widespread adoption and uptake challenging. AI, particularly NLP and ML, offer partial solutions by acting as an augmented intelligence tool. AI excels at high-volume data ingestion, automating the tedious tasks of aggregating and correlating massive amounts of historical records—overcoming common obstacles like name variations and fragmented documentation. This allows the human expert to dedicate their limited time to intricate deductive reasoning and resolving challenging genealogical conflicts.

References

Arntfield, M. (2022). *How to solve a cold case: And everything else you wanted to know about catching killers*. HarperCollins.

Arntfield, M. & Mains, K. (2016). Cold case homicides: Challenges & opportunities. In J. Swart & L. Mellor (Eds), *Homicide: A forensic psychology casebook* (pp. 299 – 314). CRC.

Chao, Sheau-yueh J. (March 2006). Sources on overseas Chinese studies: Genealogical records. *Library Collections, Acquisitions, and Technical Services*, *30*(1–2), 18–46.

Dahlquist, J., Robinson, J. O., Daoud, A., Bash-Brooks, W., McGuire, A. L., Guerrini, C. J., & Fullerton, S. M. (2024). Public perspectives on investigative genetic genealogy: Findings from a national focus group study. *AJOB Empirical Bioethics*, *15*(4), 280–290. https://doi.org/10.1080/23294515.2024.2336904

David, L. T. (2024). Supporting the use of genetic genealogy in restoring family narratives following the transatlantic slave trade. *Am Anthropol*. Mar; *126*(1), 153–157. doi: 10.1111/aman.13939. Epub 2023 Oct 25. PMID: 38312167; PMCID: PMC10836826

deGroot, N. F., van Beers, B. C., & Meynen, G. (2021). Commercial DNA tests and police investigations: A broad bioethical perspective. *Journal of Medical Ethics*, *47*, 788–795. doi: 10.1136/medethics-2021-107568

Dutchen, S. (2023, August 3). Historical DNA study connects living people to enslaved and free African Americans at early ironworks. *Harvard Medical School*. https://hms.harvard.edu/news/historical-dna-study-connects-living-people-enslaved

Fatumo, S., Chikowore, T., Choudhury, A., Ayub, M., Martin, A. R., & Kuchenbäcker, K. (2022). Diversity in genomic studies: A roadmap to address the imbalance. *Nature Medicine*, *28*(2), 243–250. https://doi.org/10.1038/s41591-021-01672-4

Genealogical Proof Standard. (n.d.). *National Genealogical Society*. https://www.ngsgenealogy.org/going-to-the-next-level/understanding-genealogical-proof/

Glynn, C. L. (2022). Bridging disciplines to form a new one: The emergence of forensic genetic genealogy. *Genes*, *13*(8), 1381. https://doi.org/10.3390/genes13081381

Guerrini, C. J., Wickenheiser, R. A., Bettinger, B., McGuire, A. L., & Fullerton, S. M. (2021). Four misconceptions about investigative genetic genealogy. *Journal of Law and the Biosciences*, *8*(1), lsab001. https://doi.org/10.1093/jlb/lsab001

Guerrini, C. J., Bash Brooks, W., Robinson, J. O., Fullerton, S. M., Zoorob, E., & McGuire, A. L. (2024). IGG in the trenches: Results of an in-depth interview study on the practice, politics, and future of investigative genetic genealogy. *Forensic Science International*, *356*, 111946. https://doi.org/10.1016/j.forsciint.2024.111946

Hazel, J. W., & Clayton, E. W. (2021, January 20). Law enforcement & genetic data. *Hastings Center for Bioethics*. https://www.thehastingscenter.org/briefingbook/law-enforcement-and-genetic-data/#:~:text=Since%201994%2C%20the%20U.S.%20Department,assisted%20in%20over%20540%2C000%20investigations.

Johnston, M. (2021, November 29). The hunt for a killer. *TorontoLife*. https://torontolife.com/city/inside-the-hunt-for-christine-jessops-real-killer/

Kilgannon, C. (2025, December 7). Cold case inquiries hampered after genealogy site revisits terms of use. *The New York Times*. https://www.nytimes.com/2025/12/07/nyregion/ancestry-dna-police.html

Kling, D., Phillips, C., Kennett, D., & Tillmar, A. (2021). Investigative genetic genealogy: Current methods, knowledge, and practice. *Forensic Science International: Genetics*, *52*, 102474. https://doi.org/10.1016/j.fsigen.2021.102474

Lasyone, C., Budowle, B., Mittelman, K., & Mittelman, D. (2025) Investigative and policy impacts of forensic genetic genealogy in the identification of human remains. *Forensic Science International: Synergy*, *11*, 100651. https://doi.org/10.1016/j.fsisyn.2025.100651

Levenson, E., & Casarez, J. (2025, March 1). Over two years after four students were fatally stabbed in Idaho, the defense strategy emerges. *CNN.com*. https://www.cnn.com/2025/03/01/us/bryan-kohberger-trial-defense-dna-evidence

Liu, Y., Sun, C., Si, H., Peng, Z., Gu, L., Guo, X., & Song, F. (2024). Bibliometric analysis of kinship analysis from 1960 to 2023: Global trends and development. *Frontiers in Genetics*, *15*, 1401898. https://doi.org/10.3389/fgene.2024.1401898

McEwen, J., Pino, N., Raphael, A., Renna, K., Boyer, J., & Brody, L. (2021). Investigative genetic genealogy: Ethical, legal, and social issues and directions for future research. *Forensic Genomics*, *1*, 91–98. https://doi.org/10.1089/forensic.2021.0008

McNair, M. (2020, October 21). Calvin Hoover's family 'devastated' to learn police believe he killed Christine Jessop. *CBC News*. https://www.cbc.ca/news/canada/toronto/hoover-family-devastated-by-murder-accusation-1.5771340

McNamara, M. (2018). *I'll be gone in the dark: One woman's obsessive search for the Golden State Killer*. HarperCollins.

Moore, C. B., Dolan, D. D., Yarmolinsky, R., Cho, M. K., & Soo-Jin-Lee, S. (2023). The ELSI virtual forum, 30 years of the genome: Integrating and applying ELSI research. *J Law Med Ethics*, *51*(3), 661–671. doi: 10.1017/jme.2023.109. Epub 2023 Dec 13. PMID: 38088602; PMCID: PMC11068442.

Mulcahy, B. L. (2024, April 1). *Genealogy research tips: AI and its impact on genealogical research*. https://libraryaware.com/1159/NewsletterIssues/ViewIssue/eb26d9aa-ff19-435e-a3a2-82fc423d7380?postId=0ece8dff-6040-40d1-9589-6002b60c1fbf

Saey, T. H. (2021, March 4). *DNA databases are too white, so genetics doesn't help everyone. How do we fix that?* https://www.sciencenews.org/article/genetics-race-dna-databases-reference-genome-too-white

Rabideau, M. (2025, 4 April). The revolutionary impact of AI on genealogy and historical research. *ManyRoads*. https://www.many-roads.com/2025/04/04/the-role-of-artificial-intelligence-in-genealogy-and-historical-research/
Salazar, G. (2024, January 24). Unraveling the past: AI and the evolution of genealogy. *AWIS*. https://awis.org/resource/unraveling-the-past-ai-and-the-evolution-of-genealogy/
Sessa, F., Esposito, M., Cocimano, G., Sablone, S., Karaboue, M. A. A., Chisari, M., Albano, D. G., & Salerno, M. (2024). Artificial intelligence and forensic genetics: Current applications and future perspectives. *Applied Sciences*, *14*(5), 2113. https://doi.org/10.3390/app14052113
Tanner, A. (2024, August 15). AI and genealogy: Advancements you can use. *FamilySearch*. https://www.familysearch.org/en/blog/ai-developments-genealogy
Totenberg, N. (2013, June 3). Supreme Court rules DNA can be taken after arrest. *NPR*. https://www.npr.org/2013/06/03/188397999/supreme-court-rules-arrest-dna-collection-reasonable
US Department of Justice (2019, September 24). Department of Justice announces interim policy for emerging method to generate leads for unsolved violent crimes. *Justice.gov*. https://www.justice.gov/archives/opa/pr/department-justice-announces-interim-policy-emerging-method-generate-leads-unsolved-violent
Wang, H. (2023). The popularization of Chinese genealogy. In *The general theory of China's genealogy*. Springer. https://doi.org/10.1007/978-981-15-6377-5_8ttps://doi.org/10.1016/j.lcats.2006.07.019, 19
Wickenheiser, R. A. (2022). Expanding DNA database effectiveness. *Forensic Science International: Syngery*, 4, 100226. https://doi.org/10.1016/j.fsisyn.2022.100226

20

FACIAL RECOGNITION TECHNOLOGY IN US POLICING

Crime Control, Officer Safety, and Racial Equity Implications

Thaddeus L. Johnson and Natasha N. Johnson

Introduction

Facial recognition technology (FRT) has rapidly emerged as a critical tool in United States (US) policing. Law enforcement primarily uses this algorithm-based technology to match faces from crime-scene images or video against large digital repositories such as mugshot databases and driver's license records (Bromberg et al., 2020). Police adoption has expanded from limited pilots in the early 2000s to widespread use by federal agencies and a substantial share of local departments by 2020 (Garvie et al., 2016; US Government Accountability Office, 2022). Departments increasingly rely on FRT to identify suspects, improve clearance of serious crimes, and deter offending by raising the certainty of apprehension and conviction (Barranco, 2023; Beety, 2022). For example, police in Maryland reportedly used FRT to help dismantle a violent criminal ring, leading to over a dozen indictments and disrupting planned shootings (Parker, 2020).

However, critics emphasize FRT's implications for privacy and civil rights, potential accuracy differentials across demographic groups, and the risk that agencies over-rely on algorithmic outputs in investigations (Brayne, 2020; Ferguson, 2017; Garvie et al., 2016). Performance testing has documented demographic differentials in some systems (e.g., by race, sex, and age), although accuracy has improved substantially and varies widely by vendor, data quality, and threshold settings (Grother et al., 2022; Leslie, 2020; Sham et al., 2023; Yucer et al., 2022). High-profile misidentifications, including the arrests of Robert Williams in Detroit and Nijeer Parks in New Jersey, illustrate the stakes when a face-search result is treated as more than an investigative lead (Fussell, 2020;

DOI: 10.4324/9781003671312-20

Perano, 2020). These cases are consequential but anecdotal; they do not establish how often such errors occur. In most cases, the breakdown is often owed to investigative workflow failures (e.g., thresholds, review, documentation, and corroboration) rather than a single deterministic decision by the algorithm.

Even when functioning as intended, FRT can reinforce existing patterns of uneven enforcement if it is deployed and queried primarily where police attention is already concentrated. From this position, downstream disparities are more plausibly operational (where and how the tool is used) than purely algorithmic (how well the model matches faces), because adoption decisions, camera placement, and investigative workflows are shaped by local priorities and historical deployment patterns (Brayne, 2020; Ferguson, 2017). FRT thus enters democratic policing at the intersection of crime-control promise and governance choices about discretion, transparency, and accountability.

This chapter synthesizes findings from three empirical studies on police use of FRT and public safety outcomes in US cities. To date, these studies by Johnson and colleagues (2022, 2024, 2025) constitute the only published, multi-jurisdiction empirical evidence on FRT in policing that moves beyond law review debate and laboratory tests to examine enforcement outcomes. Collectively, they assess FRT's impact in three key areas:

1 The relationship between police FRT applications and changes in violent crime and arrest patterns.
2 The combined effects of FRT alongside other surveillance tools, such as body-worn cameras (BWCs) and fixed cameras, on violent police–citizen encounters.
3 The association between police FRT adoption and shifts in Black–White arrest disparities.

We integrate insights from these studies to clarify FRT's benefits and pitfalls, identify what remains unknown, and discuss implications for criminological theory and law enforcement.

We approach this review through three conceptual lenses:

1 Deterrence theory (does FRT deter crime or unwanted behaviour by increasing the certainty of identification and punishment?)
2 Technological governance (how do policies and organizational choices mediate FRT's impacts?), and
3 Social equity (does FRT reinforce or mitigate inequities in law enforcement outcomes?).

Taken together, these lenses underpin what we term a surveillance–deterrence–equity (SDE) framework for understanding FRT's role in contemporary policing.

The chapter concludes with recommendations for future research, technology policy, and responsible FRT deployment in law enforcement.

Background and Theoretical Frameworks

Deterrence Theory and Surveillance Technology

Deterrence theory helps explain how FRT might shape crime and police–citizen interactions. Classic frameworks hold that people are less likely to offend when they perceive a high risk of swift, certain, and sufficiently severe punishment (Barnum & Pogarsky, 2023; Beccaria, 1764/1963; Nagin, 2013). Empirical syntheses find that certainty of punishment exerts a more consistent deterrent effect than severity, while evidence on swiftness (celerity) is limited and mixed (Nagin, 2013).

FRT applies deep-learning algorithms to detect, extract, and match a face against millions of stored images (Lozano et al., 2021). In policing, this technology may strengthen deterrence by accelerating identification from surveillance images and increasing the perceived certainty of apprehension. By linking incidents to identifiable individuals, FRT can raise expectations that serious offenders will be recognized and arrested. Public awareness of camera coverage and FRT may further deter offending by increasing the perceived detection risk (see Piza et al., 2015).

Consistent with this logic, studies on closed-circuit television (CCTV) surveillance systems indicate modest crime reductions in environments where detection risk is salient (Piza et al., 2019). BWC studies indicate that perceived recording can shift behaviour by reducing citizen complaints and, in some settings, police use of force (Ariel et al., 2015; Lum et al., 2019). Yet deterrence effects are not automatic; they depend heavily on context and perception. People must perceive a credible risk of punishment for deterrence to operate (Nagin, 2013; Paternoster, 2019). If offenders do not know that police have FRT capabilities, the technology cannot meaningfully alter their cost–benefit calculations. Conversely, if FRT applications are publicized through signage, community outreach, or news coverage, it may contribute to a perception of ubiquitous monitoring and post-hoc identifiability, reinforcing deterrent effects (Brayne, 2017).

Deterrence theory also assumes some degree of rational or quasi-rational calculation in which people weigh anticipated costs and benefits (even if imperfectly) before acting (Cornish & Clarke, 1986; Paternoster, 2019). In high-crime contexts or among impulsive, intoxicated, or highly distressed actors, the deterrent effect of any sanction or technology may be limited because immediate pressures, emotions, or constraints overshadow longer-term risks (Piza et al., 2015).

Technological Governance and Policy Mediation

Technological governance refers to the rules, policies, and organizational practices that shape the use of technology and structure how power, discretion, and accountability are distributed around data-driven tools (Ferguson, 2017). In the context of police FRT, governance encompasses how agencies regulate face recognition, what oversight mechanisms exist, and how transparency and accountability are maintained within departments and to the public (Garvie et al., 2016).

A core lesson from the broader Artificial Intelligence (AI) governance literature is that governance is not a single policy lever (Batool et al., 2025; Nelson & Gorichanaz, 2019). Instead, it spans multiple levels (e.g., organizational, industry, national, and international) and should cover the full system life cycle, including pre-deployment design and procurement, deployment and use, and post-deployment monitoring, evaluation, and revision (Batool et al., 2025; Nelson & Gorichanaz, 2019). In policing, this life-cycle view matters because procurement decisions (vendor selection, thresholds, integration with other systems) can lock in downstream practices and risks long before an officer runs a single search.

Police agencies began using FRT before clear regulatory frameworks were in place, and early adopters often deployed it with limited legislative or judicial oversight (Garvie et al., 2016). Some cities voluntarily constrained FRT's use to serious crimes, including Detroit, where policy limits face recognition to violent felonies and other serious offenses (Ng, 2020). In contrast, New York City reportedly used it for lower-level crimes such as theft and shoplifting (Garvie et al., 2016; Ng, 2020). Other jurisdictions, including San Francisco, enacted preemptive bans, citing civil-rights and civil-liberties concerns about pervasive monitoring (Lee, 2019). These divergent approaches underscore that FRT's effects are likely mediated by governance choices rather than determined by the technology alone.

Good governance of police technology balances crime-control objectives with safeguards for rights and equity through transparency, accountability, and continuous evaluation (Ferguson, 2017; Richards & King, 2014). Transparency includes notifying communities about FRT use and publishing policies that define who may be searched, which databases are queried, and how long data are retained (Richards & King, 2014). It also includes communicating operational guardrails, so the public can understand what technology can and cannot do (Batool et al., 2025; Nelson & Gorichanaz, 2019). Accountability includes auditing FRT searches, requiring supervisor approval or judicial authorization in defined circumstances, and imposing clear consequences for misuse (Garvie et al., 2016; Joh, 2016).

Operationally, this implies specifying:

- Who is responsible (command staff, analysts, vendors, oversight bodies)?
- What is governed (data sources, thresholds, match review, documentation, retention, sharing)?

- When is it governed (design/procurement, deployment/use, post-incident review)?
- How is it governed (policies, training, technical controls, audits, and public reporting)?

At a minimum, agencies should require that FRT outputs be treated as investigative leads, subject to documented corroboration, rather than standalone probable cause. Established identification systems offer a useful analogy. Automated Fingerprint Identification System (AFIS) searches typically return a candidate list that must be evaluated by a trained examiner rather than treated as a definitive identification (Ulery et al., 2011). Similarly, the Combined DNA Index System (CODIS) database "hits" trigger an inter-laboratory confirmation process. Laboratories exchange information to verify the match, and many jurisdictions retest or otherwise confirm underlying profiles before proceeding (Federal Bureau of Investigation, 2017; Federal Bureau of Investigation, 2025). Translating this lesson to FRT, policy should explicitly require that a face-search result be logged as a lead and corroborated with independent evidence before it can contribute to probable cause.

Technological governance also encompasses inter-agency coordination and information-sharing. Because offenders move across jurisdictions, neighbouring agencies may need to coordinate FRT deployment and data-sharing to avoid creating "safe havens" for lawbreakers. This should also help maximize regional deterrent effects (Johnson et al., 2024). Coordination also matters because governance gaps at one level (e.g., local policy) can be widened or narrowed by national and international standards and oversight regimes. As such, AI governance research increasingly emphasizes this multi-level alignment as a precondition for trustworthy technology deployment (Batool et al., 2025; Nelson & Gorichanaz, 2019).

Social Equity and Justice Considerations

Equity is a recurring theme in debates about police surveillance technology, but it helps to separate two questions: how the model performs and how the technology is used. Claims of inherent bias are common, yet audits and government evaluations show a mixed picture. Error rates can differ across demographic groups in some systems and contexts, while performance varies widely across algorithms and has improved among top-performing vendors (Buolamwini & Gebru, 2018; Grother et al., 2022). Separately, operational choices about where cameras are placed, which cases are prioritized, and when searches are initiated shape who is most likely to be searched and investigated. The core equity issue is therefore whether governance can keep differential error and differential exposure from translating into unequal enforcement outcomes.

Equity concerns typically arise through two pathways. First, differential error refers to performance gaps across groups. Benchmark tests show variation by phenotype, age, and gender, but the size of these differences depends heavily on the vendor, image quality, and threshold settings, and leading systems have improved markedly (Buolamwini & Gebru, 2018; Grother et al., 2022). Crucially, differential error does not, by itself, produce wrongful arrests. Errors become consequential when agencies treat low-confidence matches as probable cause, fail to document verification, or bypass corroboration practices that are standard in other biometric workflows (Ulery et al., 2011).

Second, differential exposure can persist even when accuracy is high. Research on data-driven policing suggests that when surveillance resources are disproportionately directed to the same neighbourhoods and problem types, investigations and enforcement contacts can expand there even under race-neutral rationales (Brayne, 2017; Lum & Isaac, 2016; Richardson et al., 2019). If FRT is layered onto those practices through camera placement and search prioritization, disparities may widen because surveillance is unevenly distributed—not necessarily because the algorithm systematically misidentifies one group (Moy, 2021).

In this context, Johnson et al. (2022), analyzing more than 1,100 US cities, report larger Black–White arrest rate gaps in jurisdictions using facial recognition than in those that do not. These patterns are consistent with selection and use effects. FRT may be adopted by agencies with distinct enforcement profiles or deployed in ways that intensify investigative attention in particular settings. The study does not isolate a single mechanism (algorithmic error versus operational deployment) and should not be read as proof that the technology is inherently discriminatory. The most defensible takeaway is governance-centered. That is, agencies should audit usage and outcomes, set thresholds and review requirements, and monitor whether FRT deployment coincides with widening disparities.

Equity frameworks also emphasize downstream impacts on community trust and legitimacy. Procedural justice research shows that perceived unfairness or intrusiveness reduces willingness to cooperate with police and comply with the law (Gau & Brunson, 2010; Sunshine & Tyler, 2003). If communities experience FRT as an added layer of monitoring in already heavily policed areas, it may further erode legitimacy and civic trust, with spillover consequences for public safety (Alang et al., 2022; Stuart, 2016).

An Integrated Surveillance–Deterrence–Equity Framework

Together, these lenses suggest that FRT is best understood as part of a broader surveillance regime that raises identification certainty, reallocates discretion and power, and reshapes legitimacy. We propose an integrated framework with three interacting components (see Figure 20.1):

1 Surveillance intensity (the density and connectivity of tools such as FRT, fixed cameras, and BWCs),

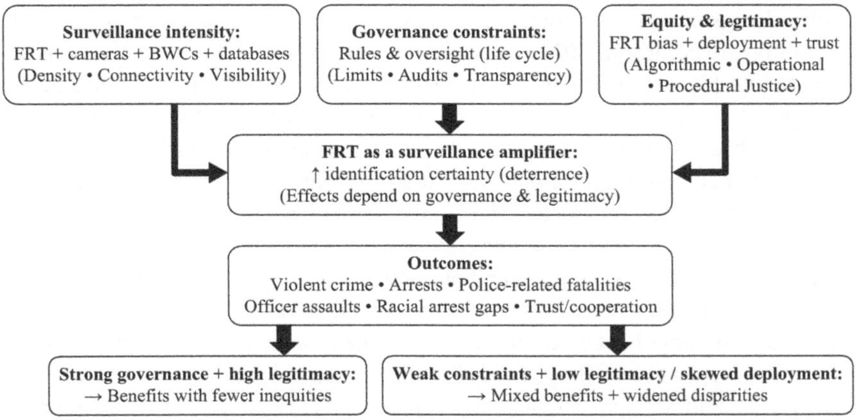

FIGURE 20.1 SDE Framework: Surveillance–Deterrence–Equity (FRT in Policing)

2 Governance constraints (policies, oversight, and transparency mechanisms that channel how those tools can be used), and
3 Equity and legitimacy (where surveillance is concentrated and how communities experience it).

Within this framework, FRT operates less as a standalone tool and more as a surveillance amplifier. In high-surveillance settings with strong governance and high legitimacy, greater identification certainty may reduce crime and lethal force without substantially widening disparities. In low-legitimacy settings with weak constraints and racially skewed deployment, the same increase in certainty may reduce some lethal incidents (i.e., homicide, police killings) while elevating non-lethal resistance and coinciding with wider arrest disparities. The studies by Johnson et al. can be read as tests of the SDE framework across various enforcement contexts.

State of the Literature on Police FRT

Before turning to these studies, we situate Johnson et al.'s contributions in the broader FRT and surveillance literatures. Research on FRT in policing builds on scholarship on algorithmic accuracy and bias, surveillance governance, and data-driven policing. Technical evaluations by the US National Institute of Standards and Technology show large improvements in face-matching accuracy over the past decade, substantial variation across software and systems, and persistent demographic differentials by race, sex, and age (Grother et al., 2022).

Legal and civil-liberties analyses examine how FRT deployments implicate constitutional protections, particularly when paired with large-scale image collection from social media, driver's license databases, or other government repositories (Ferguson, 2017; Garvie et al., 2016). Watchdog investigations estimate that FRT-enabled law enforcement networks permit face searches across images of more than 117 million American adults—often without explicit legislative authorization or robust oversight—and report uneven Black representation in mugshot and other image databases used for searches (Garvie et al., 2016).

A parallel literature situates FRT within a broader "stack" of police technologies, including predictive-policing systems, automated license-plate readers, and networked CCTV. Hotspot and predictive-policing research show that data-driven tools can intensify surveillance in already over-policed neighbourhoods and magnify racially skewed enforcement when underlying data reflect historical and structural bias (Brayne, 2017; Lum & Isaac, 2016).

Privacy and surveillance scholars connect these dynamics to theories of the panopticon, datafication, and algorithmic governance, arguing that contemporary surveillance architecture, including FRT, can deepen power asymmetries by normalizing continuous monitoring and automated decision-making (Lyon, 2018). At the same time, evaluations of BWCs and CCTV suggest that, under specific conditions, surveillance can reduce crime, use-of-force incidents, and citizen complaints (Ariel et al., 2015; Lum et al., 2019). These studies highlight how policy design, training, and organizational culture shape technological impacts.

Against this backdrop, the three Johnson et al. studies occupy an important niche. They move beyond lab accuracy tests, litigation, and case study critiques to conduct multi-city analyses of how police FRT relates to crime, arrests, racial disparities, and lethal and non-lethal violence. Their work helps bridge the gap between technical evaluations of FRT and empirical research on its real-world consequences.

Data, Methods, and Limitations for the Three Studies

The three studies summarized here draw on publicly available panel data from US cities and municipal police departments over time. They combine measures of crime, arrests, police-related fatalities, officer assaults, and FRT adoption with demographic and socio-structural indicators. Analytically, the work relies on generalized difference-in-differences and doubly robust estimators, pairing city and year fixed effects with controls for crime levels, population characteristics, and other policy changes.

However, important study limitations warrant discussion. FRT adoption is not random, and adopting cities may differ in unobserved ways (e.g., political priorities, reform capacity, organizational culture). Deployments also often coincide with other technologies or reforms, complicating attribution of effects uniquely to FRT. Measurement is typically at the agency-adoption level rather than encounter-level usage, and the arrest disparity analysis is based on city-level rather than individual-level data. Accordingly, the estimates are best read as rigorous associational evidence about FRT as part of a broader policing regime, not as definitive causal effects of FRT in isolation.

Effects of FRT on Violent Crime and Arrests

Johnson et al. (2024) provide longitudinal evidence on FRT's impact on violent crime and arrests (homicide, robbery, aggravated assault, and rape) using data from 268 US cities from 1997 to 2020. Generalized difference-in-differences models indicate an average 14 percent decrease in city homicide rates following FRT deployment. Robbery and aggravated assault show small negative associations that do not reach standard levels of statistical significance. Early adopters (cities that implemented FRT in the mid-2000s) experienced larger average drops in homicides than late adopters, suggesting that sustained use of FRT over many years may confer cumulative benefits.

Johnson et al. (2024) posit two main mechanisms are at play: 1) improved identification and 2) general deterrence. By quickly identifying suspects from surveillance footage or witness photos, FRT can lead to faster arrests of violent offenders. Awareness that police can identify suspects from video evidence may also discourage some premeditated violence. These crime-reduction effects, however, are specific to street crimes. Reported rapes do not decline with FRT use, likely because many occur in private settings where public surveillance is less relevant.

A related question is whether FRT leads to more arrests for felony violence. Johnson et al. (2024) find no significant increase in violent crime arrests associated with FRT deployment. The only near-significant change is a slight decrease in aggravated assault arrests in cities with FRT. The absence of an arrest spike suggests that FRT is not simply a dragnet leading to mass arrests. Instead, it may improve arrest efficiency and help pinpoint key offenders without increasing the volume of enforcement actions. Within the SDE framework, these patterns are consistent with the idea that increases in certainty, when embedded in relatively stable governance regimes, can reduce some forms of serious violence without substantially expanding enforcement reach.

FRT, Use of Force, and Officer Safety

The second reviewed study by Johnson et al. (2025) examines police-related fatalities (PRFs) and assaults on officers in relation to agencies' adoption of FRT and other surveillance technologies across 508 US city departments in 2016 and 2020. Departments using FRT exhibited substantially lower PRF rates on average. Net of controls, FRT adoption was associated with an estimated 37 percent reduction in total PRFs relative to non-FRT agencies. The decline, however, is heterogeneous. Fatalities of White civilians fall in FRT-using cities, whereas

Black civilian fatality rates decline significantly only when FRT is paired with dense fixed-camera networks.

The authors argue that FRT, particularly in camera-saturated environments, can shift encounter dynamics in ways that avert lethal outcomes. When suspects perceive that video evidence plus identity confirmation will be decisive, the payoff to violent resistance or flight may diminish. Likewise, officers who expect their actions to be recorded may escalate more cautiously. In this account, FRT and cameras operate as a form of mutual deterrence that reduces lethal outcomes.

Despite this, FRT is associated with higher rates of assaults on officers. Where agencies do not use FRT, additional fixed cameras are largely unrelated to officer assault rates. Where agencies do use FRT, greater camera density correlates with higher assault levels. Johnson et al. call this a deterrence paradox in which heightened identifiability may reduce PRFs while increasing non-lethal resistance. Conceptually, these patterns extend classic deterrence theory by foregrounding surveillance intensity and legitimacy. That is, the certainty of identification and the immediacy of observation appear to reshape behaviour in ways that depend on how communities experience and interpret police surveillance.

Racial Disparities in FRT-Assisted Policing

Using data from over 1,100 US cities, Johnson et al. (2022) estimate how FRT adoption relates to racial differences in arrests. In doubly robust models[1], FRT adoption is associated with higher overall arrest rates for Black residents and lower rates for White residents. This divergence yielded meaningfully higher Black–White arrest-rate ratios in adopting cities, even after adjusting for crime, demographics, and other factors.

These results are consistent with the possibility that FRT, like other surveillance tools, can interact with existing deployment strategies in ways that widen observed arrest gaps. The evidence does not imply that the algorithm itself is the primary driver of racial inequality, nor does it establish the prevalence of misidentification-based arrests. A more cautious interpretation is that FRT can shift investigative capacity and attention, and that without clear use restrictions, documentation, and corroboration requirements, those shifts may fall unevenly across communities. In SDE terms, high surveillance intensity combined with weak governance and low baseline legitimacy may concentrate the burdens of heightened enforcement certainty in Black communities.

Synthesis, Policy, and Implications

The three reviewed studies provide some of the clearest insights to date into how police FRT use is related to crime, officer–citizen encounters, and arrest outcomes. Overall, the evidence points to measurable public-safety benefits alongside governance challenges that can include officer-safety tradeoffs and uneven arrest patterns. Specifically, FRT adoption is associated with reductions in homicides and civilians killed by police in some settings. However, FRT deployment is also linked to higher rates of assaults on officers and larger overall Black–White arrest gaps in city-level data. These findings underscore that outcomes depend on how FRT is deployed, governed, and integrated with other surveillance tools, rather than suggesting a single, uniform effect of the technology across jurisdictions.

Fixed-camera density, BWC saturation, and policy constraints shape whether FRT saves lives, exposes officers to greater risk, widens disparities, or some combination of the three. Within the SDE framework, FRT's impacts are best understood as contingent on surveillance intensity, governance constraints, and baseline legitimacy, rather than as uniform effects that travel unchanged across places. Accordingly, the studies by Johnson and colleagues represent an early quasi-experimental examination of FRT's real-world impacts, providing empirical grounding for debates about AI-enabled policing.

Technology Policy and Deployment Recommendations

Policymakers should create clear, enforceable frameworks governing police FRT use. These rules should specify permissible uses (e.g., serious felony investigations) and prohibit high-risk uses (e.g., random, real-time crowd scanning or low-level offenses absent exigent circumstances). Policies should require agencies to audit FRT usage and outcomes by demographic, including minimum accuracy thresholds, and prohibit arrests based solely on a match without independent corroboration.

Agencies should be as transparent as possible without jeopardizing investigations. This involves publishing FRT policies and, ideally, annual transparency reports that summarize volume, case types, and compliance metrics. Community engagement is vital. Cities can hold town halls, convene citizen advisory committees, and include community representatives in decisions about FRT and other surveillance technologies.

Officers and analysts using FRT should undergo specialized training on technical limitations, legal boundaries, and bias awareness, with an emphasis on treating each FRT match as an investigative lead rather than proof of guilt. Given evidence that police FRT deployment is associated with higher officer assault rates, training should also prepare officers for increased suspect resistance in camera-rich environments.

Strong data management policies are essential. Agencies should set limits on how long facial data are stored, specify who can access it, and prohibit FRT data from being used for unrelated purposes. Systems should incorporate audit trails logging every search and provide remedies for those misidentified, including expungement/correction mechanisms and clear, accessible processes to challenge and correct errors.

Agencies should avoid an "all-or-nothing" approach when deploying FRT-enabled surveillance applications. Evidence suggests targeted deployment focused on violent crime can produce benefits with fewer downstream harms. Departments should calibrate the mix of complementary technologies, pairing FRT with an appropriate level of fixed cameras while avoiding nonstrategic saturation with BWCs. Where agencies raise equity concerns, the response should be concrete and operational: define permissible uses, set thresholds, require documented review and corroboration, and publish audit results on searches and outcomes by demographic. Agencies should be willing to suspend or modify uses that are error-prone, poorly governed, or associated with widening disparities.

Finally, responsible deployment means preserving the human element in policing. FRT should inform police work, not replace human judgment. Officers should be encouraged to treat FRT matches as leads and continue practicing proven investigative principles, including talking to witnesses, assessing context, and exercising discretion in ways that respect community norms.

Future Research Directions

Future research should build on these early studies in at least five main ways. First, encounter-level analyses are needed to illuminate mechanisms. Linking FRT usage logs with BWC footage and incident reports would allow researchers to compare suspect and officer behaviour in FRT-assisted versus non-FRT encounters. Such analyses can clarify when FRT contributes to de-escalation, when it heightens resistance, and which situational or organizational factors moderate these effects.

Second, scholars should examine longer-term trajectories and policy change. As additional years of data become available, quasi-experimental studies can test whether crime-control benefits persist, intensify, or fade and whether racial disparities widen, plateau, or shrink as agencies revise policies and oversight. Comparing jurisdictions that ban FRT, adopt strict statewide regulation, or rely on local ordinances would help identify governance models associated with better public safety and equity outcomes.

Third, interdisciplinary work is needed to improve algorithmic performance and deployment decisions. Collaborations among computer scientists, criminologists, and legal scholars can evaluate commercial systems on criminal justice-relevant image datasets, with particular attention to cross-racial accuracy. Agencies can then use these findings to guide procurement and incorporate uncertainty flags that discourage overreliance on marginal matches.

Fourth, community-centered research should examine how residents experience FRT-enabled policing. Surveys, focus groups, and participatory projects can assess public awareness, perceived benefits, and perceived harms, including effects on reporting, cooperation, and democratic oversight. Parallel qualitative work with officers and supervisors can illuminate how FRT and related tools shape perceptions of danger, discretion, and legitimacy. Lastly, as departments adopt additional AI tools, research should assess how FRT operates within this evolving "stack" of technologies.

Conclusion

FRT in policing is a clear example of how technological innovations can yield both promise and peril. Peer-reviewed research by Johnson and colleagues offers an early look at reality. FRT makes policing more effective and, in some respects, more humane, but it can also entrench inequalities and introduce new risks. Theories of deterrence, technological governance, and social equity must evolve to account for these findings, recognizing that surveillance technology effects are conditional on usage patterns, organizational choices, and social context.

For practitioners and policymakers, the mandate is straightforward. Do not adopt FRT blindly. Adopt it cautiously, guided by evidence, constrained by conscientious policy, and accompanied by rigorous evaluation. In the broader future of policing, this means treating FRT and related tech not as inevitable upgrades, but as governance choices that must be justified in terms of safety, equity, and legitimacy. Under those conditions, it is possible to envision a future in which facial recognition is used in ways that enhance public safety and justice without sacrificing civil rights and public trust.

Note

1 Doubly robust modelling is a statistical weighting approach to make fairer comparisons using observational data. They adjust the results in two ways. First, it weights observations so FRT and non-FRT adopting jurisdictions are more similar statistically on key characteristics. Then, by modelling the outcome (arrest rates), the estimate is considered "robust" because it is reliable even if one of those two steps is misspecified, so long as the other is reasonably correct.

References

Alang, S., VanHook, C., Judson, J., Ikiroma, A., & Adkins-Jackson, P. B. (2022). Police brutality, heightened vigilance, and the mental health of Black adults. *Psychology of Violence*, *12*(4), 211–2020. https://psycnet.apa.org/doi/10.1037/vio0000418

Ariel, B., Farrar, W. A., & Sutherland, A. (2015). The effect of police body-worn cameras on use of force and citizens' complaints against the police: A randomized controlled trial. *Journal of Quantitative Criminology*, *31*(3), 509–535. https://doi.org/10.1007/s10940-014-9236-3

Barnum, T. C., & Pogarsky, G. (2023). Revisiting the role of sanction risk perceptions in deterrence policy. In *Routledge handbook of evidence-based criminal justice practices* (pp. 151–157). Routledge.

Barranco, P. (2023). Match up: Increasing disclosure of facial Recognition technology with criminal discovery rules. *Duke Journal of Constitutional Law & Public Policy, 18*(1), 135–168.

Batool, A., Zowghi, D., & Bano, M. (2025). AI governance: A systematic literature review. *AI and Ethics, 5*, 3265–3279. https://doi.org/10.1007/s43681-024-00653-w

Beccaria, C. (1963 [1764]). *On crimes and punishments* (translated by Henry Paolucci). Bobbs-Merrill.

Beety, V. (2022). Considering "machine testimony": The impact of facial recognition software on eyewitness identifications. *Duquesne Law Review, 60*(2), 271–282. https://dsc.duq.edu/cgi/viewcontent.cgi?article=3933&context=dlr

Brayne, S. (2017). Big data surveillance: The case of policing. *American Sociological Review, 82*(5), 977–1008. https://doi.org/10.1177/0003122417725865

Brayne, S. (2020). *Predict and surveil: Data, discretion, and the future of policing*. Oxford University Press.

Bromberg, D. E., Charbonneau, É., & Smith, A. (2020). Public support for facial recognition via police body-worn cameras: Findings from a list experiment. *Government Information Quarterly, 37*(1), 101415. https://doi.org/10.1016/j.giq.2019.101415

Buolamwini, J., & Gebru, T. (2018). Gender shades: Intersectional accuracy disparities in commercial gender classification. In *Proceedings of Machine Learning Research* (Vol. 81, pp. 1–15). http://proceedings.mlr.press/v81/buolamwini18a/buolamwini18a.pdf

Cornish, D. B., & Clarke, R. V. (1986). *The reasoning criminal: Rational choice perspectives on offending*. Springer-Verlag.

Federal Bureau of Investigation. (2017). *CODIS and NDIS fact sheet*. https://www.fbi.gov/how-we-can-help-you/dna-fingerprint-act-of-2005-expungement-policy/codis-and-ndis-fact-sheet

Federal Bureau of Investigation. (2025). *National DNA Index System (NDIS) operational procedures manual*. https://le.fbi.gov/file-repository/ndis-operational-procedures-manual-version-11-070122.pdf

Ferguson, A. G. (2017). *The rise of big data policing: Surveillance, race, and the future of law enforcement*. New York University Press.

Fussell, S. (2020, June 24). *A flawed facial-recognition system sent this man to jail*. WIRED. https://www.wired.com/story/flawed-facial-recognition-system-sent-man-jail/

Garvie, C., Bedoya, A., & Frankle, J. (2016). *The perpetual line-up: Unregulated police face recognition in America*. Georgetown Law Center on Privacy & Technology. https://www.perpetuallineup.org

Gau, J. M., & Brunson, R. K. (2010). Procedural justice and order maintenance policing: A study of inner-city young men's perceptions of police legitimacy. *Justice Quarterly, 27*(2), 255–279. https://doi.org/10.1080/07418820902763889

Grother, P., Ngan, M., & Hanaoka, K. (2022). *Face recognition vendor test part 2: Identification*. NIST. https://pages.nist.gov/frvt/reports/11/frvt_11_report.pdf

Joh, E. E. (2016). The new surveillance discretion: Automated suspicion, big data, and policing. *Harvard Law & Policy Review, 10*(1), 15–42.

Johnson, T. L., Johnson, N. N., McCurdy, D., & Olajide, M. S. (2022). Facial recognition systems in policing and racial disparities in arrests. *Government Information Quarterly, 39*(4), 101753. https://doi.org/10.1016/j.giq.2022.101753

Johnson, T. L., Johnson, N. N., Topalli, V., McCurdy, D., & Wallace, A. (2024). Police facial recognition applications and violent crime control in US cities. *Cities, 155*, 105472. https://doi.org/10.1016/j.cities.2024.105472

Johnson, T. L., Johnson, N. N., Lea, R., & Hartman, M. A. (2025). Police facial recognition systems, surveillance, and racial differences in police lethality in U.S. cities. *CrimRxiv.* https://doi.org/10.21428/cb6ab371.60569323.

Lee, D. (2019, May 15). *San Francisco is first US city to ban facial recognition*. BBC News. https://www.bbc.com/news/technology-48276660

Leslie, D. (2020). Understanding bias in facial recognition technologies. *arXiv preprint*. https://arxiv.org/abs/2010.07023

Lozano, I. A., Molina, J. M., & Gijón, C. (2021). Perception of artificial intelligence in Spain. *Telematics and Informatics*, *63*, 101672. https://doi.org/10.1016/j.tele.2021.101672

Lum, C., & Isaac, W. (2016). To predict and serve? *Significance*, *13*(5), 14–19. https://doi.org/10.1111/j.1740-9713.2016.00960.x

Lum, C., Stoltz, M., Koper, C. S., & Scherer, J. A. (2019). Research on body-worn cameras: What we know, what we need to know. *Criminology & Public Policy*, *18*(1), 93–118. https://doi.org/10.1111/1745-9133.12412

Lyon, D. (2018). *The culture of surveillance: Watching as a way of life*. John Wiley & Sons.

Moy, L. M. (2021). A taxonomy of police technology's racial inequity problems. *University of Illinois Law Review*, *2021*, 139–192.

Nagin, D. S. (2013). Deterrence in the twenty-first century. *Crime and Justice*, *42*(1), 199–263. https://doi.org/10.1086/670398

Nelson, J., & Gorichanaz, T. (2019). Trust as an ethical value in emerging technology governance: The case of drone regulation. *Technology in Society*, *59*, 101131. https://doi.org/10.1016/j.techsoc.2019.04.007

Ng, A. (2020, January 24). *NYPD's facial recognition use raises civil-rights questions*. CNET News. https://www.cnet.com/news/police-are-using-facial-recognition-for-minorcrimes-because-they-can/

Parker, J. (2020, July 16). *Facial recognition success stories showcase positive use cases of the technology*. Security Industry Association. https://www.securityindustry.org/2020/07/16/facial-recognition-success-stories-showcase-positive-use-cases-of-the-technology/

Paternoster, R. (2019). How much do we really know about criminal deterrence?. In *Deterrence* (pp. 57–115). Routledge.

Perano, U. (2020, December 31). *Facial recognition tech under spotlight after 3rd false arrest*. Axios. https://www.axios.com/2020/12/31/facial-recognition-tech-new-jersey-false-arrest

Piza, E. L., Caplan, J. M., Kennedy, L. W., & Gilchrist, A. M. (2015). The effects of merging proactive CCTV monitoring with directed police patrol: A randomized controlled trial. *Journal of Experimental Criminology*, *11*(1), 43–69. https://doi.org/10.1007/s11292-014-9211-x

Piza, E. L., Welsh, B. C., Farrington, D. P., & Thomas, A. L. (2019). CCTV surveillance for crime prevention: A 40-year systematic review with meta-analysis. *Criminology & Public Policy*, *18*(1), 135–159. https://doi.org/10.1111/1745-9133.12419

Richards, N. M., & King, J. H. (2014). Big data ethics. *Wake Forest Law Review*, *48*, 393–432.

Richardson, R., Schultz, J., & Crawford, K. (2019). Dirty data, bad predictions: How civil rights violations impact police data, predictive policing systems, and justice. *New York University Law Review Online*, *94*, 15–55. https://www.nyulawreview.org/online-features/dirty-data-bad-predictions

Sham, A. H., Aktas, K., Rizhinashvili, D., Kuklianov, D., Alisinanoglu, F., Ofodile, I., … & Anbarjafari, G. (2023). Ethical AI in facial expression analysis: Racial bias. *Signal, Image and Video Processing*, *17*(2), 399–406. https://doi.org/10.1007/s11760-022-02246-8

Stuart, F. (2016). Becoming "copwise": Policing, culture, and the collateral consequences of street-level criminalization. *Law and Society Review*, *50*(2), 279–313. https://doi.org/10.1111/lasr.12201

Sunshine, J., & Tyler, T. R. (2003). The role of procedural justice and legitimacy in shaping public support for policing. *Law & Society Review*, *37*(3), 513–548. https://doi.org/10.1111/1540-5893.3703002

Ulery, B. T., Hicklin, R. A., Buscaglia, J., & Roberts, M. A. (2011). Accuracy and reliability of forensic latent fingerprint decisions. *Proceedings of the National Academy of Sciences*, *108*(19), 7733–7738. https://doi.org/10.1073/pnas.1018707108

US Government Accountability Office. (2022). *Facial recognition technology: Federal Agencies' Use and Related Privacy Protections*. https://www.gao.gov/products/gao-22-106100

Yucer, S., Tektas, F., Al Moubayed, N., & Breckon, T. P. (2022). Measuring hidden bias within face recognition via racial phenotypes. In *Proceedings of the IEEE/CVF Winter Conference on Applications of Computer Vision* (pp. 995–1004).

INDEX

Note: bold page numbers indicate tables; italic page numbers indicate figures; page numbers followed by n indicate notes.